ART AND POLITICS IN
RENAISSANCE ITALY

ART AND POLITICS IN RENAISSANCE ITALY

British Academy Lectures

SELECTED AND INTRODUCED BY
GEORGE HOLMES

Published for THE BRITISH ACADEMY
by OXFORD UNIVERSITY PRESS

Oxford University Press, Walton Street, Oxford OX2 6DP

Oxford New York
Athens Auckland Bangkok Bombay
Calcutta Cape Town Dar es Salaam Delhi
Florence Hong Kong Istanbul Karachi
Kuala Lumpur Madras Madrid Melbourne
Mexico City Nairobi Paris Singapore
Taipei Tokyo Toronto

and associated companies in
Berlin Ibadan

First published 1993
Paperback edition 1995

British Library Cataloguing in Publication Data
Data available

ISBN 0–19–726159–0

Printed in Great Britain
on acid-free paper
at the University Press, Cambridge

CONTENTS

LIST OF PLATES

INTRODUCTION

THE nineteenth century witnessed a number of grandiose sorties by English writers into the world of Renaissance Italy: Ruskin's *Stones of Venice*, Pater's *Renaissance* and J. A. Symonds' *History of the Italian Renaissance*, for example. It also saw a substantial amount of serious, detailed scholarship. For a long time Edward Moore's was the best edition of Dante's *Divina Commedia*. One of the last works produced in the age before World War I, *Botticelli*, published in 1908 by Herbert Horne, who bequeathed the Museo Horne to Florence, is still regarded with veneration by experts. Among the authors whose lectures make up this volume, one, C. M. Ady (d. 1958), belonged by ancestry and in spirit partly to that world. She was the daughter of Julia Cartwright, writer of a still useful two-volume life of Baldassare Castiglione and something of the generous sweep of the Victorian imagination can be discerned in her contribution. Miss Ady was the author of a number of important historical works, including *Pius II*, *The Bentivoglio of Bologna* and *Lorenzo dei Medici and Renaissance Italy*. Our other authors belong to a different world which has existed since the English retired from their control of Tuscan *palazzi* and, to some extent perhaps, withdrew from the attempt to conceive the Renaissance world as a whole. They are essentially inhabitants of the world of professional scholarship.

The lectures reprinted here are all, with the exception of those by Wilde and Wind, which are 'Aspects of Art Lectures', 'Italian Lectures', founded as a result of the endowment of Mrs Angela Mond in 1916, which are now delivered every other year. All the lectures in this volume deal, roughly speaking, with the period 1400–1520. This does not imply any judgment on the dates when the 'Renaissance' began or ended. Nor does it arise from disparagement of lectures dealing with earlier or later periods. It is simply that there happens to be a convenient group of lectures within this time-limit which it seemed sensible to publish together. 1400 to 1520 will probably be thought by most people to be at least a large and central section of the Italian Renaissance and it provides a certain amount of coherence. 'Renaissance' is at best a vague word associated in our minds with particular kinds of visual art and with extreme enthusiasm for Antiquity. Applying it to a period of Italian history inevitably links it loosely with other non-cultural phenomena, also represented here. The lectures particularly illustrate the success of English writers in improving our understanding of two aspects of Italy in this period. The first is the art of Florence and Rome. The second is the political background to the great cultural flowering of Italy. They all contain statements of research which are currently useful.

Some of our authors can reasonably be regarded as springing from native British traditions which have little to do with either the Courtauld or the Warburg Institutes. Daniel Bueno de Mesquita (d. 1989) was a Cambridge historian and a pupil of C. W. Previté-Orton who took up the political history of Milan as his field of research. His monograph on *Giangaleazzo Visconti* was followed by many years of work in the Milanese archives, with more interest in the Sforza period, of which the lecture printed here is a fruit. It is a striking example of his exceptionally precise and delicate scholarship. No other British author has had such a command of the Milanese sources. Bernard Ashmole (d. 1988) (he was indeed associated with the Warburg Institute but only after he had become established) was an Oxford-trained classical archaeologist, not a Renaissance historian. His interest in Cyriac of Ancona arose, no doubt, from interest in the lessons which a classicist could learn from the work of a very early predecessor, but it is equally interesting to those wishing to place Cyriac in his Italian environment. His lecture illustrates the importance of the recovery of antiquity as a part of the evolution of Florentine art. Cecil Grayson and Denys Hay are both distinguished living scholars, one in Italian literature, the other in history, whose intellectual roots are to be found in the Oxford of the thirties and forties. Grayson investigates Alberti's work on Italian grammar, adding to our understanding of a great humanist who was also, unusually, a serious writer in the vernacular. Hay, writing on Flavio Biondo, is concerned with the development of the historical sense which was a fundamental part of the Florentine Renaissance of the Quattrocentro. Both Alberti and Biondo, in different ways, were men whose writings linked the two centres of Florence and Rome.

The most important factors in the development of Italian Renaissance studies in Britain in the twentieth century, however, have been the events of the 1930s: the establishment of the Courtauld Institute, the Warburg Institute's move from Hamburg to London, and the immigration of refugee scholars to England. Roughly speaking the Courtauld has concentrated on art history, the Warburg on 'the history of the classical tradition', which has also included much distinguished art history. Both have strengthened the study of cultural history in Britain and particularly the cultural history of the Renaissance period. These events of the 1930s were of course interrelated. The Warburg was itself a refugee. The Courtauld was affected by immigrants. It is partly as a result of these new elements in British life that Britain has made a very considerable contribution to the subject of this book in the post-war period.

One of the immigrants, who had originally nothing to do with either the Courtauld or the Warburg, was Nicolai Rubinstein. Rubinstein is the author of a magisterial work on *The Government of Florence under the Medici, 1434 to 1494.* More recently he has been the general editor of the Letters of Lorenzo de'Medici, a publication which is appearing in many volumes, sponsored by the Warburg jointly with the Istituto Nazionale di Studi sul Rinascimento, the Renaissance Society of America, and the Harvard University Center at I Tatti. He has established a school which has made enormous contributions to the political history of Florence. His pupils and their publications have been legion, by no means all British. This is an example, of a kind perhaps rather rare in British academic life, of the impact which a single master can have on a subject. Rubinstein's Florentine school now has a parallel in a lively Venetian school of British scholars. The most obvious centre of Venetian work in recent decades has been the University of Warwick, which annually sends a number of undergraduates, with teachers, to reside and work in Venice for a term. One of the managers of this school is represented in our collection: Michael Mallett, a scholar who has been involved both in Venetian history—he collaborated with Sir John Hale in the publication of a book on the organisation of armies at Venice in the fifteenth and sixteenth centuries—and also in Florentine history, as the editor of several of the volumes of Lorenzo de'Medici's letters. He contributes a notable lecture on the style of international relations in the age of Lorenzo which involves a number of Italian states.

Among the refugees of the 1930s was Johannes Wilde (d. 1970) who came to London from Vienna in 1939 and taught at the Courtauld. He did not publish very much but he was an inspiring teacher and must certainly be counted among those who contributed strikingly to the creation of a strong school of Renaissance art history in London. He is well known of course for the posthumous books on *Venetian Art from Bellini to Titian* and *Michelangelo*, published after his death by friends and pupils. One of Wilde's British pupils was John Shearman whose lecture on the Vatican Stanze has a natural link with Wilde's on the Sistine Chapel. Shearman himself has of course been an important contributor to the history of art in the sixteenth century in both Florence and Rome in books on *Andrea del Sarto, Raphael's Cartoons* and *Mannerism*. Another refugee, Edgar Wind (d. 1971), came to England with the Warburg, then moved to the United States, to return to Britain as the first Professor of the History of Art at Oxford in 1955. Wind's Oxford lectures and his BBC broadcasts aroused enormous fascination in a very wide range of amateurs as well as experts. His great collection of essays on *Pagan Mysteries of the Renaissance*, published in 1958, has contributed perhaps more than any other work to making English-speaking readers aware of the fascinating connections between art and philosophy suggested by scholars in the German tradition. His study of part of the Sistine ceiling makes a suitably splendid end to this series of lectures about a spectacular epoch.

The immigration of the 1930s is easily associated with the ideas of Aby Warburg, the founder of the Institute, and with neo-platonism. In fact the events of the 1930s did not have the effect of popularising any particular doctrine or ideology. What they did was to re-enforce standards of high scholarship by providing two centres of expertise in London by which these standards have been maintained and promoted. They have tended of course to encourage the learned article and the austere monograph rather than books appealing more superficially to broader interest groups which were perhaps commoner in the days of Herbert Horne and Julia Cartwright—though this is not of course meant to suggest that either of those was guilty of superficiality. But the articles and monographs are the bedrock on which all sound writing has to be based. We should be grateful that levels of scholarship have been so decidedly raised in this country over the past sixty years. As far as quality is concerned British scholarship in the Italian

Renaissance field has at present nothing to fear from foreign competition. Quantity of course is another matter, and there the British position is weaker. But perhaps it is worth saying at this point that there are quite a large number of notable scholars in this field not represented in this volume and from whom it would be invidious to pick out particular names.

There are some areas in which the British contribution to Italian Renaissance studies has not been very strong. Obvious ones are the history of commerce and the history of religious movements. To make a contrast with our nearest neighbour, there has been no one in this country to stand comparison with Fernand Braudel, Jacques Heers or André Vauchez. On the other hand France has been relatively weak where Britain has been strong: in art history and political history. One of the strong elements in the British tradition has been the willingness to take detailed political history seriously, to struggle with the interpretation of particular individuals and events. It is delicately exemplified in Bueno de Mesquita's lecture, 'travelling hopefully in the wake of Ludovico's conscience, observing the fears and aspirations that marked its progress and the compromises that attended its discharge'. This is not of course the only virtue that these lectures exhibit but it is a central historical quality.

The lectures particularly illuminate three areas of Italian Renaissance history. The first is the development of humanism in the early fifteenth century. Flavio Biondo, Cyriac of Ancona and Alberti were three outstanding and distinctive figures in that world. Biondo and Alberti were both major actors in the growth of the new learning at the papal court. Biondo was one of the inventors of the idea of the Middle Ages as a chasm between classicism and modernity. Alberti, philosopher, littérateur and art critic, was perhaps the most original genius among the humanists since Petrarch. Cyriac, eccentrically pursuing his enthusiasm for archaeology along the routes of the Venetian galleys, was the first to bring home to Italians an accurate view of the relics of antiquity in Greece.

Rubinstein, Mallett and Bueno de Mesquita are all experts on the politics of the late fifteenth century. Their minute examination of events brings to life in the only possible way two great and very different princes of Northern Italy, Lorenzo de'Medici and Ludovico Sforza. Lorenzo can be seen as the patrician banker operating continuously within the republican world of Florence. Ludovico is the duke of Milan, concerned in a princely manner with the problems of ecclesiastical patronage.

Finally the lectures of Shearman, Wilde and Wind take us into the great blossoming of the visual arts in early sixteenth-century Rome where Florentine artistry was given a grander opportunity by papal patronage. The central figure is of course Julius II who paid for Michelangelo's painting in the Sistine Chapel but the story of the Vatican Stanze also runs through Leo X's pontificate. The fever of artistic creation by Michelangelo and Raphael against the background of the invasions of Italy is what most people probably think of as the climax of the Renaissance.

Regarded in perspective the British contribution to Renaissance scholarship in the last half-century has been enormous. It has defined the forces at work both in political experience in the city states and in artistic endeavour. It is arguable that a new synthesis which will relate the societies of the cities and the papal court with the religious and artistic manifestations of the age is now the greatest need. Historians still operate to some extent within the framework created by Burckhardt in the mid-nineteenth century. The reason for this is partly that expertise in separate aspects of the Renaissance world now confines scholars to a lifelong involvement in one discipline. It is impossible to be an expert in both art and politics at the level attained by the authors of these lectures. And yet another section of the historical world, which, as it happens, is not represented in these lectures, is late medieval and Renaissance economic history, which has made strides beyond the dreams of Burckhardt's contemporaries in the present century. Though we find it difficult altogether to escape from Burckhardt, however, our modern conception of the Renaissance has been changed substantially by the new insights provided by research in the last fifty years. The revelations of scholarship contained in these lectures are an essential part of the new material. They enable the reader to see where the subject now stands.

MORALS AND MANNERS OF THE QUATTROCENTO

THERE are moments in history when events combine to give to the members of a certain class and nation the opportunity to fashion the mode of their existence after the ideal of the good life as they see it. The vicissitudes of the world outside their own borders do not affect them. Classes less fortunate than themselves live by ministering to their needs. Within the privileged circle in which they move they are free to pursue their peculiar tastes and interests; nothing hinders them in the performance of their duty according to the conception of it which they themselves have formed. Athens experienced such a moment in the age of Pericles; so did England in the period which preceded the first Reform Bill. Then not only the great political families but the country gentry in whose circles Jane Austen moved were able to a considerable extent to shape their lives after the pattern which they admired. Few men and women, however, have enjoyed so unrestricted an opportunity for self-expression as the ruling families of Quattrocento Italy; none were more richly endowed with the qualities which enabled them to use it to the full. Contemporary sources of various kinds give an intimate picture of their daily life. Each city had its chroniclers who found in the doings of their *signori* their most congenial theme. Men of letters attached to the court celebrated the tournaments, the weddings, and the funerals of the ruling house in prose and verse. The *signori* themselves were voluminous letter-writers, and their correspondence reveals their personal point of view, their friendships, their enmities, and their idiosyncrasies. Their artistic ideals are embodied in the palaces and churches which they built, and in the paintings and sculpture executed at their orders. With so much material available it seems worth while to try and draw some general conclusions as to the Renaissance way of life. To do this, consideration must be given not only to how the members of Italian society lived—what they wore, what they ate, how they employed their time—but to how they thought it was desirable to live. The loyalties which they recognized, the standard of conduct which they set before them, and the ideals of which they dreamed must be taken into account. A forty years' acquaintanceship—shall I say friendship?—with the leading families of the Quattrocento is my excuse for making the attempt.

The hey-day of the Italian princely families corresponds roughly to the second half of the fifteenth century. It begins when the promoters of the Italian League of 1455 made it their object to establish, in the place of the conflicts of the first half of the century, a regime of peace and friendship between the powers of Italy. It ends when the effects of the French invasions made themselves felt throughout the peninsula. If the golden age was short, the full enjoyment of its delights was the privilege of a comparatively small circle. Some six or seven families with their friends and dependants made up what may be termed Italian society. Of these, the most important politically were new-comers on the scene. Cosimo dei Medici's achievements in Florence enabled his sons and grandsons to emerge from the ranks of the Florentine *popolo* into those of the old princely families. When Milan threw open her gates to Francesco Sforza, it made princes of the descendants of a *condottiere*, the native of an obscure village in Romagna. With the accession of Ferrante, the illegitimate son of Alfonso of Aragon, to the throne of Naples, and the severance of his kingdom from the dominions of his Spanish cousins, he and his children became almost purely Italian in their outlook and interests. While the size and wealth of their dominions assured to the rulers of Florence, Milan, and Naples a preponderating influence in the politics of the day, the tone of the society in which they moved was set by the older Italian families. Este of Ferrara, Gonzaga of Mantua, Montefeltro of Urbino, as well as the lordlings of Romagna, belonged by birth to the feudal nobility, and the traditions of chivalry were maintained at their courts. The captains of their forces, the lords of local castles, and the members of cadet branches of ruling families who formed their entourage, owed them personal loyalty. On the other hand, their right to rule over their respective cities had been conferred on them by the sovereign people. In relation to the citizens they were not feudal lords but chosen heads of the republic, whose primary function it was to further the well-being of the city. This fusion of the atmosphere of the feudal court with that of the free republic, of the *vita cavalleresca* with the *vita civile*, is perhaps the most distinctive feature of Italian society. Court and city were part of a single whole. The daily life of both was marked by simplicity and informality, magnificence being reserved for public ceremonies. Talent was the key to all doors and friendships were formed regardless of class distinction. Ties of personal friendship bound Lorenzo dei Medici to the Neapolitan Prince, Federico of Aragon. Ercole d'Este, Duke of Ferrara, was on terms of affectionate intimacy with Giovanni Bentivoglio, who was only the leading citizen of Bologna. Baldassare Castiglione, prince of courtiers, found the friend of his heart in Raphael, a craftsman of Urbino.

'There are two things in the world which I desire more than any other; one is the perpetual triumph of this city and her liberty, the other the glory of our house, not only in my lifetime but for ever.'[1] In recognizing as his twin loyalties city and family, Guicciardini speaks as a representative Italian of the ruling class. His opinions resemble those of earlier Florentine political philosophers. Matteo Palmieri, in his *Vita Civile*, a work which a recent writer describes as 'the finest blending of humanism with the Florentine civic spirit',[2] speaks of man as filled with the desire for the perpetual glory and prosperity of his *patria* (the *patria* of an Italian is always his city) and the continuous welfare of his descendants. The function of a good father, says Leon Battista Alberti in *La Famiglia*, is 'always in every thought to have before him the welfare and tranquillity of his whole family'.[3] In the same work he declares that injury to *patria* is as impious an act as violence done to a father. The city despots, both in their theory of government and in their practice, were guided by the same principles. 'It is often necessary to treat the people as one treats children, that is, to act for their good in a way which they dislike.' So wrote Sante Bentivoglio to Francesco Sforza when a threat to the independence of Bologna obliged him to resort to the highly unpopular measure of introducing armed forces into the city.[4] Contemporary opinion revered Sante as one of the wisest rulers of his age. His attitude towards Bologna and her citizens shows the despot at his best, looking upon himself as the father of his people, and holding himself responsible for their material and spiritual well-being. Lords of cities built churches, and founded monasteries, libraries, and hospitals. Among these last, the *Ospedale Maggiore* in Milan founded by Francesco Sforza is a noteworthy example. Vasari describes it as 'so well built and

[1] *Opere inedite*, ed. Canestrini, vol. x, p. 4.
[2] H. Baron, *History*, Mar. 1938, p. 323.   [3] Bk. I, p. 31, ed. Pellegrini, 1911.
[4] Archivio di Stato, Milano, Potenze Estere, Romagna, 24 May 1459.

arranged that it has not its equal in Europe',[1] and it continues to-day to carry on its beneficent work. In times of scarcity, which were of frequent occurrence, corn from the granaries of the *signori* was sold to the citizens at moderate prices. Streets were paved and widened, and housing conditions were improved. Princes were indefatigable in writing letters to their friends on behalf of individual citizens requiring help of many kinds. Recommendation of candidates for university professorships, of soldiers of fortune, painters, preachers, or bank-clerks, pleas for those who have been wrongfully imprisoned, or who cannot collect their debts or their wife's dowry—such matters form a substantial part of the correspondence of the ruling families.

While the duty of providing for the welfare of their city and its inhabitants was a determining motive in the conduct of Italian princes, the needs and interests of their family constituted an even higher claim on their allegiance. For the most part this involved no conflict of loyalties, for without the good will of the citizens they could not hope to maintain their family in power. 'Every ruler', wrote Isabella d'Este, 'should set greater value on the hearts of his subjects than on fortresses, money, or men-at-arms, for the discontent of the citizens is a more serious cause of war than the enemy at the gate.'[2] No considerations of patriotism were, however, allowed to stand in the way of the advancement of the family. Nowhere as in Renaissance Italy was the good of the city so ruthlessly sacrificed to family ambition. The fierce family rivalries which destroyed the peace of civic life arose from the fact that the despots, both official and unofficial, were themselves citizens. Other citizen families, while they might acquiesce in the supremacy of the ruling house for the sake of the advantages which it brought to the city, could never overcome their resentment of a success which exceeded their own. Any sign of weakness or failure on the part of the despot was greeted as an opportunity for his overthrow and their own advancement. 'If', wrote Guicciardini, 'the root of discontent lies in the desire of the citizens for liberty, in order that they may share the honours, and take part in the government, then no good rule on the part of the despot will be able to destroy it; for all his beneficence he will never be without fear.'[3]

---

[1] *Vite*, vol. iv, Filarete.

[2] 28 Feb. 1495. Luzio-Renier, *Delle relazioni di Isabella d'Este Gonzaga con Ludovico e Beatrice Sforza*, Arch. Stor. Lomb., 1890, p. 622.

[3] *Considerazioni intorno ai Discorsi del Machiavelli*, p. 27 (Scritti politici, ed. Palmarocchi, Bari, 1933).

Examples of the truth of his words are to be found not only in his own Florence but in almost every Italian state. In 1478 the rival banking family of Pazzi tried and failed to overthrow the Medici by murdering Lorenzo and his brother during High Mass in the Cathedral. In 1494 members of the ring of merchant families who had stood highest in the Medici counsels succeeded in driving Lorenzo's son from Florence. The enmity shown by a faction of the nobility to the Sforza dukes made Milan an easy prey to the French. Gian Giacomo Trivulzio, whose family had long been in opposition to the ruling house, and who had received a personal affront from Duke Lodovico, preferred the service of a foreigner to that of a rival. Thus, when Louis XII's conquering armies entered Milan they were led by a Milanese. Typical of this canker at the heart of Italian society is the misery brought upon Bologna by the rivalry between the Bentivoglio and the Malvezzi. The two families were nearly related; both had identified themselves with the cause of Bolognese independence. But the Bentivoglio were first in the city, and the Malvezzi could not be content with the second place. After years of smouldering enmity a plot on the part of the Malvezzi to seize the Bentivoglio Palace and murder the entire family was discovered on the eve of its being carried into effect. The immediate consequence was the destruction of the Malvezzi; those who escaped death were pursued from court to court in Italy by the vengeance of the Bentivoglio. Within Bologna there remained an aftermath of fear and hatred, which led ultimately to the fall of the Bentivoglio, and the subjection of the city to the direct rule of the Papacy.

If excessive love of family was a cause of crime and suffering it was also responsible for one of the most pleasing features of Italian society, its preoccupation with the cares and joys of family life. In court circles, as elsewhere, the children were not kept in the background but shared in the pursuits of their elders. Their education, their health, and, later on, their marriages and their careers were the subject of much thought and correspondence on the part of their parents. Lodovico Sforza was a devoted and even over-anxious father. 'Signore Ercole has not been very well yesterday and to-day, as he is cutting his teeth and has been in some pain. Although his indisposition is slight, Signor Lodovico has been much distressed and displeased—more so than is necessary.'[1] So wrote Agostino

[1] Archivio di Stato, Milano, Potenze sovrane, Massimiliano, Vicende personale, 27 Feb. 1494.

Calco to his brother, Lodovico's chief secretary, from the Villa Sforzesca at Vigevano. This was the favourite residence of the ruler of Milan and his wife, Beatrice d'Este, where they and their two little boys lived a simple country life. Here the Emperor Maximilian spent three weeks in the summer of 1496, forming a lasting friendship with the whole family, and asking that the elder boy might bear his own name. So Ercole became Massimiliano, and in the autumn of that year his tutor reported from Milan that he had 'adopted a very good manner of living'. He rose early and breakfasted according to the doctors' orders on two pieces of bread spread with some form of paste. He then heard mass at the church of St. Maria delle Grazie, 'with great pleasure', returning with a good appetite for dinner. All day long he was good and happy and slept well at night.[1] Later there is a report of a visit to the boy's uncle, Cardinal Ascanio Sforza, to whom the five-year-old Massimiliano recited some of Aesop's fables. There are letters from the children themselves telling of their doings, sending affectionate messages, and making small requests after the manner of children all the world over. 'I am sending my groom Paolino to ask if you will please send me some live animals so that I and the duke of Bari can play with them in the garden, now that you are not here.'[2] When Massimiliano wrote this letter to his father Beatrice d'Este was dead and the light had gone out of the Milanese court. More then than ever were his children the objects of Lodovico's devotion.

The educational theories of the Renaissance are too well known to require elaboration here. It may, however, be worth while to consider what end princely parents had in view when they were at pains to secure the leading scholars of the day as tutors to their children, and followed the progress of their studies with unremitting interest. Their desire for each child was, it seems, that he should become a specialist in the art of living, able to play suitably and effectively whatever part might be assigned to him upon the stage of life. According to the humanists, the model of good living lay in the study of letters. By this means youth would be made familiar with the classical world, which, in the opinion of the age, represented the norm of the good life. Children would learn to know and to admire the heroes of antiquity and would model their own conduct on the classical virtues—valour, wisdom, moderation, devotion to the public good. Thus the boys and girls of the Quattrocento

[1] Loc. cit., Oct. 1496. [2] Loc. cit., Oct. 1498.

realized that attention to their books was a sure way to please their parents.   At the age of eleven Lorenzo dei Medici was working with Gentile Becchi who described him as 'well on with Ovid', although not apparently an enthusiastic scholar. 'Lorenzo is well', wrote the tutor to Piero dei Medici, 'but your absence is always in his mind. Do not ask how he enjoys his present studies. In all other matters he is obedient, and since you are not here, the fear of transgressing makes him more diligent.'[1] Another frequently enjoined precept was that of moderation in eating and drinking. This, with good manners at table, was urged upon Galeazzo Maria Sforza among the *Suggerimenti di buon vivere*[2] addressed to him by his father on his attaining the age of sixteen. Francesco's chief purpose in laying down these rules for his son was that Galeazzo should, when the time came, prove himself a worthy Duke of Milan. Thus he must cultivate the justice and mercy which befits a ruler, he must show politeness to all according to each man's rank, he must learn to keep his temper and to do without that which he cannot get by honest means; he must pay no attention to slanderers and he must choose good horses. The same spirit inspires the letter of advice which Lorenzo dei Medici wrote to his son Giovanni on his taking up his residence in Rome as a cardinal. A cardinal's hat for Giovanni was for long Lorenzo's dearest ambition, and the Florentine agent in Rome laboured to this end for at least four years. At one moment he even suggested that the obstacle of Giovanni's youth might be overcome by removing his name from the baptismal register and getting witnesses to swear that his age was not thirteen but fifteen.[3] When at last, at the cost of many *fiorini*, the goal was won, Lorenzo's chief thought for his son was that he should be 'a good ecclesiastic'. He notes with pleasure that during the last year the boy has been several times to confession and communion without being reminded by anyone, and urges him to persevere in these duties. He warns him of the temptations to which he will be exposed in Rome, 'that sink of all iniquities', and advises him to model his conduct on those of the Cardinals who are 'learned and good men, of holy life'. He recommends him to 'eat plain food and take much exercise', also to get up early; by so doing his health will benefit and he will have time in which to think over and arrange all

---

[1] Archivio di Stato, Firenze, Medici avanti il Principato, xvii, 158; cf. Maguire, *The Women of the Medici*, p. 201, London, 1927.

[2] Ed. Orano, Rome, 1901.

[3] Picotti, *La Giovinezza di Leone X*, pp. 658–9, Milano, 1928.

the business of the day. As a cardinal he is first of all a servant of the Church, but he can at the same time serve his city and family. He will be the link between Church and city, *e la casa ne va colla città*.[1] These two letters are typical of the standards of the day. Francesco Sforza, like Lorenzo, had been unscrupulous in the methods which he employed to secure the exaltation of his house. When, however, high position was attained, honour demanded that it should be filled with distinction.

The recognition among the ruling classes of Italy of the claims of city and family upon the loyalty and service of the individual is not open to question. Was there any like recognition of the claims of religion? Many conflicting elements go to make up the answer. Among them is the fierce anti-clericalism shown in the public opinion of the age, and the scepticism which, for many thinking men, made of Christianity at best a philosophy rather than a faith. On the other hand account must be taken of the general acceptance of religious observance as a part of the good life, and the honouring of piety as a virtue which adorns the character and enhances the reputation of princes. 'There are few priests who are learned or even honest,'[2] wrote Leon Battista Alberti; his views were prevalent throughout Italy, more particularly in Rome and in the states of the Church. Roman society, as may be gathered from Lorenzo dei Medici's reference to it, was a by-word for profligacy and luxury, but the root cause of the feeling against ecclesiastics is probably to be found in the temporal power of the Papacy. The use of spiritual sanctions to further political ends aroused bitter resentment. The greed and unscrupulousness with which the Popes strove for territorial aggrandizement for themselves and their families robbed the Church of respect. Giovanni Bentivoglio expressed the opinions of all those who acknowledged the Pope as their suzerain, when in a reply to a request from the Duke of Ferrara to take part in the defence of the Italian mainland against a Turkish attack, he wrote:

He who is responsible for the oversight of our religion, must do as Christ did when he said 'I have given you an example'. Such action would befit him more than trying to drive the unhappy lords of Romagna from their states, and keeping Italy in such vexation and turmoil as to make others more inclined to desire the coming of the Turk than to oppose it. If he (the Pope) would lay aside personal

[1] Fabroni, *Laurentii Medicei Magnifici vita*, vol. ii, pp. 308–12, Pisa, 1784.
[2] *La Famiglia*, Bk. IV.

ambition and consider the common good and the welfare of our faith and our religion, I am convinced that lords, cities, and all men of good will would be ready to play their part.[1]

When this letter was written Cesare Borgia was in the midst of his campaigns of conquest in Romagna, arousing Italy to ever greater fear and hatred of the Papacy. The injury done to the cause of religion by the Popes of his day and by the lesser clergy whom their example corrupted, made Guicciardini include among those things which he most desired to see before his death 'the world freed from the tyranny of these rascally priests'.[2]

Criticism of the clergy, notwithstanding the due performance of *il culto divino* in court and city, was a matter to which the lords of Italy devoted much care and interest. Lent preachers were engaged from various parts of Italy after careful inquiry into their qualifications, and it was the custom of the court to attend the courses arranged in the principal church of the city. The sight of the chief politicians, merchants, and thinkers of Florence with faces upturned to his pulpit in the Duomo, no doubt helped to create in the mind of Savonarola the impression which he formed of the capacity of the Florentines for religion. Duke Federico of Urbino records that Vespasiano ruled his household as if it had been a monastery. Galeazzo Maria Sforza sought singers from Picardy and Flanders for the choir of his private chapel. At the court of Ferrara, Friday was observed by the singing of Psalms while rose-water for the hands went round at the beginning of dinner; choice dishes of fish, vegetables, and sweets made up for the absence of meat. It was counted a sign of grace on the part of the Este children that, of their own wish, they renounced their privilege of exemption from fasting in order to share in the Lenten fare of their elders. As a reward for their devotion they were given pastry, whipped cream, and marzipan.[3] Isabella d'Este practised the art of mental prayer, commending her state, her husband, and her children to God by this means. On hearing this, her half-sister, Lucrezia Bentivoglio, wrote to ask that she would let her into 'these secrets of the heart', in order that she too might learn the prayer of contemplation.[4] Among the leading men of the day who showed a real love of the

[1] *Carteggio dei principi esteri*, Archivio di Stato, Modena, 19 Sept. 1500.
[2] *Scritti politici e ricordi*, p. 243, ed. Palmarocchi, Bari, 1933.
[3] Bellonci, *Lucrezia Borgia*, pp. 389–90, 614, Milan, 1939.
[4] Luzio, *Isabella d'Este di fronte a Giulio II*, Arch. Stor. Lomb., 1912 pp. 331–4.

things of the spirit was Cosimo dei Medici. He had his cell at San Marco to which he retired for rest and prayer. He read and discussed Plato's *Summum Bonum* with Marsilio Ficino. The letter of thanks which he wrote to Pope Pius II for his condolences on the death of his favourite son, expresses the mind not only of a Platonist but of a Christian. 'I never thought that it was not well with my son Giovanni; he has passed from death to life. For that which we call life is death; there is the true life which is eternal.'[1]

'Devotion to God is the duty of all and especially of princes. . . . It is impossible to rule rightly one's self or others without the aid of God.' Such are the maxims laid down by Castiglione in *Il Cortegiano*.[2] Admirable as they appear they conceal a characteristic weakness in the philosophy of his time. Religion, like learning, or proficiency in the art of war, was treated as an attribute of the perfect prince; its end was the greater glory not of God but of man. As Sir Walter Raleigh has expressed it in his introduction to Hoby's translation of *Il Cortegiano*: 'The self-assertion of the humanists was open and unashamed: man was to train himself like a race-horse, to cultivate himself like a flower, that he might arrive, soul and body, to such perfection as mortality may covet.'[3] Whatever other loyalties he might recognize, the first duty of the man of the Renaissance was to himself. While piety prompted him to invoke divine aid in his work, his own heart and mind and will, rather than the grace of God were for him the source of *virtù*. Thus man himself became both the end and the means of all efforts after perfection. Two consequences followed from this man-centred philosophy of life. One was the divorce between religion and morality. As the determining factor in human conduct was not the service of God or neighbour but self-development, any crime was justified if it contributed to the interests of the individual. Obstacles in the way of the full exercise of princely power must be removed without hesitation or scruple. In the second place it tended to focus the attention of the leaders of Italian society on the joys of life. Self-expression easily became self-pleasing; the complete development of the human faculties was sought by means of deep draughts at the fountain of delight. How varied, how civilized, and how absorbing were the forms of enjoyment open to the privileged few may be imagined from the

[1] Fabroni, *Magni Cosmi Medicei vita*, vol. ii, p. 235, Pisa, 1788.
[2] *Il Cortegiano*, ed. Cian, Bk. IV, p. 382, Florence, 1908.
[3] Raleigh, *Some Authors*, p. 98, Oxford, 1923.

description given by the historian Corio of the court of Milan in the years which preceded the first French invasion.

Everyone believed that peace had come to stay; everyone was intent on getting rich, and all paths were open to them. Feasting and entertainments held the field; the world seemed more stable than ever before. The court of our princes was most splendid, full of new fashions, new clothes and new pleasures. There was rivalry between Minerva and Venus, everyone seeking to cultivate his abilities to the uttermost in order to adorn the goddess of his choice. While men and maidens joined the school of Cupid and flung themselves headlong into the dance of love, Lodovico Sforza, that glorious Prince, brought men of talent from all parts of Europe to honour the noble academy of Minerva. Here shone the learning of the Greeks and the poetry and prose of the Latins. Here the muses sang and the masters of sculpture and painting worked. Here the sweetest harmonies of music seemed sent down from heaven upon this most distinguished court.[1]

Of Lodovico Sforza, who presents perhaps the most perfect portrait of a Renaissance prince, it might be said that the rivalry between Minerva and Venus was fought out in his person. He is the discriminating patron of the arts who knew how to win and keep the services and the friendship of Leonardo da Vinci. He is also the man of unrestrained passions, whose mistresses-in-chief enjoyed a recognized position at the court. While he could say in all sincerity that his wife Beatrice d'Este was 'the dearest thing I have in all the world',[2] he had love to spare for Cecilia Gallerani, Lucrezia Crivelli, and the children they bore to him, as well as for other women of humbler origin who ministered to his insatiable desires. When his illegitimate daughter died, he could write to her mother 'You will be as much loved by us in the future, as if Bianca were still alive'.[3] Ercole d'Este, Duke of Ferrara, strove for righteousness more sincerely than other rulers of his age, and his peculiar hobby was the revival of classical drama at his court. Yet he, too, took illicit sexual relations so much for granted that he sent the portrait of his illegitimate daughter, painted for him by Cosimo Tura, as a gift to his affianced bride.

Among the women of the Renaissance, the devotees of Minerva and Venus were more sharply divided. Two famous ladies, Isabella d'Este and Lucrezia Borgia, are representative of two opposing types of womanhood, the one active and intellec-

[1] Corio, *Storia di Milano*, ed. Magri, vol. iii, p. 156, Milano, 1855.
[2] Letter to Francesco Gonzaga, 3 Jan. 1497; Luzio-Renier, *Relazioni di Isabella d'Este con Ludovico e Beatrice Sforza*, Arch. Stor. Lomb. 1890, p. 639.
[3] Malaguzzi-Valeri. La Corte di Lodovico il Moro. Milan, 1913, p. 499.

tual, the other the eternal feminine. Throughout the sixty-five years of her life, Isabella's devouring energy drove her on from one achievement to another. She made contact with every man of talent in her day. She would write forty or fifty letters about a single picture for her *studio*. During visits to the Milanese Court, shortly after her marriage, she showed equal enthusiasm at the prospect of seeing 'the noble city of Genoa', and over a day's hunting in an Alpine valley when she herself contributed a wild goat to the bag.[1] Her diplomacy guided the little state of Mantua through political cross-currents which would have baffled most rulers and were certainly too much for her husband. In matters of statecraft, it was common knowledge in diplomatic circles that the Marquis Francesco Gonzaga did what his Marchioness wanted (*tanto fa quanto volle la Marchesana*);[2] he once told Julius II that she was a woman with a will of her own and that when she thought fit she acted without his knowledge. Much as he admired and loved his brilliant wife, Francesco fell victim to the charms of Lucrezia Borgia. Lucrezia came to Ferrara as the bride of Alfonso, the heir to the Duchy and Isabella's brother. The alliance was prompted by political necessity. Scion of an old and proud race, the Duke of Ferrara could not like the marriage of his son with the Pope's bastard daughter, still less when, in contrast to the irreproachable virtue of his own wife and daughters, she herself was not without a past. Yet the papal suzerain of Ferrara must be propitiated, and the Ferrarese envoy in Rome did his best to present the betrothal in a favourable light. Alfonso, he wrote, would be well satisfied with his bride; she was quite pretty (*di bellezza competente*), very graceful, modest, and God-fearing; nothing wrong should or could be suspected about her.[3] In the main his optimism was justified. Lucrezia proved an excellent wife and mother, devoted to good works and so zealous in the practice of her religion as to join the Third Order of St. Francis. Yet she exercised a power over men, which Isabella with all her abilities could never wield, and life was insupportable to her without a love affair. Among the objects of her affection at Ferrara were Pietro Bembo, whose relations with her may have been purely

[1] Letters of 19 Jan. 1491 and 27 Aug. 1492, Arch. Stor. Lombardo, 1890. pp. 85, 355.

[2] Cipher despatch from Bologna, 11 Dec. 1510, cited in Arch. Stor. Lomb., 1912, Fasc. 34, p. 277; cf. also Fasc. 35, p. 143.

[3] Gian Luca Castellini to Ercole d'Este, 23 Dec. 1501; see Bellonci, *Lucrezia Borgia*, p. 266, Milan, 1939.

Platonic, but were certainly romantic, and the Marquis of Mantua. The two exchanged messages under assumed names, making Ercole Strozzi, the poet, their intermediary. Thus Francesco learned that Lucrezia loved him dearly—'much more than you think'. He replied by gifts of choice fruits and carp from Lake Garda, begging for a few lines in her own hand. When the duchy of Ferrara seemed about to fall into the clutches of Julius II, Gonzaga, as a captain of the papal forces, obtained the Pope's promise that Lucrezia should be placed in his custody, and busied himself in preparing an apartment for her reception at Mantua.[1] One of the Gonzaga ladies, on a visit to Ferrara, wrote to Isabella of Lucrezia's 'gentle and friendly disposition'. Lucrezia had inquired about fashions at Mantua, asked for patterns of Isabella's dresses offering some of hers in exchange, and expressed the hope of seeing her soon.[2] Such courtesies notwithstanding, there could have been little love lost between the sisters-in-law.

The high lights in the picture of Renaissance life in court and city were created by its festivals. Weddings of members of the ruling family, or the feast of the patron saint of the city—St. John Baptist in Florence, St. George in Ferrara, San Petronio in Bologna—provided occasions for Italian society to muster in force for a round of gaiety lasting perhaps for a week. Marriage ceremonies began with the dispatch of a noble company of gentlemen, chosen from among the bridegroom's family and friends, to fetch the bride to her new home. More than one bridal cortège made a triumphal progress through the length of Italy at this period. Perhaps the most famous was that which escorted Leonora of Aragon from Naples to Ferrara, to become the wife of Ercole d'Este. Another brought Ippolita Sforza from Milan to Naples as the bride of Leonora's brother, Alfonso, the heir to the Neapolitan throne. Ippolita spent some days in Bologna as the guest of Giovanni Bentivoglio. The decorations made the streets through which she passed look like a forest, and some thousand persons were entertained in the city. An early hint of the rivalry between Bentivoglio and Malvezzi occurs in a letter from Virgilio Malvezzi to the Duke of Milan, complaining that Giovanni had prevented Ippolita from visiting him before the party left for Florence.[3] Leonora was entertained in Rome by Cardinal Pietro Riario at a banquet of unprecedented splendour. Scenes from classical mythology such as the

---

[1] Bellonci, op. cit., pp. 517, 557, 560.   [2] Op. cit., p. 390.
[3] Archivio di Stato, Milano, Potenze Sovrane, Romagna, 19 June 1465.

labours of Hercules and the rescue of Andromeda were represented life-size in pastry. A poem written for the occasion by
Porcelio Pandoni told how the gods failed to obey Jove's
summons to a council as they were busy serving at the cardinal's
table, how Jove came in person from Olympus to fetch them,
and on hearing from the mouth of Mercury that they were
enjoying the feast too much to leave it, he was graciously pleased
to excuse them.[1] By such means did the Renaissance Papacy
vindicate its claim to the lordship both of ancient and of
Christian Rome. Next, Leonora and her train passed to Florence
to take part in the festivities of St. John Baptist's day as the
guests of the Republic. These included the customary procession
of the guilds to the church of San Giovanni, horse races, seven
scenes representing the mysteries of the Christian faith, and a
banquet at which Lorenzo and Giuliano dei Medici waited
upon the bride.[2]

The festivities arranged for gala occasions included tournaments, races for the palio, football matches, theatricals, pageants,
banquets, dances. Whatever the entertainment provided its
aim was not merely diversion or display but artistic and literary
interest. A banquet must appeal not only to the palate but to
the eye and the mind; a tournament was preceded by verse-
speaking and the combatants entered the lists as champions of
opposing arguments in an academic dispute. Every spectacle
was given a classical setting, so that the company might add to
their delights the illusion of living in the golden age. A marriage
in the next generation, that of Lucrezia d'Este to Annibale
Bentivoglio in 1487, was marked by celebrations of exceptional
variety, which serve to illustrate the characteristic features of
Renaissance merry-making. The wedding took place at Ferrara,
and in the evening members of the court gave a performance of
the *Amphitruo* of Plautus, after a version composed for the
occasion by Pandolfo Collenuccio. When, next day, the bride
and bridegroom entered Bologna they were met at the city gate
by a youth representing Hope, who appeared on a triumphal
arch and spoke appropriate verses. Six more arches spanned
the route through the city; each had its verse-speaker representing a different virtue, and the series ended outside the
Bentivoglio palace, with words of welcome from Fortitude. In

---

[1] Corvisieri, *Il trionfo romano di Eleonora d'Aragona*, Arch. Soc. Rom. di
Storia Patria, x, pp. 629–89.

[2] Corvisieri, op. cit., Appendix I, prints Leonora's letter describing the
doings in Florence.

the week which followed, every day began with Solemn Mass in one of the principal churches; then came a banquet, and a spectacle. The performances of a child-dancer from Florence made everyone exclaim, 'How could one so young be so clever!' Another evening when dancing was going on in the Bentivoglio palace, a company of young men appeared on the Piazza, where a figure dressed as Mars incited them to battle. All rushed to the great windows to watch the contest which was to decide whether Wisdom or Fortune wielded the greater power over men. The battle ended in a draw. At one of the banquets each guest had placed before him 'a stupendous work in sugar'. Cardinal Ascanio Sforza had a viper, the Visconti device adopted by his family, Lorenzo dei Medici had a peacock, the papal and Neapolitan representatives were given models of the Castello di S. Angelo and the Castel Nuovo at Naples. The *pièce de résistance* of the week was a masque, for which the libretto was written by Domenico Fosco, the theme being the triumph of Venus over Diana; Matrimony over Chastity.[1]

'How blessed is life at the villa! Vita felice et non conosciuta.'[2] Leon Battista's words serve as a reminder that the private pleasures of the Italian ruling families were centred in the country. The Villa Sforzesca at Vigevano, the Schifanoia palace on the outskirts of Ferrara, the Bentivoglio villa at Ponte Poledrano, and the ancestral home of the Medici at Caffagiolo, as well as their numerous villas round Florence, were for their owners places of rest and refreshment from the fevered life of the city. It was a common practice to keep Christmas at the villa, and also to take a spring holiday in the country round about May day. The mornings would be spent in hunting, hawking, or fishing, or simply in riding through the pleasant country-side. Giuliano dei Medici when he sketches the ideal court lady in *Il Cortegiano*, declared that he was unwilling to see her practise 'such virile and rough exercises' as jousting, hunting, and riding.[3] Many ladies, however, were enthusiastic sportswomen, and among them the Este sisters, Isabella and Beatrice. One Bolognese lady, appropriately named Diana Saliceta, was an expert huntress, and even coursed hares on foot with her dogs leashed to her arm. The hunting parties returned 'to give to

[1] The wedding is described in detail in Salembeni's *Epitalamium*, University Library, Bologna, MS. 1491, and in the *Hymeneo* of Sabadino degli Arienti; cf. Zannoni, *Una rappresentatione allegorica a Bologna* (Rendiconti della R. Accademia dei Lincei, 1891).

[2] *La Famiglia*, Bk. III, p. 395.   [3] Castiglione, *Il Cortegiano*, Bk. III, p. 263.

the body at table', as Isabella d'Este once put it, 'its share of the
delights enjoyed by the mind',[1] and after dinner there were
many pleasant ways of spending the evening. There were card
games, including one with the intriguing title of raising the dead
(*resuscitar morti*), and pall-mall, the original form of croquet.
The company danced, made music, played practical jokes on
each other, and best of all, talked. 'Conversation', wrote
Stefano Guazzi, 'is the beginning and end of all knowledge.'[2]
The Renaissance passion for conversation made exchange of
opinions on subjects of common interest not only a means of
education but a pastime. Sitting on tree trunks in the garden
of Villa Viola, and eating fruit freshly gathered from the trees,
or lingering on the banks of the river at the baths of Porretta,
the *élite* of Bolognese society discussed the rules of love, asked
riddles, and told stories. In the Castello of Milan, Lodovico
Sforza and his courtiers debated whether Dante or Petrarch
were the greater poet, or Florence or Ferrara the more beautiful
city. Meeting at the mountain sanctuary of Camoldoli, or at
Marsilio Ficino's villa near Careggi, the members of the Platonic
Academy of Florence pondered over the problems of heaven
and earth and agreed that Platonism was the means by which
philosophic minds might be brought to the Christian Faith.
So strong was the desire for self-expression, so fascinating was
the play of mind upon mind, so sharp the thrust of contending
wits that conversation lasted long into the night. Thus at
Urbino, the attributes of the perfect courtier were discussed
until 'they opened the windows on the side of the palace looking
towards the east, and saw a rosy dawn breaking'.[3]

Absorption in the art of living can alone explain the extraordinary indifference of the princely families to the dangers
which threatened their states. An aggressive policy in Italy was
no sudden whim of Charles VIII. Throughout the century,
French claims to Milan and Naples had been pressed whenever
occasion arose, yet no Italian ruler could bring himself to admit
the seriousness of the situation. All persuaded themselves that
the French would not come, and meanwhile they treated
the French claims as diplomatic weapons to be used when it
suited them in their own quarrels. The transitory effects of
Charles VIII's invasion fostered still further the illusion of
security. Before 1494 it had been thought that the French would
not come, afterwards it was cheerfully assumed that they would

[1] Op. cit., Archivio Storico Lombardo, 1890, p. 355.
[2] *La Civil Conversatione*, 1574.   [3] Castiglione, *Il Cortegiano*, p. 434.

not stay. Italian society, after suffering a temporary shock, threw itself with renewed ardour into the pursuit of pleasure. Energies were absorbed in learning and the arts, wealth was lavished on building and pageantry, military defences were neglected. With each new invasion the power of resistance to the foreigner grew less. As one by one the city states went down before aggression, the exiled families took refuge at the courts of their friends and relatives. They were received with every kindness, and their talents made a welcome addition to the circle into which they were absorbed. Yet nothing effective was done to reinstate them in their dominions. It is noteworthy that two of the principal speakers in *Il Cortegiano*, Giuliano dei Medici and Federico Fregoso of Genoa, were at Urbino because the coming of the French had driven them from their cities. So too, on the fall of Bologna, two sons of Giovanni Bentivoglio found a home with their wives' families. Annibale went with Lucrezia d'Este to Ferrara, where the latter won a place among the eight most distinguished ladies of the court in Ariosto's *Orlando Furioso*. Alessandro lived in Milan with his wife, another Ippolita Sforza, during the French occupation, and during the transitory restoration to power of her cousins, Lodovico's two sons. Here Ippolita's garden formed the setting of the *Novelle* of Matteo Bandello. Even to-day the Bentivoglio palace in Ferrara, still in the possession of the family, and the Monastero Maggiore in Milan, with its portraits of Bentivoglio donors among Luini's frescoes, recall the vanished glories of Bologna.

Survivals such as these are symbolic of the fate which overtook Italian society at the end of the Renaissance. The Quattrocento was an age of optimism. It treated the caprices of fortune as man's opportunity and placed its faith in the power of human *virtù* to triumph over obstacles in the path to success. It set itself to fashion men and women so perfectly equipped as to be able to touch with a master hand every aspect of life, and in so doing to win fame for themselves, their family, and their city. Every effort was concentrated on the development of talent. The life which the members of Italian society evolved for themselves in the process of making actual their manifold potentialities was so entrancing that living became an end in itself. They had little time or thought to spare for preventing disaffection among their subjects, or for the defence of their states against external enemies. Thus they failed to preserve the civilization which they had created, the princely families fell from power, and their cities lost their independence. Seeing all round them signs of misfortune and disaster, the men of the succeeding age lost confidence in themselves and in their power to mould events. Life appeared no longer as a battle between man and fortune, in which man might achieve victory by the exercise of his abilities, but as a game played by fortune with man. The best they could do was to enjoy life while fortune smiled on them, bow to her blows when they fell, and afterwards try to recreate what they could of the old life out of the ruins. It was the fashion of the age to ascribe failure to a malignant fate. Machiavelli's judgement on the princes of Italy who had lost their states was that they must not blame fortune but rather their own lack of initiative.

In June 1520 Antongaleazzo Bentivoglio, Apostolic Protonotary, wrote from Rome to his friend Cardinal Ippolito d'Este, recalling the years of their boyhood. He remembered, especially, the hot days when they bathed together in the River Reno, and shouted to one another in their sport. He wished that they were young again, but now they were both in the forties, and Antongaleazzo had to confess to growing fat. 'Above all things,' he wrote, 'I should like to spend a month with you, in order that we might re-live in memory "li piaceri passati di tanti anni".'[1] A middle-aged ecclesiastic indulges in sentimental regrets for his vanished youth. Yet his words have a wider significance. Already in the first half of the Cinquecento, the happy days were, for the majority of princely families, those of long ago. Italian society was living on its past.

---

[1] Dallari, *Carteggio tra i Bentivoglio e gli Estensi* (Atti e memorie della R. dep. di storia patria per Romagna, 1902, No. 664).

FLORENCE AND THE GREAT SCHISM

THERE is a famous observation about the Great Schism contained in the *Ricordi* of Gino di Neri Capponi who died in 1420 after being a prominent Florentine politician for many years. 'Do not meddle with priests, who are the scum of the earth', he said,

'in matters either of money or of the Church, except so far as concerns the sacraments and offices of the Church. The divided church is good for our commune and for the maintenance of our liberty but it is contrary to the good of the soul and therefore one should not work for it but leave it to the course of nature. As far as it is possible to be concerned solely with spiritual matters, the unity of the Church is hallowed and useful to our commune. The friendship of the pope is useful to our commune and that should not be opposed, for nothing can be achieved without the friendship of the Church.'[1]

There are several points to be noted here. First, the general contempt for priests, no doubt a common, though certainly not a universal, Florentine opinion. Second, the idea that the Schism had advantages for the commune and, other things being equal, was politically desirable. Third, the idea that the friendship of the pope was useful. For a large part of the Schism period the commune of Florence was not in fact firmly attached to one pope and showed a preference for ending the Schism. Nevertheless, Capponi gives a helpful indication of the sceptical realism with which ecclesiastical affairs were approached which is worth remembering when considering the affairs of the Schism. The one important thing that he did not touch on, and which is perhaps even more important for the historian, was that a united papacy could be a dangerous threat to Florence. It could be a threat in the

[1] G. Folena, '"Ricordi" politici e familiari di Gino di Neri Capponi', *Miscellanea di studi offerta a A. Balduino e B. Bianchi* (Padua, 1962), pp. 35–6.

straightforward political sense that popes might present a military danger to the contado as near neighbours or a danger to commerce by the use of the interdict which freed debtors to businessmen. It could be a threat in a more complicated way to intellectual life by forcing Florentines into subservience to religious orthodoxy or alternatively into an anxious religious nonconformity. The dominant concern of Florentine politicians in international affairs, during the Schism as at all other periods, was to cope with the recurrent threat of invasion or blockade, presented by one external power after another in the turbulent world of Italy. Sometimes the pope presented this threat, sometimes another power, and this was what mattered more than anything else in Florence's relations with the world. The Great Schism, which extended from 1378 to 1415, began with Florence at the mercy of a superior papal power, which Gino Capponi may have forgotten by 1420, and ended with a weak and friendly Papacy in a subservient position towards Florence. This contrast was in part the result of a fundamental weakening of the Papacy's relations to the European world. Florence, as its closest neighbour, was more affected by this change than any other major power. I would like to suggest in this lecture that this transformation in relations with the Papacy was of the greatest importance in the evolution of the Florentine mind.

Let us begin by looking briefly at the evolution of Florentine international politics during the Schism period.[2] The War of the Eight Saints between Florence and the Papacy, which had lasted more than three years, was finally ended in the year the Schism began by the peace made in October 1378 which was a Florentine humiliation, involving restitution of church property which had been seized and a substantial fine to the Papacy. Peace was hastened on the one hand by Florentine exhaustion which had led to the Ciompi revolt and on the other hand by the anxiety of Urban VI, the new Roman pope elected in 1378, because the Schism had begun and the new Avignon pope, his rival, was crowned three days after the peace. I shall return later to the War of the Eight Saints and its implications.

The end of the War of the Eight Saints was followed within a

[2] Florentine involvement in international politics during the Schism period is best followed in rather old accounts, notably F.-T. Perrens, *Histoire de Florence depuis ses origines jusqu'à la domination des Médicis* (Paris, 1883), Vols 5 and 6 and N. Valois, *La France et le Grand Schisme d'Occident* (Paris, 1896–1902). There is also useful material in Gene Brucker's *The Civic World of Early Renaissance Florence* (Princeton, 1977).

few years by a new series of dangers resulting from the conflict for the succession to the throne of Naples between Charles of Durazzo, a member of the Neapolitan Angevin royal family, supported by the Roman Pope Urban VI, and Louis of Anjou, the brother of the King of France, supported by Avignon. Charles invaded Florentine territory and occupied Arezzo in 1380, to be bought off by a large loan. Louis of Anjou then came South with an army commanded by the mercenary captain Enguerrand de Coucy who occupied Arezzo as Charles had done. Florence summoned her mercenary captain Sir John Hawkwood and prepared for serious warfare, which was only averted by the blessed relief of Louis's death in September 1384.

The Louis of Anjou episode was followed by a more serious threat from Milan which lasted intermittently from 1385 to 1402. The cause of the trouble was the wish of Giangaleazzo Visconti of Milan to establish links with Tuscan towns, a policy which Florence quite rightly saw as a threat of encirclement which would squeeze her out of her dominant position in Tuscany. The conflict blew up into a serious war, lasting from 1390 to 1392, in which Florence spent considerable sums of money on sending Hawkwood into Lombardy. It blew up again in the War of Mantua, lasting a year from 1397 to 1398, in which Florence, responding to the threat of Milanese links with Pisa and Siena, had some success in importing French support into Lombardy. Finally it led to the war between 1400 and 1402 provoked by the intolerable tightening of the Milanese stranglehold by links not only with Pisa and Siena but also with Bologna, Perugia and Lucca. This episode ended, like that of Louis of Anjou, with the relief of Giangaleazzo's death in 1402 when Florence seemed to be on the brink of disaster.

After the breathing-space, which allowed Florence in 1406 to complete its perfidious acquisition of Pisa, prepared incidentally by serious consideration of a plan to change from the Roman to the Avignon obedience in order to facilitate the purchase of Pisa from marshal Boucicaut, came the next threat from the aggressive Ladislas king of Naples, explicitly aiming at the conquest of Florence. In the spring of 1408 Ladislas had advanced through the Papal State, which he was reputed to be negotiating to buy from the Roman pope Gregory XII, and was breathing fire in the direction of Florence. It was at this point that the cardinals of both the Roman and the Avignon obediences took the step of breaking with their popes and organizing a council to heal the Schism. These events happened at Lucca and Pisa. We can read in the *consulte* of this period that the main Florentine reaction was terror at the prospect of offending Ladislas, which might be done easily by breaking too violently with Gregory XII or by appearing to favour Avignonese cardinals who would be supporters of the French claim to the throne of Naples. With some hesitation Florence allowed the council to take place on her territory at Pisa. During the Council in 1409 Florentine terror redoubled, for Ladislas had now advanced to Arezzo. In face of this threat the Florentine oligarchy decided that it must call in a counterbalancing power and envoys were sent to Louis II of Anjou suggesting that he should make an expedition to conquer Naples from Ladislas with Florentine financial support. He came, Ladislas withdrew, and Florence then lost all interest in Louis of Anjou. But two years later Ladislas was again dangerously on the offensive. Pope John XXIII the pope of the new, third Pisan obedience, established by the Council of Pisa, was driven out of Rome and sought refuge in Florence. Once again the city was terrified of doing too much to offend Ladislas. John XXIII spent five months in the suburbs of Florence but was never admitted to the city, though he had influential friends in it. Ladislas had already shown what damage he could do by persecuting Florentine merchants in Naples and the city was not prepared to risk anything worse. It was not until the following year when Ladislas, like Louis of Anjou and Giangaleazzo before him, died, that Florence could breathe again. By that time, 1414, John XXIII was far away in the clutches of King Sigismund and the Council of Constance, which was to end the Schism, was about to begin.

I have listed this series of events, rather tedious to us but exciting enough for Florence at the time, to emphasize the thread of pressing concern with military danger which ran through the Schism period. It was entwined in a complicated way with the problem of obedience to the popes and the Florentines were always willing to abandon their obedience to Rome if pressing political needs suggested it. As the Schism wore on and popes became increasingly impotent, the political respect which they enjoyed in the city declined to zero. This decline of papal power was the most important result of the Schism as far as Florence was concerned. Although it was a reduction in the political importance of the popes it had, however, positive effects in helping to encourage a different attitude of mind in Florentine intellectual circles.

The decade from 1375 to 1385 can be seen in perspective as the last age of medieval Northern-European intervention on a large scale in Tuscany, the last of those episodes stretching back through the fourteenth and thirteenth centuries which should be put in line with the earlier invasions by members of the families of Wittelsbach, Luxemburg, Valois, Anjou and Hohenstaufen. In this case the main operators in central Italy were Sir John Hawkwood and Enguerrand de Coucy and their low status has prevented recognition of their importance. The only book about Hawkwood was published exactly one hundred years ago by a wealthy English amateur, John Temple-Leader, who employed an Italian, Giuseppe Marcotti to work in the archives.[3] There are in fact still hundreds of unpublished letters in the archives of Florence, Siena, Lucca and elsewhere recording dealings with Hawkwood and he remains a great unsung villain, neglected by the Italians as a despicable barbarian and by the English as a pretentious adventurer. Behind Hawkwood and Coucy stood the imperial figure of Pope Gregory XI, the last medieval ruler of the whole of Christendom, who invested vast sums of Northern European money in Italian warfare.[4] It was the last period in which the Papacy was able to behave in that way. By the end of the Schism the popes were in general reduced to minimal expenditure derived from their imperfectly controlled State in Italy, though John XXIII did receive some taxation money from the North. The Schism was followed by a century of an essentially Italian papacy operating on a scale very much smaller than that of the popes before 1378. Their efforts between 1375 and 1378 had also been the last epoch of large-scale Northern intervention in

[3] J. Temple-Leader & G. Marcotti, *Sir John Hawkwood (L'Acuto) Story of a condottiere* (London, 1889). On Enguerrand de Coucy see H. Lacaille, 'Enguerrand de Coucy au service de Grégoire XI', *Annuaire-Bulletin de la Société de l'Histoire de France*, **32** (1895); L. Mirot, 'Sylvestre Budes et les Bretons en Italie', *Bibliothèque de l'Ecole des Chartres*, LVIII, LIX (1897–8). Papal–Florentine relations in the early Schism years have been reviewed by E. -R. Labande, 'L'attitude de Florence dans la première phase du Schism', *Genèse et Debuts du Grand Schisme d'Occident*, Colloques Internationaux du Centre national de Recherche Scientifique, No. 586 (Paris, 1980).

[4] On Gregory's expenditure see K. H. Schäfer, *Die Ausgaben der apostolischen Kammer unter den Päpsten Urban V und Gregor XI, Vatikanischen Quellen zur Geschichte der päpstlichen Hof- und Finanzverwaltung 1316–1378* (Paderborn, 1937), Vol. 6; J. Glénisson, 'Les Origines de la révolte de l'etat pontifical en 1375', *Rivista di Storia della Chiesa in Italia*, **5** (1951); L. Mirot, 'Les rapports financiers de Grégoire XI et du Duc d'Anjou', *Mélanges d'Archéologie et d'Histoire*, **17** (1897). The later decline of papal financial resources was described by P. Partner, 'The "Budget" of the Roman Church in the Renaissance Period', E. F. Jacob (ed.), *Italian Renaissance Studies* (London, 1960) and there is a valuable account by J. Favier, *Les finances pontificales à l'époque du grand schisme d'occident, 1378–1409* (Paris, 1966).

Italy by any power before 1494. This transformation of the international scene was in my opinion one of the most important reasons for the successful emergence of classicist humanism in Florence, the main point I wish to make in this lecture.

The War of the Eight Saints from 1375 to 1378 was a conflict between Florence and the pope. It produced intense feeling in the city which found an outlet in exceptional taxation pressure on the clergy—they were to be squeezed according to one contemporary 'usque ad feces'[5]—in the confiscation of ecclesiastical property, which was sold, in greater tolerance to heretical *fraticelli*, in outbursts of popular religion which filled the churches, and also, among the more devoted adherents of the guelf cause, in expressions of conviction that a war against the pope could never be successful.[6] The strong popular feeling of hatred for the papacy at this time was expressed, for example, in a poem by Franco Sacchetti who compared Pope Gregory XI to Nero, Attila and the Saracens. His barbarian troops had devastated Faenza, delivered lands near Piacenza like Judas to the 'Breton pigs' and allowed the troops of the Cardinal of Geneva to rape Cesena. He deserved to be known as Pope 'Guastamondo', waster of the world.[7]

This conflict produced a complete schism between the papal court and the proto-humanists at Florence in the immediate aftermath of the deaths of Petrarch and Boccaccio. Petrarch's admirer and successor Coluccio Salutati was Chancellor of Florence and his diplomatic correspondence defending and promoting the Florentine cause was a powerful element in the city's aggressive policy. Salutati brought into play all the resources of his command of the classics and his belief in the superiority of Italy and of the republican system of government. His letter on behalf of the commune of Florence to the Romans in January 1376 is a good example of his style. He urged the Romans to rebel in defence of their liberty against the tyranny emanating from the papal court, to act in the tradition of Horatius Cocles and Mutius, the Roman

[5] A. Gherardi (ed.), *Diario d'anonimo fiorentino dall'anno 1358 al 1389*, in *Cronache dei secoli xiii e xiv* (Florence, 1876), p. 232.

[6] Florentine conflict with the Papacy during the War of the Eight Saints is dealt with by A. Gherardi, 'La guerra dei Fiorentini con papa Gregorio XI detta la guerra degli Otto Santi', *Archivio Storico Italiano*, Ser. 3, Vols 5–8 (1867–1868), and R. C. Trexler, *The Spiritual Power. Republican Florence Under Interdict* (Leiden, 1974). For reactions within Florence see the articles by M. Becker, 'Florentine Politics and the Diffusion of Heresy in the Tracento' and 'Church and State in Florence on the Eve of the Renaissance, 1343–1382', *Speculum*, **34** (1959), **37** (1962).

[7] Franco Sacchetti, *Il Libro delle Rime*, ed. A. Chiari (Bari, 1936), pp. 206–9.

republicans, to remember that their city had once been the capital of Italy and the whole world, not to be seduced by the blandishments of the clergy but to join in the defence of Italy against barbarian subjection.[8] The registers of the commune of Florence for this period are full of letters in which Salutati presented the Florentine cause with similar rhetorical splendours not only to the Italian cities but to every European prince from the Emperor himself downwards. In a private letter to a Franciscan theologian in November 1375 he put the Florentine case in a different, more considered way. Florence was not at war with the church. It had taken up arms, as always, to defend its liberty, not against the Church but against foreign invaders, enemies of the Italian name, sent to reduce Italy to miserable prey. The pope's power was almost limitless because he could release debtors and allies from their contracts. The only resource available to the city was military action against his barbarous mercenaries.[9]

In these circumstances it was not surprising that Salutati should write to Francesco Bruni, a Florentine papal secretary, in July 1377 urging him to leave the papal court and its iniquities. Men living as he did were corrupted by the society of the rich. The prelates of the Roman court were wealthy men, enemies of poverty, corrupted by simony and every other vice, whom St Peter would reprove. Bruni should leave them and allow reason to oppose the senses. It was surprising indeed that the study of the classics did not teach him a better course of action.[10] At this time the breach between Florentine humanism and the papal court was complete and Salutati was the flagbearer in the vanguard of a ferocious anti-papal crusade lasting for more than three years. The religious enthusiasts of the *fraticelli* heresy and the humanists of Salutati's circle had, of course, nothing in common in the intellectual basis of their beliefs but they were united by a purely political struggle of the city against the pope, caused originally by the difficulty of procuring grain from the papal state during the famine of 1375,[11] later by the depredations of English and Breton mercenaries, by the enormous costs of warfare and by the dire

---

[8] Archivio di Stato, Florence, Signori-Carteggi, Missive 1ª Cancellaria, 15, fo. 40. Cf. R. G. Witt, *Coluccio Salutati and his Public Letters* (Geneva, 1976), pp. 51–2.

[9] To Fra Niccolò Casucchi da Girgenti, F. Novati (ed.), *Epistolario di Coluccio Salutati* (Rome, 1891–1905), Vol. 1, pp. 213–18.

[10] *Epistolario*, Vol. 1, pp. 263–76.

[11] J. Glénisson, 'Une administration médiévale aux prises avec la disette, la question des blés dans les provinces italiennes de l'état pontifical en 1374–1375', *Le Moyen Age*, **57** (1951).

commercial effects of the papal interdict which hampered Florentine merchants all over Europe. The War of the Eight Saints was
the last and worst in a long line of Florentine conflicts with the
Pope and the only one which had serious implications for the
development of humanism, largely because of the unique position
of Salutati, the heir of Petrarch, whose office in the city gave him a
prominent political role.

The quarter-century following the War of the Eight Saints, the
period of the pontificates of the two Roman popes Urban VI and
Boniface IX, 1378 to 1389 and 1389 to 1404, witnessed a long
relaxation of tensions between Florence and the papacy whose
relations resumed their normal course of intermittent friendship
and dispute, minor quarrels about the appointment of bishops,
and a recovery of the dominant position held by Florentine
merchants in the management of papal finances. Apart from his
diplomatic correspondence Salutati sent several private letters to
the papal curia during this period which show that he no longer
regarded it with hatred. In 1393 he wrote to the pope thanking
him for an expectative provision for his son Piero and again on
behalf of his son Jacopo, who was granted a rectory in the diocese
of Pistoia. In later years he wrote again on behalf of a member of
his family and also about a request for a marriage dispensation.[12]
Relations between Florence and Rome were, however, much
complicated by the moves towards ending the Schism which
emanated from France after the beginning of the pontificate of
the second Avignonese Pope Benedict XIII in 1394. Already in
that year Benedict made moves to negotiate with Boniface through
Florence. In January 1395 Salutati, who was, of course, involved
in these political moves as Chancellor, wrote a private letter to
Benedict XIII, with whom he seems to have exchanged a copy of
the Odyssey for a Plutarch, thanking him for the honour of a
letter and praising his wish to end the Schism.[13] In the last year of
Boniface's pontificate, 1404, several Florentine letters indicated a
wish to bring the two opposing popes together. These tendencies
were much strengthened by the accession of Innocent VII,
succeeding Boniface at Rome in 1404, a more pliant pope who
was in serious trouble in Rome throughout his short pontificate
from the pressure of Ladislas of Naples, and also by the Florentine
wish in 1405 to 1406 to use the help of Marshal Boucicaut and
Benedict XIII in securing Pisa.

[12] *Epistolario*, Vol. 2, pp. 434–5; Vol. 3, pp. 661–3, 665–7, Vol. 4, pp. 255–9,
263–4.
[13] *Epistolario*, Vol. 3, pp. 53–7.

The election of Innocent VIII in 1404 marked the beginning of
the gradual downfall of the Roman curia of the Schism. Two
relatively weak popes, Innocent VII and Gregory XII, led in a few
years to the Council of Pisa and then to the Council of Constance.
The main point that I wish to make in this lecture is that these two
pontificates created a quite new situation in the relations between
Rome and the papacy which was an extreme contrast to the
situation during the War of the Eight Saints and which allowed a
new grouping and a new attitude among the Florentine humanist
circle which now became divided between Florence and Rome. In
order to present this view I wish to distinguish between two stages
in the evolution of Florentine humanism. The first took place in
the period from 1395 to 1405 when Salutati was still alive and the
Florentine-curial link was not yet fully in existence. The second
was in the succeeding decade from 1405 to 1415 when the link
was fully established and the Roman papacy was collapsing. This
evolution of Florentine-curial relations is, I believe, much more
important in the history of Renaissance classicism at this period
than the political crisis of the Florentine war with Milan which has
been given such prominence in recent writing.[14]

The native Florentine school of humanism which existed
immediately before 1405 was created principally by two men:
Salutati himself, as an enthusiastic promoter of the study of
classical literature, and the Greek visitor Manuel Chrysoloras,
who was an enthusiast for everything in the classical world. It was
almost certainly Salutati who persuaded the commune of Florence
to invite Chrysoloras to Florence as a teacher of Greek in 1396.
He came in 1397 and stayed until 1400. Not much is known about
Chrysoloras apart from the rather general praise lavished upon
him by his disciples. His letter to John Paleologus about the city of
Rome, however, indicates that he was the teacher most likely to
have extended Florentine humanism beyond the well-established
attachment to Latin literature, not only into an appreciation of
Plato and other Greek authors, with which he was obviously
concerned, but also into linking classical literature with classical
architecture and sculpture. His description of Rome praised its
ancient buildings in the architectural manner of the Greeks, its
triumphal arches, its Latin inscriptions and also its sculptures in
the style of a Phidias or a Praxiteles.[15] This letter shows a breadth

[14] Notably by H. Baron, *The Crisis of the Early Italian Renaissance* (Princeton,
1955).
[15] J. -P. Migne (ed.), *Patrologia graeca* (Paris 1857–60), clvi, cols. 23–53. See M.
Baxandall, *Giotto and the Orators* (Oxford, 1971), pp. 80–3. On Chrysoloras in
general G. Cammelli, *Manuele Crisolora* (Florence, 1941).

of appreciation which might have been available to Petrarch but which was not normal in the attitudes of Salutati and his friends. Chrysoloras should be restored to the pre-eminent position he once had among the creators of the Renaissance.

His pupils in Florence included, apart from Salutati, Niccolò Niccoli, Leonardo Bruni, Poggio, Roberto Rossi, Palla Strozzi, Jacopo Angeli da Scarperia, and Vergerio. These men were the creators of Florentine classicism and it is fairly clear that they existed as a group in the very first years of the fifteenth century. The record of their beliefs is contained in Bruni's *Dialogus*, composed in 1401, in Vergerio's *De Ingenuis Moribus*, 1402, and in Giovanni Dominici's *Lucula Noctis* of 1405. Bruni's *Ad Petrum Paulum Istrum Dialogus*, dedicated to Vergerio, which is commonly dated to 1401, records two discussions in which the participants were Bruni, Coluccio Salutati, Niccolò Niccoli and Roberto Rossi.[16] It is modelled to some extent on Cicero's *De Oratore*. The aim of the work is to put forward two opposed points of view about culture: one that emphasizes the hopeless weakness of modern writings and ideas in comparison with those produced in the age of Cicero, many of which are now lost; the other allowing value to the native Florentine tradition of the fourteenth century in the writings of Dante, Boccaccio and Petrarch. It is the former naturally, that interests us. Niccoli is made to argue that philosophy, which was taken by Cicero from Greece to Italy and which is also to be found in the later writings of Cassiodorus and Chalcidius, is now hopelessly lost. All the texts are corrupt. Modern philosophers lay down Aristotle's ideas as law and do so in inelegant language and they do not really understand what Aristotle said. Modern dialectic is dominated by Oxford logicians with a list of barbaric names.

The reason for this weakness is primarily the lack of good texts and of masters fit to teach them. We lack texts of Cicero, Livy, Sallust, Pliny and Varro. Dante wrote poor Latin and had the affrontery to prefer the tyrant Caesar to Brutus the defender of liberty. Petrarch was like a painter who claimed to be another Apelles but could not in fact draw a straight line and his *Africa* was greatly inferior to Virgil's *Aeneid*. One letter of Cicero and one poem of Virgil would be worth all his writings. In the second

---

[16] E. Garin (ed.), *Prosatori Latini del Quattrocento* (Milan–Naples, 1952), pp. 44–99. There is a recent study of the controversies about the Dialogus by D. Quint, 'Humanism and Modernity: A Reconsideration of Bruni's *Dialogues*', *Renaissance Quarterly*, **38** (1985).

conversation Niccoli withdrew most of his calumnies of the Florentine writers, which he said he had put forward only to provoke Salutati, and the discussion ends with a happy agreement on the great virtues of modern Florence. That does not very much matter. What is interesting is that we find sketched here a statement that the recovery of Latin writing and of its philosophical attitudes are essential, exactly the point of view which animated the humanists of the Florentine school. The probability is that the views attributed to Niccoli here—sufficiently in agreement with half-a-dozen later literary evocations of him[17]—and those attributed to Salutati, the grand old defender of Florentine culture, convey a reasonably good impression of their opinions in real life. In the manner common in *quattrocento* dialogues we have famous characters, recognizable but with an added spice of parody or satire to improve the reader's pleasure.

Niccoli's gracious withdrawal of his views about the ancients and the moderns in the later part of the dialogue does not alter the fact that he had stated them. And we can tell, in fact, from the correspondence of Salutati and Bruni a few years later that the two views attributed to Niccoli and Salutati in the first part of the dialogue were true statements of opinions held in their circle. Salutati wrote two well-known letters to Poggio, who had gone to Rome, in December 1405 and March 1406, shortly before his death, reproving him for the sarcastic observations about modern writers contained in letters to Salutati and Niccoli, insisting against him that Christian authors were superior to pagan and that Petrarch had much to recommend him.[18] Salutati, in contrast to Poggio and Niccoli, attached enormous value to classical literature but also insisted at the same time on putting it within a Christian framework. Like Boccaccio before him, he believed that classical stories were valuable if they were given allegorical interpretations which revealed a meaning acceptable to Christian ethics. As far as their beliefs went, Christians were always preferable to pagans. But it is clear that the effect of the instruction

---

[17] Niccoli's opinions have recently been re-examined by P. A. Stadter, 'Niccolò Niccoli: winning back the knowledge of the ancients', *Vestigia Studi in Onore di Giuseppe Billanovich* (Rome, 1984), Vol. 2, and his contemporary reputation by M. C. Davies, 'An emperor without clothes? Niccolò Niccoli under attack', *Italia Medioevale e Umanistica*, **30**, (1987).

[18] *Epistolario*, Vol. 4, pp. 126–45, 158–70. There are modern works on Salutati by B. L. Ullman, *The Humanism of Coluccio Salutati* (Padua, 1963), and R. G. Witt, *Hercules at the Crossroads. The Life, Works, and Thought of Coluccio Salutati* (Durham, N. Carolina, 1983).

given by him and by Chrysoloras had been to create a small group which adopted a much more indiscriminate classicism which asserted the general superiority of the ancient to the modern world. This point of view was represented again by Vergerio's *De Ingenuis Moribus* which proposed an ideal liberal education without any reference to Christian precepts.[19] A liberal education should consist of history, moral philosophy, to teach men the secret of true freedom and eloquence. No mention was made of the subjects principally valued in contemporary university education.

The views held by the extreme classicists at Florence were attacked in 1405 by the Dominican preacher Giovanni Dominici in his book *Lucula Noctis*. Dominici's view was quite simply that Christianity and pagan literature were incompatible. The arguments in favour of pagan writings as a support to Christianity were quite valueless. Christians would do better to ignore them and take up manual labour. 'Sacred writings are neglected', he said,

'books of faith uncared for, the writings of pagans are bound in silk, decorated with gold and silver, read as precious things, and all the schools of Christians—Christians in name only—resound day and night, holy days included, with the words of pagans.'[20]

Dominici's words refer, recognizably, to the classicists' obsession with manuscripts which is often indicated by their letters. And his argument is clearly true. The group represented by Niccoli, Poggio and Vergerio did indeed favour a general attachment to

---

[19] 'Petri Pauli Vergerii De Ingenuis Moribus et Liberalibus Studiis Adulescentiae etc.', ed. A. Gnesotto, *Atti e Memorie della R. Accademia di Scienze, Lettere ed Arti di Padova*, **34** (1917). There are recent studies of Vergerio by D. Robey: 'Vergil's statue at Mantua and the defence of poetry: an unpublished letter of 1397', *Rinascimento*, **20** (1969); 'P. P. Vergerio the elder; republicanism and civic values in the work of an early humanist', *Past and Present*, **58** (1973); 'Humanism and Education in the Early Quattrocento: The "De ingenuis moribus" of P. P. Vergerio', *Bibliothèque d'Humanisme et Renaissance*, **42** (1980); 'Humanist views on the study of poetry in the early Italian Renaissance', *History of Education*, **13** (1984).

[20] R. Coulon (ed.), *Beati Iohannis Dominici Cardinalis S. Sixti. Lucula Noctis* (Paris, 1908), Chap. 13. There are more recent studies of Dominici by P. Da Prati, *Giovanni Dominici e l'Umanesimo* (Naples, 1965) and C. Mésoniat, *Poetica Theologia. La 'Lucula Noctis' di Giovanni Dominici e le dispute letterarie tra '300 e '400* (Rome, 1984) but the most useful account of his life in the period considered here remains that by H. V. Sauerland, 'Cardinal Johannes Dominici und sein Verhalten zu den kirchlichen Unionsbestrebungen während der Jahre 1406–15', *Zeitschrift für Kirchengeschicte*, **9** (1887).

classical culture which would, if accepted, create an alternative lay culture which would have no place for Christian beliefs and this attitude of mind did become dominant a generation later in the important writings of Bruni, Alberti and, most of all, Lorenzo Valla.

A new stage in the circumstances of the Florentine humanist group resulted from the move by Bruni to the papal curia at Rome in April 1405 and the death of Salutati in May 1406. Salutati's death meant that a restraining hand was removed from the group. Salutati had been a supporter of traditional religious assumptions and a defender of the Florentine intellectual tradition of Dante, Boccaccio and Petrarch. Poggio had moved to the papal curia in 1402 as secretary to the Cardinal of Bari. By 1404 he was scriptor. After working for popes Innocent VII and Gregory XII he became a scriptor for the Pisan popes Alexander V and John XXIII. Later on he became a secretary.[21] Bruni went to Rome in April 1405 and quickly became a secretary to Innocent VII.[22] His acceptance and promotion were evidently due to Salutati's enthusiastic recommendaton. Bruni described in a letter the reception of Salutati's letter to the pope about him, read aloud in a group including several cardinals, who expressed doubts about his youth but were moved by the gravity and ornamentation of the letter and by the charity of Salutati's praises. He claimed that he, Bruni, had impressed the pope by a reply he wrote to letters from the Duke of Berry which surpassed a version submitted by Jacopo d'Angeli, incidentally another member of the Florentine circle, and according to his own account he quickly became important in curial business.[23] Bruni remained with the

[21] On Poggio's career at the papal court in this period, see W. von Hofman, *Forschungen zur Geschichte der Kurialen Behörden vom Schisma bis zur Reformation* (Rome, 1914), Vol. 2, p. 110; E. Walser, *Poggius Florentinus* (Berlin, 1914), pp. 19–41. Cf. M. C. Davies, 'Poggio Bracciolini as rhetorician: unpublished pieces', *Rinascimento,* **22** (1982).

[22] On Bruni's career at the papal court see von Hofmann, op. cit., Vol. 2, pp. 107, 110; C. Vasoli, 'Leonardo Bruni', *Dizionario Biografico degli Italiani,* Vol. 14 (1972). There has been a great deal of modern work on Bruni by H. Baron in *The Crisis of the Early Italian Renaissance; Humanistic and Political Literature in Florence and Venice at the Beginning of the Quattrocentro* (Cambridge, Mass., 1955); and *From Petrarch to Leonardi Bruni* (Chicago–London 1968). There is a recent addition by C. Griggio, 'Due lettere inedite del Bruni al Salutati e a Francesco Barbaro', *Rinascimento,* **26** (1986).

[23] L. Mehus (ed.), *Leonardi Bruni Arretini Epistolarum Libri VIII* (Florence, 1741), Vol. 1, pp. 1–3; F. P. Luiso, *Studi su L'Epistolario di Leonardo Bruni* (Rome, 1980), pp. 5–8.

courts of Innocent VII and Gregory XII. In the middle of 1408 he said he intended to stick by Gregory although the pope was being abandoned by his cardinals, but in April 1409 he in fact moved to the council at Pisa because he said he now believed that the action against Gregory was necessary since he had been so misled by his advisers.[24] Both Poggio and Bruni therefore eventually went North with John XXIII to be present at the Council of Constance. The papal court also included at this period, among humanists having very close connections with the Florentine group, Jacopo Angeli da Scarperia, who became a scriptor under Boniface IX in 1401 and later on was a scriptor under John XXIII,[25] and Vergerio, who joined the curia in 1405 and then rejoined the court of John XXIII in 1414 to become one of the four *votorum scrutatores* at the Council of Constance.[26] A discourse by Vergerio has survived in which he urged the court of Gregory XII to give way to the other side in order to end the Schism and deplored the failure of Innocent VII to do this.[27] There was, then, a distinct Florentine humanist group of functionaries entrusted with writing at the papal court which lasted through the pontificates of Innocent VII, Gregory XII and John XXIII from 1405 to 1415.

Throughout the period from 1406 to 1415 our knowledge of the humanist circle depends mainly on the correspondence between Poggio and Bruni at the papal court and Roberto Rossi and Niccolò Niccoli at Florence. There are few letters from the hand of Poggio surviving from this period, though those that we have are important, and none of course from Niccoli. But there is a large number of important letters from Bruni, which present a vivid picture of the relations between the four men and constitute our main source of information for a decade of Florentine humanism. The two important things that emerge from this correspondence are, first, the intense pursuit of strictly humanist objectives—the search for manuscripts, exchange of manuscripts, admiration for Plato, observation of Roman remains—

[24] *Epistolarum Libri VIII*, Vol. 2, pp. 21, 22; Luiso, op. cit., pp. 50–2.

[25] von Hofmann, op. cit., Vol. 2, pp. 108, 255; R. Weiss, 'Jacopo Angeli da Scarperia (*c*. 1360–1410/11)', *Medioevo e Rinascimento Studi in onore di Bruno Nardi* (Florence, 1955), Vol. 2.

[26] L. Smith, 'Note cronologiche vergeriane', *Archivio Veneto-Tridentino*, **10**, (1926).

[27] C. Cambi, 'Un discorso inedito di Pier Paolo Vergerio il seniore', *Archivio Storico per Trieste, l'Istria e il Trentino*, **1**, (1981–2).

and, secondly, the curious combination of the secretaries' self-conscious importance at the curia resulting in their ability, for instance, to help in securing benefices, with a classical detachment from the purposes of the great religious organization they were serving. 'If I thought that what is done here', Bruni wrote to Niccoli from the Council of Constance in 1414 'and what is said here interested you, I would tell you about the acts of the council and give you a commentary on everyday affairs. But, if I know you well, your attitude is that you not only do not care to know about these things but you prefer to be ignorant of what you call the tedious behaviour and absurdities of men'. I think therefore, Bruni went on, that the best thing I can do is to describe my journey through the Alps. He mentioned with amusement that one of the things he had seen was a marble slab surviving from the Roman period with an inscription nearly worn out by the reverence of the faithful which turned out on examination with a humanist eye to record the names 'not of the saints of Christ but of the persecutors of the Christian faith'.[28]

One personage whom the humanists encountered at the papal court in the period immediately preceding the Council of Pisa was their old intellectual critic Giovanni Dominici. Dominici was sent to Rome by the commune of Florence in November 1406 after the death of Innocent VII with the mission of influencing the conclave of cardinals which eventually elected Gregory XII. Contrary to custom, Bruni reported, Dominici was allowed to address the cardinals in conclave through a window but they reported their intentions to him rather than acceding to his suggestions.[29] Florence was by this time actively in favour of a union of the two popes to end the Schism and although still in the obedience of Rome was receiving envoys from Benedict XIII. Dominici, however, was won over to the side of Gregory XII and remained at his court. The commune wrote to him in May of the following year, 1407, saying that he was dismissed from his employment as envoy and that if he wished to be paid his salary he must return to Florence.[30] He did not. He remained with Gregory after the pope had turned against the conciliar idea and was made a cardinal in 1409 among those appointed to fill the gap caused by the flight of Gregory's cardinals to the Council of Pisa. Bruni replied in 1408 to a letter from Roberto Rossi asking what he

[28] *Epistolarum Libri VIII*, Vol. 4, p. 3; Luiso, pp. 81–2.
[29] *Epistolarum Libri VIII*, Vol. 2, p. 3; Luiso, p. 26.
[30] Sauerland, 'Cardinal Johannes Dominici', p. 248.

thought about Dominici since there were various opinions about
him in Florence. Bruni wrote thoughtfully that he regarded
Dominici as outstanding as a man of learning and eloquence. He
held it against Dominici, however, that when he was made a
bishop by the pope he immediately gave up his support for
conciliar union. Bruni hoped that he was moved by wisdom and
not ambition; nevertheless, he could not help liking him.[31]
Poggio, characteristically, took a rather more light-hearted and
critical view. Many years later he wrote a dialogue about hypocrisy
in which he gave Dominici a prominent place. He recalled that
when Dominici had been in Florence he had been a successful
preacher against public immorality, had secured the abolition of
games of dice in the festivals of May Day and had attacked license
in female clothing. When he joined the court of Gregory XII, he
joined the crowd of hypocrites and won Florentine disapproval by
becoming first bishop of Ragusa and then a cardinal. Poggio
recalled that in those days, when he was in the middle of
everything at the court of Gregory, he had been present at a
dinner where Dominici, recently arrived in Rome, had criticized
the pope's policy. 'I told him', Poggio said, 'the offer of a
cardinal's hat will change your opinion ... And, as I had predicted,
so it fell out.'[32] Poggio presumably remembered the attack on the
point of view he shared which had been delivered by Dominici in
Florence and took pleasure in the failure of the rigid Gregorian
line to which Dominici had been faithful when the humanists all
joined the court of the Council's pope John XXIII. The latter was
of course also an old ally of Florence and a financial associate of
the Medici.[33]

If we looked at the letters of ordinary, non-humanist laymen
visiting the papal court and the councils, we would no doubt find
their observations equally dispassionate and sceptical. In that
sense the only significance of the humanists' remarks is that they
were couched in good Latin and are more amusing as sentences
composed for deliberately classical compositions. Their importance, however, becomes much greater if we place them in
context. In the first place the humanists were important in papal
business. It was not only that their position at the curia gave them
an influence in securing benefices as the letters from Niccoli and

[31] *Epistolarum Libri VIII*, Vol. 2, p. 19; Luiso, p. 49.

[32] *Centra hypocritas dialogus*, reprinted in Poggius Bracciolini, *Opera Omnia*, ed.
R. Fubini (Turin, 1966) Vol. 2, pp. 73–4.

[33] G. Holmes, 'How the Medici became the Pope's Bankers', N. Rubinstein
(ed.), *Florentine Studies* (London, 1968).

others asking for their assistance showed. Bruni claimed that he had refused the offer of a bishopric made to him by Innocent VII.[34] The really important thing was that scriptors and secretaries wrote the pope's major political letters. They were employed to do this because their command of classical Latin carried weight in the diplomatic world. Giangaleazzo remarked that Salutati's letters written as Chancellor of Florence were worth a squadron of cavalry[35] and that was why Salutati's recommendation secured Bruni his place in the curia. The composition of such letters inevitably made them privy to all the secrets of their masters. It is remarkable that such detached observers should have been in control of supremely important ecclesiastical affairs.

Secondly, humanist activity at the curia was significant because it was accompanied by a passionate and continuous pursuit of classical culture, accompanied no longer by the restraining hand of Salutati. In Bruni's letters his frequent reports of curial affairs and his complaints about the turbulent war-ridden society about which the papal court moved are only intervals in a torrent of classical enthusiasm. Roman remains were observed. Bruni's description of the ancient monuments at Rimini in 1409 led him on to reflections on the superiority of ancient republican institutions in the city. The essence of a city he said was a magistracy with the power to summon citizens, a point connected with his interest in the Roman-republican origins of Florence.[36] Poggio was at this time already beginning the investigations which were to lead him many years later to compile the first list of Roman inscriptions. The letters contain many references to the exchange of treasured manuscripts between the classicists. Bruni writes to Niccoli in 1406 about a three-way exchange of Greek manuscripts between them and Antonio Loschi, also at that time at the papal court.[37] There was evidently a constant interchange of manuscripts between them. The connection with Loschi, who was also a papal secretary under Gregory XII and John XXIII, should remind us, incidentally, that classical friendship between the humanists was more important than the temporary political opposition which had placed Loschi and Salutati in opposite camps in the war

---

[34] *Epistolarum Libri VIII*, Vol. 2, p. 11; Luiso, pp. 35–6.
[35] Ullman, *Humanism of Coluccio Salutati*, p. 14.
[36] *Epistolarum Libri VIII*, Vol. 3, p. 9; Luiso, p. 63.
[37] *Epistolarum Libri VIII*, Vol. 10, p. 19; Luiso, pp. 23–4.

between Florence and Milan.[38] Bruni displayed a keen interest in
the translation of Plato about which he several times wrote to
Niccoli. Above all, the vision of the classical world, which this
acquaintance with monuments and manuscripts inspired, was
accompanied by an enthusiastic exaltation of the ancient world
for its superiority to present times as shown by its literature, its
philosophy and its political deeds. 'We are in these times' wrote
Bruni in 1408 'small men (*homunculi*) in whom greatness of soul is
not lacking but the material is certainly lacking for the amplifica-
tion of our name and glory.' In comparison with the deeds of
Minutius and Marcellus 'what have we which is similar or equal?
What is great or admirable apart from study and letters?'[39] This
depreciation of modern men and events in comparison with the
ancients had been deplored by Salutati. It was now given free
rein. It was encouraged by the humanists' consciousness that,
being in contact with the very cockpit of modern christianity and
politics, they knew everything about the corrupt and disordered
world in which they lived and could see clearly its inferiority to the
glories of ancient civilization. There can have been no time in
European history when antiquarianism produced a more vivid
sense of the superiority of a past age, worthy of the total
dedication of the student in the hope of imitating and recreating
it in the present. This was the state of mind which was to lead to
the total classicism of the Florentine renaissance, the attempt to
imitate not only Roman methods of writing but Latin letters,
Roman architecture, Greek sculpture and Platonic philosophy,
the whole panoply of revival and rebirth which was to make up
the classical renaissance.

The culmination of Florentine humanist effort in the late
Schism period was, from one point of view at any rate, Book I of
the *History of the Florentine People* which Leonardo Bruni composed in 1415 to 1416, immediately after he had returned to
Florence from the court of Pope John XXIII.[40] This told the
story of Florence from its foundation by Sulla in the Roman
republican period until the Guelf–Ghibelline disputes in the

---

[38] Loschi's life was first recounted by G. da Schio, *Sulla vita e sugli studi di
Antonio Loschi vicentino* (Padua, 1858). There is a recent investigation of part of it
by D. Girgensohn, 'Antonio Loschi und Baldassare Cossa', *Italia Medioevale e
Umanistica*, **30** (1987).

[39] *Epistolarum Libri VIII*, Vol. 2, p. 1; Luiso, p. 47.

[40] *Leonardo Bruni Aretino Historiarum Florentini populi libri XII*, ed. E. Santini &
C. di Pierro (Rerum Italicarum Scriptores, XIX, iii, Città di Castello, 1914–26),
pp. 5–26.

thirteenth century. The book presented the original Florence as a city established under the inspiration of the Roman republic whose remains were still visible in Bruni's day. He mentioned the aqueduct by which water was brought into the town, the theatre outside the walls, now incorporated into the city, the temple which was now the Baptistery. These people, he said, had built in imitation of Rome itself. They had a capital and forum, public baths, a temple of Mars. This was the city to which Cicero and Sallust had referred, in Bruni's estimation, and no doubt in his remarks we see the humanist assumptions about the buildings of contemporary Florence which deluded Brunelleschi into his confusion of Roman and Romanesque architecture. Florence was in fact poor in Roman remains but classical enthusiasm encouraged its devotees to create a political chronology based on literary sources, while exaggerating the archaeological evidence in order to strengthen the essential Romanism to which they were attached.

The decline of the Roman Empire began, said Bruni, at the time when Rome, having abandoned liberty, began to serve the emperors. Augustus and Trajan were worthy rulers, but after them came disaster. 'Liberty ended in the imperial name and after liberty virtue also departed.' 'Under Julius Caesar how many lights of the republic were extinguished.' The idea of imperial decline, perhaps taken over from Orosius, was converted into a conception of the loss of liberty and with liberty of the civilization that went with it. With these sentences the Gibbonian conception of history was inaugurated. Bruni also had a clear idea of the long period of decay caused by the barbarian invasions. After that flood had passed he said, 'cities throughout Italy began to grow and flourish and to raise themselves up into their early authority', *pristina auctoritas*. The distinction of ancient and medieval history, the decline and recovery of civilization were present to his eyes.

When Bruni was back in Florence writing his *History of the Florentine People* his friend Poggio was still at the Council of Constance to which he had gone as a secretary of Pope John XXIII. There are no elaborate published literary pieces from Poggio at this time but there is an oration about the clergy and there are various letters which convey a distinct impression of an individual mind and attitude. The oration about the clergy is an attack on clerical behaviour which might have come from any sharp-minded observer, distinguished only by its wide-ranging criticism of hypocrisy and financial greed and by the charming

Latin in which it is couched.[41] The letters seem to me more interesting because Poggio presents himself in them as an employee of the curia observing the Council of Constance with the enlightened detachment of an observer, watching a collection of people and events to be described with the parallels and the insights of classical authors. In the period before Martin V's election in 1417 he wrote to Francesco Pizzolpassi advising him not to come to Constance before a pope was elected because the discussion in the Council might have disastrous effects and constructing parallels at some length between ecclesiastical disputes and the political quarrels of the last days of the Roman republic.[42] The most remarkable thing that Poggio wrote at Constance however was his letter to Bruni about the trial and burning of the Czech heretic Jerome of Prague dated 30 May 1416.[43] Jerome evidently made a profound impression on Poggio. It was not for him, Poggio said significantly to decide who was right or wrong. What impressed him was the language of the martyr which approached the *facundia priscorum,* the eloquence of the ancients, the arguments, the demeanour, the faith with which he answered adversaries. His dignity resembled that of another Cato. His behaviour when he was burnt was close to the constancy of soul of the Stoics. His acceptance of death claimed comparison with Mutius and Socrates. In all these writings one must of course allow a certain force to the passionate devotion to the Latin tongue which Poggio characteristically showed. The power of composition, *ratio dicendi,* was what separated men from animals and Poggio was at that time conducting his expeditions from Constance to nearby abbey libraries in search of manuscripts of Cicero and Quintilian which would improve the literary powers of modern humanity. But beyond this purely linguistic aspect of his outlook there was also an acceptance of the classical point of view which made the proceedings on which his income depended appear to him barbarous so that he appears in his writings almost as an anthropologist observing the deplorable behaviour of a curious sect. This is an

[41] *Oratio Patres Reverendissimos,* reprinted in *Opera,* Vol. 2, pp. 13–21. Cf. R. Fubini, 'Un' Orazione di Poggio Bracciolini sui Vizi del clero scritta al tempo del concilio di Costanza', *Giornale Storico della letterature Italiana,* **142** (1965).

[42] A. Wilmanns, 'Ueber die Brifsammlungen des Poggio Bracciolini', *Zentralblatt für Bibliothekswesen,* **30** (1913), pp. 459–60, reprinted *Opera* (Turin, 1969) Vol. 4, pp. 320–1.

[43] T. de Tonellis, *Poggii Epistolae,* reprinted in *Opera,* Vol. 3 (Turin, 1963), letter I, p. 2; Poggio Bracciolini, *Lettere,* ed. H. Harth, (Florence, 1984), Vol. 2 pp. 157–63.

attitude which classicism has never ceased to encourage but it is interesting to see it so clearly presented already by Poggio.

It might be objected that, in emphasizing the extreme classicism of Bruni and Poggio, I am presenting a one-sided view. I do not think that this is so. Bruni, Poggio and Niccoli, from whose hand nothing remains but who is shown clearly by the others' letters to share their point of view, remained close friends for many years after 1415 and presided over the Florentine Renaissance, not only its literary manifestations but also the artistic side developed by Brunelleschi and Donatello with the patronage of Cosimo de' Medici. It is therefore worth noticing that this group flourished and blossomed in the last decade of the Schism in political circumstances which were exceptionally favourable to its attitudes.

I have ignored in this lecture two notable compositions of the classicists in the period before Salutati's death which have attracted much valuable attention as expressions of their political interests. I mean Salutati's reponse to the invective of Antonio Loschi[44] and Bruni's *Laudatio Florentinae Urbis*.[45] These are both defences of the virtues of republicanism as exemplified in the Florentine constitution and they are no doubt responses to the threat of Milanese tyranny. I have neglected them because they seem to me to be of relatively subsidiary importance in the evolution of humanism and it may be helpful, in contrast, to present humanism against the ecclesiastical background, whose importance has been rather underestimated in recent writing. The really important point about humanism was not that it was republican but that it was thought by some people to be pagan. In one sense the most important document about early humanism was Dominici's *Lucula Noctis* in which the point was fully and correctly stated. The reason why humanism developed so extravagantly at that period was partly that the humanists had an exceptionally easy relationship with the centre of ecclesiastical power at the papal court. This was made possible by the events of the late Schism period which gave both the city of Florence and the individual humanists unparalleled power over the papacy. It is of course extremely dangerous to state general links of causation of this kind between political and cultural movements. There are so many accidental factors involved which determined the careers of individual humanists and helped to shape their outlook. Nevertheless it seems to me impossible to imagine Florentine humanism evolving

[44] Garin, *Prosatori Latini*, pp. 8–37.
[45] H. Baron, *From Petrarch to Leonardo Bruni*, pp. 232–63.

in the way it did if it had been faced by a powerful papacy defending orthodox values and on the other hand easy to see it in the circumstances of ecclesiastical confusion in which their city had a crucial power over popes and councils and they were valued functionaries of the papal bureaucracy. They were not heretics anxious to fight the church. They were aesthetes who were largely indifferent to it and the acceptance of its generous salaries for their invaluable literary expertise gave them the easiest position for the adoption of an alternative set of values which could not be condemned quite simply because they were indispensable. The Schism, which was the collapse of the medieval papacy, provided the setting for the promotion of the Renaissance.

CYRIAC OF ANCONA

CYRIAC of Ancona—the name, because of its natural music, is familiar to many who know little of the man; and not a few respectable students of classical antiquity are unaware that his contribution to our knowledge of ancient monuments and inscriptions is substantial, and that as an archaeological observer he was at least a century ahead of his time. That is my excuse for beginning with a brief sketch of his life.[1]

Born in 1391, he began travelling when only nine years old, in the company of his mother's brother, who was a merchant; and many of his journeys, especially the earlier, were primarily commercial. Later he was often given diplomatic missions—for instance, as a trusted envoy of Pope Eugenius IV: but whatever the ostensible purpose of his journey, he seems never to have neglected a chance of searching out and recording the remains of classical antiquity.

At the age of thirty he studied Latin systematically, and learnt Greek at Constantinople four years later. In 1433, by which time, apart from extensive travels in Italy, he had already visited Sicily, Dalmatia, Egypt, and both the Ægean and Constantinople twice, he joined the Court of Sigismund at Siena, entered Rome with him for his coronation as Emperor, and remained to guide him among its antiquities. For this he was highly qualified, since he had studied and made drawings of the monuments of Rome nine years before. Two years later—1435—he visited Illyria, Epirus, and Greece: in 1436 the pyramids of Egypt; Athens, and the Peloponnese. Then, after a stay of six years in Italy, he went east again in 1443; in 1448 travelled a second time through the Peloponnese; was with Mahomet II at the siege of Constantinople in 1453, and died at Cremona about 1455.[2]

[1] This is based on R. Sabbadini's excellent article in *Enciclopedia italiana* x (1931), p. 438, *s.v.* CIRIACO. It is a pleasure to acknowledge the generous help of other scholars, especially Mr. Charles Mitchell and Professor R. Weiss.   [2] See E. Jacobs, *Oriens* ii, 1949, p. 15.

The fruits of these travels were a number of letters, and six volumes of Commentaries, which together must have contained a vast quantity of antiquarian material: descriptions, drawings and measurements of buildings, drawings of sculpture—even of curious animals such as the white elephants of the island of Meroe—and many copies of inscriptions. The Commentaries probably perished in the fire which, in 1514, destroyed the library of Alessandro and Costanzo Sforza at Pesaro: but before this disaster Cyriac's friends, and other humanists of the next generation, had drawn on them freely, and we possess some of the extracts they made. These—several of them illustrated— together with fragments and copies of the letters, and with the manuscript life of Cyriac by Francesco Scalamonti, continued by Felix Felicianus, and printed by Giuseppe Colucci in 1792, are our chief source for his movements, his work and his character.[1] There are, in addition, two manuscripts believed to have been written and illustrated by Cyriac himself, which ought naturally to be the first criteria for his distinctive lettering and his draughtsmanship.

There would not be time to discuss, or even to review, in a single lecture, all the problems connected with the transmission of Cyriac's writings and drawings. I propose therefore to confine myself to one theme only, namely his fidelity when recording antiquities. This may seem difficult when we have little that is autographic, and when we lack the evidence to establish the exact relationship of the other surviving manuscripts to those written by him which have since been lost. Nevertheless it is still possible to pass a judgement which, within its limits, can be shown to be perfectly sound. On the scale of truth we may not know the highest level Cyriac reached, but we can usually fix the level below which he did not fall.

On the fragments attributed to his own hand we can obviously pass a direct judgement, especially if the objects he is describing survive. But even when dealing with copies of his lost journals and letters, we can still rest assured that a copy, although it may be less accurate, can hardly be more accurate than the lost original. To put it very simply: Cyriac draws a building or a piece of sculpture: the copyist has this drawing before him, but has never seen the original object: he may therefore, in copying Cyriac's drawing, depict that object less accurately than Cyriac

[1] Mr. Charles Mitchell is preparing a new edition of the *Life* which will contain much material previously omitted; M. Jean Colin is on the point of publishing a comprehensive study of Cyriac.

did, but he cannot, except by sheer accident or inspired guess-work—making an architectural form more orthodox, for example—depict it more accurately. Thus, if we have two versions by two copyists of one of Cyriac's drawings of an object—an object out of reach of the copyists themselves—it is safe to say that the version which reproduces the original object more faithfully is also more faithful to Cyriac; and, conversely, Cyriac is entitled to the credit for any detail, in either of the drawings, that is more accurate than the same detail in the other. With inscriptions the matter is a little different. Superior knowledge of Greek or Latin might enable the copyist, if Cyriac had blundered, to produce a superior version. I have laboured this apparently simple point because it does seem that neglect of it has allowed scholars to wander—or even walk briskly—down misleading by-paths.

On this basis, then, I propose to examine a series of Cyriac's records (his alleged original manuscripts or copies of them) of various kinds of antiquities—sculpture, architecture, ancient sites—with the purpose of demonstrating that not only was he trying to make a true record of the objects, but was succeeding so well that he occasionally puts later investigators to shame. I shall then discuss the question of his imaginative reconstruction of ancient monuments, as distinct from his record of actual remains. Finally, I shall show an example of how he can first record an antiquity and then indulge his imagination in interpreting it, not to deceive, but as a light-hearted fantasy.

In order to avoid presenting an unnecessarily complicated picture of the problem—which is certainly complex enough—I shall confine myself in the main to five only of the extant manuscripts, and shall endeavour to indicate the special character of each.

They are, first, the Codex Ambrosiano-Trotti, which is believed to be Cyriac's own record of his journey through the Peloponnese in 1448:[1] second the Codex Hamiltonianus, which bears a dedication to Pietro Donato, bishop of Padua: for this too the claim has been made that Cyriac both wrote and illustrated it.[2] Next, the Codex Barberinianus in the Vatican, compiled by the architect Giuliano di San Gallo and his son Francesco about 1500.[3] Fourth, the Codex Manzoni, which, though exceedingly rough, sometimes throws light on the other

[1] Sabbadini in *Miscellanea Ceriani* (1910), p. 237.

[2] Michaelis, *Arch. Zeit.* xl (1882), pp. 367 ff.; Mommsen, ibid., pp. 402 f.

[3] Chr. Hülsen, *Il libro di Giuliano da Sangallo: Codice Vaticano Barberiniano Lat. 4424* (1910).

manuscripts;[1] and, lastly, the Codex Ashmolensis, compiled by Bartholomaeus Fontius in the generation after Cyriac, which includes copies of certain drawings by Cyriac that have not otherwise survived.[2]

Clearly, any manuscript that can be identified as from Cyriac's own hand is of the utmost importance, and this claim has been advanced for the Codex Ambrosiano-Trotti, from which Plate I, *a* is reproduced. Sabbadini makes out a strong case for its being the autographic record of Cyriac's second journey to the Peloponnese in 1448, and if we accept the claim this manuscript must form a touchstone for any other claimants.[3] The drawing is a fair sample of its contents, depicting one of a well-known class of Hellenistic tomb-reliefs; this particular specimen has disappeared, but one resembling it, now in Berlin, will serve for comparison with the drawing (Plate 1, *b*):[4] the heroized dead, at a sacred banquet, are approached by worshippers, and in the background, seen through a window, is the horse which both marks the status of the hero and symbolizes his journey to the next world. Two things are obvious in Cyriac's drawing. One is the determination to reproduce the details of the relief as accurately as possible. The second is the untutored character of the draughtsmanship: he not only has little style of his own, and, one would say, had never had drawing-lessons: but he also usually fails to convey the style of the original. He makes the figures look like living beings and not like sculpture: see, for instance, how the horse has come to life and has put its head through into the room. There is no fantasy: he is all for facts: and despite the lack of style and the vague anatomy, there is not the slightest difficulty in recognizing the kind of relief intended.

Now if the date 1448 be accepted, this is the work not of a novice, but of a man in his fifties, who had been drawing antiquities for thirty years or more. We could not therefore possibly expect any radical change in his style later on, and anything he had drawn before would be likely to be even less facile —more unsophisticated—than this. This is an important point,

[1] Hülsen, op. cit., p. 37.

[2] The substantive publication is by F. Saxl in *Journal of Warburg and Courtauld Institutes*, iv (1940–1), pp. 19–46, see also *Hesperia*, xii (1943), pp. 115 ff. (Lehmann).

[3] loc. cit. n. 1, p. 27; where Sabbadini claims other smaller fragments of manuscripts as autographs, including that in the Vatican quoted in n. 2, p. 39.

[4] C. Blümel, *Staatl. Mus. zu Berlin. Katalog der gr. Skulpt.* iii, no. K 100, p. 69, pl. 81.

as one sees on turning to look at the second manuscript which claims to be from Cyriac's own hand. This, the Hamilton Codex in Berlin, has played a major part in the forming of judgements on Cyriac's whole attitude towards antiquity. Its claim to be an autograph by him rests partly on the handwriting, partly on a dedication inscribed in it which reads as follows:

R.D. ⟨Reverendissimo Domino⟩ Petro Episcopo Patavino
Kyriacus Anconitanus.

We know of Cyriac's friendly relations with Pietro Donato, Bishop of Padua, and the dedication seems explicit enough. Do the contents substantiate the claim?

The drawing (Plates 2 and 4, *b*) depicts a Doric temple with a sculptured pediment, which, the inscription informs us, is 'ingens et mirabile Palladis divae marmoreum templum'—in short the Parthenon. It is the West front, where in the pediment was represented the contest of Athena and Poseidon for the land of Athens. The two deities had driven up each in a two-horse chariot and had arrived in the centre of the pediment—Athena on our left, Poseidon on our right. Very little now remains of these sculptures: we know from the drawings made by Jacques Carrey in 1674 what the composition was (Plate 4, *a*):[1] he was a quick and unattractive but remarkably faithful draughtsman, who shows clearly the remains of Athena and Poseidon, the chariot of Athena (Poseidon's was already destroyed), their charioteers, and various minor personages. The Hamilton manuscript has eliminated Poseidon altogether, and gives instead a single female figure who seems concerned only with the horses. The others present seem to be mostly children, and mostly winged.

This drawing must have been based on Cyriac's first studies in Athens in 1436, for he did not visit it again until 1447, the year of Donato's death. How does it agree in style and general feeling with the drawing (Plate 1, *a*) which is supposed to have been done twelve years later? Hardly at all. Here you have a draughtsman who, within his limitations, is an able one, neat and accomplished; who can sketch in a fairly complicated pose, for example, the crouching figure in the centre; but whose mis-statements are almost unthinkable in the man who made the

---

[1] H. A. Omont, *Dessins . . . attribués à J. Carrey*: on the question of the authorship of the drawings see also Ch. Picard, *Man. d'archéol. grecque: Sculpture*, ii, p. 401, n. 1.

drawing of the Hellenistic relief in Plate 1. The draughtsman here is not interested in reproducing exactly what was in the pediment: on the contrary, he deliberately tricks out all the figures with wings in a quite irresponsible way. Facts take second place to fantasy.

These features may raise a doubt in our minds: but there are even more serious grounds for disquiet, which appear when we turn to the third of our manuscripts. This is the Barberini manuscript in the Vatican, begun in 1465 by the architect Giuliano di San Gallo, who did most of the drawings: he was helped by his son Francesco, not born until 1494, who knew Latin, and added the inscriptions. The manuscript contains much that is not taken from Cyriac: what was taken—and it seems to have been done about 1510—was transferred on to noble sheets of parchment nearly eighteen inches high by fifteen inches wide, from the pages of a book about a quarter the size; and the pictures have been shuffled a good deal in the process, sometimes by accident, sometimes deliberately (Plate 3).[1]

Here there appears again the drawing of the Parthenon (the inscription above is similar though not identical) (Plates 3, 5) and if the current hypothesis, first advanced by Mommsen,[2] is correct, that the Hamilton Codex is Cyriac's autograph, this San Gallo manuscript, where it differs from the Hamilton, ought always to be inferior, being only a copy. And in one respect it is obviously less accurate, namely in the columns, where the capitals have been transformed from the Doric of the real building into a kind of Composite. But corrupt though it may be in that detail, it seems to reproduce the pediment more accurately than does the Hamilton manuscript: the proportions are less stilted, and the figure on the right of the centre, who, as we have seen, should be Poseidon, although more sketchily drawn and somewhat ambiguously clothed, does seem to have a beard. Below the temple in both manuscripts are other drawings. The Hamilton Codex (Plate 2) tells us that they are the friezes (*listae parietum*), and in the San Gallo manuscript it can be clearly seen that they are indeed intended for part of the frieze of the Parthenon: on the right a horseman, then some oxen and an attendant (Plate 5). The horseman could be from the West or the North frieze; the others must be from the North: for on the South frieze both horsemen and oxen face right. The next two figures could be some of the old men shown as taking part in the procession on

[1] See Hülsen, op. cit., p. 38.
[2] *Jahrb. der K. Preuss. Kunstsammlungen*, 1883, pp. 80 ff.

PLATE 1

a. Drawing from Codex Ambrosiane-Trotti

b. Relief in Berlin

PLATE 2

Page from Codex Hamiltonianus

THE PARTHENON

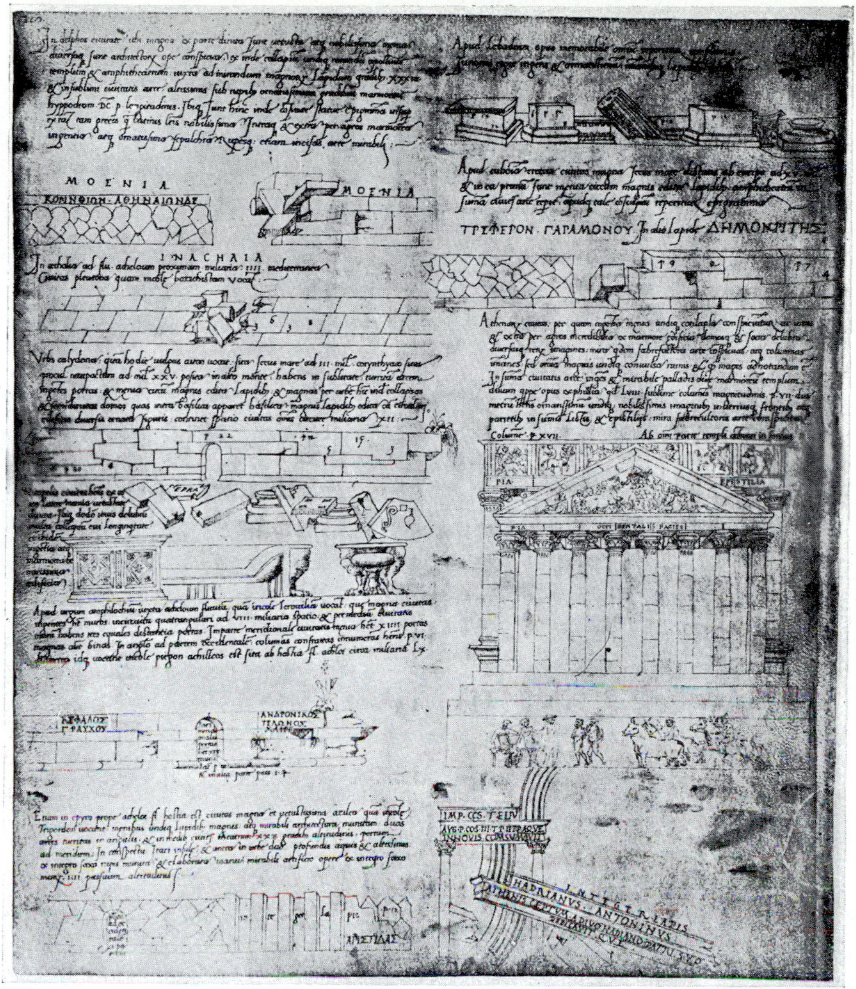

PLATE 3

Page from Codex Barberinianus

ANTIQUITIES OF GREECE

PLATE 4

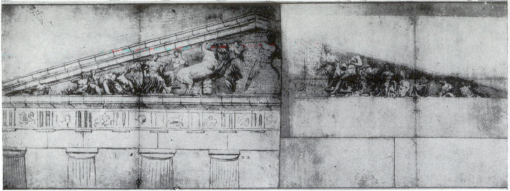

a. Drawing of West pediment of the Parthenon, about 1674

b. Drawing from Codex Hamiltonianus. (Cf. Pl. 2)

c. Drawing from Codex Barberinianus. (Cf. Pl. 3)

d. Part of the frieze of the Parthenon, East side

PLATE 5

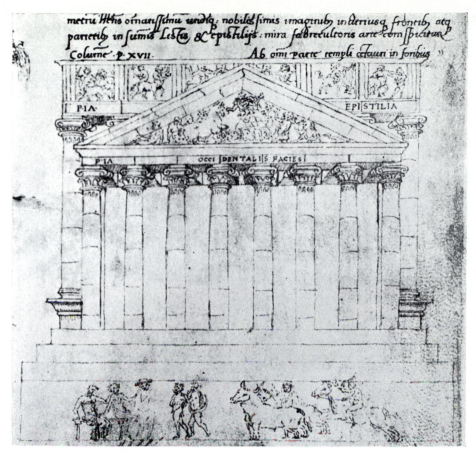

Drawing from Codex Barberinianus. (Cf. Pl. 3)

THE PARTHENON

PLATE 6

a. Engraving by James Stuart

b. Restoration by Nicholas Revett

THE GATEWAY OF HADRIAN'S AQUEDUCT, ATHENS

PLATE 7

a. Codex Barberinianus. (Cf. Pl. 3)

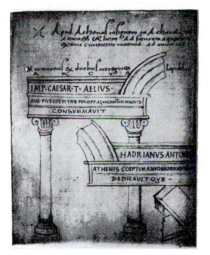

b. Codex Hamiltonianus

c. Codex Manzoni

THE GATEWAY OF HADRIAN'S AQUEDUCT, ATHENS

PLATE 8

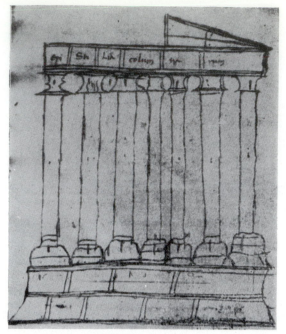

a. Codex Manzoni

b. Codex Hamiltonianus

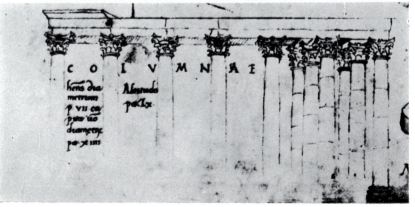

c. Codex Barberinianus

THE TEMPLE OF ZEUS OLYMPIOS, ATHENS

PLATE 9

a. The Temple of Zeus Olympios, Athens

b. Oeniadae:drawing from Codex Barberinianus. (Cf. Pl. 3)

PLATE 10

a

b

c

d

Four pages from Codex Ashmolensis

THE TEMPLE OF HADRIAN AT CYZICUS

PLATE 11

a. Castel S. Angelo, Rome

b. Drawing in Modena

THE MAUSOLEUM OF HADRIAN

PLATE 12

Page from Codex Ashmolensis
THE MAUSOLEUM OF HADRIAN

PLATE 13

a.

b.

Details of a bronze door, St. Peter's, Rome
THE MAUSOLEUM OF HADRIAN

PLATE 14

a. Cast from a rock-crystal in Berlin

b. Drawing from Codex
Barberinianus

c, d. Statue of giant, Athens

e. Drawing from Codex Hamiltonianus

PLATE 15

Page from Codex Barberinianus

ANTIQUITIES OF GREECE AND ASIA MINOR

PLATE 16

Drawing from Codex Barberinianus. (Cf. Pl. 15)

the North frieze;[1] and on the left, despite the deplorably sketchy drawing, a slab of the East frieze can be recognized. There are only six seated figures facing right on the frieze of the Parthenon, so we must make our choice from them; and the most promising candidate is the slab on which are seated Poseidon, Apollo, and Artemis (Plate 4, d). What distinguishes it from the others is that both Poseidon and Apollo are raising their hands, as are the figures in the San Gallo drawing.

In the Hamilton manuscript two of the same slabs are reproduced, but they have been curiously transformed (Plate 4, c). The figures have been given a completely three-dimensional existence as if they were in a painting, with no suggestion of their sculptural character at all. Moreover, although they are only sketched in, they are most ably done, and possibly by a hand different from that which drew the pediment above. Look for instance at the skilful way in which the relative position of the figures in space is suggested.

How can we explain the greater accuracy of the San Gallo manuscript over the Hamilton, if the Hamilton is the work of Cyriac himself and the San Gallo, as we know it to be, only a copy? We have already argued that a more accurate manuscript must necessarily be closer to Cyriac: yet here we have a manuscript claimed to be the very work of Cyriac himself which is inferior in accuracy to an acknowledged copy. One begins to doubt the autographic character of some at least of the drawings. And it seems to me that as soon as one of them is admitted to be by a different hand,[2] this undermines the whole claim that the Hamilton manuscript is an autograph by Cyriac. If one part is by someone else, why not another? And if another, why not all?

Moreover, there is further evidence that seems fatal to the claim. On the same page as the Parthenon in the San Gallo manuscript (Plate 3) there appears another of the monuments of Athens, the ornamental gateway, completed by Antoninus Pius, of the reservoir in which Hadrian's aqueduct ended on the slopes of Mount Lycabettus. Today its masonry has been removed to the Royal Gardens, and even when the architects

[1] e.g. slab X (A. H. Smith, *Parthenon* (1910), pl. 44).

[2] Michaelis, for example (loc. cit. in n. 2, p. 27) acutely assesses the discrepancies between the Hamilton and San Gallo MSS., but refrains from the obvious inference that the Hamilton drawing of the façade of the Parthenon is not by Cyriac, holding rather that it is a fancy version made by him from his own original, more accurate drawing. Cf. *A.J.A.* lxii (1958), pp. 222 f. (Donaldson).

Stuart and Revett were working in Athens in the middle of the eighteenth century, only two columns remained upright, as may be seen from the drawing by Stuart (Plate 6, *a*).[1] In Cyriac's day also, only two columns remained, but in front of them lay a large piece of the rest of the archway and of the horizontal Ionic entablature: these were carved, as Cyriac recorded and San Gallo faithfully repeated, from a single block—*integer lapis* (Plate 7, *a*). It is through this record by Cyriac that we know the whole of the inscription. But although the right half of the stone had disappeared by their time, Stuart and Revett, strange to say, also recovered the full text of the inscription, as may be seen in Revett's restoration (Plate 6, *b*). They were able to do so because Jacques Spon, passing through Zara on the Adriatic in 1676, had seen a manuscript which he described as being then two hundred years old: in it was the full inscription from the gateway: Spon printed it in his book,[2] and Stuart and Revett transcribed it from there. Two hundred years takes one back to the third quarter of the fifteenth century: the manuscript at Zara was almost certainly derived from Cyriac. This, however, is by the way: to return to the point at issue, San Gallo (Plate 7, *a*) gives a tolerable reproduction of the gateway, although he transforms the Ionic columns into Corinthian; and he shows the fallen arch and entablature as they lay. We must therefore assume that they were shown thus in Cyriac's original drawing.

How then does the Hamilton manuscript, allegedly Cyriac's own, show it? (Plate 7, *b*.) Oddly enough it does not show the arch fallen in this way, but floating in the air on an even keel, and unsupported by the fallen blocks below, the nature of which the draughtsman hardly seems to understand, transforming—for instance—what was, from the evidence of the San Gallo manuscript, a neatly drawn clamp-cutting, into a meaningless flap.[3] Can we believe that Cyriac, copying his own drawings in order to give them to a friend, would have shown so little feeling for them and for the objects represented in them? For final confirmation that the original drawing by Cyriac showed

---

[1] Stuart and Revett, *Antiquities of Athens*, iii (1794), ch. iv, pp. 27–29. Pl. I (actual state); Pl. II (restored elevation).

[2] *Voyage d'Italie, de Dalmatie, de Grèce et du Levant* (1724 ed.), ii, p. 99 (with illustration): cf. p. 52, from which it seems that the manuscript was in the possession of Valerio Ponte.

[3] In the drawing by San Gallo (Pl. 7, *a*) the clamp-cutting can be seen immediately below the second syllable of DEDICAVITQUE: in the Hamilton MS. (Pl. 7, *b*) below the last syllable.

the arch lying fallen, one has only to look at the same subject in the Manzoni manuscript (Plate 7, *c*) copied neither from the Hamilton nor from the San Gallo manuscript, for it has elements which are not found in either of them. It too preserves the relative position of the fallen block.

Another drawing in the Manzoni manuscript (Plate 8, *a*) is of a more famous ancient monument in Athens, the columns of the temple of Zeus Olympios, seen from the South. Plate 9, *a* shows them as they are today. The copyist has perhaps not understood what he was drawing, for although he seems to indicate the return of the entablature on the East face,[1] he does not distinguish the columns that support it. But he does include the great podium which is an important feature of the building. And he certainly does a good deal better than the draughtsman of the Hamilton manuscript, who is alleged to be Cyriac himself (Plate 8, *b*). Here the colonnade is a single row of miniature Gothic pillars—even the lettering is Gothic—and they were surely drawn by a man who had never seen or never looked at a Corinthian capital in his life. The effect of reality is not helped by his having given the first column on the left a capital—reversed—at the base, as well as one at the top. Plate 8, *c* is San Gallo's version, which is evidently superior in some ways to the Hamilton Codex. It adds measurements; it makes the capitals look Corinthian, and it shows quite successfully not only the seven columns of the South side, but also the group of columns at the East end of the building, of which the Hamilton Codex gives not a hint. Yet this feature must have been in Cyriac's original. How otherwise could San Gallo have known of it?

The conclusion is unavoidable: the drawings in the Hamilton Codex are not autographs by Cyriac, despite the dedication. For even if Cyriac had been making drawings for his friend in haste, which might account for carelessness, could he possibly have changed his style to such an extent, and would he have done anything so inept as to put a capital where the base of a column should be, though knowing, as the evidence of the other manuscripts proves, the true form and approximately the true proportions of the real colonnade?

If we accept the dedication to Pietro Donato at its face value, to imply that the Hamilton Codex was a gift from Cyriac, then a possible explanation might be that Cyriac, wishing to make a present of an extract from his records, and having no time to copy the drawings himself, either gave them to someone else to

[1] Unless he thought that it was the corner of a pediment.

copy, or lent them to Donato, who employed someone else—
apparently more than one person—to copy them.[1] That would
not prevent Cyriac dedicating the result to Donato, however
little pleased he may have been with the attempt of the scribe
or scribes to reproduce his drawings.

These conclusions must be stressed, for the comparatively low
opinion held by some scholars of Cyriac's trustworthiness is
partly due to their using the drawings of the Hamilton Codex as
their criterion. No matter what the exact relationship of these
four manuscripts to Cyriac's originals, he is entitled, as we have
seen, to the credit for everything that is best in them; and even the
glance we have given at this selection, with that proviso in mind,
conveys some impression of his quality as observer and recorder.

Let us now turn to consider his method with ancient sites.
I have chosen a little-known site which happens to be described
and illustrated on the same page of the San Gallo manuscript
as the Parthenon and the aqueduct of Hadrian (Plates 3, 9, *b*).
This was Oeniadae in Acarnania, not far from the mouth of the
Achelous, on the upper lip of the mouth of the gulf of Corinth,
a site so well protected by marshes that in winter, as readers of
Thucydides will remember, it was considered impregnable; and
Phormio, who was stationed at Naupactus in the third year of
the Peloponnesian War with an Athenian fleet, did not venture
to attack it.[2] It was heavily fortified, and much of its fine circuit
of walls, largely of polygonal masonry, still survives, including
a number of gateways. Cyriac visited the site in 1436: San Gallo
copied his drawing (Plate 9, *b*), and his description thus:

> Also in Epirus near the mouths of the river Achelous is a great and
> very ancient city, Axilea, which the natives called Trigordon, defended
> on all sides by fortifications with large stones and marvellous architec-
> ture: two citadels with towers at the corners, and in the middle of the
> city a theatre thirty steps high. A harbour on the south in sight of the
> island of Ithaca. Also two caves in the city with very deep water sur-
> rounded by very high stone walls cut by hand from the living rock.
> Walls too of wonderful artificial work and of living rock 4 paces high.

The gate in Plate 9, *b* gives a tolerably correct impression of
the kind of masonry and the general appearance of the walls—
a combination of genuine arches with polygonal stonework—
which still exist. But what is the curious structure on the right?

---

[1] De Rossi, *Inscr. Chr.* ii. 1, p. 360, suggests that Donato himself may have
copied part.

[2] Thucydides ii. 102. For the history and topography of the city, see
Pauly-Wissowa, xvii, pp. 2204 ff., *s.v.* OINIADAI.

It is marked *integer lapis*, which in this context must mean 'the living rock', and seems to consist of five buttresses or bastions, of no obvious purpose, since for defence they would not be so effective as an unbroken surface of rock. The site of Oeniadae was excavated by an American expedition in 1900.[1] They found that on the edge of the harbour there had been a hill of solid grey limestone, rising abruptly from the water's edge. This had been cut back to form a nearly square area about 150 feet each way, leaving a number of buttress-like projections in the face of the rock. Where the hill sloped away, it had been built up to full height with polygonal masonry, as may be seen in the drawing (Plate 9, *b*). The projections had formed a series of supports for the roof of a building originally twenty feet high, the rest of the roof being carried by rows of columns running out at right angles to the rock-face. The building, of the third century B.C., had been a combination of ship-sheds and naval storehouses, with slips up which the triremes were drawn. Here again, then, there is no reason to doubt that Cyriac was endeavouring to reproduce accurately what he saw. Leake visited the site in 1809, and identified the ship-sheds, but took the projections to be of masonry because one had collapsed, and not, as Cyriac had rightly seen, of the living rock. Neither Leake nor, at first, the American excavators, saw the inscription ΑΡΙΣΤΙΔΑΣ which Cyriac recorded, and this, like the other inscriptions he shows on city-walls, some of which are clearly late funerary inscriptions, goes to prove his trustworthiness in this matter.[2]

At Oeniadae this inscription did—and does—exist, although a good deal smaller than the drawing would lead one to believe, the letters being about seven inches high. The point becomes a crucial one when an inscription is shown as being on a building that has now completely disappeared (Plate 10, *a*). The Codex Ashmolensis—our fifth and last manuscript—reproduces a series of six drawings copied from Cyriac. They are the only pictorial record of a temple which in late antiquity was reckoned the eighth wonder of the world, the temple of Hadrian at Cyzicus, on the shores of the Sea of Marmara. It seems to have been remarkable chiefly for its size, but also for its curious plan, which was in three tiers.

The temple today is nothing but a brushwood-covered mound,

---

[1] B. Powell and J. M. Sears in *A.J.A.* viii (1904), pp. 137–237; a report of the excavations, with photographs of the walls and gates.

[2] e.g. those on the walls of the Amphilochian Argos: Hülsen, op. cit., p. 41, fig. 39.

with elaborate tunnels underneath it, but when Cyriac first saw it, in 1431, he described it as being almost intact, and he did his best to prevent it being despoiled for the building of mosques in neighbouring towns, by interceding with the Turkish governor, who was of Greek extraction.

It is true that his later more detailed description shows that only about half the colonnade was standing to the full height, but since they were the largest columns in the world, and there had been more than sixty of them originally, it must have been a stupendous sight.

I have discussed elsewhere Cyriac's account of this temple:[1] sufficient here to say that there is still some question whether he saw the dedicatory epigram on the building or took it from an anthology, but little doubt that his measurements are substantially correct, for example, those of the doorway twenty feet wide and forty feet high, and of the Corinthian capital nine feet high (Plate 10, *a*, *b*); and that his drawings of the unique portico (Plate 10, *c*, *d*) and of vine-wreathed columns in other parts of the building are genuine records of what he saw on the site. Fragments of a capital from Cyzicus provide measurements close to those in Plate 10, *b*; fragments of vine-wreathed columns have been found there; and it is possible that a complete column in Constantinople once belonged to the portico.[2]

Let us now consider another side of Cyriac's activities, his drawings of the monuments of Rome. And here we are on dubious ground, for although he is stated to have studied the monuments of Rome and to have spent forty days making drawings of them in 1424,[3] we do not know what form those drawings took; whether they were 'actual state' drawings, showing the ruins as he saw them, or whether they were reconstructions, showing the buildings as they were imagined to have been in antiquity. On the assumption that they were of the second kind —imaginative reconstructions—it was once believed that his

[1] *Journal of Warburg and Courtauld Inst.* xix, pp. 179 ff. I take the opportunity of correcting three misprints in the transcription there of the Cyzicene epigram: the first line should read (as may be seen in our Plate 10, *a*)

ΕΚ ΔΑΠΕΔΟΥ ΜΩΡΘΩ ΣΕΝΟΛΛΗΣΑΣΙΑΣ

and of noting a piece of sculpture perhaps from the temple: G. Mendel, *Cat. des sculpt., Musée de Brousse* (1908), p. 27, no. 32.

[2] loc. cit. n. 1, pl. 39, *b*, *c*. Mr. Donald Strong suggests that a gravestone from Cyzicus (*Ath. Mitt.* xxix (1904), p. 289, fig. 20) where the dead man is shown beside a large Corinthian capital, may be that of a craftsman employed on the temple.

[3] De Rossi, *Inscr. Chr.* ii. 1, pp. 357, 359.

drawings had formed the basis for a series of amusing little pictures drawn about 1465 by Marcanova—the doctor-philosopher of Padua—which are preserved in Modena, and of which the Mausoleum of Hadrian (Plate 11, *b*) is a fair specimen.[1] This can hardly be considered a serious attempt to reconstruct ancient Rome from the remains. The artist could not entirely disregard the great building that still survived (Plate 11, *a*), but his picture has a scene-painter's irresponsibility, with its buildings of improbable proportions backed by hills of incredible declivity; its towers of medieval aspect; even the angel on the summit (erected in the Middle Ages); even a papal coat of arms. It is no longer believed that Marcanova's drawings owed much to Cyriac's. But there does exist a reconstruction of the Mausoleum of Hadrian which gives evidence of quite a different approach to the problem, and although it lacks that delightful air of medieval romance, and is even less successful in its proportions than Marcanova's, does show signs of being based on direct observation of the surviving building. Plate 12 shows that reconstruction as it appears in the Codex Ashmolensis.

There are other reproductions of this design, especially that on one of the bronze doors of St. Peter's in Rome, made by Antonio Filarete[2] (Plate 13, *a*, *b*). The subject is the martyrdom of St. Peter, and Rome is indicated by four of its monuments—a tree, presumably the enigmatic Golden Palm; and three which still survived, namely, the pyramid of Cestius, which was sometimes called the pyramid of Remus; the pyramid of Romulus, which stood in the Borgo Nuovo: and the Mausoleum of Hadrian.[3] The bronze doors were made between 1439 and 1445, that is to say whilst Cyriac was still alive. The proportions here are a little better, but even so it is difficult to believe that Cyriac, whose drawings of Cyzicus must have given such an accurate picture of the remains, should have gone so far

---

[1] Chr. Hülsen, *La Roma antica di Ciriaco di Ancona* (1907): cf. F. Saxl, *Lectures*, pp. 204 f. Mr. Charles Mitchell writes of these and of the set in Princeton, both of which he has studied at first hand: 'In the original series in Modena several draughtsmen are involved, I think, which implies that they were all copying a homogeneous existing series done by somebody unknown. The sister set at Princeton is exactly like the other series in general style and handling: I do not know whether one of the Modena draughtsmen did them.' L. Venturi was the first to dispute the attribution to Cyriac (*L'Arte* (1910), p. 392).

[2] M. Lazzarini and A. Munoz, *Filarete, scultore ed architetto del secolo XV* (1908).

[3] See Platner and Ashby, *Topographical Dictionary of Ancient Rome*, under PALMA AUREA (p. 382): SEP. C. CESTII (p. 478): META ROMULI (p. 340): MAUSOLEUM HADRIANI (p. 336).

astray, especially in the proportions, in the reconstruction of a building so much nearer home. The difference in dates may have something to do with it—1424 as against 1444—twenty years of additional experience. One suspects, too, that at some stage in the transmission of the design a copyist may not have done full justice to the original drawing: Filarete seems to have here been using a better copy than the scribe of Ashmolensis (Plate 13, *b*). Two things might lead one to believe that Cyriac had a hand in it somewhere. One is the careful drawing of the friezes and of the rectangular corner-capitals, which seem to preserve a record, though a slightly confused one, of the friezes that were there, as we know from other, later drawings. The second is the remarkably accurate recording of the inscriptions.[1]

We have not touched so far on another of Cyriac's interests—coins and intaglios. In the Vatican a fragment of a letter from him describes a night he spent in a ship's cabin over a collection of small antiquities, and gives us the delightful picture of a hard-bitten sea-captain, admiral of the Venetian fleet, finding time to discuss his coins and gems with a fellow enthusiast into the small hours. We know the date: it was November 1445; off Crete. Now it so happens that the piece in the collection which most interested Cyriac still exists, or did exist until the war, in the museum in Berlin.[2] In the nineteenth century it was in Florence, and when there was broken into four pieces: the cast on Plate 14, *a*, is an old one, and was taken before the accident. The original, of rock-crystal, though very large for an ancient intaglio, is a small thing, not three and a half centimetres high; and Cyriac had not quite the same opportunities of seeing the detail as the modern magnifying glass gives us.

He starts off by transcribing the signature with only one small error,[3] Eutuches Dioskouridou Aigeaios epoiei. 'Eutyches, the son of Dioscourides, of Aegae, made it.'

Dioscourides was a gem-engraver of the early Roman Imperial period, official engraver to the Emperor Augustus; and this intaglio by his son is certainly one of the masterpieces of ancient gem-engraving. Cyriac launches into a description of it with hardly any punctuation, and in a style of Latin which barely

[1] Unless Fontius copied the inscriptions. On this question see Saxl, *Journal of Warburg and Courtauld Inst.* iv (1940–1), p. 30, n. 2. On the entablature, D. Strong, *P.B.S.R.* xxi, p. 142.

[2] Fürtwangler, *Antike Gemmen*, i, pl. xlix, 11, 11*a*; pl. lxi, 21; ii, p. 234.

[3] He read ΑΙΓΕΛΙΟΣ for ΑΙΓΕΑΙΟΣ.

recognizes the existence of such a thing as a relative clause. Nevertheless his account produces an effect of breathless, even if faintly ridiculous enthusiasm. It contains one or two errors, but also some perceptive criticism, and is, in short, a very fair sample of his strength as well as his weakness. The errors arise partly from faulty observation, which is understandable when the conditions are remembered—a ship's cabin and the artificial light of the fifteenth century—partly from a mistaken theory about the identity of the person represented, who is the goddess Athena.

And to tell you something really remarkable—when Jo. Delphin (Johannes Delphinus), that keen and hard-working naval commander, had displayed a number of coins and precious gems to me when I stayed through the night in his office on board, among other things of the kind, he showed me a noble seal of crystal, of the size of one's thumb; it was engraved in very deep relief by the wonderful skill of the artist Eutyches with the portrait of Alexander of Macedon, helmeted, as far down as the breast; and for an ornament of the polished helmet two heads of rams impressed in front, with twisted horns—the very symbol of his father Jupiter Ammon: and at the very top a tiara is seen to bear on each side Molossian hounds, swift in the chase, of the highest artistic beauty: and under the helmet the prince most delicate with curls on either side, dressed in fine cloth and in a traveller's cloak with elaborate designs at the top seems to have moved his right hand[1] which is bare to the elbow, holding out his clothing becomingly from the upper part of his chest: and his face with a wonderful expression and with royal aspect directing his gaze keenly, truly he seems to show living features from the glistening stone, and also his own heroic grandeur. When you hold up the thick part of the gem right towards the light, where the breathing limbs are seen to shine out in wondrous beauty with complete solidity, and with luminous crystal shadows in the hollows, we learn who is the maker of so splendid a thing, by the Greek letters—very ancient ones, too—carved above.[2]

[1] The Molossian hounds are griffins, and the cloak with elaborate designs along the top is the aegis with its snaky edge. The right hand appears as the left hand in the impression on Pl. 14, a.

[2] 'Praeterea ut insigne admodum aliquid tibi referam, cum mihi Jo. Delphin, ille Ναύαρχος diligens καὶ φιλοπονώτατος, apud eum per noctem praetoria sua in puppi moranti pleraque nomismata preciosasque gemmas ostentasset, alia inter ejusdem generis supellectilia nobile mihi de cristallo sigillum ostendit, quod pollicaris digiti magnitudine galeati Alexandri macedonis imagine pectore tenus miraque Eutychetis artificis ope alta corporis concavitate insignitum erat, et expolitae galeae ornamento, bina in fronte arietum capita, certa Ammonii Jovis insignia parentis, tortis cornibus impressa, ac summo a vertice thyara, cursu veloces hinc inde λαργικούς molosos gerere videtur eximia artis pulchritudine, et sub galea tenuissimus [sic]

Through the spate of words one can see the genuine and intelligent pleasure that Cyriac enjoyed, and the determination to convey it to his correspondent.

We now come to an example of Cyriac's deliberate fantasy. It was not intended to deceive, and the error it involves was a genuine misunderstanding, not a falsification. The origin of the idea was the torso which appears in the San Gallo manuscript as if it were standing under the arch of the Augustan aqueduct at the Porta Tiburtina in Rome (Plate 14, *b*). Assuredly it never stood in this position, nor even in Rome. The Hamilton Codex gives a truer hint and shows it near the monument of Lysicrates, in Athens (Plate 14, *e*); and that is where it really belongs, for it is one of those serpent-legged giants which stood outside the Odeion of Agrippa when it was reconstructed in the second century A.D. (Plate 14, *c*, *d*).[1] It had been much mutilated, and there was some excuse for Cyriac making an incorrect inference about its sex; but whether he turned a blind eye or not, the final product, on another page of the San Gallo manuscript, is a symbol apt enough: 'Kumodoke, supreme goddess of the nereid nymphs' (Plate 16).[2] She holds a sixteen-oared galley in her hand; two dolphins disport themselves in front of her, and she wears a dolphin cap. The same page contains two drawings of Santa Sophia in Constantinople, which

hinc inde capillamentis princeps suctili velamine et peregrino habitu elaboratis a summitate listis amictus, dexteram et nudam cubitenus manum, veste summo a pectore honeste pertentantem, videtur admovisse, et gestu mirifico facies regioque aspectu acie obtuitum perferens, vivos nempe de lapide nitidissimo vultus, et heroicam quoque suam videtur magnitudinem ostentare. Cum et ad lucem solidam gemmae partem objectares, ubi cubica corporalitate, intus sublucida et vitrea transparenti umbra mira pulchritudine membra quoque spirantia enitescere conspectantur, et tam conspicuae rei opificem suprascriptis inibi consculptis literis graecis atque vetustissimis intelligimus.' *Cod. Vat.* 5237, fol. 515 *b*, transcribed by G. B. de Rossi, *Bull. d. Inst.* 1853, p. 54.

[1] Homer Thompson in *Hesperia*, xix (1950), p. 107, no. 9. Miss Alison Frantz has kindly allowed me to reproduce her photographs of the torso. Reisch (*Ath. Mitt.* 1889, p. 219) was the first to identify Cyriac's model.

[2] ΚΥΜΟΔΟΚΗΙ ΝΗΡΗΙΔωΝ ΝΥΜΦΑωΝ ΥΠΕΡΤΑΤΗΙ ΘΕΑΙ. The dative shows that it is an invocation. Reisch (loc. cit. in n. 1, p. 220) quoted the passage from the Schedel MS. published by O. Jahn (*Bull. d. Inst.* 1861, p. 183) '*bis septem munita remigibus navi honorifice altoque aequore Nympharum Nereidum choro comitante*' . . .; and Mr. Mitchell cites the passage in another letter (Florence, *Bibl. Naz. MS. Tang.* 49, f. 11) '*nec non nympharum nereydum nostrarum praeclarissimarum ⟨sc. choro⟩ favitante*'. There is also the better known invocation to the Chian and other nymphs mentioned by Saxl (loc. cit. in n. 2, p. 28), p. 31 n. 1.

must also be copied from Cyriac (Plate 15); and the appearance of Kumodoke in this context can hardly be without significance. It has been suggested that she stood as a dedication on the front page of the book of Cyriac's from which the San Galli drew their material;[1] but I do not think it has been suggested to whom that dedication was made. We can surely guess. The galley, lovingly drawn, would be one in which Cyriac himself had travelled. There was a person in whose ship, in November 1445, he had studied the intaglio of rock-crystal; and in one of whose ships he had sailed, in December 1446, to Constantinople. Would it be unjust to Cyriac's sense of humour to recognize in the elderly dolphin—less care-free in expression than the others, and longer in the beak, who, tucked under her arm, is clearly in the special care of the goddess—the friend whose name it echoes, Jo. Delphin?[2]

Whether that be so or not, the device must once have served as an envoy. Perhaps we can appropriately make it serve again as ours.

[1] Hülsen (op. cit. in n. 3, p. 27), p. 38.

[2] Cyriac describes a ship as 'Delphinia' on more than one occasion; but the most pertinent is in 1446: '*ex Pontica navigatione Delphinia trireme per Bosphorum VI Iduum Decembrium die regiam Byzantion*' (G. Targioni Tozzetti, *Rel.*[2] 1773, v, p. 441, quoted in de Rossi, *Inscr. Chr.* ii. 1, p. 373).

ACKNOWLEDGEMENTS

Plate 1a after *Miscellanea Ceriani*, Milan, 1910; 1b after Blümel, *Katalog. d. gr. Skulpt. III*; 2, 3, 4b, 4c, 5, 7, 8, 9b, 14b, 14e, 15, 16 after Chr. Hülsen, *Il libro di Giuliano da Sangallo* (1910); 11b after Chr. Hülsen, *La Roma antica di Ciriaco di Ancona* (1907); 6a, 6b after Stuart and Revett, *Antiquities of Athens* (1794); 11a, 13a, 13b from photographs by Alinari; 14c, 14d from photographs by Miss Alison Frantz.

FLAVIO BIONDO AND THE MIDDLE AGES

ONE of the paradoxes of historical writing is that even its
ablest practitioners are soon neglected. Indeed, where their
ability has been literary they suffer at the hands of posterity
even more than their fair share of oblivion, ending up (in our
own day) in the limbo of the prescribed books for public exami-
nations or the pit of postgraduate theses. Yet, even unread,
certain historians exert an influence over later ages which en-
sures them a kind of anonymous immortality. Their immediate
successors transmit an interpretation which, in the hands of later
exponents, is divorced from its first begetters. This is particularly
true of historiography prior to the second half of the nineteenth
century, prior to the monograph and the learned journal.
Nowadays we are all obsessed with our indebtedness to others
and ransack the scholarly literature of our immediate predecessors for parallels to observe and precedents to quote. And we are
as suspicious of literary graces as earlier critics were offended by
their absence: it can become almost insulting to say that a contemporary writes well. It is, in short, easier far to assure oneself
a niche in a bibliographical Pantheon by a gnarled and ungracious investigation into some small and intricate historical
problem than by a survey, however delightful, of a big subject.

These reflections are pertinent to a consideration of the writer
on whom I am privileged to lecture today. Flavio Biondo in a
sense stands at the threshold of a world where, for the first time,
history could be presented either as art or as science. His reputation in his own day was to some degree determined by his
response to this question; and more recently he has been singled
out for praise because he is supposed to have chosen erudition at
the expense of artistry. My purpose in what follows will be to
examine in some detail Biondo's most famous work, the *Decades*,
a history covering the period from the fall of Rome to the middle
of the fifteenth century. It can be stated confidently that it is
talked about more often than it is read, as is the case with the
works of all the main Renaissance historians.

Historical writing was extraordinarily luxuriant in medieval Italy. It provides evidence of an interest in the past on the part both of scholars and, with the emergence of vernacular narratives, of an ever widening lay public. It may well be that this was one of the features of Italian cultural life most propitious to the development of the new values of humanism. Certainly humanism encouraged further extensions of historical activity in Renaissance Italy, although in ways which have seemed to many to be unfortunate. If one compares a fine example of the vernacular chronicle with a fine piece of humanist history— Villani with Bruni, for example—there does seem to be a frigidity in the latter, an air of unreality and artifice, absent from the earlier writer. But the gains offered by the new methods were great. In an accomplished historian like Bruni or Poggio we find first of all a commendable concentration on the form and style of presentation foreign to the earlier Tuscan writers, whose felicities are accidental. More important still, we sometimes find an anxiety to display motives which is not often seen in the rambling narration, however picturesque and lively, of less sophisticated writers: the humanist historian, in short, often had an axe to grind; he was a publicist, and his work was addressed to men of affairs. In any event the vernacular writers continued to thrive, picturesque as ever; even if we neglect them their contemporaries did not.[1] Both sources, the humanist Latin and the vernacular, contributed to the formation of the historiography of Machiavelli and Guicciardini.

The analysis of Renaissance historical writing which is accepted at large today owes much to a short chapter in Burckhardt's book.[2] Starting from this Fueter elaborated a sharp distinction between what he called the Rhetorical school, stemming from Bruni, and the Scholarly school. The first was, he argued, by far the more influential since it placed humanism at the service of the city and the dynasty. At its best it was brilliantly apologetic, at its worst it was a feeble imitation of the Livy so admired by all its practitioners. For the rhetoricians the first aims were to persuade and to please, and stylistic brilliance and purity was a necessary condition of success, for the histories of cities or princes were not meant to convince within the area of the writer's loyalty but at large in Italy. Bruni, Poggio, Accolti were Florentine chancellors; Sabellico was a pensioner of the Vene-

[1] See V. Rossi, 'Storia litteraria d'Italia', *Il Quattrocento*, new ed., Milan, 1938, pp. 182–8 and refs.

[2] *Civilization of the Renaissance in Italy*, part III, ch. viii.

tian state; Pontano was a servant as well as the historian of King
Ferrante, as Crivelli and Simonetta were successively secretaries
as well as biographers of Francesco Sforza.[1] Opposed to the
rhetorical historians were the laborious disciples of erudition, of
history for its own sake, whose scientific interests transcended
loyalty to a state: of these the luminaries were Calchi at Milan,
Valla the critic of the Donation of Constantine, Pomponio Leto
the Roman antiquary; their master was Flavio Biondo.[2]

This Burckhardt–Fueter interpretation has been very widely
accepted, for few of us have had the occasion to read carefully
the old editions where most of this literature is still enshrined.
We take on trust the truth of what has entered the canon of
Renaissance interpretation, and see the game being played
according to the rules determined for us by Fueter. These rules
can be summarized in his own words: the imitation of classical
models (especially in respect of a rhetorical approach), and a
'secularization of history' which involved jettisoning a providential view of history and all that went with it, notably the outmoded universals of empire and papacy, and the miraculous.
These characteristics were approved of by Fueter, but he argued
that with the excessive regard to style went a neglect of chronology, a distortion of institutional realities, and a perverse glori-
fication of men and states.[3] Recent studies of Leonardo Bruni
have disputed some of these strictures:[4] the present paper may
show that an examination of the founder of the 'learned school'
leads to other modifications in hitherto received opinions.

Before we examine Flavio Biondo's place in the traditional
picture we must look for a moment at his life, which has some
light to throw on his writings. It is a life devoid of much excite-
ment.[5] Born at Forlì in November or December 1392, educated

[1] E. Fueter, *Geschichte der neuern Historiographie*, 1911; later editions, so far
as the matters discussed here are concerned, seem to add nothing to the
second which appeared revised as a French translation by E. Jeanmaire
(Paris, 1914), which I accordingly use; the relevant pages are 10–60.

[2] Fueter, pp. 128–36.

[3] Ibid., pp. 10–18.

[4] E. Santini, intro. to *Leonardi Aretini historiarum Florentini populi libri xii*,
RR. II. SS., xix pt. 3, pp. i–vi; B. L. Ullman, in *Studies in the Italian Renaissance*, Rome, 1955, pp. 321–44.

[5] The introduction to B. Nogara's *Scritti inediti e rari di Biondo Flavio*, 'Studi
e testi', no. 48, Vatican 1927, supersedes all earlier biographical accounts of
which the most valuable was the short study of A. Masius, *Flavio Biondo, sein
Leben und seine Werke*, Leipzig, 1879. Unless otherwise noted the following
account is based on these authorities. There is an extended notice of Nogara's
book by A. Campana in *La Romagna* (Imola), xvi (1927), 487–97, and a

at Cremona, he and his family were buffeted by all the political storms which raged in the Romagna. One of his earliest memories was being held in his father's arms to see the comet which, as it soon emerged, betokened the fall of Gian Galeazzo Visconti.[1] When he was thirty a revolution in Forlì led to his exile. By this time he was already, it seems, occasionally employed by his city and already on intimate terms with Guarino da Verona. The next years are filled by a series of posts significant of the openings increasingly available to the humanist-trained scholar: secretary of the Venetian Francesco Barbaro at Vicenza and Bergamo, of Pietro Loredano at Brescia, of Capranica (governor at Forlì) and, in 1432, of Vitelleschi then governor of the March of Ancona. From Vitelleschi's service Biondo passed, early in 1433, to the service of the pope: in 1434 he was appointed to the papal secretariat. So far his career gave promise of an active participation in public life, with high promotion as its natural end. And for a time this must have seemed likely not only to Biondo but to his fellow administrators. He was charged with important negotiations on behalf of the pope in Romagna and at Venice in 1434. He followed Eugenius IV to Florence, when the pope escaped from Rome in that year, and he was then involved in negotiations with Sforza.

His biographers, following a lead given by Paolo Giovio,[2] make this year a turning point in Biondo's life: from now on he is supposed to have abandoned interest in a political career, realizing that his marriage, which had occurred in 1423, would preclude the very highest ecclesiastical responsibilities and rewards. Yet there are some grounds for doubting this, or at any rate for arguing that too little has been made of Biondo's public importance after 1434. In the first place, in 1437, when Leonardo Bruni despaired of securing a proper reward from Humphrey Duke of Gloucester for his Latin version of Aristotle's *Politics* and wished to give it to Eugenius IV, he chose Biondo as his agent—presumably because the latter had the pope's ear.[3] Second, he was fairly prominent in the negotiations with the Greeks at Ferrara and Florence which culminated in the ill-fated union of

valuable review by R. Sabbadini in the *Giornale storico della letteratura italiana*, xciii (1929), 182–6. See now Additional Note below, p. 90.

[1] *Decades*, ed. Basle 1531 (the edition hereafter quoted for this work and the other main books by Biondo), p. 392, a corrupt passage in printed texts; see Nogara, p. xxiv and note.

[2] Quoted Nogara, p. lxxiv, note.

[3] Cf. R. Weiss, *Humanism in England during the XVth Century*, Oxford, 1941, pp. 48–49.

July 1439. In fact he was one of those who attested the act of union[1] which he quotes verbatim in his history.[2] Third, when Thomas Bekynton, anxious to secure a bishopric, was distributing gifts to influential members of the Curia in 1441 he was advised to include Biondo among the recipients, which he did.[3] And fourth, in 1449, two years after the election of Nicholas V, Biondo was forced to leave the Curia, to which he did not return until early in 1453. What led to this fall from favour we do not know. Biondo referred to the machinations of an enemy unnamed.[4] Aeneas Sylvius explained it as the common fate of favourites of the old pope in the early years of his successor: this can be supported, though Pius II may not have known this, by the careful way Biondo removed from the master copy of his *Italia illustrata* flattering references to Nicholas V after the latter had died. Nogara, Biondo's most recent and most scholarly biographer, has the flattering explanation that in the flippant milieu of *abbreviatores* like Poggio, Biondo's purity led to his victimization. Whatever the truth in all this, it remains clear enough that Biondo, as late as 1449, was important enough to have important enemies. In my judgement we should date his withdrawal from active participation in papal politics from 1450 rather than from 1434. What is clear is that for the rest of his life he played only a very small part in public affairs. He was in the papal secretariat until his death in June 1463. 'He died a poor man, as was proper for a scholar', commented Pius II. He was buried in S. Maria in Aracoeli on the Capitol, heart of that Rome which formed the centre of so much of his writing.

To his writings we must now turn.[5] All are of interest, but I shall only pause here to indicate those of directly historical content. These are in fact more substantial than his treatises on philology, education, or crusades, which are paradoxically better understood than the major books, for they have been printed or reprinted with all the aids of modern scholarship and typography. The four big books—*Roma instaurata* (1440–6), *Italia illustrata* (1448–53), the *Decades*, and *Roma triumphans* (1456–60)

---

[1] Nogara, p. lxxxii.　　　　　　　　　　[2] *Decades*, pp. 550–1.

[3] *Correspondence of T. Bekynton*, ed. G. Williams, Rolls Series, i. 169–72, 241–2. This is not mentioned by Nogara.

[4] Quoted Nogara, p. cxiv.

[5] A brief chronology of composition and publication is attempted below in Appendix I (pp. 88–9), as this is not to be found in Nogara or elsewhere.

—have all to be studied in sixteenth-century folios, where the pages of dense type, the absence of paragraphs, the frequent errors of the printer, and the absence of adequate lists of contents and indexes are all formidable obstacles to ready comprehension, let alone pleasurable reading. (This is often the penalty of a certain amount of popularity in the late fifteenth and the sixteenth century: a manuscript by a relatively unimportant and uninfluential Renaissance writer has more chance of being published critically in our own day than the work of an author, however important, who achieved print in or near his own time.)

The *Italia illustrata* has naturally been given more attention than the others, for in it Biondo achieved a new and fruitful combination of geography and history, of antiquities and contemporary observation. This was undoubtedly the inspiration of the larger and better-written surveys of Aeneas Sylvius, and leads on to the scholarly geographers of the next century. It has been made the subject of a short essay;[1] this has been outmoded, however, by the publication of additional material.[2]

A proper understanding of the *Roma instaurata* and *Roma triumphans* must wait, as Professor Momigliano has pointed out, until we find someone willing to write a history of antiquarian thought in Italy.[3] In a sense they were the most rapidly superseded of all Biondo's books, for they stimulated a host of other topographers and antiquaries who were better equipped. As we shall see, they throw some light on the general aims of their author as historian.

The biggest and probably the most important of Biondo's works was the *Decades*. How may this be briefly described? It consists of forty-two books, running from the seizure of Rome by Alaric in A.D. 410 down to the peace of Cavriana in the autumn of 1441. Arranged in decades of books, the first ten extend to January 754; the second ten to the election of John XXIII in 1410; the third, beginning with a retrospect to the death of Gian Galeazzo in 1402, goes down to November 1439; the fourth contains two books, the first covering 1440 and the

---

[1] Johann Clemens Husslein, *Flavio Biondo als Geograph des Frühhumanismus*, Würzburg, 1901.

[2] Such as Nogara prints from two manuscripts, one at Florence (Riccardiano 1198) and one at the Vatican (Ottoboniano 2369), op. cit., pp. 219–39; and A. Campana discusses Cod. Classense 203 at Ravenna in 'Passi inediti dell' "Italia illustrata" di Biondo Flavio', *Rinascita* (Florence), i. (1938), 91–97.

[3] A. Momigliano, *Journal of the Warb. and Court. Institutes*, xiii (1950), 289 n.

second (which was not in the early printed editions)[1] covering
1441. It will be observed that far more space is devoted to the
forty years of the fifteenth century than would seem to be justified by the broad aim of the author: furthermore one should
note that the fourteenth century is practically concentrated into
one book, II. x, of thirty-five pages.[2] But these dates and proportions tell us nothing. What is the book about? To answer that
question we must consider how it was composed.

In the late 1430's Biondo, an established member of the papal
Curia, an author recognized by the scholars of Florence and
Venice, turned to writing history. From the first reference to
this, in a letter of 1440 to Francesco Barbaro, we must infer that
he was drawn to contemporary history, the scope of his work
being described as being 'mainly the changes in the Italian
scene', *maximis quae Italiam agitant rerum varietatibus.*[3] The four
books here referred to began in 1417, circulated in manuscript
among the author's friends and were subsequently added to
until, revised, and now beginning at 1402, they had reached
twelve books and the final terminus of the whole work by some
point in 1442. Eleven of these were in fact circulating and had
attracted favourable comment. In 1443 the Italian content of
this portion of the work is expressly stated by Biondo in a letter
to Alfonso of Aragon: *quae . . . ubique in Italia sunt gesta.*[4] But at
this stage a bigger plan had emerged: the author sends Alfonso
the first eight books of a new section, beginning with the fall of
Rome, and explains that he deliberately wrote the contemporary
portion first and only later turned back to the earlier centuries.

That in fact the author had had the whole work before him
when he began writing in 1439 has reasonably been doubted.
But besides the letter of 1443 to Alfonso there is another piece of
evidence that by about 1442 he had extended the work back to

---

[1] A portion of IV. ii was printed by G. Williams in *Bekynton Correspondence*,
ii. 327–38, from Corpus Christi College, Cambridge, MS. 205; Nogara, who
printed the whole of IV. ii from two Vatican manuscripts, was not aware of
this text, which contains, in an illuminated initial on f. 1, what appears to be
a portrait of Biondo, much defaced. See further below, p. 66.

[2] See below, Appendix II, for a sketch of the periods covered by each book.
In a letter to Francesco Sforza written at the end of his life Biondo summarized the chronology as follows: 'La mia prima deca, longa de anni CCCC,
uene fino ad VIIJ^c ab incarnatione. La seconda ariua al MCCCC; la tertia,
piena di geste de annj XLIJ, dal MCCCC uene fin a la pace . . . a Marti-
nengo . . .', Nogara, pp. 211–12.

[3] Nogara, p. 103, and cf. intro. pp. lxxxiii–lxxxiv.

[4] Nogara, p. 148.

the fall of Rome. I have mentioned that Bekynton sought his friendship with a gift. This produced from Biondo a letter, dated from Florence on 18 June 1442, in which he writes that Bekynton's present has given him great pleasure and that he hopes to reciprocate very soon by sending something which, since his English correspondent lacks nothing in the material sense, shall be for his solace and enjoyment.[1] What Biondo in fact sent was a copy of the twelve completed books of his history, the volume now being in the library of Corpus Christi College, Cambridge.[2] Now there are several manuscripts which contain the third decade and one or both books of the fourth. But this copy can be assigned with confidence to the months immediately after June 1442 and it already contains in the opening words of decade III a reference to the earlier sections of the work. So precise in fact is the reference to the author's joy in having completed his task of resuscitating a thousand years in twenty books[3] that we can hardly question that some kind of draft of the earlier decades was indeed completed by about 1442, even if only eight books of the first decade were fit to be sent to Alfonso early in 1443. Biondo himself gives us a clue when in the first pages he indicates that his work covers a thousand and twenty years—*in praesens tempus* (which would be 1442).[4] Certainly it was later polished: he tells us this himself in a letter of 1444 which refers to the work being in the hands of copyists;[5] and events of November 1443 are mentioned in decade I, ix.[6] Early in 1444 we find him

[1] *Bekynton correspondence*, i. 241–2: '. . . quae jocunditatem offerat at aliquod ornamentum'.

[2] MS. 205; G. J. Vossius, *De historicis latinis libri iii*, Leyden, 1651, p. 585; *Bekynton Correspondence*, i, p. xxxii; M. R. James, *Descr. Cat. of the MSS. in . . . Corpus Christi College*, i. 494–5. I have to thank Mr. R. Vaughan for arranging for me to consult this manuscript.

[3] Corpus Christi MS. 205, f. 1r: 'Laetanti iam mihi et exultanti non obscuram magis quam sepultam mille annorum historiam uiginti librorum uoluminibus in lucem, certumque ordinem reduxisse. . . .' Cf. ed. Basle, 1531, p. 392, where the same words occur.

[4] See passage quoted below, p. 67, n. 4; as noted below, p. 76, Biondo put the fall of Rome in A.D. 412.

[5] 'Historiae meae, quibus limandis hactenus insudavi, in librariorum manibus sunt, quarum exemplum ut habeas curabo. . . .' Nogara, p. 154.

[6] Nogara, p. ciii. It would be useful as a check to find other unequivocal indications in the first two decades of events in the 1430's and 1440's. But the only other such points that I have noted—a reference to Bruni's version of Procopius early in the first decade and another to Eugenius IV's escape from Rome in book iv of the second decade—are not helpful: the first could have been written at any point in or after 1441 and the second in or after 1434 (*Decades*, pp. 43, 236).

anxious to have an earlier draft returned so that only one version may circulate.[1] By October 1453 Biondo himself claims that his work is now dispersed through all Europe. We may fairly summarize all this by saying that by 1442 the whole work existed in draft and that the final version was circulating by 1452, if not considerably earlier.[2]

The account I have given of the composition of the *Decades*, which differs a little from those previously accepted,[3] was proffered as preliminary to an attempt to define the scope of what, in its contemporary aspect, Biondo had defined as 'Italian history' when discussing decade III. He hardly tells us in the work itself what precisely he intends to cover in the earlier portions. It is, he says at the start, to cover the deeds of the thousand and thirty years since the Goths captured the city.[4] It is from the fall of Rome that a new epoch must be dated: Livy's history was called 'ab urbe condita'; and his (we may infer) *ab inclinatione imperii*.[5] But the Roman empire was a bigger affair than Italy itself. And so the story is at first filled by 'those things which happened in the former provinces of the empire beyond the Alps and outside Italy',[6] where, he laments later on, the rule of Rome

[1] Nogara, p. 161. Nogara dates this letter 1446: but advances as his reason the congratulations with which it begins, which he says arise from E. Barbaro's promotion to the see of Verona (16 November, 1443, cf. Eubel, ii. 265, and not October, as in Nogara, p. civ, n. 127). In 1446 he may perhaps have felt so dissatisfied with the second decade as to refer to it as unwritten save for the first book; but this letter is undated in the original and parts of it are evidently corrupt: Nogara, p. 162.

[2] I do not think the undated letter asking Sforza for details of Visconti origins, *c.* 1450–1 (Nogara, p. cv), suggests that the work was still unwritten in its fourteenth-century parts—though the fourteenth-century portion is a hurried piece of writing (above, p. 65); any more than that may be inferred from the letter of December 1454 (Nogara, p. 168) asking for materials for Genoese history.

[3] Nogara's interpretation is neatly digested by V. Rossi in the revised version of his *Quattrocento*, as cited above, p. 60 n. I differ in considering that the *Decades* were to all intents finished by the mid-1440's.

[4] *Decades*, p. 3: 'Visum est itaque operaeprecium a me factum iri, si annorum mille et trigenta quot ab capta a Gothis urbe Roma in praesens tempus numerantur, ea inuolucra et omni posteritati admiranda facinora in lucem perduxero.'

[5] Ibid., p. 10: 'Annus . . . qui et salutis Christianae duodecimus et quadringentesimus fuit, nobis primus erit ab inclinatione imperii constitutus'; see the whole passage of which this is the end, and below, p. 76.

[6] Ibid., p. 55: 'Haec quidem in Romanis quondam prouinciis Transalpinis et extra Italiam tunc fiebant'; and cf. the letter to Barbaro of (?)1444: 'praeclara optabiliaque in Romano olim imperio, in Italia, in Venetis, in Liburnis inserta sunt gesta', Nogara, p. 161.

is a thing of the past.[1] The scope of the first eight books of the
first decade (i.e. down to about A.D. 600) may fairly be described
as an account of the former provinces of the empire, with the
stress laid on events in Italy.[2] He summarizes this himself by
saying he has described not only the decline of the empire, but
also the devastation of Rome and Italy.[3]

Soon, however, we may detect a change in the author's aim.
Already in book ix of the first decade he explains that much
could be written of the former provinces—Gaul, Spain, England,
and the rest. But they all continue in independence, and his
prime task is the decline of Rome.[4] Yet Rome was now the heart
of another kind of universal state: the *orbis christianus* is mentioned—very significantly he abandons the dating *ab inclinatione
imperii* at this point—in 'the year of the incarnation of our Lord
700'. And the first decade ends with a frank disclaimer of any
intention of a general account of the Franks.[5] Later on we are
told that the deeds of Otto I outside Italy are beyond his scope.[6]
Thereafter, though we have references to the provinces, the
wider horizon might be described as Christian rather than imperial: it is as an extension of Christendom that Charlemagne's
campaigns are presented;[7] it is for this reason that the relief of
the Holy Land is described as the finest deed of any pope;[8] and
this explains the very full account of the Crusades in the Middle
East and elsewhere. From the fourth book of the second decade
to the end of the eighth book, from the Council of Clermont to

[1] *Decades*, p. 100: '. . . quod neque in Galliis, neque in Hispaniis, aut Ger-
mania, siue in insula Britannia, et prouinciis quae Danubium adiacent, aliqualis
ultra fuit Romano imperatori aut Romanae reipublicae iurisdictio'. And
compare the passage p. 365 where, on Petrarch's authority, Cola di Rienzi's
reinvocation of ancient Rome is described as causing favourable comment in
the non-Italian provinces of the old Empire.

[2] Cf. ibid., pp. 111, 115–16; and the remarks on Africa and Spain in the
last book of the first decade, pp. 136–7.

[3] Ibid., p. 150.

[4] Ibid., p. 133.

[5] Ibid., p. 148. On the dating see further, below, p. 76.

[6] Ibid., pp. 182–3: 'Multa interim maximaque, et quidem praeclarissima
in regnis Franciae et Germaniae Otho gesserat, quae nostrae intentioni parum
accommoda omittimus.'

[7] Ibid., p. 161: 'Erant autem tunc in Romani olim imperii Europae
prouinciis res turbulentissimae. . . . Dumque tot in locis rem bene gererent
Christiani. . . .' In so far as the older area is referred to at this stage it is only
the European provinces which are involved, e.g. p. 176: '. . . cum multis
Europae prouinciis, tum Italiae. . . .'

[8] Ibid., p. 207: '. . . facinus . . . maximum excellentissimumque omnium
quae fuerint pontificis Romani cuiuspiam ductum.'

the fall of Acre in 1291, the non-Italian material is virtually restricted to accounts of the Crusades.[1]

Before Biondo reaches the third decade and the events of the fifteenth century he has, of course, begun narrowing his interest to that intensive concentration on Italy which, as we have seen, he himself recognized as his aim in the later books. How did he view Italy? What is the range of his interest in Italian affairs? There are some tantalizing glimpses of a general interpretation of Italian history. In an early passage of the *Decades* Biondo consoles himself for the shame of the fall of Rome by contemplating the rise of a new Italy: let us be encouraged by narrating the beginnings of the new cities, the glory of a splendid people, which were to restore to Italy her lost dignity: Venice, Siena, Florence, and the rest re-establish for Italy the glory of fallen Rome.[2] But this proves a dead end. Biondo does not deal adequately with any city save Venice, whose origins (not surprisingly in view of his intimacy with Venetians) are discussed at some length.[3] The rest are merely mentioned, if at all, in a perfunctory line or two. Another theme, rather more substantial this time, is the need for peace in Italy. He seems to have accepted that the barbarian invaders of Italy soon became Italians:[4] thereafter Italy is disturbed either by foreign attack —by aggressive Greeks under Justinian, later by Germans and French[5]—or by domestic warfare. This deep-rooted desire for *pax in Italia* accounts, of course, for the panegyric on Theodoric[6] which Machiavelli later helped to form into a significant strand in Italian historiography. Popes are praised for their efforts to secure peace in the peninsula: so Honorius III[7] and so, in his

[1] Ibid., pp. 215–332. Note here *passim* the use of 'nostri' for 'Christiani'. And note the references, pp. 267–8, to crusading in Spain, and pp. 318–19 to Louis IX in Tunis.

[2] Ibid., p. 30: '. . . sed dedit animos, et ut omni absterso pudore scriberemus, nos pulit spes proposita narrandae originis nouarum urbium, praestantissimorumque populorum decus, quorum et nouae sobolis excellentia, non parua ex parte Romanam restituit Italis dignitatem. Videmus nanque dei nostri rebus Italiae indulgentissimi benignitate, multum creuisse Venetam, Senensem, Ferrariensem . . . ciuitates . . . per quarum opes, uirorumque qui in illis coaluerunt uirtutem, et dignitas adest et gloria Italiae Romana rei-publica destitutae.'

[3] Venetian origins are discussed on pp. 41–42.

[4] Ibid., p. 95: after 72 years the Goths are now *omnes in Italia geniti et nutriti.*

[5] Ibid., p. 389: Alberico da Barbiano praised for driving the *externam militiam* from Italy.

[6] Ibid., pp. 33 ff.

[7] Ibid., p. 276.

own day, Martin V, who attempted to pacify the papal states when he failed to secure a more general settlement;[1] Benedict XII on the other hand is rebuked for having legitimized the tyrants of Lombardy—however wise it may have seemed at the time.[2] The schism of 1378 is stated to be a disaster for Italy as well as for the whole of Christendom.[3] The poisonous rivalries of Guelf and Ghibelline call forth a stinging passage: *ea infausta rebus Italiae nomina*. The scourge continues to our own day, Biondo goes on, and Italians treat each other worse than they had formerly been treated by the barbarians: town against town, region against region, one section of the population against another group—only Venice has been spared this cause of division.[4]

Yet such passionate moments do not represent a steady argument and when Biondo comes to the events of his own day in the third and fourth decades alarums and excursions become his theme. As we shall see, the third decade represents a different kind of history in more ways than one compared with what goes before, and I shall have occasion to suggest that it is more stylishly composed, more 'humanist'.[5] But we should be wrong to think that the concentration on war was a product of Biondo's humanist aspirations. It was, unhappily for him and his contemporaries, the true condition of his times in the Italy which was now his main theme. 'Italy was now quiet', he writes of the peace of April 1428, 'and this had happened seldom enough in previous centuries'.[6] But the peace lasted only four months and later on Biondo describes such a period as 'rather an interval between upheavals', and noted that the lull corresponded to winter months when campaigning was suspended.[7] The whole work ends with the peace of Cavriana in the autumn of 1441.[8] But this terminus represented nothing very significant for Biondo.

One can, of course, feel disappointed that the political scene in early fifteenth-century Italy is treated by Biondo in strictly inter-state terms. The internal history of the cities is hardly touched on. For example, the rise of the Medici is very cursorily treated[9] and the affairs of Forlì are given a prominence which,

---

[1] *Decades*, p. 458.
[2] Ibid., p. 362.
[3] Ibid., p. 375.
[4] Ibid., p. 288.
[5] Below, p. 75.
[6] *Decades*, p. 446: 'quiescebat Italia, quod multis anteactis seculis raro contigisse constabat.'
[7] Ibid., p. 562: 'uel quies, uel ea erat a motibus uacatio.'
[8] Nogara, p. 28.
[9] *Decades*, p. 489.

though natural, is disproportionate: for the rest, only Bologna's internal politics are discussed with any fullness,[1] and Rome's in so far as they impinged on papal action. Yet to critics who accused him of not seeing the trees because of the wood Biondo could have replied fairly enough—'how else could I have done it?' No general history of the peninsula could have displayed the detailed internal history of Florence or Genoa or Naples. As it was Biondo again and again[2] bemoans the difficulty of organizing this material in his third decade. Anyone who has tried to write or lecture on Italian history in the early fifteenth century will sympathize with his embarrassment.

The account given above of what the *Decades* are about does not end up with any simple picture. But it seemed worth while demonstrating the varieties and changes in the scope of various parts of the work because some rather ambitious claims have been made for it. An Italian critic has seen in it a picture of the final stage in Orosius's doctrine that world monarchy had moved from the East to Carthage, from Carthage to Rome—the eternal nature of the final *translatio imperii* being secured by the Christian religion.[3] That pagan Rome was justified for Biondo by becoming the centre of Christianity we cannot doubt. A passage of great eloquence comes at the end of his survey of the antiquities of the ancient city in the *Roma instaurata*. He sweeps away the legionaries and the temples and proclaims a new Rome: Christ is *imperator*, the city now the seat of an eternal religion, its citadel and dwelling place: of old men feared the name of Rome, now they worship it.[4] My point is that such a view does not colour

---

[1] Ibid., p. 446. At p. 497 Biondo rejects the possibility of writing succinctly of the internal history of Naples, or even of mastering adequately the factions, 'qui ter quaterque diuersa secuti sunt studia'.

[2] Ibid., p. 459: 'Distrahent uero scribentem, tam diuersae inter sese, quam frequentes ac propemodum continuae rerum Italiae agitationes . . .'; p. 514: '. . . nihil est operosius, quam cum gesta in regione una scribere aggressi fuerimus, ita dicendi cursum moderari, ut eodem tempore alibi gestorum ratio habita uideatur.'

[3] L. Colini Baldeschi, *Studio critico sulle opere di Flavio Biondo*, Macerata, 1895, p. 8, or (more accessibly, perhaps) in *La Nuova Rassegna* (Rome), 1894, pp. 1024–37.

[4] *Roma Instaurata*, p. 271: 'Viget certe uiget adhuc, et quanquam minori diffusa orbis terrarum spacio solidiori certe innixa fundamento urbis Romae gloria maiestatis. Habetque Roma aliquod in regna et gentes imperium, cui tutando augendoque non legionibus, cohortibus, turmis et manipulis, non equitatu peditatuque opus, nullo nunc delectu militum, qui aut sponte dent nomina, aut militare cogantur eductae Roma et Italia copiae in hostem ducuntur, aut imperii limites custodiuntur. Non sanguis ad praesentem

the *Decades*, though at one point it is reflected there. 'Then', he writes of the conversion of the English, 'Rome again began to rule Britain and this was accomplished by the use of a better kind of warfare than of old, the preaching of Christ's servants and the authority of the pope.'[1] This view of a transcending Christian mission is elsewhere in the *Decades* only suggested in Biondo's account of the Crusades.[2]

Another kind of erroneous judgement falsifies the range of Biondo's book. Fueter writes: 'Italy is in the foreground, but the history of other countries is always summarised'; 'this man without a native land had written the history of the whole of Christendom'.[3] This is just not true. Let us glance at the glimpses of English history in the *Decades*. There are references, and not much more, to St. Augustine's mission of conversion,[4] to Cnut's visit to Rome,[5] to Henry II's reconciliation with the pope after the murder of Becket,[6] to John's submission to Innocent III,[7] to Henry III's quarrel with de Montfort (apropos the intervention of Clement IV),[8] and (apropos the career of Albergati) to papal efforts at Arras to heal the Anglo-French war.[9] From these fugitive points one could hardly construct even the briefest account of English history. It is true only in a very limited sense that the *Decades* are a general history of medieval Europe: we should note that Biondo himself complains when discussing the tenth and eleventh centuries that his sources deal too much with the former provinces of Rome, and tell him far too little about 'the Roman empire, the popes of Rome and even less about affairs in Italy'.[10] One reason for these shifts in emphasis is laid bare

seruandam patriam effunditur, non mortalium caedes committuntur. Sed per dei nostri et domini nostri Iesu Christi imperatoris uere summi, uere aeterni religionis sedem, arcem, atque domicilium in Roma constitutum, ductosque in illa ab annis mille et quadringentis martyrum triumphos, per dispersas in omnibus aeternae et gloriosissimae Romae templis, aedibus, sacellisque sanctorum reliquias magna nunc orbis terrarum pars Romanum nomen dulci magis subjectione colit, quam olim fuit solita contremiscere. Dictatorem nunc perpetuum non Caesaris, sed piscatoris Petri successorem, &c.'

[1] *Decades*, p. 110: 'Tuncque coepit urbs Roma per arma solito feliciora, seruorum scilicet Christi praedicationem et summi pontificis autoritatem, Britanniae insulae et eius incolis Saxonibus Anglicis denuo imperare.' Cf. Bede's praise of Ethelbert, who had learned that 'seruitium Christi uoluntarium, non coacticium esse debere', ed. Plummer, i. 47.

[2] It is, of course, also revealed in Biondo's Crusading treatises written between 1452 and 1454; see below, Appendix I, no. 5.

[3] Fueter, pp. 128, 132.   [4] *Decades*, p. 110.
[5] Ibid., p. 192.   [6] Ibid., p. 252.   [7] Ibid., p. 275.
[8] Ibid., p. 313.   [9] Ibid., p. 493.   [10] Ibid., p. 177.

when we turn to the two related problems of Biondo's sources and the construction and style of exposition he adopted.

The first of these questions—his sources—must not detain us long. Decades I and II were analysed from the viewpoint of the sources in a brief dissertation published in 1881.[1] It may be summarized and supplemented as follows. Biondo used a number of general historical compendia: the Liber pontificalis, Sigebert of Gembloux, Martinus Polonus, Vincent of Beauvais, Giovanni Villani are the most important; and with these we may link the crusading writers, notably William of Tyre and Jacques de Vitry. To these he added certain sources more limited in scope and often more valuable historically: Paulus Diaconus, Jordanes, Gregory the Great, the *Gesta regum Francorum*, Einhard, are his main authorities for the period up to the ninth century. For the tenth to the thirteenth he depended greatly on the general chronicles I have mentioned, as well as on Ptolemy of Lucca and the great Venetian chronicle of Andrea Dandolo. In his early fourteenth-century passages good use is made of the works of Dante (including valuable references to letters which are otherwise not known)[2] and for the mid-fourteenth century Biondo draws very freely on Petrarch's letters.[3] Events in the third decade are, of course, those for which Biondo is himself a first-hand witness, but we are sometimes very conscious of his dependence on information provided by correspondents: there can be no doubt that Biondo's narrative of the defence of Brescia in 1438 and 1439 depended on the account of its Venetian hero, Francesco Barbaro, in whose service Biondo began his career.[4]

In addition to narrative sources and the letters of Dante and Petrarch, Biondo made occasional use of documents and archaeological material. Papal privileges are quoted,[5] so is Gratian's *Decretum*,[6] papal registers,[7] and other documents.[8] The third decade contains among other things references to letters by Eugenius IV,[9] the bull of union between the Latin and Greek

[1] Paul Buchholz, *Die Quellen der Historiarum Decades des Flavius Biondus*, Naumburg, 1881.

[2] On this see M. Barbi, 'Sulla dimora di Dante à Forlì', *Bull. della Soc. Dantesca*, ser. 1, no. 8 (Florence, 1893), 21–28.

[3] *Decades*, pp. 329, 334, 364–70 *passim*.

[4] Ibid., pp. 528 ff.   [5] Ibid., p. 165.

[6] Ibid., p. 184; cf. p. 280.   [7] Ibid., pp. 193, 198, 200, 203.

[8] Ibid., pp. 313, 387.   [9] Ibid., p. 475.

churches which is given *in extenso*,[1] while the terms of the settlement with the Armenian church are fully rehearsed.[2] That the author of *Italia illustrata* and *Roma instaurata* should include frequent references to old buildings is hardly surprising and a long list could be drawn up of such passages. They are particularly full for the north of Italy[3] and frequent for Rome,[4] though they contain disarming anachronisms which warn us of Biondo's limitations as an historian of art.[5]

Such a list is, I think, impressive, and rightly so. But I have introduced it at this point in order to finish what I have to say about the scope of the *Decades*, which, as we have seen, shifts gradually from a large view of the old Roman world at the start to a narrow concentration on Italy at the end. The reason for this is that, whatever Biondo's merits as a critic (and to these I shall devote a word shortly) he was in the last resort the victim rather than the master of his sources. He does not take all his materials and spread them out in a fundamentally reconstructed story. Rather he has one main source and sticks to it, using other writers for supplementing his narrative. Thus Paulus Diaconus supplies the skeleton of his narrative of the fifth century.[6] The account of the Goths comes from Procopius, largely it seems from the version of Leonardo Bruni.[7] Then he reverts again to Paulus Diaconus down to the mid-eighth century.[8] From the ninth century down to the Crusades his main account is drawn out of Ptolemy of Lucca, who, with Villani, is the basis for the rest of the second decade.[9] These main sources partly account for the emphasis which the history of Biondo has from time to time; we may reflect that, doubtless involuntarily, he thus transmitted fairly truly the changing horizons of earlier periods.

The composition, style, and structure of the *Decades* demand a moment's consideration: they have been neglected from this point of view and here again, under the influence of Fueter, we have regarded Biondo's book as all of a piece. It is, in fact, very far from being that and, just as we have seen that the content

---

[1] *Decades*, pp. 550–1; cf. Hefele-Leclercq, *Histoire des Conciles*, VII. ii. 1038–40.

[2] *Decades*, p. 559; Hefele-Leclercq, VII. ii, 1079–80.

[3] e.g. *Decades*, pp. 14, 44 (Ravenna), 167 (Venice).

[4] e.g. ibid., pp. 97–98, 123, 275–6, 280, 325, 373.

[5] Theodolinda's church at Monza, p. 113; cf. *Italia illustrata*, p. 364.

[6] *Decades*, pp. 14–38.

[7] Ibid., pp. 38–98. Biondo himself points out that Bruni's *De Bello Italico adversus Gothos* is just a version of Procopius: ibid., p. 43; on Biondo's use of Bruni cf. Buchholz, pp. 33–38.

[8] *Decades*, pp. 98–149.   [9] Ibid., pp. 174–392.

changes, so, but much more drastically, we can observe a sharp
transition in Biondo's manner of exposition. There is a tremen-
dous difference between the third decade (and what he added
of a fourth) and what goes before. The contemporary part,
written first, betokens far greater attention to stylistic pre-
occupations. This strikes a reader of the work as a whole very
forcibly. The differences are as follows. First, there is an avowed
concern with style. Decade III begins with a long passage describing the anxieties of an historian from the viewpoint of
linguistic propriety.[1] How can an historian of the post-Roman
world deal with a vocabulary which has no exact parallels in
the writers of antiquity? As Biondo points out, the Romans had
no artillery of a modern kind and war in particular is full of
terminological pitfalls. The other great field of embarrassment is
found in place-names, and here he refers us to what he has
written on this in his *Italia illustrata*.[2] We are used to accepting
such an awareness of stylistic problems in Leonardo Bruni and
in what Fueter called the 'school of Bruni': but we have been
led to suppose that Biondo is free of it.[3] There is, however, more
to it than that. I think one must admit that he was not a writer
of sparkling Latin; but one must note on the other hand that on
occasions he tried very hard to be fashionable[4] and that once or
twice he produces very gripping and lively passages: such as, for
example, his account of his own adventurous journey from the
Curia to Venice in the summer of 1434[5] and the dramatic escape
of Eugenius IV from Rome shortly afterwards, so vividly described that Biondo has (wrongly) been regarded as an eye-
witness.[6]

In all these points Biondo is, we might say, of 'the school of
Bruni'. And so he is in three other features of the third decade.
There is an almost total absence of precise chronological statements: 'at the same time, just after this, meanwhile';[7] these are
the conjunctive phrases which lead us on from one point of time
to another. In the whole of this part of the work, covering as it
does a period of forty-two years, there are only two dates—at the
start of each of the two books of the fourth decade. It is true that

[1] Ibid., pp. 393–6.
[2] Ibid., p. 395. Cf. *Ital. illus.*, p. 294.   [3] Fueter, p. 129.
[4] See e.g. the Ciceronian diction on p. 407: *regina . . . orat, obsecrat, obtestatur,*
&c.
[5] Ibid., pp. 479–80 (cf. Nogara, pp. lxvi-lxvii).
[6] Ibid., pp. 481–4.
[7] 'interea, quo tempore, non multi intercesserunt dies', &c.

the attentive reader will observe that from the seventh book of the third decade the author gives in effect a book to a year;[1] prior to that he must not let his attention wander or he will be lost indeed. Second, like Bruni and the classical models admired at the time, the third decade is full of set battle pieces; their bulk obtrudes itself as disproportionate even granted that the period was full of wars.[2] And, finally, the modern part has many speeches: about a tenth of the pages devoted to the years 1400–42 are filled by direct speech.[3]

When we compare this with the first two decades we can see how differently they were composed. There is no indication of concern over vocabulary or style; there are no extended descriptions of famous actions, bellicose or otherwise; there are some speeches, but very few and much shorter.[4] And (praise be) there are plenty of dates. At first Biondo ambitiously tried to construct a chronology from the fall of Rome and up to the year 1000 we occasionally meet an *annus ab inclinatione imperii*,[5] a rather uncertain indication as Biondo put his catastrophe in the year A.D. 412. But soon this affectation is discarded. Once, in the year 700, he gives us the year of the Incarnation,[6] and from A.D. 1000 it is invariably used by him, to the great solace of the reader. I have noted seventy-two dates,[7] or on average one in every five or six years from 1000 to 1400. Here again we must attribute these practices to the sources Biondo was using.[8]

The composition and style of the various parts of Biondo's *Decades* thus reflect in many ways the authorities on which he depended, and in particular the moment when he passes from a dependence on others to the description of the events of his own lifetime. The change in manner between the first two

[1] See Appendix II.

[2] e.g. *Decades*, pp. 456–7, 462–3, 488–9, 494, 497–9, 528–42, 572–4.

[3] Ibid., pp. 402, 405, 421–31, 437, 475, 477, 484, 503, 518, 573; Nogara, p. 20.

[4] I have noted only the following: pp. 47, 78–79, 84–85, 197, 207–8. Cf. p. 216 where Biondo announces that 'the speech which Robert the Monk (of St. Remy) puts into Bohemund's mouth may be omitted'.

[5] *Decades*, pp. 10, 13–14, 25, 26, 30, 43, 120, 133, 170, and in the titles of books *passim*; cf. above, p. 67.

[6] Ibid., p. 136.

[7] These are mostly (but not completely) shown in marginalia in the Basle edition of 1531.

[8] And so also the use of regnal year of pope and emperor, p. 101. If the third decade is devoid of dates of years, it is fairly liberally provided with months and days: among these we may note a number referring not to the Roman calendar but to saints' days: pp. 485, 490, 498, 537.

decades and the contemporary portion may have a further explanation. Aulus Gellius had recalled a distinction made between *annales* and *historia*;[1] and this was referred to, at about the time Biondo was at work, by his friend Guarino da Verona.[2] *Historia* differed from *annales* both in being the work of an observer of the events in question and in laying bare motives[3] which would account for the great space which, as already pointed out, is allotted to speeches in the third decade. There is, however, no evidence that Biondo himself was aware of these differences in approach and in general there seems little reason to suppose that the structure of the work has much significance. There seems to me to be little behind the division into decades, though we know that this is in fact how he saw the books himself, for so he refers to them on several occasions.[4] If it was to Livy's work he tacitly compared his own[5] his model's decades did not offer much encouragement to treat the division as significant; for Biondo a decade, we may be sure, meant only ten books, whatever it had meant to Livy. Nor can one find much behind the division into books. Perhaps this absence of sharply defined endings also stems from Livy. However that may be, the books in Biondo's *Decades* end and begin for the most part without much obvious necessity. Again and again a book stops with some indication that a new subject demands a fresh start, but the new book belies this.[6] Even when, in the modern part, virtually a whole book is devoted to one subject (as in III. ii which really deals entirely with the great debate at Venice in 1425 on the Florentine alliance), the author seems unconscious of it, though he gradually becomes aware that after 1437 he is giving a book to a year and ending at the autumn hibernation of the armies.[7] If one lists the main dates covered by each book[8] one can get the

---

[1] *Noct. Att.* v. xviii.

[2] R. Sabbadini, *Il Metodo degli umanisti*, Florence, 1922, p. 79: letter to Tobia del Borgo, 1446.

[3] Aulus Gellius, loc. cit.: 'Historiam ab annalibus quidam differre eo putant, quod, cum utrumque sit rerum gestarum narratio, earum tamen proprie rerum sit historia, quibus rebus gerendis interfuit is, qui narret.' He then quotes Sempronius Asellio on the need for a historian 'quo consilio quaque ratione gesta essent, demonstrare'.

[4] 'Tres historiarum mearum decades' (1453), Nogara, p. 167; 'la mia prima deca' (1463), ibid., pp. 211–12; the manuscripts enumerate thus: *Quartae decadis liber secundus incipit*, &c.

[5] Biondo refers to Livy's decades as such, Nogara, p. 211.

[6] Ibid., p. 238; '. . . ut liberiore animo ampliorique spacio narrare possimus'; cf. pp. 255, 276, 304, 481.

[7] Ibid., p. 561.   [8] See Appendix II.

impression of a kind of symmetry which in reality is absent.
Most books end with a cluster of insignificant events and yet
this effect of a dying fall reflects no conscious artistry but only
the annalistic framework within which Biondo worked. He
called it *ratio temporis*.[1] And chronology makes him mince up
what look like being indestructible historical units. His elaborate
and lengthy account of the first crusade[2] is sawn in half to insert
a comment on affairs in Italy;[3] his very full account of the war
between Venice and Genoa in 1378–80 is interrupted by a sentence dealing with the obedience of the schismatic popes.[4] And
so with all the central events of his own day, though in this
contemporary section (as we have seen) he frequently bemoans
his inability to organize his material.[5] We cannot blame Biondo
for making an *Odtaa* of the past: it was what most of his contemporaries were doing, what their revered classical exemplars
did, and it was what the medieval chronicler had done, in that
interval the history of which Biondo had set himself to write.
Nor can we discern in Biondo any novel view as to the historian's
mission. He subscribes to the conventional attitude: that history
is the means by which the great man's fame is handed down to
posterity.[6]

I have spent some time in a criticism of Biondo (and, by
implication, of those who have given him extravagant praise).
In turning by way of conclusion to estimate his value and his
influence I shall have occasion to sing his praises. And in the
first place we must recognize him as being the first medieval
historian. He takes this place by virtue of the book which I have
laboriously considered, which runs from the fall of Rome to the
Renaissance. 'All who cherish literature know', he wrote to
Alfonso of Aragon in 1443, 'that for twelve hundred years the
Latins have had few poets and no historians. From Orosius
onwards events are obscure. Today we have many who interest
themselves in verse, speeches and letter-writing, translating a
great deal from Greek into Latin and popularising some of the
mysteries of knowledge in an elegant manner, but not under-

---

[1] e.g. on pp. 296, 481, 550.   [2] Ibid., pp. 217–230.
[3] Ibid., p. 228.   [4] Ibid., pp. 378–84.
[5] See above, p. 71 and n. 2.
[6] Nogara, pp. 150–2 (letter to Alfonso, 1443); pp. 185–9 (second letter to
Galeazzo Sforza, 1458); p. 211 (letter to Francesco Sforza, 1463): 'La quale
gloria sempre ha habuto questa conditione in ciascuno grande et uirtuoso
homo, che tanto è durata e amplificata, quanto ha habuto bone et sollide
historie scripte, etc.'

taking the large historical work which is called for.'[1] Biondo, in short, realized on the one hand that there was a gap to be filled, and on the other that to fill it would not be a particularly fashionable activity, and so (as he says elsewhere himself) not likely to bring him any material rewards.[2] He thus at any rate tried to get outside his own period and is entitled to our esteem on that account. It was probably a more difficult step to take than merely to realize, as he did, that the *studia eloquentiae* were again flourishing in Italy.[3] The revival of letters is not equated by him with a brave new world: he had the future of his ten children to think about and no patron to relieve him of the embarrassments of the active life so praised by Florentine 'progressives'.

Recognizing and chronicling the *medium aevum*, even if not using the phrase, constitutes a major claim to the esteem of posterity. There are other aspects of the *Decades* that are meritorious: while it is true that many of the errors in his sources are transmitted uncorrected by Biondo,[4] it is also true that he frequently subjects them to criticism: his discussion of Procopius,[5] of the Liber pontificum,[6] of the chronology of Vincent of Beauvais and other thirteenth-century writers,[7] of the uncritical use made of Martinus Polonus,[8] are only a few examples of the sharp asides in which this critical acumen is displayed. Equally significant is his awareness that his sources have greater authority when they are dealing with events of their own time: thus he remarks on Ptolemy of Lucca's closeness to the diffusion in Italy of Guelf-Ghibelline rivalries;[9] for the same reason Dante

---

[1] See the full passage, summarized above, in Nogara, p. 148.

[2] To Giacomo Bracelli, 10 December 1454: 'sed quicquid et qualicumque iudicio dignum sit, quod dicturus sum, uelim credas me, qui nulla ad scribendum spe pecuniaria sim adductus; nullam ab auaritia et ingratitudine iniuriam existimare': Nogara, p. 168; cf. Masius, p. 30.

[3] Biondo's concern with humanism as such deserves separate treatment. It is briefly discussed by Wallace K. Ferguson, *Renaissance in Historical Thought*, New York, 1948, pp. 22–23. The key text is the long passage in *Italia illustrata*, pp. 345–8, which surveys the men of letters stemming from John of Ravenna: cf. G. Voigt, *Wiederbelebung des classischen Alterthums*, 3rd ed., Berlin, 1893, i. 219–220, 245. In the *De Verbis Romanae Locutionis*, Nogara, p. 125, Biondo describes the barbarous Latin of some of his colleagues in the Curia, 'Gallos, Cimbros, Teutonos, Alamannos, Anglicos, Britannos, Pannoniosque . . . qui . . . illiterati et penitus idiotae dici possint.'

[4] Buchholz, p. 6.

[5] *Decades*, pp. 43, 64–65.

[6] Ibid., p. 140.

[7] Ibid., p. 180.

[8] Ibid., p. 237.

[9] Ibid., p. 289; on Paulus Diaconus's authority see below, p. 80, n. 3.

is frequently advanced both as actor and source.[1] Nor are we
entirely dependent on the internal evidence of the *Decades* for
our knowledge of Biondo's care over his authorities. Several
letters have survived which show him asking for help: to Alfonso
of Aragon for Spanish sources, to Giacomo Bracelli for a Genoese
chronicle, and to Francesco Sforza for details of early Visconti
history.[2] Even more interesting are three manuscripts at the
Vatican which show Biondo at work gathering his materials.
The first is the history of Paulus Diaconus which contains many
annotations in the hand of Biondo.[3] Another has particular
relevance for an English historian, for it is the *British History* of
Geoffrey of Monmouth.[4] There is no case here of Biondo annotat-
ing the text: it contains only one devastating final comment on
the utter waste of time it had caused him:[5] 'I have never come
across anything so stuffed with lies and frivolities.' Another
manuscript seems to contain a sheet of notes made from a copy
of the *Liber Pontificalis*.[6]

Biondo's decision not to classicize the terminology of his
sources has been much admired[7] and undoubtedly it had a
certain boldness about it at a time when Bruni and Poggio were
both his contemporaries and fellow graduates of the Curia.
Some of the modern admiration is, however, due to an attitude
of censure taken towards the 'rhetorical' writing of humanist
historians, which has been much exaggerated.[8] If we are grateful
to Biondo for giving us words like 'Manganellae et bricolae',
'feudatarius', 'barchae', 'gonzardi', 'banderesii', 'bombardae',[9]
we must accept in him equally a neglect of the beautiful, and an
indifference to good taste which might have deprived him of
merit had not the vernaculars come to the rescue. Indifference
justly describes his attitude to literature, for he was not unaware
of the felicities of good writing, as we may see from his praise of

[1] *Decades*, pp. 331–2, 338, 342.
[2] Nogara, pp. 147, 168, cv and n.
[3] Cod. Vat. Lat. 1795. Cf. Nogara cvii and n., where the impression is
unintentionally conveyed that Biondo's animadversions are mostly hostile.
Most of the annotations in the manuscript are in fact summaries or notes
drawing attention to a passage. On fol. 49ᵛ Biondo identifies the author as an
Italian because he says *nostrum Adriaticum*; fol. 66ᵛ: *Nota auctor proximus fuit his
temporibus*.
[4] Cod. Vat. Lat. 2005.   [5] Ibid., fol. 69.
[6] Cod. Urb. Lat. 395, fol. 231ᵛ, *ex priuatis scriptis blondi*.
[7] Fueter, p. 129; Nogara, p. cviii.
[8] See above, p. 61, n. 4.
[9] *Decades*, pp. 264, 275, 373, 377, 378, 383. There are many others.

Bruni, whom he calls *scriptor aetate nostra clarissimus.*[1] In any case we must not exaggerate Biondo's stylistic ineptitude. As already observed, he makes intermittent efforts to polish his style in the third decade and succeeds there in attaining some passages of sustained effect. In any event, judged by the standards of fourteenth-century Latin, he wrote well. Even among practitioners of what Fueter would have us regard as the 'rhetorical school' he found admirers of his competence. For example, Cardinal Prospero Colonna invited Biondo, as well as Bruni, Poggio, and other admitted stylists, to suggest emendations to his Livy,[2] and he was praised as a writer by Leodrisio Crivelli, the first of the Sforza humanist historians.[3]

Careful handling of sources, concentration on a new and significant period of time, these are major titles to recognition as an important scholar. But Biondo's sense of the conjunction of events, of the causal element is less impressive, because very much less in evidence. The chronicling pattern of writing, of course, hardly lends itself to elaborate analysis of motive. But none the less in a work which it has been claimed inaugurated scientific history,[4] an historian whom his admirers have compared with Vico,[5] in the event seldom uncovers the springs of human action. It is not that Biondo shelters behind the providential view of history, to which he would have subscribed, as we may see (*pace* Fueter) from the frequent record he gives of both miracles and saints.[6] God is occasionally invoked as a cause but

[1] Ibid., p. 43. Cf. above, p. 75.

[2] Giuseppe Billanovich e M. Ferraris, 'Le "emendationes in T. Livium" del Valla, e il Codex Regius di Livio', *Italia medioevale e umanistica*, i (1958), 248.

[3] Leodrisio Crivelli 'de vita Sfortiae vicecomitis', Muratori, *Scriptores* (1731), xix. 629: '. . . vir in scribendo aeque exercitatus ac doctus, . . . multa . . . felici stylo complexus est.'

[4] P. Villari, *N. Machiavelli e i suoi tempi*, 2nd ed., 3 vols., Milan, 1895–7, i. 143; cf. iii. 203.

[5] L. Barozzi e R. Sabbadini, *Studi sul Panormita e sul Valla* (R. Istituto di Studi Superiori . . . in Firenze), Florence, 1891, p. 222.

[6] Fueter, p. 131: 'As with other humanists, he finds no place for legends and miracles'. Miracles: *Decades*, pp. 24, 52, 85, 108, 131, 191, 220–1, 252 (St. Thomas of Canterbury), 281 (St. Francis), 297 (St. Stanislaus), 323 (St. Gregory X); other canonizations: ibid., pp. 283 (St. Dominic, St. Anthony of Padua, Queen Elizabeth of Hungary), 297 (St. Edmund of Canterbury), 309 (St. Clare), 313 (Aquinas and Bonaventure), 335 (St. Louis), 348 (Celestine V); with these may be linked the translation of St. Augustine's remains to Pavia, p. 142, and the translation of St. Mark to Venice, pp. 172–3. See p. 172 for a criticism of J. de Voragine and other hagiographers; and cf. *Roma instaurata*, pp. 271–2, for a list of the holy places in Rome.

seldom (and this is the point) in an avenging or rewarding capacity: the galaxy of splendid cities which rose in Italy after the fall of Rome is attributed to the grace of God:[1] and so is the universal devastation of the Black Death.[2] But I have only observed two occasions when the wrath of God is advanced—for barbarian attacks on Italy[3] and for the loss by Heraclius of the Asiatic provinces of the empire.[4] Fortune makes even rarer appearances than God.[5] Human nature, grasping, superstitious, always ready to take risks, sometimes appears in Biondo's pages: Saladin is driven by ambition,[6] Sforza overplays his hand.[7] But there are besides these explanatory moments a few passages where political situations are analysed in political terms.

'No cause for the overthrow of the declining empire appears more effective', writes Biondo in what is really his only general comment on the coronation of Charlemagne in 800, 'than the conflict now begun between Rome and Constantinople'.[8] This is an important observation, and later he has other notes on the disastrous effects of the rivalry of Greek and Latin.[9] Again, he sees justly the consequences for northern Europe of the division of the Empire after Charlemagne's death,[10] just as later he rightly attributes the Angevin connexion with Naples to the abiding fear inspired in the papacy by Frederick II.[11] I have already mentioned his account of the Guelf-Ghibelline distractions of thirteenth-century Italy: he does not see their social origins in the Italian communes; but he does see their prolonged deleterious effects.[12] To the long vacancy between the death of Nicholas IV in 1292 and the election of Celestine V in 1294 he attributes the failure of the union of the churches agreed on at Lyons and the continued war between England and France, with all the evil results that flowed from both events.[13] A very interesting passage examines the difficulties in securing a Venetian-Florentine alliance in 1425: ancient hatreds were exacerbated by trade rivalries and in particular by competition from Pisa in the Eastern trade.[14]

---

[1] *Decades*, p. 30: *dei nostri . . . benignitate* (see above, p. 69, n. 2).
[2] Ibid., p. 365: 'ut omnes una deus ruina populos prostraturos uideretur.'
[3] Ibid., p. 108.   [4] Ibid., p. 125.
[5] Ibid., pp. 477, 483.   [6] Ibid., p. 256.
[7] Ibid., p. 477; and cf. other instances, pp. 333, 401.
[8] Ibid., p. 166: cf. pp. 163–4.
[9] Ibid., p. 309.   [10] Ibid., p. 175.
[11] Ibid., p. 313.
[12] Above, p. 70; cf. *Decades*, pp. 315, 353, 374.
[13] Ibid., p. 333.   [14] Ibid., p. 421.

These passages suggest that Biondo was a sufficiently shrewd commentator on politics. Why, then, does he exercise his talents so rarely? Aside from his own disinclination, and it must be conceded that reflecting about the past is a more exacting occupation than baldly narrating it, there is one reason which springs to mind. Biondo was a servant of the pope, writing his history at a time when the papacy was more involved than ever before in shifting political alignments. Properly to comment on either the past or the present might have involved Biondo in censure or dismissal. In all the welter of factional history Biondo's work has, in fact, a kind of detachment which is both rare and salutory; in particular he frequently gives us a view which is in striking contrast with the victorious versions embodied in what might be called the Whig tradition of the Florentines.[1] And by detachment should not be meant a Guelf or pro-papal attitude to the past. A student of Biondo has claimed that he had 'l'animo profondamente religioso e Guelfo'[2] on the grounds that he was hostile to Lombards, and to German emperors. This does not seem evident from a reading of the *Decades*. The popes play a very small part in the early *Decades*[3] and there is, significantly, no reference to the Donation of Constantine, the genuineness of which Valla had just attacked, and no moralizing on Canossa.[4] It is true that we know from Biondo's other writings[5] that he saw Christian Rome as the shining successor of the old empire. But this did not provoke him into a blind defence of the papacy: it would be hard to say whether his picture of Frederick II is harsher than that of Boniface VIII,[6] and he is capable of criticizing, albeit indirectly, the Italian prelates of his own day.[7] It is true that he hardly supported the conciliar programme and from his pages no just appraisal of the debates at Constance or Basle can be made. We should perhaps discriminate, however, between his treatment of Basle and Constance. He deals with neither in any detail, but against the bitter remarks he makes about the fathers at Basle we should place the much more

[1] Cf. *Decades*, p. 374, on the attitude to the papacy of the Florentines, *populi in res nouas semper procliues*.

[2] Colini Baldeschi, *Studio critico*, p. 5.

[3] Popes are mentioned only on pp. 24 and 36, in the first three books. Cf. the sketchy treatment of Innocent III, pp. 275–6.

[4] Ibid., p. 200.

[5] Above, pp. 71–72, and Colini Baldeschi, pp. 8–10.

[6] Cf. the unflattering picture of Urban VI, *Decades*, p. 385.

[7] Ibid., p. 435: Albergati praised as a saintly man, 'cui ecclesia rarissimos aetate nostra habuerit praelatos adsimiles'.

sympathetic account he gives of Constance, and note that he quotes (somewhat incorrectly) the terms of the decree *Frequens*.[1]

He was not a publicist. He had no argument to press; it is this which really distinguishes him from a good many of his humanist contemporaries and which led to a somewhat disparaging view of him among some of them. Biondo himself regarded his work as successful and applauded, and reported in 1443 to Leonello d'Este that he had received the praises of Francesco Barbaro and Pier Candido Decembrio, and had heard that Leonardo Bruni was also favourably impressed by it.[2] Note the approval of Bruni, which Biondo had heard about, he says, through mutual friends: the point is worth mentioning for Fueter wrote 'a humanist like Bruni found it distasteful to be compromised by a public acknowledgement of this too well-informed historian', and others have only too glibly repeated what Fueter almost literally invented.[3] His work was thus in good repute with leading humanists at Venice, Milan, and Florence. But his reputation extended beyond Italy. In 1453 Biondo says that copies of the *Decades* are distributed throughout Europe, and ten years later he says there are copies in England, Spain, France, as well as Italy, more than fifty copies being sold.[4] Yet these signs of esteem are recorded for us by Biondo himself, and very soon we have less flattering judgements from other sources. Pius II wrote of him:

He wrote a universal history which is a painstaking and useful work. Blondus was by no means a good stylist. He did not revise carefully what he had written and took pains to write a great deal rather than the essential truth. It would be most valuable if some learned and stylish author would polish and emend his works.[5]

[1] *Decades*, pp. 399 (Constance), 477, 514, 527 (references to Basle).

[2] Nogara, pp. 146–7.

[3] Masius, p. 33, drew attention to the letter in which Biondo reported the reaction of his friends: from the fact that Bruni had not written to Biondo (up to that point) and (I suppose) from the phrase '. . . eamdem historiam, ut amici retulerunt, aliis *me absente* laudaverit' constructed his theory of Bruni's squeamish repugnance. I can see no other grounds for the statement in Fueter, p. 132. For an example of glib repetition I can refer to my introduction to *Anglica Historia of P. Vergil*, Camden Society 1950, p. xxvii.

[4] 'Tres Historiarum mearum decades, quae iam disseminatae in omni Europa sunt . . .', Nogara, p. 167; '. . . disseminate per Anglia, Spagna, Franza, quanto per Italia . . . chè per la christianitate in ogni natione e prouintie sono molti uolumi de mie historie, de quali oltra cinquanta sono gosti a chi li a uoluti oltra ducati quaranta per uno', ibid., p. 212.

[5] See the full passage, *Commentarii*, Frankfurt, 1614, p. 310, quoted Nogara, p. cxi, n. This judgement is echoed by Voigt, ii. 492.

And even a minor poetaster like Cleofilo could write equivocally of the man and the historian.[1]

If imitation is flattery, Biondo had little enough of it. Among the very numerous contemporaries of his who were composing apologia his lack of party spirit was itself an irritation. Crivelli, whose praise of Biondo's style has been referred to already, found him sadly lacking as a source of information on the history of the Sforza;[2] Platina as apologist of the Gonzaga of Mantua is even sharper in his strictures.[3] The point, however, is that he was widely used. Pius II put his own advice into practice by making an abridgement of the first two decades[4] and this work had considerable influence, not least because in this form Biondo became one of the prime sources of Platina's *Lives of the Popes*,[5] the most generally influential and long-lived of all humanist Latin histories. What may be described as the most influential of the vernacular Italian histories, Machiavelli's *Florentine History*, equally depends greatly on the *Decades*.[6] Practically every sixteenth-century scholar must have turned to the *Decades* for factual information[7] and when Pius II's epitome appeared in the Italian translation of Lucio Fauno[8] Biondo's work was made available to a much wider public.

[1] As the epigram is unprinted I give it from Cod. Vat. Lat. 5763, fol. 36ᵛ.

De Blondo historico

Blonde Latinarum scriptor celeberrime rerum
Æmiliae splendor, gloria, fama, decus,
Te Liui superat tantum facundia, quantum
Res tua Romana distat ab historia.

On Cleofilo, Francesco Ottavio of Fano, d. 1490, see Tiraboschi, vi. 925. For a few other judgements of Biondo see Apostolo Zeno, *Dissertazioni Vossiane*, Venice, 2 vols., 1752, i. 233–4.

[2] Muratori, xix. 629.   [3] Ibid., xx. 815.

[4] See Appendix I below, no. 2. It is to be noted that Pius did not correct the mistakes of fact which he had earlier stigmatized.

[5] G. Gaida discusses Platina's indebtedness fully, *Platynae historici liber de vita . . . omnium pontificum*, R.R. II, SS., III. i, intro., pp. liv–lvii.

[6] Villari, *Machiavelli*, iii. 206–73 passim and, for nature of the borrowings in book i, L. La Rocca, *Il primo libro delle 'Istorie florentine' di N. Machiavelli e del parallelismo con le 'Decadi' di F. Biondo*, Palermo, 1904.

[7] The following are given as instances, not as a complete list—Bartolomeo Scala, Wimpfeling, Meisterlin: Fueter, pp. 30, 227, 242; Sabellico: Nogara, p. cxi, n. 142; Donato Giannoti: Villari, *Machiavelli*, iii. 223; Giambullari: Colini Baldeschi, p. 5; Paulus Aemilius: doctoral dissertation on 'Gaguin and Aemilius', by Miss K. Davies, Edinburgh (1954); Polydore Vergil: D. Hay, *P. Vergil*, pp. 56, 86; Girolamo della Corte: M. Barbi, *Bull. della Soc. Dantesca*, no. 8 (1893), pp. 24–25. Cf. M. Bandello, *Novella* IV. viii.

[8] Venice, 2 vols., 1543–4, repr. 1547. Fauno translated Pius II's epitome

In this way Biondo may justly be said to have laid his imprint on the writing of history in subsequent centuries: his digest of the materials became the common property of the much more exact scholars who followed him. Sigonius, Muratori in the *Annali d'Italia*, Sismondi in the *Républiques italiennes* follow more or less a path hacked out by their unassuming predecessor. They do so, of course, from the sources themselves; but then so did Biondo, and many of the authorities quoted for the events of the early fifteenth century by Sismondi for instance are sixteenth-century historians like Scipio Amirati, or even fifteenth-century writers such as Poggio or Simonetta, who had used Biondo in their turn. Here I am, of course, referring to the third decade covering Biondo's own lifetime which has been unduly neglected as a primary source.[1] There are even some nourishing morsels to be found in the second decade where the author calls on family memories, such as his grandfather's account of the effects of the Black Death in 1348,[2] or the picture he was given by old men of the wretched remnants of Louis of Anjou's army straggling home across the Romagna in 1384, naked and unarmed.[3]

At the start of this paper the point was made that Biondo stood at a moment when it was possible to choose between writing history as a form of artistic literature and writing history without such pretensions. I do not think Biondo made such a conscious choice, nor do I think all contemporaries attributed as much importance to it as we have been led to suppose. I trust it will also be agreed that so far as Biondo himself is concerned he fits ill into a rigid antithesis between rhetoric and learning: there are moments when he is consciously rhetorical, more frequent moments when he is careless of this and reflects the carelessness of his sources, those writers of the Middle Ages whose epoch his own work helped to define. Yet whether or not we can call the

of the first two decades, and himself epitomized as well as translated books xxi–xxxi. (The work includes Italian versions of R. Volaterrano 'delle cose d'Italia' and Sabellico 'dell' antichità' d'Aquileia'). For another sixteenth-century translation of the first decade in a MS. at Forlì, see F. Cavichi, 'La prima delle "Historiarum Decades" di F. Biondo volgarizzata da A. Numai', *Atti e memorie della R. deputazione di storia patria per le provincie di Romagna*, ser. iv, vol. viii (Bologna, 1918), 281–96.

[1] For praise of Biondo's accuracy see P. Partner, *The Papal State under Martin V*, 1958, p. 90, n. 4: 'not only the fullest, but the most reliable historian of these events' (at Bologna in 1428).

[2] *Decades*, p. 366.

[3] Ibid., p. 385.

pedantic and ungracious researchers of the sixteenth and seventeenth centuries Biondo's 'school', there is no doubt that at that
time a division developed between the antiquarian and the
more popular writer of history. However cherished Biondo may
have been by the former, he was out of favour with the latter,
whose subjects were either nationalistic or confined to contemporary affairs. Yet his own theme in the *Decades* had a celebrated
reincarnation. It was appropriate that, when scholarship and
literary artistry came together again in the eighteenth century,
one of the resulting masterpieces was another *Decline and Fall of
the Roman Empire*.

APPENDIX I

Dates of Composition and Publication of Flavio Biondo's Principal Writings

NOT included in this list are the letters, of which there are not many and of which a good account is given by Nogara (above, p. 61, n. 5). Two of these are in effect short treatises: Nogara, pp. cxlvi–cxlvii, 170–89. Biondo's first recorded scholarly work is a transcription of the *Brutus* (Cicero *de Oratore*), Nogara, p. xxxvi. I note manuscripts in British libraries.

1. 1435. *De uerbis Romanae locutionis*: a treatise on whether there had been two Latins, one literary and one popular. Ed. prin., Rome, ?1470 (with no. 3); reprinted by G. Mignini, *Propugnatore*, vol. 23 (1890); and by Nogara, pp. 115–30.

2. 1439 onwards (see above, pp. 102 ff.). *Historiarum ab inclinatione Romani imperii decades III, libri xxxi.*[1] Ed. prin., Venice, 1483; Venice, 1484 (with Pius II's epitome); Basle, 1531 (with nos. 3, 4, 6); Basle, 1559 (with nos. 3, 4, 5*d*, 6). Pius II's epitome, Rome, 1481; in *Opera Omnia*, Basle, 1551 and 1571; Helmstadt, 1700; L. Fauno's translation of the epitome, Venice, 1543–4; Venice, 1547.[2] Book xxxii printed in part in G. Williams, *Bekynton's Correspondence* (Rolls Series), ii. 327–38, and in full by Nogara, pp. 3–28.

3. 1444–6. *Roma instaurata.*[3] Three books on the topography of ancient Rome. Ed. prin., Rome ?1470 (with no. 1); Verona, 1481–2 (with nos. 4, 5*d*);[4] Venice, 1503 (with nos. 4, 5*d*); Venice, 1510 (with nos. 4, 5*d*); Turin, 1527 (with no. 4); Basle, 1531 (with nos. 2, 4, 6); Basle, 1559 (with nos. 2, 4, 5*d*, 6). L. Fauno's Italian translation (and of no. 4), Venice, 1543, 1548, 1558.

4. 1448–53. *Italia illustrata.*[5] A description of Italy, province by province. Ed. prin., Rome, 1474;[6] Verona, 1481–2 (with nos. 3, 5*d*); Venice, 1503 (with nos. 3, 5*d*); Venice 1510 (with nos. 3, 5*d*); Turin, 1527 (with no. 3); Basle, 1531 (with nos. 2, 3, 6); Basle, 1559 (with nos. 2, 3, 5*d*, 6).[7] L. Fauno's Italian translation (and of no. 3), Venice, 1543, 1548, 1558.

[1] Corpus Christi College, Cambridge, MS. 205 (see above, p. 66).

[2] See above, p. 85, n. 8.

[3] Brit. Mus., MSS. Harl. 4913, Add. 21956, Add. 17375 (incomplete; a coat of arms on f. 1 suggests that this manuscript belonged to a member of the Becchi-Nettoli family of Florence—I have to thank Mr. M. Maclagan for help in connexion with this).

[4] A variant noticed in M. Pellechet, *Catalogue général des incunables des bibliothèques publiques de France*, ii. 17.

[5] Brit. Mus., Sloane MS. 2456; Balliol College, Oxford, MS. 286.

[6] A variant noticed in Pellechet, ii. 16.

[7] A few extracts in G. B. Pio's miscellanea on Rome (P. Victor, P. Laetus, &c.), Bologna, 1520, sig. II i–kkiv.

5. 1452–4. Writings advocating a crusade:
   (a) *Oratio . . . coram imperatore Frederico et Alphonso Aragonum rege*: O. Lobeck, *Programm des Gymnasiums zum heiligen Kreuz*, Dresden, 1892, pp. xvii–xxii; Nogara, pp. 107–14.
   (b) *Ad Alphonsum Aragonensem . . . de expeditione in Turchos*: Nogara, pp. 31–51.
   (c) *Ad Petrum de Campo Fregoso . . . Genuae ducem*: Nogara, pp. 61–71.
   (d) *De gestis Venetorum* or *Consultatio an bellum uel pax cum Turcis magis expediat reipublicae Venetorum*.[1] Ed. prin. Verona, 1481–2 (with nos. 3, 4); Venice, 1503 (with nos. 3, 4); Venice, 1510 (with nos. 3, 4); Basle, 1559 (with nos. 2, 3, 4, 6); and in J. G. Graevius, *Thesaurus* (1722 ff.), V. i.

6. 1456–60. *Roma Triumphans*. Ten books on the religion, government, armies, and customs of ancient Rome. Ed. prin. Mantua ?1472; Brescia, 1482; Brescia, 1503; Venice, 1511; Basle, 1531 (with nos. 2, 3, 4); Paris, 1533; Basle, 1559 (with nos. 2, 3, 4, 5*d*). L. Fauno's Italian translation, Venice, 1544; Venice, 1549.

7. 1459–60. *Populi Veneti historiarum liber i*. An incomplete account, ending in the early sixth century: Nogara, pp. 77–89.

8. 1460. *Borsus, siue de militia et iurisprudentia*. A treatise dedicated to Borso d'Este: Nogara, pp. 130–44.

[1] Bodleian Library, MS. Laud Misc. 718.

APPENDIX II

The Decades: Periods Covered by each Book

I. i. A.D. 412–23
  ii. to 476
  iii. to 536
  iv. to 538
  v. to 541
  vi. to 546
  vii. to 575
  viii. to 602
  ix. to 685
  x. to January 754

II. i [xi]. to 806
  ii [xii]. to 961
  iii [xiii]. to October 1097
  iv [xiv]. to 1123
  v [xv]. to 1177
  vi [xvi]. to 1215
  vii [xvii]. to 1240
  viii [xviii]. to 1291
  ix [xix]. to 1332
  x [xx]. to 1410

III. i [xxi]. to February 1424
  ii [xxii]. to January 1426
  iii [xxiii]. to September 1429
  iv [xxiv]. to autumn 1431
  v [xxv]. to May 1434
  vi [xxvi]. to August 1435
  vii [xxvii]. to December 1437
  viii [xxviii]. to March 1438
  ix [xxix]. to April 1439
  x [xxx]. to November 1439

IV. i [xxxi]. to autumn 1440
  ii [xxxii]. to October 1441.

ADDITIONAL NOTE

Major revisions, such as references to literature that has appeared since the lectures were first printed, have not been made in this volume. One later publication must however be mentioned here. Almost as soon as my lecture was in print Professor Ricardo Fubini published a lengthy life of Flavio Biondo in the *Dizionario Biografico degli Italiani*, vol. 10 (Rome, 1968), pp. 536–559. He gives an extensive bibliography. As with my lecture Professor Fubini depends heavily on the book by Nogara which is referred to above, pp. 61–2 n. 5.

LEON BATTISTA ALBERTI AND THE BEGINNINGS OF ITALIAN GRAMMAR

IT is a commonplace of criticism to speak of the 'universality' of Alberti's genius, and to hold him up as a figure representative of the multifarious interests of Renaissance man. Yet it would be true to say that this 'universality' in him is exceptional rather than typical. No one in his century embraced such a wide range of studies and practical skills. At the same time, though his range was broad, covering both literary and scientific subjects, his learning and understanding were no less profound. The designation of Alberti as a dilettante by some critics (starting from Burckhardt) admits the breadth but overlooks this depth of his studies; but more than that, it fails to recognize what is most characteristic of the man and his achievements: the ability to grasp the essentials of any subject and to contribute in some way to its advancement, either by making a discovery or by writing a treatise—in other words the power of originality. It is this quality of mind combined with wide knowledge and experience that makes him a pioneer and a key figure in the culture of fifteenth-century Italy, in the arts, in literature and language, and in certain sciences. The fact that certain developments and tendencies in these different fields were in some form present in his time and among his contemporaries, in no way diminishes the importance of his initiative as a writer or as an inventor. It was he and not they who composed this or that treatise, devised this or that instrument; and it is a distortion of the truth to regard him as a mouthpiece of others' ideas and practice.

If we want proof of his initiative and originality we can easily draw up an impressive list of 'firsts'. In the arts he wrote the first modern treatises on painting and perspective, on sculpture and on architecture, treatises whose importance and influence are too well known to need elaboration here. In literature and language he was the first to write on emblems and on ciphers; the first to adapt classical metres to Italian poetry; the first to imitate the Virgilian eclogue in Italian; the first to compose humanistic works in the Italian vernacular, whose use he championed in an age of predominant Latinity. In the sciences he occupies a first place in geographical surveying and map-making, while inventions in the fields of optics and hydraulics have also been attributed to him with a high degree of probability. In architectural practice his remarkable originality has long been recognized in the buildings he designed and super-vised in Rimini, Florence, and Mantua; whilst on some of these buildings we find, if not the first, at least some of the earliest examples of the Renaissance revival of antique Roman characters taken from medals and monuments. This brief list, which is not exhaustive nor adequate to indicate the full extent and nature of Alberti's achievement, may here suffice to show that he stands at the beginning of a wide range of developments in Renaissance art, letters, thought, and science.[1]

In the context of such diverse original contributions it is perhaps no surprise to find that Alberti was also the first to write a grammar of the Italian language, and to do so, as I hope to show, some sixty years before the far better known and more influential works of Fortunio and Bembo. The grammar in question has been known for half a century, but, although Alberti has been regarded as a strong possible candidate for its author-ship, no firm proof has until recently been offered that it is in fact his work. The object of this lecture is to demonstrate his authorship and to discuss the character and the importance of the grammar in the history of the Italian language during the Renaissance period.

That Alberti composed some kind of grammar is confirmed by his own words in the treatise on ciphers (*De Cifris*) written about 1466; in which, speaking of the different pronunciation of *u* and *v*, hitherto rendered by the same letter, he mentions that he had proposed a distinction in this case: 'alibi cum de litteris atque caeteris principiis grammaticae tractaremus' (elsewhere when I dealt with letters and other principles of grammar).[2] The context of this remark in *De Cifris* is pre-dominantly Latin, and there is consequently no certainty that Alberti was referring to a work about Italian grammar. At the

[1] These facts are well enough known to need no complete bibliography here. For details see my article on Alberti in *Dizionario biografico degli Italiani*, i (Rome, 1960), 702–9; on antique lettering see also G. Mardersteig, 'L. B. A. e la rinascita del carattere lapidario nel Quattrocento', in *Italia medievale e umanistica*, ii (1959), 285 ff. (but cf. M. Meiss, in *Art Bulletin*, xlii (1960), 97 ff.).

[2] A. Meister, *Die Geheimschrift im Dienste der Päpstlichen Kurie* (Paderborn, 1906), 127.

same time, there exists no known Latin grammar attributed or attributable to him, and no other allusion to such a possible Latin work occurs in any other of his writings.

Confirmation that Alberti did write a grammar of the vernacular is found in a letter of Giovanni Augurello which is quoted by Mario Equicola in his *Libro di Natura d'Amore*:

He was an extraordinary man learned in many disciplines, who, as I have heard, observing the excellence of the Tuscan language, decided to draw up for the first time rules taken from the writings of Dante, Petrarch and Boccaccio, even though he was himself a Tuscan; and he began from the first principles, for, perceiving that the Latin alphabet could not fully express the syllables and words of Tuscan, being in a sense a foreign language alien in part to Latin, he created a new alphabet taking some letters from Latin and adding others . . . . He probably made a fine job of it, like his other excellent works in Latin and vernacular in many branches of learning and especially in architecture and painting, all of which I sought assiduously and found with great delight whilst I was in Florence. But I was never able to discover this work on language; but it was there, according to the reports of reliable persons.[1]

Although Augurello does not name this 'extraordinary man', it is not difficult from the description to identify him as Alberti. Augurello was in Florence between 1474 and 1476, within two years of Alberti's death, and his testimony therefore carries the authority of a near contemporary.[2] Furthermore, his reference to a grammar begun from 'first principles' and to the creation of a new alphabet corresponds fairly closely to Alberti's own allusion in his *De Cifris* to orthographical reforms and grammatical principles. Yet one part of Augurello's letter raises considerable doubts about the reliability of his evidence: the statement that Alberti drew his grammatical rules from the works of Dante, Petrarch, and Boccaccio—'even though [Augurello adds] he was himself a Tuscan'. This apparently curious qualification needs comment, for it seems to indicate surprise on Augurello's part: it is strange to him, in other words, that a Tuscan like Alberti should base the grammatical rules of the vernacular, not on modern usage, but on the great Tuscan writers of the preceding century; for in doing so he would have been anticipating a principle of linguistic codification established only at

[1] Quoted and discussed by C. Trabalza, 'Una singolare testimonianza sull' Alberti grammatico', in *Miscellanea Torraca* (Milan, 1912), reprinted in his *Dipanature critiche* (Bologna–Trieste, 1920), 41–71.

[2] On Augurello see now R. Weiss, in *Dizionario biografico*, cit., vol. iv, 1962.

the beginning of the sixteenth century. I will return to this important point later. Suffice it to say here that the attribution of such a principle of imitation to Alberti would not only be an anachronism, it may be excluded *a priori*. For there is no evidence in his works of adherence to the linguistic models of those great writers. Everything points instead to the probability that, if and when writing of Tuscan grammar, he would base himself on contemporary usage and seek assistance from the forms and rules of Latin. It seems likely, therefore, as has been suggested, that Augurello's letter, which we know only through Equicola, may be of quite a late date, and consequently coloured by the ideas prevailing at the time of its writing. Besides, as he himself says, he never saw Alberti's work on this subject; he speaks from report, and quite probably from memory at some distance in time. It seems not impossible, then, to accept his confirmation of Alberti's composition of a Tuscan grammar containing orthographical reforms without accepting all the details of his description.

If this work of Alberti's was about in Florence in 1474, where could it have been and where is it now? To the first part of the question we may answer that it was possibly in the hands of a relative of Alberti, but soon afterwards passed into the library of Lorenzo de' Medici; to the second part that the complete original is now lost, but a manuscript copy, made in 1508, is now in the Vatican library. An inventory of the Medici library drawn up in 1495 contains a volume: *Regule lingue florentine*— without name of author—which is no longer extant.[1] Codex Vaticanus Reginensis 1370 contains a grammar, copied, as the subscription says, from a manuscript in the Medici Library in Rome in December 1508, and therefore most probably from those missing *Regule*; yet this likewise has no author's name, nor even a title. A later hand added simply: 'Della Thoscana senza auttore.' How then can it be said that this is Alberti's work?

Since the first discovery of the grammar at the end of the nineteenth century,[2] though other attributions have been

[1] E. Piccolomini, 'Delle condizioni e delle vicende della Libreria Medicea privata dal 1494 al 1508', in *Arch. Stor. Ital.*, 3rd ser., xix, 101 ff. and 254 ff.; xx, 51 ff. (on p. 64, item 357, the entry in the 1495 inventory).

[2] It was first mentioned by A. Torri in his edition *Della lingua volgare di Dante libri due tradotti da G-G. Trissino* (Leghorn, 1850), xxxvi–xxxvii; and more accurately described by P. Rajna, *Il trattato De Vulg. Eloqu.* (Florence, 1896), xliv–xlviii. The text was published by C. Trabalza in an appendix to his *Storia della grammatica italiana.* (Florence, 1908), 531–48 (see also 13–22).

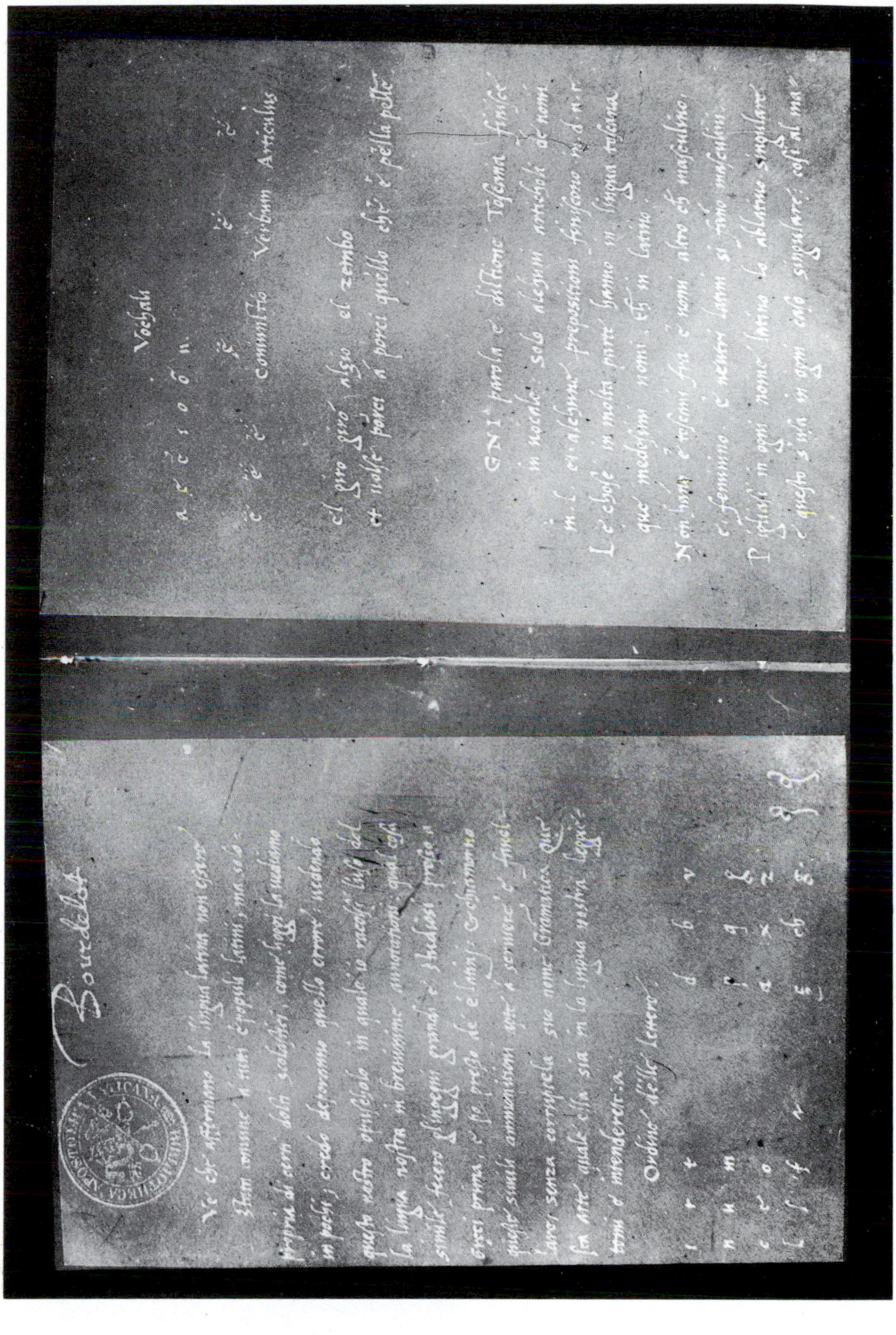

PLATE 17

Cod. Vat. Reg., fo. 1 r-v

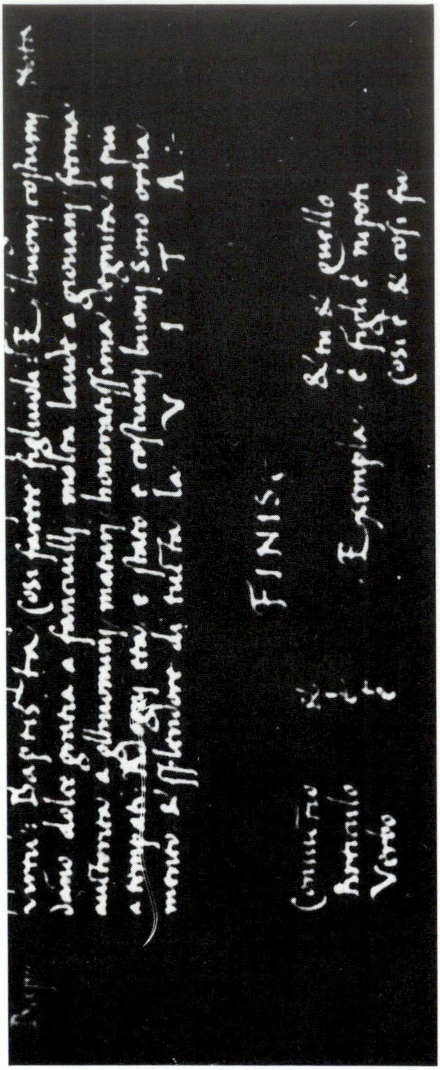

PLATE 18

a. Cod. Gadd. 84 (Bibl. Laurenziana, Florence), fo. 7ʳ

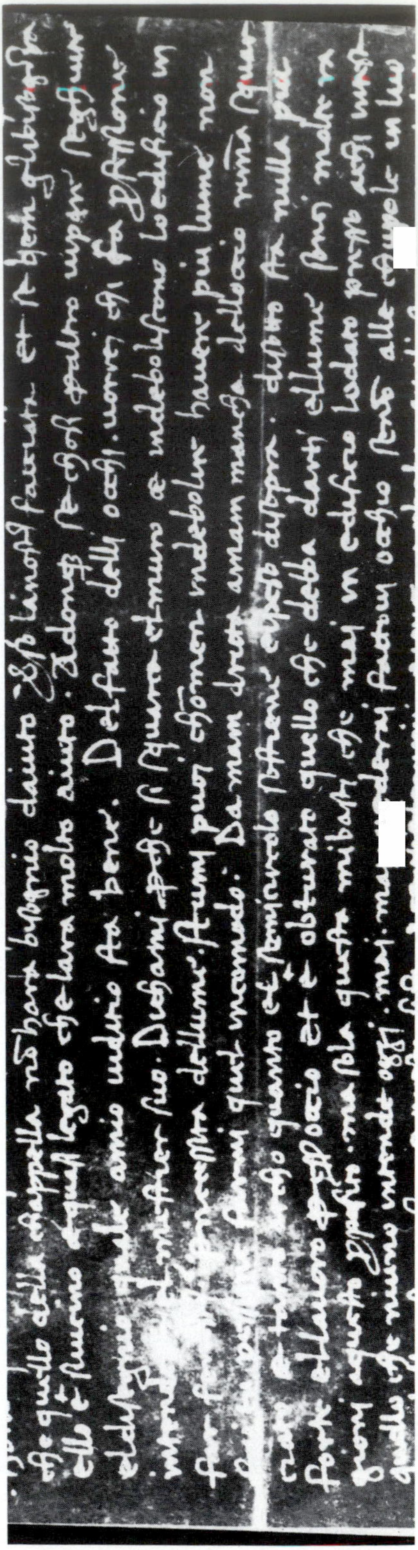

b. Autograph letter of Alberti, Pierpont Morgan Library, New York

PLATE 19

a. Cod. II. IV. 38 (Bibl. Naz., Florence), fo. 103ᵛ

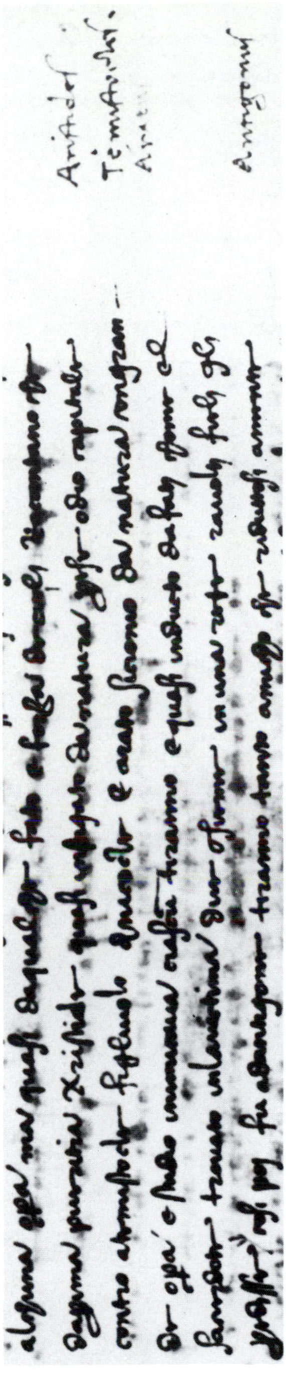

b. Cod. II. IV. 38 (Bibl. Naz., Florence), fo. 113ʳ

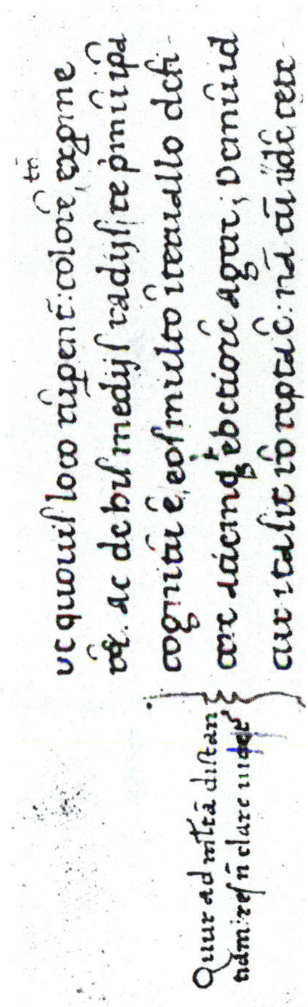

c. Cod. 146 (Bibl. Class., Ravenna)

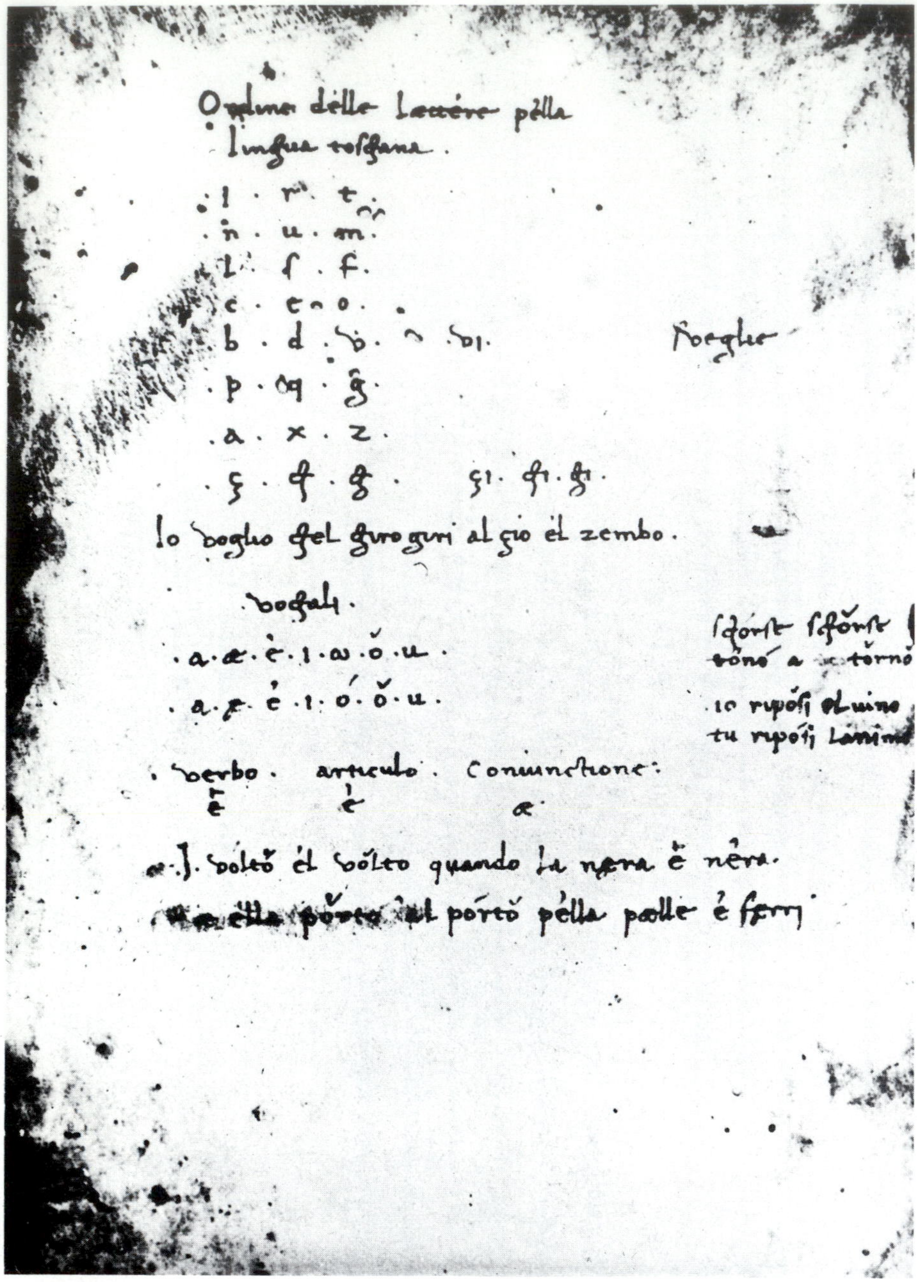

PLATE 20

Cod. Moreni 2 (Bibl. Riccardiana, Florence)

advanced, Alberti's authorship has been regarded as most probable, partly on the evidence already mentioned, and partly on the basis of elements in the text itself, starting from the character of the brief preface to the grammar, which reads as follows:

Those who affirm that the Latin language was not common to all the Latin peoples but possessed only by a few learned scholastics, as we see is the case today, will, I believe, quit this error when they see this work of mine in which I have brought together in brief form the usage of our language. Great and learned minds did the same first among the Greeks, and then among the Romans; and they called such norms of correct writing and speaking, Grammar. What this art consists in in our language, read me and you will understand.

This statement may certainly at first sight seem very curious; and to one eminent scholar fifty years ago it appeared to contain a *non sequitur*.[1] Yet another scholar, F. Sensi, already perceived that it showed some correspondence with parts of the proem to Book III of Alberti's *Della Famiglia*, and that both were strictly related to the Florentine debate of the mid-1430's reported in Flavio Biondo's *De Locutione Romana*, as to whether Rome had two different languages, Latin and vernacular, or one, Latin, from which the vernacular in some sense later derives.[2] The matter may best be clarified by quoting at some length from Alberti's proem to Book III of *Della Famiglia*:

Italy was on many occasions invaded and occupied by various peoples: Gauls, Goths, Vandals, Longobards, and other such like barbarous uncivilised nations. And as necessity or inclination dictated, the Italians, partly to be better understood, partly to please their masters in their discourse, learned this and that foreign tongue, and the foreign invaders similarly accommodated themselves to ours, I believe introducing many barbarisms and corrupt forms of speech. As a result of this mixture our original pure and cultured language became progressively more spoiled and corrupted. Nor can I agree with those who, marvelling at such a loss, affirm that the common language we now use existed continuously in Italy at that time and earlier, declaring

[1] V. Cian, 'Le Regole della Lingua Fiorentina e le Prose Bembine', in *Giorn. Stor. della Lett. Ital.* liv (1909), 120–30 (especially 124).

[2] F. Sensi, 'Un libro che si credeva perduto (L. B. A. grammatico)', in *Fanfulla della Domenica*, xxvii (1905), 34, reprinted in *Bibliofilia*, vii (1906), 211–12; and 'Ancora su L. B. A. grammatico', in *Rendiconti del R. Istituto Lombardo di Sc. e Lett.* xlii (1909), 467–75. For the debate and its context, see my inaugural lecture, *A Renaissance Controversy: Latin or Italian* (Oxford, 1960).

themselves unable to believe that women of that age could know what even very learned men now find obscure and difficult in the Latin language, and consequently they conclude that that language, in which men of learning wrote, was a sort of scholastic art and invention . . . . I would like to ask these people in what language if not in Latin any of the ancients wrote, not on matters of learning, but on ordinary everyday things, to their wives, sons and servants. . . . And I would ask them if they think it less difficult for foreigners to speak correctly and properly the language we use today than it is for us to speak that used by the ancients. Do we not see how difficult it is for our servants to express themselves so as to be understood, simply because they do not know how and are unable from their experience to vary the cases and tenses and make the agreements our language also demands. How many women there were in ancient times praised for their eloquence in Latin . . . ! And why should the ancient writers have striven so arduously to benefit their fellow citizens by writing in a little-known language? But it seems inappropriate to expatiate further on this matter here; perhaps I will discuss it more fully elsewhere.[1]

This passage, when read beside the short preface to the Vatican grammar, clarifies the historical perspective in which the grammar should be seen. The vernacular is a corruption of Latin due to barbarian influences; but fundamentally it is still in a sense the Latin language. It is not a survival of an ancient vernacular which co-existed in ancient times with Latin. It possesses cases and tenses and requires agreements just as Latin does. In writing of this matter in 1437–8 Alberti shows here clear awareness, not only of a kind of historical evolution, but also of grammatical principles inherent in the modern language; and he proposes to discuss the matter further elsewhere. This 'elsewhere' could well be the Vatican grammar, for in the same context of the preface we have just quoted, the purpose of the grammar becomes clear: to dispel the error of believing that Latin was and is the language of a few, and therefore distinct and different from the vernacular, the grammar will show their continuity in words and forms and by using the categories of Latin grammar. It will thereby prove that the vernacular is also a regular, grammatical language, and that its origins lie, not in an ancient language different from Latin, but in Latin itself. It is, therefore, a kind of historical grammar. It is not difficult to imagine from the evident correspondences of outlook and expression in the passages quoted that the author of the grammar and the *Famiglia* are the same person.

[1] Translated from the Italian text in L. B. Alberti, *Opere volgari*, ed. C. Grayson, i (Bari, 1960), 154–5.

The imagination has, however, other and still more convincing evidence to rest on. The grammar begins, immediately after the brief preface, with a table of letters in which not only is a distinction made between the forms of *u* and *v*, but accents are used to differentiate between open and close vowels; which accords closely, as scholars were quick to perceive, with the statement in *De Cifris* about orthographical reforms. Sensi also laid stress on a phrase used in the grammar to exemplify the difference between the perfect and the past definite: 'Hieri fui ad Ostia, oggi sono stato a Tibuli': this would identify the author as a Tuscan resident at the time of composition in Rome—which fits Alberti's situation in the years after 1443. The presence of gallicisms and germanisms in the text could also be explained, if Alberti were the author, by his residence in cosmopolitan Rome and his journeys abroad with Cardinal Albergati. Finally, the conclusion of the grammar seemed to echo the spirit of civic pride and usefulness typical of Alberti: 'Fellow citizens, I beseech you, if my efforts are of some avail with you, to welcome this desire of mine to honour our land, and to correct rather than criticize me if you find any mistakes in its execution.'

These were, in brief, some of the main arguments advanced in favour of Alberti's authorship up to 1912, the year in which Trabalza found and published the Augurello letter. This confirmed that Alberti wrote an Italian grammar, but gave it, as we have seen, a character alien to Alberti's outlook, and remote also from the basis of the Vatican grammar, which has nothing to do with Dante, Petrarch, and Boccaccio. In the intervening years opinions have remained divided with the balance of probability inclined in Alberti's favour.[1] It is now possible to ascribe the Vatican grammar to him with absolute certainty, both on further examination of internal evidence and on fresh external evidence which has very recently come to light. I will deal first with the internal evidence.

Analysis of the language of the grammar in the Vatican MS. shows that it abounds in words and phrases typical of Alberti's usage; in almost every case exact correspondences and parallels are to be found in his Italian works. These are too numerous to

---

[1] L. Morandi's attribution to Lorenzo de' Medici (or even Leonardo da Vinci) was early rejected (see his articles in *Nuova Antologia*, Aug. 1905, Oct. 1909; also his volume *Lorenzo il Magnifico, Leonardo da Vinci e la prima grammatica italiana* (Città di Castello, 1908)). Various other names have been put forward: Landino, Poliziano, Pulci. The present view is summed up by B. Migliorini, *Storia della lingua italiana* (Florence, 1960), 267.

illustrate fully here.[1] I select, as examples, two lexical elements which appear to me particularly decisive: first the verb *congettare* which occurs at the end of the grammar evidently with the sense of 'to compose'. 'Si questo nostro opuscolo sarà tanto grato a chi mi leggerà, quanto fu laborioso a me el *congettarlo*, certo mi dilecterà haverlo promulgato . . . .' It is so rare that I can find it in no dictionary or glossary, and one might even be tempted to think it an error, were it not for the fact that this verb occurs in an autograph letter written in 1470 by Alberti to Lodovico Gonzaga, Marquis of Mantua, about his design for the church of S. Andrea. Alberti criticizes the model prepared by Manetti, finding it unsuitable for the marquis's purpose. He goes on: 'Pensai e *congettai* questo qual ve mando. . . . S'el ve piaserà darò modo di notarlo in proportione . . . .'[2] It is apparent from this example that the verb *congettare* is literally a term of art meaning 'to sketch': it is the first step in architectural design, followed, after general approval, by complete drawings in proportion, as the basis for actual construction. This meaning has, by a happy coincidence, been amply confirmed but a few days ago by the publication of a volume on the architect Filarete, who used the term frequently: the author, knowing the example of the substantive *congetto* in Alberti's *Pittura*, believes, in my opinion correctly, that Filarete inherits it from Alberti.[3] It is very significant that Alberti should use this verb when speaking of his grammar; for its use in this context clearly indicates that he regarded the work in the nature of a 'sketch'— the first outline, as it were, for the construction of a grammatical edifice 'in proportione'.

The second example is the participle *seiuncto*, a crude Latinism used adjectivally in the grammar with the meaning 'separate'. This word is likewise missing from the dictionaries, and the only other example I can find is in Book IV of Alberti's *Famiglia*.[4] At the same time, it is typical of a long series of Albertian

---

[1] A full analysis will shortly be available in a new edition of the Vatican grammar to be published during 1964 by the Commissione per i Testi di Lingua, Bologna. The material of the present lecture was collected during preparation of this edition in 1961–2.

[2] Archivio Gonzaga, Mantua, F. II. 8. Published by G. Mancini, *L. B. Alberti Opera inedita* (Florence, 1890), 291–2.

[3] P. Tigler, *Die Architekturtheorie des Filarete*, Berlin, 1963 (*Neue Münchner Beiträge zur Kunstgeschichte*, Band 5), 149 ff.

[4] Ed. cit., p. 326, line 17. In the grammar the word is used of prepositions: 'Prepositioni che caggiono in compositione et anchora s'adoperano *seiuncte*. . . .'

lexical innovations based on Latin. The kind of coincidence exemplified by these two cases is too precise to be attributable to mere chance.

Yet an even closer link between the grammar and Alberti appears in features hitherto unnoticed or not completely understood. Besides the distinction between *u* and *v* there appear in the table of letters at the beginning of the grammar certain accents distinguishing open and close vowels; and in particular two signs which differentiate the verb *e* (3rd pers. sing. present tense of *essere*) and the article *e* (masc. plur.) from *e* (conjunction) [Plate 17]. The presence of double and triple dots over these signs, which are merely for reference (and incidentally are absolutely characteristic of Alberti's usage in manuscripts corrected by him), baffled earlier scholars, one of whom supposed some connexion with Arabic.[1] Disregarding the dots, therefore, we see that the signs themselves come in fact from Greek, and in the case of *e* verb and *e* article are quite simply the signs of the rough and the smooth breathing applied here to a purpose quite different from their true significance. In which event, unless I am mistaken, we have here the first attempt to adapt Greek orthographical features to Italian, anticipating by more than half a century, in spirit if not in form, the more conspicuous reforms of Gian Giorgio Trissino.[2]

This use of the Greek breathing in the grammar links it in a surprising way with Alberti, because I cannot find that anyone else used such signs at that time. It features as a substitute for the letter *h* in Latin manuscripts between the ninth and the eleventh centuries, but does not seem to have been continued thereafter or reintroduced in later times.[3] As far as I have been able to discover, it does not appear in any Latin or Italian

---

[1] F. Sensi, article cited in *Rend. R. Ist. Lombardo*. Cf. also C. Trabalza, *Storia della grammatica . . .*, cit., 533, 535. For the use of the 'puntini di richiamo' by Alberti cf. the facsimile of his corrections facing pp. 50 and 62 of my ed. of *Musca, Vita S. Potiti*, (Florence, 1953).

[2] On accents in Italian orthography in the sixteenth century see B. Migliorini, 'Note sulla grafia italiana del Rinascimento', in his *Saggi linguistici* (Florence, 1957), 197 ff. (especially 223–4).

[3] For medieval Latin see Sir E. Maunde Thompson, *Introduction to Greek and Latin palaeography* (Oxford, 1912), 64; M. Prou, *Manuel de paléographie*, Paris, 4th ed., 1924, 187; M.-Th. Vernet, in *Bull. d'Information de l'Institut de Recherche et d'Histoire des Textes*, n. 8 (1959), 9, 14, 29; (for a rare example of the twelfth century) B. Bischoff, *Die Süddeutschen Schreibenschulen und Bibliotheken in der Karolingerzeit*, i (Leipzig, 1940), 140, 198. Against this background must be seen the very rare examples of the fifteenth century cited below at (*a*) and (*b*).

manuscript of the fifteenth or sixteenth centuries except the following, all of them Alberti manuscripts:

1. Cod. Gaddiano 84, Biblioteca Laurenziana, Florence. This manuscript of the late fifteenth century contains two works of Alberti.[1] It is not autograph; but at the end of one of the works, *Cena familiaris*, there appears a table almost exactly similar to that of the grammar, showing the same distinction between verb, article, and conjunction [Plate 18 *a*]. Here the form of the conjunction is slightly different, and the smooth breathing has become a mere vertical line, but the rough breathing is unmistakable. Apart from this table there is no trace of these signs in the texts transcribed in this manuscript. Yet any doubts that the presence of this table in a completely Albertian manuscript may be fortuitous are removed by our second example.

2. Autograph letter from Alberti to Matteo de' Pasti, 18 November 1454, now in the Pierpont Morgan Library, New York.[2] This is the well-known letter about the form of the Tempio Malatestiano at Rimini, and it provides the most convincing example for our argument, for it contains two instances of the rough breathing on *e* verb [Plate 18 *b*, lines 2 and 8]. Alberti does not use the sign consistently throughout the letter, nor introduce other similar signs; but this fact does not lessen the importance of the two cases, which have no parallel outside these manuscripts.

Two other examples show the use of the rough breathing sign in a different and more conventional way—that is, as it featured in medieval Latin manuscripts. If what I said earlier about this use of the sign is true, then the following cases are unique in the Italian fifteenth century, and consequently may be of some interest to palaeographers:

(*a*) Cod. II. IV. 38, Biblioteca Nazionale, Florence, contains the largest single collection of Alberti's Italian works, including the *Famiglia* with autograph corrections and additions. Although there is no trace of Greek signs in these, there are two cases of Greek names written (I believe by Alberti himself) in Latin form with the Greek rough breathing in place of *h*: Teophrastus, Temistocles [Plate 19 *a*, *b*].[3]

---

[1] For a description see *L. B. A. Opere volgari*, ed. cit., 450-1.

[2] *L. B. A. and the Tempio Malatestiano: An autograph letter from L. B. A. to Matteo de' Pasti*, ed. with introduction by C. Grayson (New York, 1957, with facsimile).

[3] In the margins of ff. 103*v* and 113*r* respectively. On this manuscript see *Opere volgari*, ed. cit., 367 ff.; and for the corrections, *Lingua Nostra*, xvi (1955), 4, 105 ff.

(*b*) Cod. 146, Biblioteca Classense, Ravenna, which contains Alberti's *De Pictura* (in the Latin text). This is not autograph, but certainly contemporary with the author. There are some indications, however, that Alberti had a hand directly or indirectly in this copy; and one of these is the presence of a single instance of the rough breathing for *h* in the word hebetiorem (written: ἑbetiorem). [Plate 19 *c*].[1]

Amid the great bulk of Alberti's work these isolated examples attest at most to a sporadic use of these signs in practice. They are, nevertheless, a powerful link with the Vatican grammar, and taken together with the linguistic correspondences already indicated, as well as the other external and internal evidence of which we spoke, they suffice to prove beyond reasonable doubt that Alberti was its author.

The very recent discovery of a single folio in what would appear to be Alberti's hand, containing with small but not insignificant variants the material which in the Vatican grammar immediately follows the preface, namely the table of letters, serves to remove any possible doubt about Alberti's authorship [Plate 20].[2] The variants referred to are such as to suggest that the autograph page represents a trial or earlier stage in the composition of the grammar; but it has the advantage over the Vatican copy of the finished work in showing more clearly the exact nature of some of the orthographical innovations proposed by Alberti. These were evidently modified in transcription by the amanuensis of the Vatican MS. In the case of *u* and *v*, the form of *v* corresponds closely to the reference in *De Cifris* to the proposal to write the letter 'hasta inflexa'. Other cases of consonants, where the Latin alphabet is inadequate to represent the pronunciation of Tuscan, Alberti resolves as follows; the velar pronunciation of *c* and *g* by a

[1] For more detailed consideration of this manuscript see my article on 'L. B. A.'s *costruzione legittima*', in *Italian Studies*, xix, 1964.

[2] This folio (in Cod. Moreni 2, Biblioteca Riccardiana, Florence) was independently discovered by Dott.ssa C. Colombo, and examined in her article, 'L. B. A. e la prima grammatica italiana', in *Studi Linguistici Italiani*, iii, 1962 (published in Nov. 1963), which touches on some of the evidence already assembled by me and used in this lecture (I am grateful to Sig.na Colombo for advance information of her discovery given to me in June 1963). The fragment adds the final proof of Alberti's authorship, but also raises problems, some of which are briefly discussed here, and will be more extensively examined in an additional note to my ed. of the grammar (see n. 1, p. 98). Meantime the plates here reproduced (17 and 20) give some opportunity for comparison with the Vatican MS.

fusion of these letters with *h*: the distinction between the voiced and voiceless pronunciation of *z* by *z* and *ç* respectively. And these forms are summed up in the exemplary line: 'Io voglio chel ghiro giri al çio el zembo.' None of these forms were without precedent in vernacular orthography, but they here enter a system, and appear more clearly in the autograph fragment than in the Vatican MS.

The representation of vowel sounds in the fragment is, on the other hand, somewhat puzzling, for Alberti here offers two seemingly alternative solutions, with variations in the forms used for open *e* and open *o*. The form for *o* of the second line has entered his examples in the margins and at the foot of the page; but the form for *e* is confused in the examples of made-up sentences: *nęra* and *pœlle*. These discrepancies, which show inconsistency on Alberti's part in the fragment, do not appear in the Vatican MS., where the system corresponds closely to the second line of the autograph. The system in the latter (i.e. the fragment) is as follows: open *o* is distinguished by the acute accent; close *o* by an inverted circumflex; open *e* (and *e* conjunction) by what appears like a diphthong œ, and is probably simply a version of the ampersand (as frequently used by Alberti elsewhere); close *e* by a form of the smooth breathing (or, possibly, an apostrophe); while both these are distinguished from the verb *è*, which carries the rough breathing sign.

In the Vatican MS. this system is simplified further by the removal of the acute accent from open *o*. This fact, and the absence of discrepancies, indicate that the Vatican version derives from another, later, redaction of the grammar by Alberti. None the less, the fragment clarifies certain details, and adds final confirmation to an already overwhelming case in favour of Alberti's authorship of the Vatican grammar.

One part at least, therefore, of Augurello's description of Alberti's grammar is certainly correct: that it attempted to remedy the inability of Latin letters to represent the sounds of Tuscan by introducing new letters and forms. For this purpose Alberti quite clearly had recourse to Greek, and in this, in general, he anticipated both the problems and the proposals of the sixteenth-century reformers of Italian orthography. It is interesting to speculate as to where Alberti got the idea of borrowing elements from Greek. He undoubtedly knew Greek, but it seems possible that this direct knowledge was not the sole inspiration.[1] I suggest as a probable intermediary the

[1] Cf. G. Mancini, *Vita di L. B. A.*, 2nd ed. (Florence, 1911), 44–46.

well-known *Institutiones Grammaticae* of Priscian; for this work not only appears to have provided the scheme and some of the details for Alberti's grammar, but also to have constituted a principal source for his *De Cifris*. Were further proof needed that he wrote the Vatican grammar, this coincidence would offer still more evidence for the attribution.

Priscian's *Institutiones* open with a lengthy treatise on letters and syllables in Latin and Greek, which would seem to have nothing in common with the beginning of the grammar, where the letters are disposed according to their form.[1] It is much more evidently like the *De Cifris*, which like Priscian begins with an inquiry into *litterarum elementa* and their composition in sylla- bles, and for the purpose uses elements and examples which seem to derive directly from the *Institutiones*. Yet Priscian's first book not only contains a clear statement on the dual nature of the letter *u* as both vowel and consonant (I, 17), but deals on three separate occasions with the use and significance of the sign of the Greek rough breathing (I, 12, 24–26, 47). Some words and phrases of Priscian are also echoed in the grammar, and suggest that the *Institutiones* were present in Alberti's mind when he wrote it.[2] This seems to be confirmed by the order in which Alberti deals with the grammatical categories, which corre- spond in all but one particular with Priscian's. The sequence in Alberti's grammar is: noun, pronoun, verb, preposition, adverb, interjection, conjunction, construction. In Priscian's order verb precedes pronoun. Whatever the reason for this difference, the fact remains that Alberti's scheme appears based on Priscian in general and in some of its details.[3] One instance of details, for example, is that the grammar, under prepositions, deals first with those occurring in composition, and then distinguishes pre- positions according to whether they are mono- or polysyllabic.

[1] References included in the text are to the edition of M. Hertz, *Prisciani . . . Institutionum Grammaticarum Libri XVIII*, in the collection edited by H. Keil, *Grammatici Latini* (Leipzig, 1864).

[2] Cf. e.g. the statement in the grammar: 'Ogni parola o dictione Toscana finisce in vocale . . .', with Priscian, *Inst.* i. 9.

[3] For the various schemes in relation to Italian grammar in the sixteenth century see the excellent article by M. Corti, 'Marco Antonio Carlino e l'influsso dei grammatici latini sui primi grammatici volgari', in *Cultura Neolatina*, xv (1955), 196–222. The order of verb and pronoun in Alberti's scheme may have been influenced either by Donatus or by the pseudo- Priscian *De nomine, pronomine et verbo*. For other correspondences between Priscian, *De Cifris*, and the grammar, I must refer to my forthcoming edition, cit. supra.

Priscian had done exactly the same, dividing them more minutely, however, into prepositions of one, two, or three syllables. Again, under construction, the *Institutiones* conclude with a section dealing, *inter alia*, with solecisms and barbarisms; correspondingly we find at the end of the grammar some observations on errors in agreement of number and tense, *nomi barberi* and other *vizi del favellare*.

It would be wrong to pretend that the grammar, a very brief though highly original work, borrowed from the *Institutiones*, which is a vast grammatical-philosophical treatise, more than the scheme, nomenclature, and some particulars of the strictly grammatical part, together with some inspiration regarding letters and orthographical signs. Yet this debt is, in my view, sufficient to show that the first Italian grammar follows, not, as Trabalza wrote, 'gli schemi della grammatica generale latina', but more specifically the model of Priscian; and this same model subsequently served Alberti for another purpose when writing about ciphers in the 1460's. I say 'subsequently' because the grammar must have been composed some sixty or more years before the only surviving complete copy of 1508. It is not possible at present to ascribe a date to the recently discovered autograph fragment; but we may deduce something from the other documents mentioned. I would suggest the letter to Pasti of 1454 as a *terminus ante quem*. The *Cena* is difficult to date, but the corrections on the *Famiglia* MS. suggest a date some ten years earlier than that letter.[1] This would accord more closely with the character of the grammar itself, which, as already mentioned, takes us back to the disputes of the 1430's and the proem to Book III of Alberti's *Famiglia* (1437–8). The example involving Ostia and Tivoli, now we are sure of Alberti's authorship, indicates his probable residence in Rome, that is, after 1443. We may, therefore, with reasonable confidence ascribe the completion if not the entire composition of the grammar to that year or soon after, and certainly to the time when the controversy over the language of Rome was still warm and actual.

Quite apart from that specific context it would seem natural if not indeed inevitable, that the first grammar of Italian, whenever conceived, should base itself on the model of Latin. In this context, however, the Latin basis of Alberti's grammar is dictated by something more than convenience or tradition;

---

[1] The *Cena* was written some time after the *Famiglia* (cf. *Opere volgari*, cit., 346); the autograph corrections to MS. II. IV. 38 were probably made before 1443, and perhaps even before 1437 (cf. ibidem, 378–80).

it is a necessary and integral part of the proof that modern Tuscan is its historical if somewhat corrupted descendant, that this vernacular, rather than being a fortuitous or chaotic language, falls by nature into the rules and categories of ancient grammar. Hence the demonstrative rather than preceptive character of Alberti's work. The motive behind its composition is not so much to teach people how to speak and write Tuscan correctly (though this is also implied in the preface), as to show that it possesses a regularity parallel to that of Latin. This major, indeed almost exclusive, purpose is all the more striking because of the author's complete lack of awareness of any other problems of the kind which preoccupied and agitated later generations of grammarians. He addresses his Tuscan grammar to his fellow citizens the Florentines, to those who possess this language and can check and emend his work—to a narrow audience, that is, and without concern for the wider implications of the term 'Tuscan'.[1] There is no assertion within this term of Florentine superiority, no shadow of intention to impose it on others or to rival other regional languages. In other words, there is no wider feeling for an Italian context. The only and constant term of comparison with Tuscan, apart from incidental references to gallicisms and germanisms, is Latin.

The grammar is similarly lacking in literary concerns or prejudices. Its subject and source is ostensibly modern usage: 'l'uso della lingua nostra.' No appeal is made to the past or to literary tradition by way of justifying the existence and virtue of this present language. No mention is made of Dante, Petrarch, or Boccaccio. This is all perfectly in character with the outlook and writings of Alberti; and this feature alone of the grammar should have been sufficient to disqualify several of the candidates put forward at various times for its authorship. In the generation of Lorenzo de' Medici and Cristoforo Landino, failure to include the literary giants of the Trecento would be unthinkable both in theory and practice. With Alberti we are at the beginnings of a new historical awareness and justification by practical utility of the vernacular: an awareness limited to the Latin origins, which dictates dependence on Latin for its regularity as well as for its present and future enrichment. This accounts also for the presence of Latinisms within the Tuscan usage of Alberti's grammar, as it explains the character of the language of his Italian prose writings. To this outlook the generation of Lorenzo

[1] The 'dedication' is contained in the conclusion to the grammar, cit supra, p. 97.

added a new enthusiasm for the Tuscan literary tradition as a demonstration and justification of the abilities of the vernacular. Later, writers and grammarians of the sixteenth century strove to discount the dependence of the vernacular on Latin typical of Alberti, and to remove the stigma of corruption on the modern language implicit in the fifteenth-century theory of its origins. Principal guarantee of its independence, purity, and regularity became, from Bembo onwards, the literary usage of the great writers of the past.[1]

For this reason alone it is curious that some direct debt of Bembo's *Prose della volgar lingua* to Alberti's grammar should have been argued by Vittorio Cian, for the two works are poles apart in their approach to the regularization of the vernacular: Bembo essentially literary, imitative of the great writers of the past, convinced that a language exists only because such authors have used it; Alberti essentially practical, accepting its existence as an unquestioned fact, and finding its elements in contemporary usage. Cian's argument was based in part on the belief that the Vatican copy of Alberti's grammar was made by Bembo himself. This is undoubtedly not the case; nor are there any other sure grounds for thinking that Bembo had direct knowledge of Alberti's work. The presence of this copy in the Vatican miscellany, which also contains a *De Vulgari Eloquentia* annotated by Bembo, is almost certainly due to a later collector.[2] None the less, whatever the differences of outlook separating these two grammarians and the ages in which they lived, it is still very significant that in 1508, when linguistic controversy was rife, especially in Rome and Urbino, someone with privileged access to the Medici library should have had Alberti's grammar copied; and furthermore, perhaps not long after that date, someone else was sufficiently interested in the work to beg, borrow, or steal the original. As neither original nor copy had the author's name we can be sure that in both cases interest was focused on the content.[3]

[1] On the growth of these ideas, see also my article, 'Lorenzo, Machiavelli and the Italian language', in *Italian Renaissance Studies*, a tribute to the late Miss C. M. Ady (London, 1960), 410–32.

[2] Cf. V. Cian, article cit. supra. My statement is based on comparison of various Bembo autograph manuscripts with the text of the grammar in Cod. Reg. Lat. 1370. For a more detailed description of this manuscript, its composition and history, see my forthcoming edition of the grammar.

[3] The Medici library was acquired (and brought to Rome) by Giovanni de' Medici on 29 April 1508, and made available to scholars from early in 1510; so that whoever made the Vatican copy in 1508 had special access to the library. See Piccolomini's article, cit. supra, n. 1, p. 94.

Beyond these elements we have little more than conjecture on which to base consideration of the fortune and influence of Alberti's grammar. When Augurello was searching for it in 1474, its existence was evidently known about in Florence, but no one else seems to have been as anxious to find it; and even when it became Medici property, still in Lorenzo's time, though lacking the author's name, no one seems to have been concerned to identify it or make it known. This silence is a clear indication that however dated by the end of the century was the particular controversy over the language of Rome from which Alberti's grammar took its start, his initiative in grammatical thought was a good half-century before its time. When others, as it were, catch up with him at the turn of the century, the situation is already much more complicated by parochial, interregional, and literary concerns. The absence of these complications was in a way an advantage to Alberti rather than a disadvantage. It permitted him to formulate his rules based on usage with great simplicity and brevity. Such an enterprise in the sixteenth century will appear to some quite hopeless in the face of the inevitable questions: what usage? whose usage? present usage? literary usage? and so on. No grammar could begin without explicitly or implicitly resolving the 'questione della lingua'.

These remarks are meant to characterize Alberti's grammar, not to exalt it as a model; it is short and schematic; it omits much, and it includes some things that are, to say the least, curious. The usage it represents is to some extent, inevitably, a personal one, in which popular forms and words co-exist with cultured and latinizing forms and words. But I do not see here, as Cian remarked, 'almost a contradiction between his often latinate exposition and his theoretical inclination for the live language of Tuscany'.[1] There was not and could not be a contradiction in these terms in Alberti's mind. To imagine it would mean ascribing to him a concept of usage of a much later age. There is no opposition or confusion in his work between live usage and learned forms, for no such consciousness of limits was present in him. These criteria come later, for aesthetic more than historical reasons; their absence in Alberti is precisely what permits and explains the co-existence, bland and unproblematic, of learned and popular elements in his grammar.

It seems possible to suppose, nevertheless, that Alberti's grammar was not without some influence in grammatical thought of the sixteenth century. Even though Augurello

[1] Article cit., 125.

apparently never saw it he knew at least, correctly, that it contained proposals for orthographical reform. It is true that none
of the particulars of these, with the exception of the acute and circumflex accents, figures in the orthographical treatises of the sixteenth century; which argues the absence of direct influence of
the text. But Augurello was not likely, with his marked linguistic interests, to have kept the information to himself in his long
and varied career and among his many like-minded friends.
The awareness of a problem is the first step towards its solution;
and it was not essential to know Alberti's proposals for the
knowledge of his awareness to bear fruit. Some reform of the
written language was undoubtedly dictated by the advent of
printing; but the orthographical question as Alberti had seen
it, as Trissino will see it, is scientific and academic rather than
strictly practical.[1] It is not a necessity, as the development of
modern Italian clearly shows, for it has shrugged off most
attempts to interfere with the Latin alphabet, and since the
sixteenth century has given up even some elements of that.
Whilst it may be possible to see a precedent for this kind of
reform in the humanists' concern for the correct orthography of
Latin, Alberti appears to have been the first to conceive an
interest in phonetics and pronunciation, and to devise some
way of bridging the gaps between sounds and representation in
the modern language. These are specialized interests which
enjoy considerable fortune in the sixteenth century and beyond;
and I would like to think of Alberti not merely as a precursor,
but as the initiator either through the seed of the problem
spread by Augurello, or even through some other knowledge of
Alberti's work.

In the more strictly grammatical field it is hardly legitimate
to suppose even an influence of a very general nature. At most
he was probably known and would excite interest as a forerunner,
the first to have seen the possibility of an Italian grammar. Its
basis was either unknown or irrelevant to the concerns of a
later age; or it was misrepresented by involvement with these
concerns, as we have seen in the other part of Augurello's
description, which would have Alberti's grammar founded on
Dante, Petrarch, and Boccaccio. Not that the grammatical

---

[1] C. Trabalza, *Storia della grammatica italiana*, cit., 95, describes it as 'un
problema d'estetica', which 'risorse col risvegliarsi del sentimento artistico e
del culto della forma nel Rinascimento'. For the orthographical reformers
of the sixteenth century, see B. Migliorini, *Storia della lingua italiana*, cit.,
367–72.

direction founded on the study of these authors represented the exclusive tendency or the final solution of linguistic regularity arrived at by sixteenth-century grammarians. Amid the vast quantity and complexity of writings on language, one fundamental problem was constantly present—the reconciliation or opposition of literary tradition and modern usage. The sense of Florentinity, which sat lightly on Alberti's shoulders, became for many an incubus, an obsession, making the dilemma of that choice or reconciliation all the more acute. The ownership of Dante, Petrarch, and Boccaccio, and the most lively modern idiom of Italy was in this sense an embarrassment, and one which did not afflict non-Tuscans. Yet it also imposed greater obligation, which was ultimately met in its own way by the Accademia della Crusca. This feeling of the natural superiority of the Florentine language was at least as old as the time of Dante, and was alive and vigorous during Alberti's lifetime. So much so that only perhaps a Florentine born and reared in exile, and who lived the greater part of his life outside Florence, could have composed a grammar like this one, exempt from even the slightest taint of *campanilismo*. When compared with later works of this kind, this appears as not the least remarkable feature of this grammar.

In publishing it for the first time (and so far the only time) in 1908, Trabalza alluded in passing to the fact that this grammar accepts the terminology of Latin grammar.[1] But he did not observe, and the fact has apparently so far been overlooked, that this implies the back-dating of many lexical elements of Italian in this field to the middle of the fifteenth century, elements which according to historical dictionaries did not make their appearance until at least the middle of the sixteenth century. Examination shows, indeed, that, as far as is known, some of the terms used by Alberti are hitherto undocumented before the seventeenth or even the nineteenth centuries.[2] It is unlikely however, that he invented all of them or their Italian form. Some of the terms he uses are already to be found in Dante and in fourteenth-century texts; and this suggests that others may well already have existed, even though they were not used

---

[1] Op. cit., 21.

[2] Here are some examples: *avverbio, appellativo, articolo, asseverativo, caso, congiugazione, dizione,* &c. (not documented until the sixteenth century); *congiunzione, monosillabo* (subst.) (not documented before seventeenth century); *anormale* (not documented before nineteenth century); *interrogatorii* (subst.) (not hitherto documented at all).

in a vernacular grammar and have not come to light in other documents. They were doubtless commonly employed in the teaching of Latin grammar by means of the vernacular; and from this tradition, which as yet has been insufficiently studied, Alberti might well have drawn.[1] To Alberti the adaptation of Latin terminology to Italian would come naturally, though not necessarily unconsciously. In other fields, where Alberti was aware of being the first writer of modern times, è.g. in painting and architecture, he was obliged to create a technical vocabulary, whose originality has only recently been investigated and emphasized by Gianfranco Folena.[2] If we want further confirmation of this quality as a linguistic pioneer, and of Alberti's consciousness of being an innovator in technical terminology and expression, this time in Latin, we have only to read the opening sentences of Book VI of his *De re aedificatoria*, where he speaks of the 'difficulties (which) every moment arose either in explaining the matters, or inventing names, or methodising the subject'.[3] The ambition to find 'arti e scienze non udite e mai vedute', to improve on or fill the gaps in the inheritance of antiquity, brought Alberti face to face with the problems of communication.[4] These were not questions of style, but more fundamental problems of basic materials needed to convey a practical and useful message; and if they were not to hand, they had to be made. In this context we must appreciate his frequent protestations of efficiency rather than elegance of expression; and in this context we may see also the linguistic innovations of his grammar.

The grammar which we now know to be certainly Alberti's work, has this and all the other marks of his original and inventive mind. If it is not possible to attribute to it much weight in determining the later development of Italian grammatical thought, this does not lessen its significance as a unique achievement. As he writes at the conclusion of his treatise on painting,

[1] For examples of bilingual grammars cf. R. Sabbadini, in *Studi Medievali*, i (1904), 280–92; A. De Stefano, in *Rev. des langues romanes*, xlviii (1905), 495–529; B. Terracini, in *Romania*, xl (1911), 435, n. 4. For general observations and other manuscript material see especially C. Trabalza, *Storia . . .*, cit., chap. i, 40–41 and relative notes.

[2] 'Noterelle lessicali Albertiane', in *Lingua Nostra*, xviii (1957), 1, 6–10.

[3] Quoted from the translation by J. Leoni, ed. J. Rykwert (London, 1955), 111. The Latin text has: '. . . frequentes difficultates et rerum explicandarum et nominum inveniendorum et materiae pertractandae . . .'.

[4] The phrase quoted comes from the dedication of the *Pittura* to Brunelleschi (cf. edition of L. Mallè (Florence, 1950), 54).

excusing its possible defects: 'no art exists which did not have its beginnings in things full of errors; nothing is born perfect.'[1] The first and most essential step is that it should be born. Italian grammar takes that first step through the agency of Leon Battista Alberti. Or, to use his own architectural terminology, he prepared the first *congetto* of Italian grammar, and left to others the task *di notarlo in proportione*.

[1] Ed. cit., 114 (my translation).

LORENZO DE' MEDICI: THE FORMATION OF HIS STATECRAFT

WHEN I was asked to choose the topic of this lecture, I was hoping that my lecture would coincide with the publication of the first three volumes of the edition of Lorenzo's letters. I make use in it of some of the letters and the commentary included in these volumes, which cover, roughly, the first ten years of Lorenzo's ascendancy in Florence. This has obviously much facilitated my task, but new evidence, of which there is a great deal, also poses a fresh challenge; and I must admit that Lorenzo's opening words in his *Comento* strike a chord: 'Assai sono stato dubbioso e sospeso se dovevo fare la presente interpretazione'—'I have been in great doubt whether I should undertake the present interpretation.'

Lorenzo's father, Piero di Cosimo de' Medici, died on 2 December 1469, a month before Lorenzo's twenty-first birthday. On the following day, a delegation from a large meeting of leading citizens, which had decided to preserve Lorenzo and his brother Giuliano in 'reputazione e grandezza', 'in prestige and greatness', came to the Medici palace and asked Lorenzo to assume the authority his father and grandfather had exercised in Florence.[1] The vagueness of these terms reflects the indeterminate nature of the Medici regime. Since the days of Cosimo, the political power of the Medici had been exercised, within the framework of the republican constitution, by a variety of controls, primarily of the elections to the Signoria and other high magistracies; and their ascendancy depended

[The following abbreviations will be used: ASF = Florence, Archivio di Stato; ASM, SPE = Milan, Archivio di Stato, Archivio Sforzesco, Potenze Estere; MAP = Florence, Archivio di Stato, Archivio Mediceo avanti il Principato; *Lettere* = Lorenzo de' Medici, *Lettere*, vols. i and ii, ed. R. Fubini (Florence, 1977), vol. iii, ed. N. Rubinstein (Florence, 1977).]

[1] See N. Rubinstein, *The Government of Florence under the Medici, 1434 to 1494* (Oxford, 1968), pp. 174-5.

upon the support of a substantial section of the patriciate. Like the regime itself, succession to its leadership was therefore a matter of political, not of constitutional, arrangement; and like the survival of the regime, it depended on the loyal collaboration of its supporters. The improvised and unofficial character of the meeting of 2 December, which decided the succession of Lorenzo, was entirely in keeping with a situation in which his succession was clearly not felt to be a foregone conclusion. Conditions differed, in fact, from those after the death of Cosimo five years earlier. In 1466 the Medici regime had been seriously threatened by citizens who had hitherto backed it; its electoral controls had been temporarily abolished and statutory elections by lot of the Signoria restored; Piero's death could be the signal for another republican attempt to curb, or even destroy, Medici power. While the apparent unanimity of the decision, to preserve Lorenzo's and Giuliano's 'grandezza', shows their father's success in consolidating and unifying the Medici regime, during the last three years of his life, the question remained of what meaning was to be attached to that 'grandezza'; more precisely, what role the elder of the two sons of Piero was to play within the regime.

The answer depended, above all, on the willingness of Piero's principal supporters to accept the authority of Lorenzo on the same terms as they had accepted that of his father. A Medici could not take their collaboration for granted in the same way as could an Italian prince that of his counsellors, and differences in age and experience could count for a great deal: at the time of Piero's death, his most influential follower, Tommaso Soderini, was 66, while Lorenzo was only twenty. Lorenzo's youth was, moreover, liable to sharpen rivalries within the Medici regime. In fifteenth-century Florence such rivalries were liable to be compounded by conflicting loyalties to foreign states. At the end of 1469, the Duke of Milan and the King of Naples were pursuing different policies in the war Pope Paul II was waging against Roberto Malatesta of Rimini, and both were trying to win over Florence to their side by enlisting the support of leading citizens.[1] Unlike the King of Naples, Galeazzo Maria Sforza was also trying to strengthen Lorenzo's position in Florence.

After the death of Filippo Maria Visconti in 1447, Cosimo de' Medici had persuaded the Florentine government to back

[1] G. Soranzo, 'Lorenzo il Magnifico alla morte del padre e il suo primo balzo verso la Signoria', *Archivio Storico Italiano*, cxi (1953), pp. 50–1.

Francesco Sforza in his bid for the duchy of Milan, and had himself provided the financial means which enabled Francesco to achieve success. Ever since, friendship with the Sforza had been a cornerstone of the foreign policy of the Medici. It had also provided them with an invaluable external insurance of their ascendancy, and indeed security, at home. When Piero had been threatened by his opponents in 1466, Galeazzo Maria Sforza had sent troops to the Florentine frontier; four days after Piero's death, he writes to the Florentine Signoria recommending to them 'Lorenzo and Giuliano . . . whom, owing to the love we have always nourished for that house, we hold . . . dear as if they were our own sons'. And he adds that although he was confident that they would not be required, he had ordered his troops in the territories of Bologna and Parma to obey, if necessary, the orders of the Signoria: 'and we are ready, in such a case, to come in person with the rest of our troops'.[1] But if the close relationship between the Medici and the Sforza benefited the Medici, it was also useful to the Sforza, and not only for reasons of foreign policy. The Sforza court relied heavily on the Milan branch of the Medici Bank; as Raymond de Roover has shown, between 1460 to 1467, the debt of the Sforza to the bank had increased from about 53,000 to no less than 179,000 ducats.[2] Both for political and financial reasons, it was in the interest of Galeazzo Maria Sforza to secure Lorenzo's position in Florence; for political reasons, it was also in his interest to strengthen it. To an autocratic ruler, such as the Duke of Milan, and to his ambassadors, the slowness and complexity of decision-making in a state whose government and administration were still basically republican could be a source of irritation and frustration: it could also affect the reliability of Florence as an ally. Just as the elder statesmen of the Medici regime, whose role had been decisive in securing Lorenzo's succession, could hope to profit from it, so the Duke of Milan might hope to find the inexperienced youth more amenable to his influence and persuasion. What was at stake at the end of 1469 was not only Lorenzo's freedom of action, but also the manner in which the ascendancy of the Medici, which had been gradually and painstakingly established over more than three decades, was to be upheld after his father's death.

---

[1] R. Magnani, *Relazioni private fra la Corte Sforzesca di Milano e Casa Medici, 1450–1500* (Milan, 1910), doc. 61, pp. xxxviii–xxxix.

[2] *The Rise and Decline of the Medici Bank* (Cambridge, Mass., 1963), pp. 272–3.

Lorenzo was singularly unprepared for the tasks which awaited him. One of the foundations of Medici ascendancy had been, and still remained, the wealth of Giovanni di Bicci's branch of the family; it had helped Cosimo to build up the complex network of personal relationships and loyalties which provided the basis for his rise to power. Lorenzo had received a careful humanist education, but no business training; he also had, in 1469, little practical experience of politics. In 1466 he had been a member of the *Balìa* as a substitute for his father,[1] and Piero had sent him abroad on a few occasions; but his journeys had only incidentally assumed some modest political significance. In 1465 he went to Milan to represent Piero at the ceremony for the marriage between Alfonso of Calabria, the heir to the Neapolitan throne, and Francesco Sforza's daughter Ippolita Maria. In the following year he went to Rome and Naples; in the summer of 1469 he went again to Milan, to act, on Piero's behalf, as godfather at the baptism of Galeazzo Maria Sforza's son. The main purpose of these visits appears to have been to introduce Lorenzo into Italian court society; but Piero may have also wished in this way to acquaint his eldest son, gently, with the organization of the Medici Bank; when Lorenzo went to Rome, in 1466, he was meant to get information about the state of its Roman branch from his uncle Giovanni Tornabuoni, and to agree in Piero's name to a new alum contract.[2] But Piero seems to have been distinctly reluctant to entrust Lorenzo with diplomatic business. When he sent him to Milan for the baptism of Gian Galeazzo Sforza, he explicitly forbade him to get involved in any other matters, 'in cosa alcuna', as he was not going as an ambassador: 'I don't think it is proper', he adds, in his letter to Lucrezia on the eve of their son's departure, 'that the ducklings should teach old ducks to swim'.[3] And when, during the same journey,

[1] In December 1466 the *Balìa* admitted him in the same capacity to the Council of One Hundred, 'non obstante minori etate'. See Rubinstein, *The Government*, p. 221. On Lorenzo's education, see A. Rochon, *La Jeunesse de Laurent de Médicis (1449–1478)* (Paris, 1963), pp. 31–46.

[2] See his letter to Lorenzo of 15 March 1466, in A. Fabroni, *Laurentii Medicis Magnifici vita* (Pisa, 1784), vol. ii, p. 49.

[3] Piero de' Medici to Lucrezia Tornabuoni in Florence, Careggi, 13 July 1469 (ASF, MAP, I, 267): 'Tu sai che malvolentieri detci licentia a Lorenzo, per molti rispecti . . . et pertanto da' modo allo spaccio, et dì a Lorenzo che non esca dello ordine in cosa alcuna, et non faccia tante melarancie, non essendo imbasciadore, ch'io non determino ch'e paperi menino a bere l'oche . . .'

Lorenzo could not help getting involved in a matter concerning the war between Paul II and Roberto Malatesta of Rimini, he humbly apologized to his father: he would not have written to him about it had not the Duke expressly ordered him to do so; but he would keep his letter short, since the resident Florentine ambassador was writing to Piero at length.[1] Lorenzo's letter is dated 29 July 1469, four months before he was asked to succeed his father as head of the Medici regime.

It is not surprising that Lorenzo should write, three years later, in his family memoirs, that he had accepted this invitation reluctantly, 'as it was contrary to my age, and on account of the great responsibility and peril it involved'. He did so, he says, 'per conservazione degli amici', 'for the safety of our supporters', and of our properties: 'perché a Firenze si può mal viver ricco senza lo stato', 'because the rich live badly in Florence outside the political establishment'.[2] (No such hesitations were, incidentally, reported by the foreign ambassadors; and whatever went through Lorenzo's mind during those hours, he appears to have been remarkably in control of himself; so that the Milanese resident could write, hopefully, 'he behaves like an old man'.)[3] Lorenzo's justification of his acceptance is somewhat disingenuous: for the eldest son of Piero de' Medici it was not just a matter of participating in the ruling regime, as it was, for instance, for his sister's father-in-law, Giovanni Rucellai, who writes a year later that he 'had not been accepted by, but suspect to, the regime for twenty-seven years'.[4] What the leading citizens asked Lorenzo to accept was, in his own words, 'la cura della città e dello stato', 'the care of the regime and of the city'. The formulation, certainly not incidental, enshrines the two major aspects of Medici ascendancy.

For 'città' and 'stato' were by no means synonymous; and 'stato' should not be translated by 'state'. It signifies, in this context, as it normally does in the political vocabulary of fifteenth-century Florence, the dominant political regime—in other words, the power structure which, at a given time, formed the foundation of its government. 'Città' and 'stato'

---

[1] *Lettere*, vol. i, 21, pp. 45–6: 'perché io so m. Luigi ve ne scrive lungamente, non dirò altro, refferendomi a lui. Non harei anche fatto questo, se non per comandamento del Signore . . .'

[2] Fabroni, *Laurentii Medicis vita*, vol. ii, p. 42.

[3] Sacramoro da Rimini to Galeazzo Maria Sforza, Florence, 2 December 1469 (ASM, SPE, Firenze, 277): 'se deporta da vecchio'.

[4] A. Perosa (ed.), *Giovanni Rucellai ed il suo Zibaldone*, vol. i (London, 1960), p. 122: 'sono stato non accetto ma sospetto allo stato anni 27'.

are seen as distinct, yet closely allied: as the Florentine chancellor, Bartolomeo Scala, put it during Lorenzo's peace negotiations in Naples in 1480: 'la città che [è] congiunta collo stato', 'the city and the regime which are joined to one another'.[1] During the war of the Pazzi Conspiracy, Lorenzo once observed: 'la libertà nostra [ne va] con lo stato', 'our liberty goes together with the regime'.[2] The term I have chosen for the title of this lecture, Lorenzo's 'statecraft', is a literal translation of Machiavelli's 'arte dello stato'. The *Shorter Oxford English Dictionary* defines statecraft as 'the art of conducting state affairs', but this definition does not quite render the complex meaning of 'stato' in fifteenth-century Florence. The task which Lorenzo faced in December 1469 was to take charge of the Medici regime, and at the same time to conduct the foreign policy of the republic. In both respects, his actions were subject to considerable restraints. After initial setbacks, he succeeded in consolidating the regime, and his position in it, during the second year of his ascendancy, more precisely between January and July 1471. As far as his domestic policy was concerned, this concludes the first period in the formation of his statecraft. The development of his statesmanship in the conduct of foreign affairs was a lengthier and more gradual process, and there is much to be said for considering its formative period not to be completed until the end of the war of the Pazzi Conspiracy, in March 1480.

Lorenzo proposes 'to follow the methods of his grandfather', writes the Milanese ambassador at the time of Lorenzo's first attempt at internal reform in July 1470, 'which was to do such things as much as possible by constitutional methods', 'di far tal cose cum più civilità si potesse'.[3] These words reflect the constraints under which Lorenzo had to operate if he wanted to preserve the edifice of Medici supremacy, as erected by Cosimo. The cornerstone of that edifice was the office of the *Accoppiatori*, who were in charge of electing the two-monthly Signoria: as the Milanese ambassador put it, on it depended

[1] Bartolomeo Scala to Lorenzo in Naples, 5 January 1480 (ASF, MAP, XXXIV, 412): '. . . a voi et allo stato che è congiunto con voi, et alla città che [è] congiunta collo stato, habbi a venire la sua sicurtà'; cf. Rubinstein, 'Notes on the word *stato* in Florence before Machiavelli', in *Florilegium Historiale. Essays presented to Wallace K. Ferguson*, ed. J. G. Rowe and W. H. Stockdale (Toronto, 1971), pp. 313–26 (319).

[2] Lorenzo to Girolamo Morelli, 24 September 1478, *Lettere*, vol. iii, 332, p. 223.

[3] Quoted in Rubinstein, *The Government*, p. 178, n. 5 (3 July).

Lorenzo's power.[1] At the time of his succession, the *Accoppiatori*
were elected annually by the Council of One Hundred; but
although that council had been created under Cosimo to serve as
a reliable instrument of the regime, its decisions did not always
come up to expectation; its members were quite capable of
voting against proposals that originated with the head of the
regime, and of not toeing the line in the election to offices.
The Council of One Hundred, writes the Milanese ambassador
in the same letter of 31 July 1470, are in the process of electing
the new *Accoppiatori*, and some of its members are known to
want to appoint 'men who are not Lorenzo's', 'homini che non
fossero de Lorenzo'; but he hopes that they will not succeed:
'one will see to it that those who are elected are Lorenzo's
men'. This outcome was clearly not a foregone conclusion;
to make it so, was the purpose of Lorenzo's first attempt at
constitutional reform. Although this attempt failed, as a result of
the opposition of the Council of One Hundred, it is of considerable interest to us, since it shows Lorenzo's earliest reaction,
after his succession, to a major problem of Medici rule. According to his design, the *Accoppiatori* were to be chosen from among
the 40-odd citizens who had served in this capacity from October 1434 onwards, or at least from among their families. This
group would thus have included some of the prominent Medicean
families of the time of Cosimo, such as the Guicciardini and
Martelli, the Pitti and Ridolfi, as well as elder statesmen
such as Tommaso Soderini; in the words of the Milanese
ambassador, it would have consisted of 'tutti quisti cavalleri
principali', of 'all the leading citizens'; and it was not surprising
that Lorenzo's scheme was welcomed by them. Had it been
successful, it would have both strengthened the oligarchical
strand in Medici government, and provided Lorenzo with a
permanent élite group.[2] His proposal pointed to the past as
well as to the future. During the years before 1434, preceding the
establishment of Medici ascendancy, about sixty-five citizens
had formed the core, the inner circle, of the oligarchical regime;[3]
in 1480, the Council of Seventy became, for all practical purposes, a permanent senate with life membership. Only a few
months after his succession, Lorenzo thus felt the need to

[1] Sacramoro to Galeazzo Maria Sforza, Florence, 31 July, ASM, SPE,
Firenze, 279; see Rubinstein, *The Government*, p. 178.

[2] See ibid., pp. 177–9.

[3] See Dale Kent, 'The Florentine *reggimento* in the fifteenth century',
Renaissance Quarterly, xxviii (1975), pp. 604–10.

establish, at the top of the regime, a group of men on whom he could rely to secure the vital controls of election to the Signoria. His design reflects a hierarchical concept of the structure of the Medici regime, which is neatly spelled out, two years later, by Benedetto Dei in his account of contemporary Florentine society.[1] According to Dei, the innermost circle of the regime was divided into three sections: the top section consisted of twelve citizens, 'principali dello stato', headed by Lorenzo and Tommaso Soderini; below them was a group of eleven citizens, and at the bottom, a 'rearguard' of twenty: in all, the 'uomini del governo' amounted to forty-three citizens.

It was a measure of the limitations of Lorenzo's influence at the beginning of his ascendancy that neither this proposal, nor the alternative one of recruiting the *Accoppiatori* exclusively from those citizens who had previously held that office, was accepted; in the end, in January 1471, the council of One Hundred could be persuaded, though only just, to pass a law by which, during the next five years, the *Accoppiatori* were to be virtually appointed, annually, by their predecessors.[2] The next reform, of July that year, shows that Lorenzo had not given up the substance of his original design. The reform was carried out by one of those short-term commissions with extra-ordinary powers, *Balìe*, which the Medici and their followers had used from time to time to obtain legislation that the statutory councils could not be expected to pass; the main difficulty consisted in getting these councils to establish such *Balìe*; the alternative of summoning a popular assembly, a *Parlamento*, for this purpose, was too extreme and risky, too contrary to the orderly process of government, to be chosen except on rare occasions. That Lorenzo succeeded in obtaining from the councils the creation of such a *Balìa*—the first for five years—was a remarkable feat and showed consummate timing (he had been advised as early as the summer of 1470 to try this method). The *Balìa* of July 1471 consisted of a first group of forty citizens, who were elected by the Signoria and the *Accoppiatori* and in their turn elected the remaining 200 members of the commission. In order to enhance the reliability of the Council of One Hundred, whose legislative powers were substantially increased, these forty were to remain in office after the *Balìa* had been disbanded as permanent members of that council while the rest of its personnel changed twice a

---

[1] *Cronaca*, ASF, Manoscritti, 119, fol. 35ᵛ.
[2] For this and the following, see Rubinstein, *The Government*, pp. 180–5.

year. Lorenzo had clearly not given up his original design to insert a small élite group of leading citizens as a permanent fixture into the machinery of government. His domestic policy was beginning to show that combination of consistency of design with flexibility of execution which was to mark it in the coming years.

The *Balìa* of July 1471 was also a personal triumph over his rivals and opponents in Florence, and thus reflects the definitive assertion of his authority within the regime, as well as its unification. 'While before, other citizens were honoured and flattered just like him', writes the Milanese ambassador on 5 July, 'now everyone goes to him to recommend himself for election' to the *Balìa*.[1] Rivalries among leading citizens of the regime, and between such citizens and Lorenzo, had overshadowed Lorenzo's political apprenticeship, and had been sharpened by conflicting loyalties to foreign powers. Tommaso Soderini stands out, during this period, both as Lorenzo's principal rival and as the leading figure of the pro-Neapolitan faction in Florence. 'Messer Tommaso seems to believe', writes the Milanese ambassador in November 1470, 'that everyone ought to submit to him, so that he can become great and head' of the regime, 'et cum questo farsi grande e capo': he accordingly wants to diminish Lorenzo's status, 'in order to manage him the way he wants'; in short, he wants to be 'el timone vero de questa barcha', 'the real rudder of this ship'.[2] Two months later, Soderini promised the ambassador, in great secrecy, that he would henceforth back Lorenzo.[3] It was significant of the change in the political climate of Florence after the *Balìa* of July 1471 that in the following month Tommaso Soderini himself should have been sent to Milan, to inform the Duke of the 'consolidation and strengthening of our regime'.[4]

Galeazzo Maria Sforza had previously advised Lorenzo

[1] Sacramoro to Galeazzo Maria Sforza, Florence, 5 July 1471 (ASM, SPE, Firenze, 282): 'hora zaschuno concorre ad ello a recomandarsi per essere de li ellecti'.

[2] Sacramoro to Galeazzo Maria Sforza, Florence, 19 November 1470, quoted in *Lettere*, vol. i, 65, n. 1, p. 209.

[3] Sacramoro to Galeazzo Maria Sforza, 9 January 1471 (ASM, SPE, Firenze, 281): 'io prometto al ducha de Milano . . . che tucto quel ch'esso [i.e. Lorenzo] me accennerà essere el suo bisogno et la voglia de quel Illustrissimo Signore, el consiliarò et favorirò'.

[4] *Lettere*, vol. i, 90, n. intr., p. 320: 'stabilimento et corroboramento dello stato nostro'.

to achieve this result through a *Balìa*, that is by adopting the kind of measure Lorenzo did in the end adopt in July 1471; Lorenzo could now see, writes his ambassador in that month, 'how good the advice of Your Excellency has been'.[1] The Duke had also sent Tommaso Soderini a gift of 500 ducats to reward him for his change of attitude towards Lorenzo.[2] I have pointed to the advantages the strengthening of Medici power offered to the Duke of Milan. His relations with Lorenzo show his preference for dealing, secretly, with him and, possibly, a small number of his friends, rather than publicly with the Florentine government: this was in keeping with the personal style of diplomacy to which an autocratic Italian ruler was used. Thus, during particularly secret negotiations with the French King, Galeazzo Maria declared that he would confide everything to Lorenzo; matters of lesser importance could be discussed with his principal followers; all that was left to official contacts with the Signoria were 'ordinary and general matters', 'cose vulgare et generale', 'which were anyway public knowledge'.[3] Lorenzo did his best to conform: 'I shall follow the advice of Your Magnificence', he writes to the Sforza ambassador in Florence during the difficult negotiations in 1471 concerning the renewal of the Italian league, 'in keeping everything secret there, for these are matters in which consultation can be of little help', and he expresses the hope that the Florentine ambassador in Milan was writing about the matter 'in private rather than in public; in this way it will be easy to keep it secret'.[4] But there were limits to such secrecy: Florence was not Milan. 'Your Lordship wishes these matters to be very secret', writes Lorenzo, jointly with Tommaso Soderini and Luigi Guicciardini, to the Duke in March 1470, 'but this is difficult to achieve, in view of our methods of government', 'atteso il modo de' governi nostri'.[5] However great Lorenzo's authority in Florence, his diplomacy, like his domestic policy, was subject to manifold restraints, due to the continued functioning of republican

---

[1] Sacramoro to Galeazzo Maria Sforza, Florence, 5 July 1471 (loc. cit.): 'Possi mo Lorenzo accorgere quanto è stato bono el consiglio de Vostra Excellentia'. Cfr. Soranzo, 'Lorenzo il Magnifico . . .', p. 73.

[2] See *Lettere*, vol. i, 65, n. 1, cit., and Soranzo, 'Lorenzo il Magnifico . . .', p. 71.

[3] Galeazzo Maria Sforza to Filippo Sacramoro, 16 March 1476, quoted in *Lettere*, vol. ii, 219, n. intr., p. 170.

[4] Lorenzo to Sacramoro da Rimini, Bolsena, 28 September 1471, *Lettere*, vol. i, 94, pp. 336–7.

[5] *Lettere*, vol. i, 38, p. 106 (12 March 1470).

institutions. These restraints were, if anything, greater in the field of foreign, than in that of domestic, policy. It must have been difficult for an Italian despot such as the Duke of Milan fully to appreciate this. In monarchical states such as Milan and Ferrara and, for that matter, Naples the ruler alone possessed the ultimate authority to negotiate, conclude treaties, declare war; ambassadors had powers delegated by him alone, as had secret councils, whose function it was to advise the prince and which could take decisions only if authorized to do so by him.[1] In Florence, diplomatic affairs were the competence of the Signoria, which changed every two months, or, in time of war, of the *Dieci di Balìa*, elected for six months at a time. A measure of continuity was provided by advisory committees (*Pratiche*) of the Signoria, in which leading citizens could express their views, and whose advice, though not binding, carried a great deal of weight. But treaties had to be ratified by the councils; and while in a despotic state such as Milan or Ferrara taxes were imposed or regulated by the prince, in Florence it was the councils which had to vote the money that was required to fulfil treaty obligations or to hire troops. As we shall see, this system was modified, to the advantage of Lorenzo, in 1480; at the time of his succession, Florentine foreign policy, like that of Venice, was still essentially based on collective decision-making. Historians of the Medici, following Guicciardini who, writing about sixteen years after Lorenzo's death, telescoped things in retrospect,[2] tend to identify the foreign policy of Florence with that of Lorenzo, but in so doing they oversimplify one of the most intriguing aspects of his ascendancy. What was his role in the making, and in the execution, of decisions, and hence the extent to which he was able, and willing, to take over the conduct of foreign affairs from the official organs of government?

At the time of Piero's death, Florence was in the midst of intense diplomatic activity. Negotiations for the renewal of the Triple Alliance between Florence, Milan, and Naples had been going on for some months; they were meeting with

[1] See *Storia di Milano*, vol. vii (Milan, Fondazione Treccani, 1956), pp. 521–4; F. Valenti, 'I consigli di governo presso gli Estensi dalle origini alla devoluzione di Ferrara', in *Studi in onore di R. Filangieri* (Naples, 1959), vol. ii, pp. 19–33.

[2] F. Guicciardini, *Storie fiorentine*, ed. R. Palmarocchi (Bari, 1931), pp. 72: one of the benefits Florence owed Lorenzo was to have become 'quasi una bilancia di tutta Italia'.

difficulties, largely owing to conflicting policies pursued by
the Duke of Milan and the King of Naples in the war between
the Pope and Roberto Malatesta of Rimini.[1] After the defeat of
the papal army in August 1469 the allies were trying to induce
Paul II to conclude peace, but Galeazzo Maria Sforza, appre-
hensive of a French intervention in his duchy, proved more
accommodating than Ferrante of Naples. To settle these
differences, a meeting between representatives of the members
of the Triple Alliance was arranged to take place in Florence
in December; before the ambassadors arrived, Piero had died;
and, as a result, it was the young and inexperienced Lorenzo
who took his place in the committee of five which was appointed
by the Signoria to represent the government of Florence. The
meetings, which lasted until March, did not settle the differences
between the allies; but they did provide Lorenzo with his
apprenticeship in diplomacy. They also provided him with
invaluable experience of the way in which in Florence diplomacy could become entangled with domestic politics: the committee of five included partisans of the King of Naples as well
as of the Duke of Milan, Tommaso Soderini as well as Lorenzo.
Lorenzo, while supporting the Sforza, saw the role of Florence
as one of mediation; and Florence badly needed peace and the
renewal of the League. These matters, he writes in January
1470 to the Florentine ambassador in Rome, 'seem to me to be
among the most troublesome and difficult the city has ever
had to face'; but, he adds, this is 'perhaps because, as I have
never had to deal with such matters, they are new and therefore
more daunting to me';[2] nevertheless, 'as far as I can judge, there
is no other way, for our salvation lies entirely in the cohesion
and unity of the League'.[3] And when the Triple Alliance was
finally renewed, in July 1470, he was jubilant: 'at this moment,'
he writes to the Florentine ambassador at the Sforza court,
'we have received letters from Naples . . . They inform us that
our league has been renewed, which pleases everyone greatly
. . . As to my own personal interests ('spetialità'), I consider it
the best news I have ever received.'[4] Later in the same year,
during the tortuous negotiations for the renewal of the wider

[1] See Soranzo, 'Lorenzo il Magnifico . . .', pp. 50–9; G. Nebbia, 'La Lega
italica . . .', *Archivio Storico Lombardo*, N.S., iv (1939), pp. 125–7.
[2] Lorenzo to Otto Niccolini, 27 January 1470 (*Lettere*, vol. i, 33, p. 88):
'non havendo io mai praticato simili cose, come cose nuove mi dànno
magiore admiratione'.   [3] Ibid.
[4] Lorenzo to Angelo della Stufa, 12 July 1470, *Lettere*, vol. i, 58, pp. 172.

Italian League of 1454, Florence appeared once more in the role of mediator between Milan and Naples, and could even be described as 'examen della bilancia', 'the tongue of the balance'.[1] If, after his death, Lorenzo could be praised as the architect of Italian balance of power politics, he owed this to no small extent to his experience of Florentine diplomacy during the formative period of his statecraft.

One of the major problems of that period had been the interaction of domestic and foreign policies; and it was this interaction which was at the root of the gravest crisis his statecraft had to face, the Pazzi conspiracy. On 26 April 1478 Lorenzo and his brother Giuliano were attacked in the Florentine cathedral during High Mass; Giuliano was assassinated, but Lorenzo escaped. The assassination had been planned and organized by the Pope's nephew, Girolamo Riario, and members of the Pazzi family; the Archbishop of Pisa, Francesco Salviati, had participated in the conspiracy. Before he was summarily executed, Francesco Salviati confessed that it had been planned by Francesco Pazzi as long as three years earlier: relations between Lorenzo and the Pazzi had in fact become increasingly strained after 1473.[2] The origins and motives of the conspiracy were complex, and this is not the place to discuss them in detail.[3] I should, however, like to make two points. The events which led to the conspiracy show once more the interaction of Lorenzo's diplomacy and his private interests, his 'spetialità'; they also show how difficult it is to distinguish, in every single case, between his personal diplomacy and that of the republic. Pope Sixtus IV held Lorenzo personally responsible for the unsuccessful attempt by Florence to purchase the Romagna town of Imola from the Duke of Milan in 1473; but Florence had previously exercised a sort of protectorate over this strategically important place beyond her northern frontiers, and it was only natural that she should use the opportunity of its cession to the Duke of Milan by its lord, Taddeo Manfredi, to try to acquire a firm hold over it. In the circumstances, it was not

[1] Gentile Becchi to Lorenzo, Rome, 24 November 1470 (ASF, MAP, LXI, 30): 'Sta molto bene hora Firenze vaghegiata da tutta dua, et fia spesso examen della bilancia nel migliore partito se fiano uniti'. Cfr. *Lettere*, vol. i, 70, n. intr., pp. 232–3.

[2] Filippo Sacramoro to Bona and Gian Galeazzo Sforza, Florence, 27 April 1478 (ASM, SPE, Firenze, 294): 'erano tri anni che messer Jacobo di Pazzi l'haveva sempre importunato a questo tracto'.

[3] On the origins of the conspiracy, see now *Lettere*, vol. ii, docs. xi–xiii, nn. intr., pp. 411–12, 414; 417–18; 430–2, and 270, n. 8, pp. 467–9.

surprising that when the purchase fell through owing to the
opposition of the Pope, the Medici Bank decided not to provide
the loan to enable his nephew Girolamo Riario to acquire the
place; but the refusal to do so led to a further worsening of
relations between Sixtus IV and Lorenzo, while the fact that
the rival bank of the Pazzi made the loan, in its turn affected
relations between that family and Lorenzo.[1] In the following
year, the Pope's campaign against Niccolò Vitelli, the lord of
Città di Castello, was believed in Florence to pose a threat to
the neighbouring Borgo San Sepolcro. Lorenzo was at first
in favour of a military demonstration, but he was not alone in
this, and later changed his view in favour of a peaceful settlement.[2] Yet it was Lorenzo who was made to suffer through
punitive measures against the Medici Bank in Rome. Later
in that year, Sixtus IV created Francesco Salviati Archbishop
of Pisa, against the express wish of the Signoria, which accepted
the advice of a meeting of leading citizens that he should be
prevented from taking possession of the see: as one of them
declared, they were opposed to his appointment 'not because
he is an unworthy person, but because the city wants things to
be done differently'.[3] Again, it is difficult to isolate the responsibility of Lorenzo, who had certainly personal reasons for
disliking Francesco Salviati; as Lorenzo writes on 7 September
1475 to Galeazzo Maria Sforza, Salviati was 'linked to the Pazzi
by family ties as well as obligations of friendship', and was
'molto cosa di costoro', 'very much their man'.[4] '. . . I believe',
he writes on 14 December 1474 to Galeazzo Maria, 'that I
have been greatly wronged; . . . the offence, if it is one [of having
forbidden Francesco Salviati to take possession of the archbishopric of Pisa], . . . has been committed by the whole city, and
[the Pope] wants to take revenge for it on me alone'; and on
23 December he sums up, in another letter to the Duke, the
events that in his view had led to the present crisis in his
relations with Sixtus IV: it is not the affair of Città di Castello,

[1] See *Lettere*, vol. ii, 182, n. intr., pp. 52–3.
[2] Ibid., 171, n. intr., pp. 5–7.
[3] ASF, Consulte e Pratiche, 60, fols. 148r–149v (18 October 1474):
Giovannozzo Pitti: 'quod preter dignitatem civitatis et petitionem Magistratus
archiepiscopus pisanus creatus est molestum esse debere omnibus civibus.
Non quod archiepiscopi persona indigna sit, maxime propter familiam, sed
quod aliter ac civitas voluerit factum sit . . . Itaque censuit retinendum
archiepiscopatum in sua potestate Magistratum, donec archiepiscopus talis
sit qualem Magistratus velit . . .' Cfr. also *Lettere*, vol. ii, 182, n. intr., p. 57.
[4] *Lettere*, vol. ii, 201, p. 124.

but that of the archbishopric of Pisa; 'this is the root of every-thing', 'è quello onde procede tutto questo'. If it is true what the Pope says, Lorenzo continues, that many citizens have written to him in favour of Salviati, this is precisely the reason why he should not be allowed to take possession of his diocese, 'for since the Signoria and the members of the regime', the 'huomini dello stato', do not want him, those who do want him, and have written to this effect, must be men who do not get on with the ruling group, 'con quelli che governano'; and it would be dangerous to leave an unreliable ('sospectosa') city like Pisa in the hands of a man who was acceptable to the former and not to the latter.[1] Lorenzo could have hardly spelled out more forcefully the way in which the policies of the state and of the regime were entwined with one another and with his own personal interests. He certainly had a case for arguing that the Pope did him an injustice in holding him alone responsible for Florence's action.

His case was compounded by the bull of excommunication and interdict, which Sixtus IV issued a little over a month after the attack in the Duomo. Before 1478, the Pope had still observed formal diplomatic procedure by addressing his com-plaints about Florentine interventions in the Papal State to the Signoria;[2] his bull of 1 June 1478[3] is squarely directed against Lorenzo, the Signoria and other magistrates being implicated solely as his helpers and accomplices. Was Sixtus IV trying to tear down the public façade from the complex structure of Florentine government under the Medici, by placing the full responsibility for its actions on Lorenzo? It may not have been mere coincidence that one of his predecessors, Pius II, had described Lorenzo's grandfather as Signore of Florence in all but name.[4] If the republic handed over Lorenzo and his so-called accomplices for ecclesiastical punishment, Florence would be absolved from guilt by association, for the actions which, according to the bull, deserved punishment—from the inter-ventions in the affairs of Imola and Città di Castello to the hanging of the Archbishop of Pisa, Francesco Salviati, and the detention of the Pope's great-nephew, Cardinal Raffaele

[1] Ibid., 182, pp. 58–9; 184, pp. 69–70.
[2] See the copies of briefs addressed to the Signoria in 1474 and 1475 in ASF, Signori, Carteggi, Responsive, Copiari, 2, fols. 63ᵛ–64ʳ (28 June 1474), 64ᵛ–65ʳ (5 July 1474), 92ᵛ–93ʳ (21 October 1475).
[3] Fabroni, *Laurentii Medicis vita*, vol. ii, pp. 121–9.
[4] *Commentarii* (Rome, 1584), p. 89.

Riario-Sansoni, after the failure of the conspiracy. The point was driven home by the accusation, consistently used from now to the end of the war, that Lorenzo was a tyrant, and by the argument that the Pope was only trying to help the Florentines to free themselves from his tyranny.

For Lorenzo, the aftermath of the conspiracy was the moment of truth in more than one respect; it was also the supreme test of his statecraft, and of the cohesion of the regime. On 26 April the Pazzi had failed to rouse the people of Florence by the ancient republican slogan of 'popolo e libertà', and Sixtus IV's attempt to drive a wedge between Lorenzo and the Florentines proved to be equally counterproductive. That the 'uomini dello stato' would support the head of the regime was a foregone conclusion. Yet the question remained how the complex relationship between Lorenzo and the regime would stand up to the strain of interdict and war. The meeting on 12 June, in which leading citizens discussed, a few days after the publication of the bull, the threat of military action against Florence, provided Lorenzo with an opportunity to test the measure of their support. In a moving speech, he offered to face exile and even death if this could avert war. 'All citizens must place the common before the private good, but I more than anyone else, as one who has received from you and the fatherland more and greater benefits."[1] The reaction of the meeting could have been foreseen; its formulation is not without interest. 'Lorenzo and the house of Medici must be defended in the same way as the fatherland', says one of the speakers, 'Laurentium . . . et Medicam domum non aliter defendendam quam patrie salutem'; while another declares that Lorenzo's safety cannot be distinguished from that of the state, 'ne separari posse eius salutem a salute publica'.[2] And when, a month later, Sixtus IV wrote to the Florentines that he had no quarrel with the Florentine people itself, that, on the contrary, his only aim was to liberate it from the tyranny of Lorenzo, and that once Lorenzo was expelled, the troops he, the Pope, and the King of Naples were moving against Florence, would be used to protect her liberty, the Signoria replied that the man whom the Pope called a tyrant, the Florentines unanimously called 'the defender of our liberty', and that they were prepared, 'what-

---

[1] ASF, Consulte e Pratiche, 60, fol. 159[r–v]: 'Cives enim omnes publicam salutem debent suae anteponere; ego vero multo etiam magis quam caeteri omnes, quippe qui a vobis, a patria plura et maiora acceperim beneficia'.

[2] Ibid., fol. 160[r] (Piero Minerbetti, for the *Otto di Balìa*; Niccolò Berardi).

ever should happen, to stake everything on the safety of Lorenzo de' Medici'.[1]

After the meeting of 12 June Lorenzo must have felt confident that the leading citizens of the regime would stand firmly behind him; on the following day their declaration, that the defence of Florence and that of the Medici were one and the same thing, received an almost symbolic confirmation in Lorenzo's election to the newly appointed *Dieci di Balìa*. The Ten were an office created, with wide powers, in times of war; while it functioned, it took the place of the Signoria in the conduct of the war and of foreign policy. It was the first time that Lorenzo held an office in the government of Florence. From now onwards he was to participate almost continuously in the official conduct of government business in the public world of Palazzo Vecchio, as against the private, or semi-private one of Palazzo Medici. It might be argued that, as far as his actual influence on government was concerned, this would add only little, if anything, to his power. Yet, in the complex and sophisticated system of Medici rule, a great deal depended on the form in which it was exercised. Lorenzo's election to the *Dieci* thus constitutes a landmark in the formation of his statecraft.[2] It may also serve us as an opportunity to examine once more what was, perhaps, its central problem.

Throughout the period of Medici ascendancy, Medicean control of the Signoria was certainly not confined to the election of its members. The Ferrarese ambassador shrewdly observed, when reporting on Lorenzo's succession in December 1469: 'it is understood that the secret business ("le cose secrete"), of the Signoria will now pass through the hands of Lorenzo, as they did through those of his father', because his followers were able to control the elections to that office.[3] Pius II had said of Cosimo that 'affairs of State were debated in his house';[4] the opposition to Piero had demanded that government business be confined to the Palace of the Signoria; and after Piero's

[1] Ed. in L. Pignotti, *Storia della Toscana* (Livorno, 1820), vol. iv, pp. 117–21: 'Eiicere vis nos e civitate Laurentium de Medicis . . . Laurentium de Medicis tyrannum clamitas, at nos populusque noster defensorem nostrae libertatis . . . una omnium voce appellamus' (21 July 1478).

[2] See Rubinstein, *The Government*, pp. 219–21.

[3] Niccolò de' Roberti to Borso d'Este, Florence, 4 December, A. Cappelli (ed.), 'Lettere di Lorenzo de' Medici . . . conservate nell'Archivio Palatino di Modena . . .', *Atti e memorie delle Deputazioni di storia patria per le provincie modenesi e parmensi*, vol. i (1863), p. 250.

[4] Loc. cit.

death there were people in Florence who believed that this was now actually going to happen, but they were wrong.[1] Yet, there were limits to Medici influence on the day-to-day work of the Signoria, due to restraints imposed by ancient political traditions. It was up to the Signoria to summon the citizens they chose for consultation, and they were not bound by their advice; jointly with their two Colleges, they had the last word in the making of decisions; they had their own administrative staff, including, in particular, the chancery. I do not know whether Lorenzo saw, as a rule, all the more important letters addressed to or written by the Signoria, but he would not have had much difficulty in doing so. He had his own sources of information, often more reliable than those of the Signoria, and the Florentine ambassadors would write to him as well as to their government, often at the same time. Alamanno Rinuccini states that during his embassy to the Pope in 1475/6, he had 'as an old friend of Lorenzo's written to him privately, together with his official dispatches, about the weightiest matters'; and he adds that Lorenzo was, on one occasion, annoyed with him because he had reported the Pope's complaints about Lorenzo to the Signoria, as well as to him.[2] Lorenzo expected personal letters from ambassadors to contain more confidential information, not necessarily identical with that included in their official dispatches. They would also serve as channels through which foreign governments could communicate with Lorenzo.[3] This was one of the advantages of Lorenzo's personal diplomacy. Another concerned his own correspondence.

[1] See Rubinstein, *The Government*, p. 173. Cf. the letter of Niccolò de' Roberti, cit.: 'che fra pochi dì si abbia a ridurre ogni cosa al Palazzo'.

[2] *Dialogus de libertate*, ed. F. Adorno, in *Atti e Memorie dell'Accademia Toscana . . . La Colombaria*, xxii (1957), pp. 300–1: 'Quid vero reprehendere in me iure potest, si veteris amicitiae rationem sequutus una cum publicis litteris privatim quoque ad eum de maximis rebus litteras dabam . . .? . . . cum, adstante summorum patrum concilio, Pontifex de ipso verba quaedam graviora contra republicae nostrae decus fecisset, et privatim ad eum et publice ad summum magistratum omnia perscripsi'.

[3] During the secret peace negotiations in June 1479 the Milanese government would even dictate to the Florentine ambassador what he was to write to Lorenzo in his own name: see A. R. Natale (ed.), *Acta in Consilio Secreto in Castello Portae Iovis Mediolani*, vol. iii (Milan, 1969), p. 268 (23 June): Cicco Simonetta 'fecit legere . . . minutam litterarum scribendarum per dictum Magnificum Hieronymum [Morelli], oratorem florentinum, prefato Laurentio . . .' The minute is in ASM, SPE, Firenze, 298, and a copy of it, in Morelli's secretary's hand, in ASF, Carte Strozziane, 2a ser., 96, no. 5.

Owing to his position in Florence, his communications to foreign princes and statesman, whether relayed through ambassadors, his agents, or directly through his letters, were likely to carry more weight than those of the Signoria. His letters had the additional advantage of being technically private. In this sense, what might be broadly called his double diplomacy was really complementary to that of the official organs of government. It rendered Florentine diplomacy more flexible and, if necessary, more secret; among other things, it made it possible for Lorenzo, as it had done earlier for Cosimo, to disclaim ultimate responsibility for government decisions, on the grounds that he was only a private citizen. Lorenzo certainly had also considerable influence on the official correspondence of the Signoria. In this, as in other respects, the head of the chancery, Bartolomeo Scala, provided him with an invaluable link with the Palazzo della Signoria: a Medici client and friend of Lorenzo's, he was, unlike other palace officials, a permanent fixture in Florentine administration, enjoying what in the end amounted to life tenure.[1] At the same time, there were limits to the extent to which Lorenzo could, or would, normally determine the contents of official letters; had this not been the case it would have been hardly necessary, in 1477, explicitly to entrust Lorenzo and a few leading citizens with the drafting of letters for the Signoria, as was the case on several occasions; they formed a small *ad hoc* committee which met in the room of the Gonfalonier of Justice in the Palace of the Signoria.[2] One result of this development was that Lorenzo was now becoming more directly, indeed physically, involved in the official business of government, as transacted in Palazzo Vecchio (apart from being summoned, like other leading citizens, by the Signoria to advisory meetings, in which, moreover, he only spoke rarely).[3] On 1 May 1478 he became a member of the magistracy in charge of public security, the Eight of Ward, having been elected to it, for four months, shortly before the attack in the Duomo; but he resigned from it shortly afterwards, no doubt in order not to be personally implicated in political prosecutions.[4] His election to the *Dieci* in June thus forms yet another step in the same direction: the contrast between Palazzo Vecchio and Palazzo Medici, seen by their opponents as

[1] See Alison Brown's *Bartolomeo Scala* (Princeton, 1979).
[2] See *Lettere*, vol. ii, docs. i to xii (24 April to 29 September 1477).
[3] ASF, Consulte e Pratiche, 60, *passim*.
[4] See Rubinstein, *The Government*, p. 220.

symbolic of the system of government of the Medici, was beginning to lose some of its force. The *Dieci* were appointed for
six months at a time, but the citizens elected on 13 June were
re-elected twice, so that Lorenzo remained continuously in
office until 12 December 1479,[1] by which time he had left for
Naples to negotiate peace with King Ferrante.

In what ways did this shift of his political activities to Palazzo
Vecchio affect the development of his statecraft? He now participated officially in the formulation and execution of the foreign
and military policy of the republic, during a war which threatened its very independence. Yet at the same time, he kept
up, and if anything intensified, his private diplomacy. It
could hardly have been otherwise. Indeed, this diplomacy
acquired additional importance during the war, as did his
personal relations with foreign rulers, such as the Duchess of
Milan and the King of France, and with their ministers—
Cicco Simonetta and Philippe de Commynes. The correspondence of the *Dieci* and of Lorenzo shows in great detail how
his double diplomacy worked during the war. Their relationship
was based on a sort of division of labour, the *Dieci* being in
charge of the day-to-day conduct of military operations and
diplomatic affairs, Lorenzo more concerned with long-term
issues, and, in particular, with secret negotiations. To quote
one instance only: in Spring 1479, while official peace negotiations were going on in Rome, Lorenzo was involved in secret
talks, conducted partly through his brother-in-law, Rinaldo
Orsini, about a peace settlement with the King of Naples.
On 11 May he sent the Florentine ambassador in Milan a
copy of a letter concerning matters 'di grandissima importantia'
which he had received from his colleague in Rome, and asked
him to discuss it only with the ducal secretary, Cicco Simonetta,
'as it must be kept very secret': 'To you alone I want to tell my
views [on it], according to my free and rough nature', 'secondo
la mia natura libera et staglata'.[2] There is no reference to this
matter in the dispatch which the Florentine ambassador in
Rome sent simultaneously to the *Dieci*; nor in those of the
Milanese ambassador in Florence. The incident also illustrates,
once more, the role of personal relations in Lorenzo's diplomacy,
in this case with the powerful secretary of the Dukes of Milan.
It should be added that this type of diplomacy was not without

[1] ASF, Cento, 2, fols. 38ᵛ–39ʳ, 43ᵛ–44ʳ, 48ᵛ–49ʳ.
[2] Lorenzo to Girolamo Morelli, 11 May 1479, ASF, MAP, CXXXVII, 430.

risks: Venice was incensed by the rumours of secret negotiations, and Simonetta's fall from power, after Ludovico Sforza's
return to Milan in September 1479, was bound to be a source
of embarrassment to Lorenzo. In fact, Ludovico il Moro
proved to be much more lukewarm in his attitude to Lorenzo,
and to Florence, than Cicco Simonetta had been; and this
contributed, in the end, to Lorenzo's decision to follow the
Duke of Calabria's advice 'to throw himself into the arms of the
King of Naples', on the grounds that 'this is the only way in
which I can save the city and myself'.[1] On 6 December, he left
Florence for Naples.

Lorenzo's journey to Naples highlights some of the major
characteristics and problems of his statecraft, as it had developed
over the past ten years. If the aftermath of the Pazzi conspiracy
was a moment of truth for his ascendancy in Florence, the
setbacks and defeats of the war years provided a new challenge
to it. While the leading members of the regime appear to have
remained united behind him, there were rumblings of discontent;
in Florence too, there were people such as Alamanno Rinuccini
who called Lorenzo a tyrant who had deprived the city of her
ancient liberty; and they were probably more likely to do so
when the war was going badly.[2] Lorenzo's decision to assume
personal responsibility for the conclusion of peace thus forms
a logical sequel to his offer, in June 1478, to sacrifice himself
for the sake of Florence. What was at stake, once more, was,
in the widest sense, the relationship between Lorenzo and Florence, but the circumstances were different. In the summer of
1478, the offer might be considered rhetorical; in December
1479, it had a very real meaning. Against the background of
defeat, his speech to the meeting which was hastily summoned
on the eve of his departure, in order to inform, but not to consult,
the leading citizens of his decision, while reminding us of his
address to the meeting at the beginning of the war, had a
different ring of urgency. As the *Dieci* wrote to the Florentine
ambassador in Venice, Lorenzo expressed the belief that, since the
Pope and the King of Naples were holding him alone responsible

[1] Lorenzo to Girolamo Morelli, 25 September 1479 (ASF, MAP, L, 11):
'di gittarmi nelle braccia del Re, mostrandone che questa via sola ho da
salvare la città et me'.

[2] See his *Dialogus de libertate*, completed in April 1479 (ed. F. Adorno,
pp. 270–303). On 14 December, Cardinal Francesco Gonzaga wrote to his
brother, the Marquess of Mantua: 'Sonnosi in Firenza trovati scrittarini
sparti per la terra che dicevano: L'è pur partito el tyranno' (quoted in
G. B. Picotti, *Ricerche umanistiche* (Florence, 1955), p. 58, n. 2).

for the war, he would, by taking this decision, either help to bring about the peace which the city, and the whole of Italy, needed so badly, or find out whether it was really he who was the cause of the war or whether there was some other reason for it; and if it could be shown that 'the cause of the war did not concern him, but the republic, we ought to devote ourselves, unitedly and boldly, to our defence'.[1] By taking the initiative in seeking peace, Lorenzo thus reopened the question of the relationship between his own personal interests, his 'spetialità', and those of the republic—a question which seemed to have been settled and put aside at the beginning of the war. This is spelt out in his outburst after his arrival at Naples, as reported by the Milanese ambassadors there: his journey, he complained, had brought no advantage to his city; even were the King to give him full satisfaction as far as his private interests were concerned, this was not what he wanted if at the same time his fatherland remained dissatisfied; indeed, should this happen, he would, on his return, not be able to open his mouth in Florence.[2] The successful conclusion of the peace negotiations in Naples in March 1480 was therefore not only a diplomatic triumph for Lorenzo; it also decisively strengthened his position at home. The creation of the Council of Seventy, a few weeks after his triumphant return from Naples, must be seen as a further step in the domestic policy Lorenzo had been pursuing from the first year of his political career; but the unprecedented success of this policy, in concentrating power in this all but permanent council, would have hardly been possible without the challenge of peace Lorenzo had met single-handed.

For the journey to Naples was also a supreme test of the other aspect of his statecraft, his personal diplomacy. While the war years had enhanced the judicious blending of public and private diplomacy, they had also shown, once more, the

---

[1] The *Dieci* to Luigi Guicciardini, 6 December (ASF, Missive interne, 11, fols. 45ᵛ–46ᵛ): '. . . o veramente potere chiarire se questa cagione o veramente altra cagione è quella che fa questa guerra et perturbatione, a questo fine che, potendosi havere pace . . . , più facilmente si habbi, et non si potendo havere et inteso la cagione della guerra non essere per lui ma per il publico, si venga unitamente et animosamente alla difesa necessaria'.

[2] Pietro da Gallera and Giovanni Angelo Talenti to Galeazzo Maria Sforza, Naples, 22 December, ASMi, SPE, Roma, 86: 'se bene la Maestà del Signore Re nelle particularitate sue gli satisfacesse al tutto, che questo non saria el suo bisogno, restando mal contenta la sua patria, et . . . che'l non potesse parlare in Fiorenza, quando se trovasse che per la sua spetialità el ritornasse ben contento et nelle cose publice la città mal satisfacta'.

value of the latter, in terms of secrecy, initiative, and personal relationships. The journey to Naples epitomizes all this; prepared in well-kept secrecy, as a result of Lorenzo's own initiative, it was greatly facilitated, and incidentally rendered less dangerous than might appear, by his earlier contacts with members of the royal family of Naples. The Duke of Calabria, whom he had known since his visit to Naples in 1466, when informing Lorenzo on 4 December that two Neapolitan galleys were at his disposal, addresses him as 'My dearest and most beloved Lorenzo'[1]—somewhat surprising for a commander of the enemy army; his wife Ippolita Sforza, whose marriage ceremony Lorenzo had attended in Milan, proved a good friend and adviser during the negotiations at Naples—and apparently also good company: at one point, discussions were held up, because Lorenzo could not be found: it turned out that he was visiting her.[2] His refusal to act as official Florentine ambassador was in keeping with the personal style of his diplomacy;[3] his mandate to negotiate and conclude, which was sent to him by the *Dieci*, conferred on him great powers but also implied, by its very nature, that his actions were subject to restraints; and these were fully acknowledged by him, when, for instance, he announced in Naples that he wanted to return to Florence, because he could hope by his presence to persuade the Signoria to make concessions 'to which he did not dare agree on his own'.[4]

[1] ASF, MAP, XLV, 224: 'Lorenzo mio multo caro e multo amato . . .'
[2] The Milanese ambassadors in Naples report on 23 December (ASM, SPE, Napoli, 229) that they had been unable to find Lorenzo in order to deliver a message from the King until late that day, because he had gone to visit the Duchess: 'et non essendo el Magnifico Lorenzo nel suo logiamento, per essere andato a visitare la Illustrissima duchessa de Calabria, ne bisognò expectare insino alla nocte'. A month later, the *Dieci* wrote to her to thank her for having 'prestati grandissimi favori et adoperatovi per noi et durati ogni fatica', as they had been informed by Lorenzo (Florence, Biblioteca Nazionale, MS. Palat. 1091, fol. 45^r, 22 January 1480).
[3] The Milanese ambassador in Florence, Filippo Sacramoro, reports on 30 December 1479 (ASM, SPE, Firenze, 298) that to his question whether Lorenzo 'tenga grado de ambassatore', the *Dieci* had given him to understand that this was not the case, 'né l'havea, perché ha monstro non lo volere'; and on 6 January 1480, Lorenzo himself, writing from Naples, pointed out to the *Dieci* (ASF, Dieci, Responsive, 25, fol. 439) that he had not 'tenuto qua grado o termine di ambasciadore, ché m'è paruto meglo a proposito stare chome privato'.
[4] The mandate (a copy is in ASF, Notarile antecosimiano, B 2320, fols. 126^v–127^r) gave him full powers to conclude peace and alliances with the

The successful conclusion of the negotiations, completed after he had left Naples, forms a landmark in his diplomacy, as well as in his position as head of the regime. His official participation in the conduct of foreign policy as member of a public office, interrupted after he had ceased to be a member of the *Dieci* in December 1478, was resumed, on a different level, and on a practically permanent basis, after the creation of the Seventy in April 1480. A new magistracy, the *Otto di Pratica*, which was elected every six months from its personnel, replaced the *Dieci*, in peace as well as in war; but the Seventy took the final decisions, and Lorenzo was a member of that council. The new structure of government brought with it a further decline in the authority of the Signoria, as well as of the old statutory councils. Supreme authority in the republic was now concentrated in a council which, while meeting in the Palace of the Signoria, represented the inner circle of the regime. The contrast between Palazzo Vecchio and Palazzo Medici had been settled, though not in the way which the opponents of the Medici had envisaged. It was the beginning of a new period in the development of Lorenzo's statecraft.

King of Naples and other powers, 'prout eidem Laurentio libere videbitur et placebit'. In fact, Lorenzo kept in close contact with the *Dieci* throughout the negotiations. The Milanese ambassadors in Naples report on 13 January (ASM, SPE, Napoli, 229) that Lorenzo had decided to tell the King 'che la voglia et parer suo saria de ritornare a Fiorenza, perché con la presentia sua poteria più facilmente indure quella Excelsa Signoria a questi effecti, alli quali lui non ardiria aconsentire da si stesso'.

[*Bibliographical Note*: Lorenzo de' Medici, *Lettere*, vol. i (18 November 1460 to 12 July 1474), vol. ii (3 August 1474 to 14 March 1478), vol. iii (26 April 1478 to 5 February 1479), vol. iv (17 February 1479 to 23 March 1480), Giunti–Barbèra, Florence.]

DIPLOMACY AND WAR IN
LATER FIFTEENTH-CENTURY ITALY

'It is obvious that ever since the Roman Empire . . . Italy had never enjoyed such prosperity, or known so favourable a situation as that in which it found itself so securely at rest in the year of our Christian salvation, 1490, and the years immediately before and after.'[1] The famous words of Francesco Guicciardini at the beginning of the *Storia d'Italia* have been in the minds of all historians who have involved themselves in the debate about the state of Italy in the second half of the fifteenth century. Guicciardini's golden age of peace and stability has been echoed by those who have wished to stress the constructive balance of power, free of outside interference, achieved by the Italian League of 1455, by the growth of permanent diplomacy, and by the activities of far-sighted politicians.[2] It has been denounced by those others who have attached more importance to the tensions and fears of the period, to declining military effectiveness, to intrigue, deception, and growing social unrest.[3] But on both sides there has been a

The following abbreviations will be used in the footnotes: ASF—Florence, Archivio di Stato; ASMa—Mantua, Archivio di Stato; ASMi—Milan, Archivio di Stato; ASMo—Modena, Archivio di Stato; ASV—Venice, Archivio di Stato.

[1] Francesco Guicciardini, *La storia d'Italia*, ed. C. Panigada (Bari, 1929), i. 2; English translation by Sydney Alexander, *The History of Italy* (London, 1969), pp. 3-4.

[2] For differing approaches to this view of the period, see particularly G. Soranzo, *La lega italica* (1454-5) (Milan, 1924); E. W. Nelson, 'The Origins of Modern Balance of Power Politics', *Medievalia et Humanistica*, i (1943); R. Cessi, 'La lega italica e la sua funzione storica nella seconda metà del secolo XV', *Atti del R. Istituto Veneto di Scienze, Lettere ed Arti*, cii (1942-3); Garrett Mattingly, *Renaissance Diplomacy* (London, 1955), pp. 91-100; V. Ilardi, 'The Italian League, Francesco Sforza and Charles VII (1454-61)', *Studies in the Renaissance*, vi (1959).

[3] Among critics of the 'optimistic' approach, see particularly E. Pontieri, *L'equilibrio e la crisi politica italiana nella seconda metà del secolo XV* (Naples,

tendency to emphasize Italian military unpreparedness in 1494, either as a result of intense disunity or of peaceful coexistence. The wars of the period have tended to be described as brush-fire wars, temporary aberrations and breaks in the normal pattern of diplomatic relations, or as the result of the ambitions of over-powerful *condottieri*. Both interpretations, therefore, place empha-sis on a certain separation between war and the normal course of politics.

It is the aim of this lecture to question some of these interpreta-tions, particularly in the light of the unfolding publication of the letters of Lorenzo the Magnificent which has provided the oppor-tunity for sustained and detailed research into the Italian politics of the period.[1] This work, in which I have had the good fortune to become involved, is confirming some of the older ideas and hypotheses; it gives substance to Garrett Mattingly's vision of the importance of systematic diplomacy, and to some extent supports the views of the powerful influence of the leading military captains. But above all it is setting before our eyes the intimate connections between this diplomatic scene and the ever present threat of war and preoccupation with war.

A balance of power has been defined as a way of conducting international relations to avoid major wars by constantly adjusting alliance systems in accordance with changing military and economic strength. It involves a shift from a preoccupation with the purely local and immediate to a concern for areas not necessarily contiguous to the frontiers of the main powers involved. All this is to some extent true of Italy between 1454 and 1494, but it is particularly important in the Italian context not to see balance of power as a sort of panacea for all political ills, a universal acceptance of the need for peace and harmony, a kind of political enlightenment. It was rather a stalemate produced by economic exhaustion and a realization that the days of easy conquest had passed, even though the hegemonic aspirations remained. It was a situation which called for incessant alertness, a need to be constantly informed about the military strengths and

1946); B. Barbadoro, 'Il problema dell'equilibrio e la crisi della libertà d'Italia', *Questioni di storia medioevale*, ed. E. Rota (Milan, n.d.), pp. 455–73; F. Catalano, 'Il problema dell'equilibrio politico e la crisi della libertà italiana', *Nuove questioni di storia medioevale* (Milan, 1964), pp. 357–94; G. Pillinini, *Il sistema degli stati italiani* (1454–94) (Venice, 1970).

[1] Lorenzo de' Medici, *Lettere*, eds. R. Fubini and N. Rubinstein, i–iv (Florence, 1977–81). The volumes so far published cover the period 1460–80; vols. v and vi will be devoted to 1480–4.

intentions of rival powers, a determination to be prepared both to seize opportunities for minor gains and to counter such opportunistic moves by others. It was also a situation which was both fostered by, and itself encouraged, the growth of permanence in regimes, bureaucracies, diplomatic activity, and military establishments.

There is, of course, a danger in seeing the period too much as a whole. It is possible to suggest that the first ten years after the peace of Lodi saw a more positive balance achieved in which some Italian leaders, notably Francesco Sforza, Cosimo de' Medici, and Pius II, worked for peace, and that thereafter, despite the amount of information available to regimes through their diplomatic networks, despite the continual state of military preparedness, the tensions mounted. The shifting alliances of the post-1466 period on the whole failed to take account of changing military and economic strengths. The regimes themselves become more insecure internally and more inclined to thoughtless bellicoseness in the search for quick advantage. But behind such interpretations of gradual breakdown there tends to lie the dangerous assumption of historians that the main interest of the period lies in understanding the events of 1494. The roar of Charles VIII's guns has filled the ears of those who have studied the preceding years and conditioned their historical perspectives. One of the great advantages of the work on the Lorenzo letters is that it has concentrated the mind of the researchers involved on specific moments in the period and isolated them to some extent from the Guicciardinian 'crisis of Italy'. Such an approach suggests that while there were undoubtedly shifts in emphasis, and climactic moments, like Otranto, which profoundly affected the political scene, the underlying tensions between the Italian states remained surprisingly constant between 1454 and 1494. Milan, usually linked to France, was always suspect to Naples, fearful of Angevin, and later French, claims to its throne. Venice's fears of the Turks and of Milanese reprisal for the Lombard lands lost before 1454 were constant factors. The rising economic and naval power of Naples frightened all the other Italian states, while the hegemonic aspirations of King Ferrante in Genoa and southern Tuscany, as he sought to turn the western Mediterranean into an Aragonese lake, affected Florence and Milan in particular. The Papacy, inevitably mutable in its policies, yet had a consistent fear of Naples on its southern frontiers and of a possible Medici *signoria* on those to the north. Florence, beset by financial problems and open to interference and infiltration from all sides, conducted an economic rivalry with Venice and an increasingly apparent territorial and jurisdictional rivalry with the Papacy. In the midst of it all was the Romagna, the one significant political vacuum left after 1454 in which all the powers sought advantage and spheres of influence. Nor can the pressure on the system from outside Italy be said to have varied in any consistent manner. The dangers of French intervention and interference, and of Turkish incursion, were ever present.

It would be wrong to overturn traditional thinking to the extent of suggesting that these tensions, which created a sort of cold-war situation in Italy, generated a positive arms race. The maintenance and improvement of artillery trains was certainly a part of the military planning of most of the Italian states, and there was a growing awareness of the formidable potential of the new weapons. The Milanese artillery train in 1472 consisted of 16 large cannon which required 227 carts and 522 pairs of oxen to transport them and all the miscellaneous accessories for their use.[1] By 1471 Bartolomeo da Cremona was training 20 gunners at a time in the Venetian arsenal,[2] and in 1498 the Senate declared that 'the wars of the present time are influenced more by the force of bombards and artillery than by men at arms'.[3] But it was more the maintenance of permanent establishments of traditional forces which preoccupied governments. The Italian League of 1455, and all subsequent alliances of the period, sanctioned, encouraged, and yet sought to limit, such standing armies. The terms of the League set the size of the armies at 6,000 cavalry and 2,000 infantry for Milan, Venice, and Naples, and 2,000 cavalry and 1,000 infantry for Florence and the Papacy.[4] But undoubtedly all the states, with the exception of Florence, exceeded these levels of permanent troops in the years which followed. Galeazzo Maria Sforza in the early 1470s had detailed plans drawn up for the speedy mobilization of an army of nearly 43,000 men and the permanent effectives at his disposal numbered over 20,000.[5] Venice could count on a standing cavalry force of about 8,000 men during the 1460s and 1470s, supplemented by 2,000 professional infantry and an increasingly effective and trained select

[1] M. E. Mallett, *Mercenaries and their Masters; Warfare in Renaissance Italy* (London, 1974), p. 161.

[2] ASV, Senatus Terra, reg. 6, 49ᵛ (7 Oct. 1471).

[3] ASV, Senatus Terra, reg. 13, 64ᵛ (27 Dec. 1498).

[4] Soranzo, op. cit., pp. 192–3.

[5] E. C. Visconti, 'Ordine dell'esercito ducale sforzesco, 1472–4', *Archivio storico lombardo*, iii (1876).

militia.[1] Paul II, throughout his pontificate, deployed an army of
8,000 to 10,000 men for a series of minor campaigns designed to
strengthen his control over the papal state.[2] The Aragonese kings
of Naples were more interested in building up naval than military
strength, but by the 1470s the military ambitions of Alfonso, Duke
of Calabria, ensured that a large standing force was available, and
the influential *Memoriale* of one of his principal lieutenants,
Diomede Carafa, indicated the degree of permanence and pro-
fessionalism expected of this army.[3] The maintenance of these
forces consumed, in peace-time, about half the annual income of
the Italian states. Florence, for reasons which I have explored
elsewhere, was reluctant to undertake such expenditure and
normally maintained its standing forces at or below a minimum
level to conform with its alliance obligations.[4]

With this build up of permanent forces there was inevitably a
decline in the mercenary nature of the leadership. Captains were
encouraged to take out long-term contracts and to settle permanently within the frontiers of the state which they served. Most
of the Italian states resorted increasingly to relying on their own
subjects to provide military leadership; this was particularly true
of Naples, Milan, and the Papacy, less so of Venice; Florence
remained once again exceptional in this respect. At the same time
the increasing dependence of military forces on the state led to the
states themselves adopting that traditional feature of *condottiere*
warfare—the tendency to conduct wars of manœuvre and attrition, with the avoidance of battle and heavy loss one of the key
features. As the main responsibility for maintaining expensive and
precious troops passed from captain to state, so the anxiety not to
take unnecessary risks was also transferred. This reinforced the
whole framework of fifteenth-century war policy which was
oriented towards wars of attrition which damaged the rival state's

[1] M. E. Mallett, 'Preparations for War in Florence and Venice in the Second
Half of the Fifteenth Century', *Florence and Venice: Comparisons and Relations*, i
(Florence, 1979), 150.

[2] Mallett, *Mercenaries and their Masters*, p. 117; G. Zorzi, 'Un vicentino alla
corte di Paolo II; Chierighino Chiericati e il suo trattatello della milizia', *Nuovo
archivio veneto*, NS xxx (1915); A. Da Mosto, 'Ordinamenti militari delle
soldatesche dello stato Romano del 1430 al 1470', *Quellen und Forschungen aus
italienischen Archiven und Bibliotheken*, v (1902), 31–3.

[3] I. Schiappoli, *Napoli aragonese: traffici e attività marinara* (Naples, 1972),
pp. 25–32; P. Pieri, 'Il "Governo et exercitio de la militia" di Orso degli Orsini
e i "Memoriali" di Diomede Carafa', *Archivio storico per le provincie napoletane*,
xix (1933).

[4] Mallett, 'Preparations for war', *passim*.

economy and aimed at minor territorial gains—rather than at the annihilation of the enemy. Thus the whole tendency in the late fifteenth century for the tempo of Italian warfare to slow down and to rely heavily on tactics of manœuvre was more the result of the policy of governments than of the preferences of the captains. However, the War of Ferrara, which will be the focus of the later part of this paper and which is sometimes described, quite erroneously, as 'the last medieval war in Italy', was to prove somewhat exceptional in this respect.[1]

The fact that most of the Italian states in the second half of the fifteenth century had large permanent armies in a greater or lesser state of constant preparedness undoubtedly affected the conduct of relations between those states. But it would be wrong to overestimate the extent to which those permanent forces were normally ready for war or themselves fostered a willingness to go to war. While it was certainly true that contingents of heavy cavalry could be alerted at very short notice, and dispatched to counter or support aggressive political moves, full-scale mobilization was a very different matter. Milan was able to move relatively large bodies of cavalry to the Bolognese within days in response to tensions in the Romagna, as in June 1470 when 1,500 cavalry were sent,[2] and in May 1480 when Roberto da Sanseverino went with 3,000 cavalry to counter a papal threat to Pesaro.[3] But the mobilization of the permanent forces meant moving them over to wartime rates of pay and in some cases filling out the ranks with new recruits. It meant the paying of large advances or *prestanze* before the troops could be moved out of quarters. It meant the rounding up of additional horses and oxen for the baggage trains and the levying of the militia and pioneers to accompany the army. All this took time, and above all ready cash—a commodity of which fifteenth-century states were always short. A state like Venice, which had access to the assets in the vaults of its banks in emergency, was thus able to mobilize much more quickly and effectively than the other Italian states. This was clear in April 1480 when 400,000 ducats was needed, and quickly available, to get the army and a huge river fleet ready for the war of Ferrara. This advantage, as much as

[1] F. Secco d'Aragona, 'Un giornale della guerra di Ferrara (1482–4), *Archivio storico lombardo*, 8th ser. vii (1957), 344. For the best account of the War of Ferrara, see E. Piva, *La guerra di Ferrara del 1482* (Padua, 1893).

[2] Lorenzo de' Medici, op. cit. i. 158.

[3] ASMi, Archivio sforzesco, Potenze Estere, Firenze 299 (18 May and 2 June 1480); Dukes of Milan to Filippo Sacramoro in Florence.

any other factor, accounts for the general fear of Venetian imperialism in this period.[1]

If the presence of permanent forces contributed significantly to the conditions of *equilibrio* in which the Italian states found themselves in the second half of the fifteenth century, it was diplomacy which provided the mechanism of the system. Diplomacy to avoid war, diplomacy to prepare for war, diplomacy to end war; the two were crucially linked. Garrett Mattingly in his seminal book on *Renaissance Diplomacy* rightly countered the claims of the diplomatic theorists themselves that their main object was to preserve peace, but he underestimated the intimate connections between diplomacy and war in fifteenth-century Italy. He introduced, in fact, an unnatural separation between the two by ascribing the growth of permanent diplomacy in Italy to the unreliability of the mercenary system, and by suggesting that 'diplomacy was for rulers, war for hired men'.[2] This second suggestion is the result of a peculiarly Florentine view of Renaissance development, a view which, particularly in the field of international relations, leads to severe distortions. While it is on the whole true that the Florentine political élite had little direct experience of war and regarded diplomacy as a laudable, and indeed necessary, occupation for the good citizen, the same generalization is less applicable to the other Italian élites. In Venice the very experienced military *provveditori* and the ambassadors came from the same small social group, and were often the same men.[3] Many Milanese and Neapolitan diplomatic envoys had military experience, and not a few of them were 'hired men' in the sense of not being native-born subjects of the states which they served. Among the leading Milanese diplomats of the period were Prospero Camogli, Nicodemo Tranchedini, Sacramoro and Filippo Sacramori, Antonio Bracelli, and Sforza Bettini, all of whom were not Milanese by origin and some of whom served other states during their careers.[4] Giovanbattista

---

[1] D. Malipiero, *Annali veneti*, in *Archivio storico italiano*, vii (1843), 253. For a discussion of the fear of Venetian imperialism in this period, see N. Rubinstein, 'Italian Reactions to Terraferma Expansion in the Fifteenth Century', in *Renaissance Venice*, ed. J. R. Hale (London, 1973).

[2] Mattingly, op. cit., pp. 61–2.

[3] M. E. Mallett, 'Venice and its *Condottieri*, 1404–54', in *Renaissance Venice*, pp. 135–7.

[4] For short biographies of some of these men, see L. Cerioni, *La diplomazia sforzesca nella seconda metà del Quattrocento e i suoi cifrari segreti* (Rome, 1970), i; on Prospero Camogli, see P. M. Kendall and V. Ilardi, *Dispatches with Related Documents of Milanese Ambassadors in France and Burgundy, 1450–83*, ii (Ohio, 1971), xvi–xxi.

Bentivoglio in the service of Naples, Zaccaria Saggio da Pisa, the Mantuan envoy in Milan in the late 1470s and early 1480s, Antonio da Montecatini, Ercole d'Este's man in Florence for a number of years, are other examples of this phenomenon.[1]

That the military context within which these diplomats operated was no longer one of errant, and potentially faithless, mercenary captains is a point which has already been made. This is not to deny that a small group of prestigious captains did maintain a degree of independence and mobility in their allegiances and this enabled them to influence, but not I suggest control, the relations between the Italian states. The political roles of men like Federico da Montefeltro and Roberto da Sanseverino were of great significance in the years round the War of Ferrara and these can be well studied through the diplomatic correspondence of the period. One of the main functions of the resident ambassadors was the negotiation of the *condotte* of such men who provided the high command of the permanent armies. This was one of the points at which military organization and diplomacy were inextricably intermeshed. Similarly the negotiation of the alliances and leagues which dominated the period required detailed consideration both of those high-level contracts and of the general level of the maintenance of permanent forces.

But it was in their role as information gatherers that the diplomatic agents of the period had their closest contacts with the military world. Ambassadorial dispatches were filled with information on troop movements and dispositions, on the state of preparedness of companies, on the activities of paymasters and commissaries as indicators of impending mobilization. A dramatic improvement in the quality and flow of information was one of the principal characteristics of Italian statecraft in the second half of the fifteenth century. The resident ambassadors, more informal spies and informers, and the development of patron–client relationships in which one of the main obligations on the client was to keep his patron informed, all contributed to this. The information provided was not, of course, just military information. Reports on revenue, proposed taxes, and on the popular reactions to taxes were always welcome, although interestingly enough ambassadors rarely reported on economic conditions of a more general nature. The other main area of interest to ambassadors was the

---

[1] For Giovanbattista Bentivoglio, see *Dizionario biografico degli italiani*, viii. 633–4. Zaccaria Saggio was the Mantuan representative in Milan throughout the 1470s and the early 1480s. Antonio da Montecatini arrived in Florence in October 1478 and remained well into the 1480s.

unity of the regime to which they were accredited. The role of ambassadors in noting, seeking out, and even fostering factions within the Italian states is a fascinating area of research. The envoys of the other powers in Florence clearly encouraged the existence of pro-Milanese, pro-Aragonese, and pro-Venetian factions within the Florentine political class. This was not just a way of gaining additional inside information, but a form of calculated subversion and interference which could affect policy decisions and if necessary be directed towards undermining the political will of the Republic. Ambassadors seem to have been a good deal less scrupulous in these matters than Mattingly suggested and the question clearly has important implications for both external and internal affairs. However, it is too big a topic to open up in this paper and I want to move on from this rather general discussion to consider some detailed examples which illustrate the points I have been making, chosen from the period of the War of Ferrara.

The signing of the peace which ended the Pazzi War on 13 March 1480, and of the league between Naples, Florence, and Milan on the same day, initiated a period of two years uneasy tension which can be described as the preliminary to the War of Ferrara which broke out on 2 May 1482.[1] The alliance systems which confronted each other in the opening stages of that war were forged two years earlier in March and April 1480. The League of Naples was the recreation of an *entente* of the late 1460s and the league between Sixtus IV and Venice, signed on 16 April, was a natural counterbalance to it. The papal–Venetian league grew out of the dissatisfaction of both parties with the peace of 13 March and the desire of Girolamo Riario to find support for his Romagna ambitions. It was negotiated by Cardinal Foscari with Riario and the Pope, with active encouragement from Federico da Montefeltro who was angry at the preference being given to other *condottieri* in the Neapolitan League.[2]

In fact the Neapolitan League itself was in a good deal of difficulty in the summer of 1480. The idea, which was floated in early May, that the League should be reformulated in the light of the emergence of the rival papal league, took three months to materialize. The main reason for this delay was the difficulty which the three allies had in agreeing on a military command structure. This stemmed partly from the rivalries among the *condottieri* concerned, Ercole d'Este and Roberto da Sanseverino

[1] Lorenzo de' Medici, op. cit. iv, particularly, 367–402.

[2] E. Piva, 'Origine e conclusione della pace e alleanza fra i Veneziani e Sisto IV', *Nuovo archivio veneto*, NS ii (1901).

supported by Milan and the Duke of Calabria supported by
Naples. But more importantly the difficulty arose because of the
deep-rooted suspicion in Milan and Florence of Neapolitan
hegemonic intentions, because of the temporary internal crisis in
Milan caused by the erratic behaviour of the Duchess Bona and
the ambitions of Ludovico Sforza, and because of Florence's
apparently adamant refusal to make the financial contributions
expected of it towards the cost of the *condottieri*. The first of these
issues was exacerbated by the fact that the Duke of Calabria and
his troops were still occupying the Senese and appeared to be
bringing to fruition the long-term Neapolitan ambition to
establish a foothold in southern Tuscany. As Pierfilippo Pandolfini
remarked in a letter of 9 July to Lorenzo de' Medici, it was necessary 'to have the King as kinsman and companion, and even as
father, but not as Signore', and the Milanese appeared to concur
with this view.[1] But at the same time it was the Florentine
ambassador in Milan, Pierfilippo Pandolfini, who was most out-
spoken in his comments on the critical internal situation in Milan
itself, and his male chauvinist remarks about the instability of
female rulers were scarcely calculated to promote collaboration
between the two states.[2] However, it was the Florentine obstinacy
over money which was the most recalcitrant of the problems. This
was only in part a reflection of genuine financial difficulties
following the heavy costs of the Pazzi War. Feeling was growing in
Florence that it was being milked by its allies and that it was time
to make a stand and demonstrate that the Florentine treasury was
not bottomless.[3] Lorenzo was particularly sensitive to public
unrest over taxes, and was anxious to use the *condotta* issue to put
pressure on King Ferrante to give back the Florentine towns in
southern Tuscany which had been occupied by the Neapolitans
and Sienese during the Pazzi War.[4] These were to be persistent
themes in Florentine diplomacy in the next two years and they
illustrate well the interrelationship between military organization,
finance and broader political considerations, both external and
internal, which preoccupied the diplomats of the period.

[1] ASF, Signoria, Otto e Dieci; legazioni e commissarie, missive e responsive,
10, 263–4ᵛ (9 July 1480): '. . . se fe havere il Re per parente et compagnio, et per
padre, ma non per Signore!'

[2] Ibid. 169ᵛ–171 (2 Apr. 1480) and 177–79ᵛ (8 Apr. 1480); Pierfilippo
Pandolfini in Milan to Lorenzo.

[3] L. Landucci, *Diario fiorentino del 1450 al 1516*, a cura di I. del Badia
(Florence, 1883), p. 35.

[4] ASMi, Archivio Sforzesco. Potenze estere, Firenze 299 (25 June 1480):
Filippo Sacramoro from Florence to Dukes of Milan.

The Neapolitan League was finally renewed on 25 July 1480 and the *condotta* of Ercole d'Este as lieutenant-general of the League, which was a part of the agreement, included secret clauses specifically guaranteeing Ferrara against Venetian aggression.[1] Throughout the negotiations the threat of war in the Romagna to frustrate the ambitions of Girolamo Riario had been another constant theme which helped, in fact, to bring the League to fruition.[2]

But war in a different form was about to erupt in Italy. On 27 July, two days after the signing of the League, a Turkish fleet of 150 sail appeared off the coast of Puglia. Within days Otranto had fallen and for over a year events in Italy were to be crucially conditioned by the threatening presence of the Turk on Italian soil.[3] The Duke of Calabria and the bulk of his troops were withdrawn from Tuscany to face the new threat, and Florence saw the possibility of taking advantage of the withdrawal, and of Ferrante's new difficulties, to reclaim the lost towns. The 'insperato accidente' of Otranto, as Machiavelli described it, seemed to give diplomatic advantage not only to Florence.[4] Sixtus IV seized the opportunity to strengthen his prestige through vociferous championing of a crusade and to humiliate Ferrante by forcing him to beg for crusading funds.[5] Ludovico Sforza was able to resolve the internal crisis in Milan by taking control from the Duchess Bona without fear of Neapolitan interference. While in Venice the Senate pondered what advantage could be drawn from the embarrassment and preoccupation of Naples.

There was, of course, a widespread belief that Venice had

---

[1] F. Fossati, *Per l'alleanza del 25 luglio, 1480* (Mortara-Vigevano, 1901). For the *condotta* of Ercole d'Este, see ASF, Riformagioni, atti pubblici, cxxxviii (25 July 1480).

[2] E. Piva, 'L'opposizione diplomatica di Venezia alle mire di Sisto IV su Pesaro e ai tentativi di una crociata contro i Turchi, 1480-81', *Nuovo archivio veneto*, ns v, vi (1903); F. Fossati, 'Nuovi documenti sull'opera di Ludovico il Moro in difesa di Costanzo Sforza, *Atti e memorie della Dep. di storia patria per le Marche*, ns i-ii (1904-5); F. Fossati, *A proposito di una usurpazione di Sisto IV nel 1480: documenti milanesi* (Vigevano, 1901).

[3] C. Foucard, 'Fonti di storia napoletana dell'Archivio di Stato di Modena: Otranto nel 1480 e nel 1481', *Archivio storico per le provincie napoletane*, vi (1881), 82-3; P. Egidi, 'La politica del regno di Napoli negli ultimi mesi dell'anno 1480', ibid. (1910), 699-705.

[4] N. Machiavelli, *Istorie fiorentine*, a cura di F. Gaeta (Milan-Feltrinelli, 1962), p. 546.

[5] Foucard, op. cit., pp. 609-28; E. Carusi, 'Osservazioni sulla guerra per il ricupero di Otranto e tre lettere inedite di Re Ferrante a Sisto IV', *Archivio della società romana di storia patria*, xxxii (1909).

actually engineered the Turkish assault, and a general fear that the Venetians would use the situation to their positive advantage by initiating some aggressive move in northern Italy.[1] However, their apparent reluctance to take advantage of the situation is perhaps an indication of their passive involvement in the whole affair. It is tempting to suggest that growing tension over Ferrara and the eventual outbreak of the war was somehow linked to the Turkish invasion, but the chronology of the events does not really bear out such a hypothesis. The build up of that tension was a slow and erratic process and there is little evidence of Venice seizing with both hands the opportunity offered by the distraction of Naples.

The position of Ferrara as a Venetian satellite had been a cause of tension between the two cities for centuries. The famous *capitoli* which gave Venetians extensive commercial concessions in Ferrara, free access to the Po, and the right to maintain a Visdomino in the city who presided over the Venetian community, went back to the twelfth century.[2] In 1405 Venice had established control over the salt pans at Comacchio and forced Ferrara to buy from the Venetian monopoly, but this in turn created constant irritations over Ferrarese salt smuggling. During the Lombardy wars the Polesine had been ceded by Venice to Ferrara in return for military support and this served to create a strident faction of Venetian landowners in the area which took every opportunity to press for aggressive action against Ferrara. The marriage of Ercole d'Este to Eleanora d'Aragona, the daughter of King Ferrante, in 1472 further aroused Venetian suspicions, and it was soon clear that Ercole intended to use his new relationship with Naples and his position in the Neapolitan League of July 1480 to strengthen his position *vis-à-vis* Venice. During the negotiations over the League in the summer of 1480 Lorenzo de'Medici had expressed his concern that Ercole d'Este was likely to draw the League into a war with Venice.[3]

All this suggests that Venetian aggressiveness was not the only explanation of the war of Ferrara, and that such aggressiveness was at least in part the result of pressure from a private interest

[1] Piva, 'L'opposizione diplomatica', i. 75–89; F. Fossati, 'Alcuni dubbi sul contegno di Venezia durante la ricuperazione d'Otranto', *Nuovo archivio veneto*, NS xii (1906); A. Bombaci, 'Venezia e l'impresa turca di Otranto, *Rivista storica italiana*, lxvi (1954).

[2] ASV, Miscellanea atti diversi, 6A, *Rei Ferrariensis liber*; Piva, *La guerra di Ferrara*, i. 9–12.

[3] ASMo, Carteggio degli ambasciatori, Firenze 2 (15 July 1480): Antonio da Montecatini to Niccolo Sadoleto in Naples.

group within Venice.[1] These indications are borne out by the events of 1481 and early 1482. The first significant flickers of alarm came in January 1481 when the Venetians, after protesting about the building of houses on the Polesine frontier which were being used by salt smugglers, sent in troops to burn them down. The tremors caused by this episode ran through the diplomatic correspondence of all the Italian courts.[2] But it was like one stone dropping into a pool; the ripples had largely dispersed when in May Vettor Contarini, a fanatical anti-Ferrarese noble, arrived in Ferrara as Visdomino, and was within weeks engaged in a row with the ecclesiastical authorities which led to his excommunication.[3] Protests from Venice and harassment of Venetians in Ferrara followed. By late August Venetian protests were changing to positive counteraction and once again the diplomats of Italy were beginning to register reactions to the increasingly threatening situation. However, throughout this period there was no evidence of a Venetian military alert.

Then on 16 September Girolamo Riario arrived in Venice. He came ostensibly to cement the papal–Venetian alliance, to negotiate a *condotta* for himself, and to receive the rank of honorary noble of the city. But his ambitions in the Romagna were well known and there were even indications that he aspired to the throne of Naples itself.[4] Venetian help was crucial to these aspirations and Venetian help could perhaps be bought by a papal offer of Ferrara. It is not known how complete the agreement was between Riario and Venice at this stage, but clearly papal favour was an essential preliminary and a decisive encouragement to any move against Ferrara. Equally clearly, however, Riario was not much liked in Venice. He earned for himself a reputation for meanness by refusing to tip the oarsmen of the *Bucentaur* and the servants in the palace that were placed at his disposal, and seemed to attach little importance to the privileges conferred upon him.[5]

By this time Otranto had finally been recaptured and in a sense Venice's opportunity had passed without the Republic having made any real effort to grasp it. But by late September decisive

[1] Piva, *La guerra di Ferrara*, i. 16 and 55.

[2] ASMo, Carteggio degli ambasciatori, Firenze 2 (3 Jan. 1481): Antonio da Montecatini to Ercole d'Este.

[3] Piva, *La guerra di Ferrara*, i. 19.

[4] ASV, Dieci, misti, 20, 32 (9 Nov. 1480); Sigismondo de' Conti, *Istorie dei suoi tempi* (Rome, 1883), i. 114–15.

[5] Piva, *La guerra di Ferrara*, i. 50–3.

moves were being made. Venice began to construct three great bastions within the Ferrarese frontiers and the tide of protest now flowed the other way.[1] For two months the League debated an appropriate response; dispatches and instructions shuttled backwards and forwards between Milan, Florence, Rome, and Naples. By December Milan and Naples began to mobilize and ambassadors of the League were sent to Ferrara to offer support to Ercole d'Este and consider putting diplomatic pressure on Venice. By January Venice seemed to be set on a course for war; troops were being called out all over Lombardy, and moved from the eastern frontier to billets in the Padovano.[2] In late January Alberto Cortese, the Ferrarese ambassador in Venice, took fright at the rising tide of feeling against him and fled from the city.[3]

It was at this stage, however, that both inevitable delays in military mobilization and the intricacies of diplomatic manœuvre intervened. None of the members of the League were anxious for war; Naples was bankrupt and not very concerned about the defence of Ferrara; Florence declared categorically in February that it could spare no men or money for Ferrara until the question of the Sienese towns was resolved;[4] Milan was preoccupied with the growing rift between Ludovico Sforza and Roberto da Sanseverino and with the rebellion of the Rossi family; all felt it essential that agreement should be reached with Federico da Montefeltro about a *condotta* with the League before there could be any question of war with Venice. But Federico refused to negotiate actively until March when his current *condotta* with Naples and the Pope was approaching its expiry date.[5] There was a widespread belief that Venice was merely trying to force Ercole d'Este out of the League and would stop short of war. This may

[1] ASV, Senatus Secreta, 30, 33 (24 Sept. 1481). On 4 Jan. 1482 1,500 Venetian infantry were ordered to garrison the new bastions (ASV, Senatus Secreta, 30, 46).

[2] ASF, Otto, responsive, 2, 161 (report of Bongianno Gianfigliazzi from Ferrara of 7 Jan. 1482); ibid. 200 (report of Pierfilippo Pandolfini from Naples on 26 Jan. 1482).

[3] Piva, *La guerra di Ferrara*, i. 67.

[4] ASF, Signoria, missive, minutari, 12, 138r–138v (instructions of Otto to Gianfigliazzi in Ferrara of 11 Feb. 1482); ASMa, Archivio Gonzaga, 1627 (Zaccaria da Pisa in Milan to Federigo Gonzaga, 16 Feb. 1482).

[5] ASF, Archivio Mediceo avanti il Principato (henceforth MAP), xlv. 198 (Giangaleazzo Sforza to Lorenzo de' Medici, 5 Dec. 1481). Federico finally agreed to open negotiations with the League on 7 Mar. 1482 which was three months before the expiry of his *condotta* with Naples and the Papacy (ASF, Otto, responsive, 2, 224; Pierfilippo Pandolfini from Naples to Otto, 4 Feb. 1482).

have been true initially but Venice was increasingly encouraged by the hope of gaining the services of Roberto da Sanseverino if he defected from Milan, and by the assurances of Riario that he would bring the Pope on to its side. In late March ambassadors of the League were in Urbino waiting impatiently while Federico consulted with his astrologers about a suitable date for signing his new *condotta*,[1] and Sanseverino was on his way to Venice to conclude terms with the Republic. On 3 April this contract was signed and Venice had a significant accretion of strength to its already powerful and by now largely mobilized standing army.[2] Venice now began to prepare a large river fleet for use on the Po and some money and infantry began at last to arrive in Ferrara from its allies.[3] On 15 April Federico da Montefeltro finally signed with the League as captain-general having persuaded the allies to accept an elaborate military plan for concerted attacks on Rome and across the Adda.[4] On 30 April Sixtus IV finally offered Ferrara to Venice.[5] Two days later Roberto da Sanseverino crossed the Tartaro on a five-mile causeway prepared by Veronese pioneers and threw his army into the heart of the still largely defenceless Ferrarese state.[6]

This complex and rather abbreviated story brings out clearly some of the interconnections between diplomacy and war which I have been seeking to stress. Ambassadors were active at every point; in Ferrara they were seeking to advise and encourage Ercole d'Este in his dilemma of whether to give in or resist; in Milan they were trying to help Ludovico Sforza resolve his internal problems and get his army ready; in Florence their role was to find a solution to the problem of the Sienese towns without driving Siena into the arms of the Venetians. Meanwhile in Rome the ambassadors of the League and of Venice were alternately

[1] ASF, MAP, LI. 103 (Luigi Guicciardini and Pierfilippo Pandolfini from Urbino to Lorenzo de' Medici, 31 Mar. 1482).

[2] R. Predelli, *I libri commemoriali della Repubblica di Venezia*, *Regesti* (Monumenti storici pubblicati della R. Dep. veneta di storia patria, 1st ser. *documenti*, vols. 3, 7, 8, 10, 11. Venice, 1879–1901) v. 268-9.

[3] The Bishop of Parma, the Milanese envoy in Ferrara, reported in early April both on the Venetian preparations and that 'in quella terra non si parla altro che di guerra benchè i vecchi et più savi non la volessino' (ASF, MAP, LI. 106; Bernardo Rucellai from Milan to Lorenzo, 4 Apr. 1482).

[4] ASF, MAP, LI. 122 (Luigi Guicciardini to Lorenzo de' Medici, 15 Apr. 1482).

[5] E. Piva, 'La cessione di Ferrara fatta da Sisto IV alla repubblica di Venezia (1482)', *Nuovo archivio veneto*, NS xiv (1907), 415.

[6] Piva, *La guerra di Ferrara*, i. 76-7.

cajoling and threatening Sixtus IV; in Naples the Milanese and
Florentines had to convince Ferrante of the necessity for war; and
in Urbino they had to cope with the vagaries and ambitions of that
great prima donna, Federico da Montefeltro. Alongside all this
activity the stage was at least partly taken up by the commanding
figures of Federico and Roberto da Sanseverino without whose
participation the war was unlikely to start, and by the 50,000 men
who were gradually preparing themselves in their billets.[1]

The war itself revealed a combination of both surprisingly
new and predictably traditional elements. Bloody battles like
Campomorto and Argenta were interspersed with periods of
manœuvre and stalemate; Albanian stradiots and Turkish janis-
saries, retained in his service by the Duke of Calabria after the fall
of Otranto, fought alongside heavily armed veterans of the wars
of the 1450s; Venetian gunners experimented with gas shells and
shrapnel while their traditional river fleets were blown out of the
water by Ferrarese guns massed on the banks of the Po; tortuous
and treacherous peace negotiations alternated with the extraordinary summit strategy conferences of princes at Cremona in
February 1483 and Milan in January 1484. Through it all the
suspicions and rivalries amongst the allies remained and Venice
emerged beleaguered, outnumbered, but with the main gains at
the peace of Bagnolo in August 1484.[2]

I have deliberately avoided placing too much emphasis on the
role of Lorenzo de' Medici in the events I have been describing,
partly because he was the subject of the brilliant Italian Lecture
given four years ago to the Academy by Nicolai Rubinstein,[3]
partly because I think that, at least for this period, his political
pre-eminence in Italy has been somewhat exaggerated. Guicciardini's identification of him as the 'ago del bilancio' has been
enormously influential in later writing, and one's view of the
judgement must be conditioned not only by one's perceptions of
his actual political contribution but also by one's understanding of
the whole nature of the balance of power and the possibility of it
being influenced or controlled by individual statesmen. However,
as a well-documented example of the relationships between one

---

[1] For lists of the troops prepared by the various states for the early stages of
the war, see Biblioteca Nazionale di Firenze, Magl. xxv. 161.

[2] C. Bonetti, 'La Dieta di Cremona', *Archivio storico lombardo*, 4th ser. x
(1908); R. Cessi, 'La pace di Bagnolo dell' agosto 1484', *Annali triestini di diritto,
economia e politica*, xii (1941).

[3] N. Rubinstein, 'Lorenzo de' Medici: the formation of his statecraft',
Proceedings of the British Academy, lxiii (1977). [Reprinted in this volume.]

Italian political leader and the ambassadors of his state, his case obviously has a great relevance to any discussion of the role of diplomacy.

What exactly was Lorenzo's role in the formation of Florentine foreign policy? How did he relate both to the formally appointed ambassadors and to the official foreign-policy committees of the Republic? Through what other mechanisms did he or might he have operated to influence that policy and the political affairs of Italy? The answers to these questions cannot be the same throughout his career, nor, I suggest, can they be along the lines of steadily tightening control. In my view, a growing authority in the 1470s was to some extent interrupted and reduced in 1480, and was only gradually recovered in the later years of the decade with Lorenzo's important links with Rome and Naples.

Lorenzo's role in Florentine foreign policy depended on a number of factors. It depended, of course, on his natural position as one of the leaders of the oligarchy, a man whose opinions were influential in the *pratiche* and whose personal influence affected the way others thought and voted. This influence was increased by his carefully cultivated and well-known contacts outside Florence and by his position at the head of Florence's leading bank, with all that that meant in terms of economic standing and access to commercial and political information passed back by Medici banks agents. Equally carefully cultivated were his contacts with the foreign ambassadors in Florence all of whom tended to regard him as their main contact within the city and some of whom would bring the letters and instructions which they received from their governments to him to see before taking them to the official foreign-policy committees of the Republic. But, there is a danger in attaching too much importance to this essentially 'external' view of Lorenzo's pre-eminence in Florence. Princes, and the ambassadors of princes, disliked dealing with republican committees and were always anxious to find a leader in Florence, a stable point with which to negotiate, and through which to influence and control the city. The Milanese ambassador, Sacramoro Sacramori, reported in 1471: 'The affairs of this city have reached the point where everything depends on a nod from Lorenzo, and nobody else counts for anything.'[1] This was patently untrue but it was the way Milan wished to see it, and the way that Sacramoro, who had Lorenzo's ear, wished to see it. But in

---

[1] A. Brown, *Bartolomeo Scala (1430–97); Chancellor of Florence* (Princeton, 1979), p. 68: 'sono reducte le cose di questa città in locho che tutto consiste in uno cenno di Lorenzo, ne crediate che altri ce siano se non per uno zero . . .'.

practical terms such contacts were clearly important for Lorenzo's reputation as knowledgeable about foreign affairs.

Lorenzo also relied to some extent on personal envoys for particular missions and negotiations. But, up to 1484 at least, he does not seem to have made much use of any system of permanent personal agents and secretaries within the embassies abroad, as Guicciardini suggested.[1] Ambassadors selected their own secretaries in this period and there is very little evidence of Lorenzo corresponding with individuals in the embassies other than the ambassadors themselves.

But, finally, Lorenzo's role did depend heavily on his personal contacts with Florence's ambassadors and the extent to which they corresponded with him while on their missions. The ambassadors during the years 1480 to 1484 can be divided into three broad categories in terms of their relationship with Lorenzo. There were those who can be best described as 'Lorenzo men', whose careers depended very largely on their links to Lorenzo and whose appointment as ambassador was presumably owed to his influence. Men such as Francesco Gaddi and Baccio Ugolini come into this category and clearly regarded themselves as primarily his agents and only formally accredited by the Republic.[2] Their correspondence with Lorenzo tended to be detailed and comprehensive; all important information was passed to him. Then there was a middle group of men who were clearly closely linked to Lorenzo and on terms of intimacy with him—either through family ties, shared interests, or neighbourhood relationships within the city—and yet who had a role and an influence in the

[1] Francesco Guicciardini, *Storie fiorentine*, ed. R. Palmarocchi (Bari, 1931), p. 79.

[2] Francesco d'Agnolo Gaddi, a noted humanist and literary figure, was one of Lorenzo's most trusted envoys. He was sent to the French court in 1479, and again in May 1480 when he remained for nearly two years, first as Lorenzo's personal envoy and from Dec. 1480 as accredited ambassador of the Republic. He had the same dual role on a mission to Naples and the Duke of Calabria in the autumn of 1482. For fuller details of his diplomatic career, see L. Sozzi, 'Lettere inedite di Philippe de Commynes a Francesco Gaddi', in *Studi di bibliografia e di storia in onore di Tommaso de Marinis* (Verona, 1964). For his letters to Lorenzo during his second mission to France which indicate his very divided allegiances, see ASF, Signoria, Otto, Dieci; legazioni e commissarie, missive e responsive, 75 *passim*.

Baccio di Luca Ugolini was another of the literary figures of the Platonic Academy and the Lorenzan circle. He was sent to France and Germany in Aug. 1478, and to the abortive Council of Basle in Sept. 1482. He was also a confidant of the Gonzaga and was frequently in Mantua (A. Della Torre, *Storia dell'Academia Platonica di Firenze* (Florence, 1902), pp. 796–800).

oligarchy of their own right. Pierfilippo Pandolfini, Bernardo Rucellai, and Bernardo Bongirolami fit naturally into this category.[1] Such ambassadors tended to be more selective in the material which they sent to Lorenzo; letters to him would contain the more confidential information and news which the writer thought would be of particular interest to him personally—but referring him to their reports to the official organs of the Republic for more standard information. Finally, there were the envoys who owed nothing to Lorenzo, who stood entirely on their own feet in the oligarchy and whose attitude to him was one of differing degrees of personal friendship. Such men tended to come from an older generation—like Antonio Ridolfi, Guidantonio Vespucci, and Luigi Guicciardini.[2] The correspondence of this group of ambassadors with Lorenzo tended to be intermittent, in so far as we can tell, and rather arbitrary in the issues which were discussed.

For all these men, however, prior to 1480, there was a tendency

---

[1] Pierfilippo di Gianozzo Pandolfini was described by Antonio da Monte-catini as 'la mano drita cum la quale se segna Lorenzo, et praecipue ne le cose de fora' (ASMo, Carteggio degli ambascratori, Firenze 2; 6 Feb. 1481). But he was also a leading member of the Florentine oligarchy and the Republic's ambas-sador in Milan (Oct. 1479-July 1480), Naples (Nov. 1481–Mar. 1482), Rome (Feb.–May 1483), and at the peace negotiations at Bagnolo in Aug. 1484. His surviving correspondence both to Lorenzo and to the Otto is very extensive. Bernardo di Giovanni Rucellai was Lorenzo's brother-in-law and another noted humanist (G. Pellegrini, *L'umanista Bernardo Rucellai e le sue opere storiche*, Livorno, 1920). He was ambassador in Milan from Feb. 1482 to Oct. 1483.

Bernardo di Giovanni Bongirolami was a lawyer and a relative newcomer to the Florentine political élite, and hence perhaps more dependent than some on Lorenzo's support. He also was ambassador in Milan from Nov. 1483 to June 1484, following on important embassies to Naples and Rome in the early 1470s.

[2] Antonio di Lorenzo Ridolfi came of the older generation of Florentine politicians and had a distinguished record of public service in the 1460s and 1470s. He was chosen as ambassador to Rome in Apr. 1480 because he was known to be on good terms with Sixtus IV (ASF, Signoria, missive originali, 4, 67–8; 16 May 1480). He remained in Rome until Dec. 1480.

Guidantonio di Giovanni Vespucci was a lawyer and very experienced diplomat. He was ambassador in France in 1479 and 1480, and in Rome for much of the period between 1481 and 1484. His letters to Lorenzo, many of which survive in ASF, MAP, are notable for their selectivity in the matters discussed, and a tendency to draw a clear distinction between his official duties as ambassador and the private business of the Medici which he handled.

Luigi di Piero Guicciardini was, like his brother Jacopo, one of the most experienced politicians in Florence and a man whose prestige and seniority made him something of a rival to Lorenzo. He was ambassador in Venice in the first half of 1480, and together with Pandolfini negotiated the *condotta* with Federico da Montefeltro in Mar./Apr. 1482.

to use Lorenzo as a sort of filter for secret and confidential information, for unverified rumour and gossip, and for expressions of opinion by the ambassador himself. At this time dispatches were addressed to the Signoria in peace-time and were frequently discussed in the Pratica and read out to ambassadors of the foreign powers.[1] These were not the best forums for the discussion of confidential issues and the revelation of the secrets which the Florentine ambassadors had learnt. So, such information was sent to Lorenzo in the knowledge that he would know how to insert it into the policy-making process. Up to 1480 Florence lacked a small semi-permanent foreign-policy committee which could appropriately handle confidential business and long-range policy like the Consiglio Segreto in Milan, and so 'the secret affairs of this government will now pass through the hands of Lorenzo, as they passed through those of his father' as the Ferrarese ambassador put it in 1469.[2]

However, part of the constitutional reforms of April 1480 was the setting up of such a foreign-policy committee—the Otto di Pratica.[3] Eight leading members of the new Council of Seventy held the responsibility for six months and ambassadors were specifically encouraged to report fully on confidential and secret affairs to the new committee.[4] The development was seen as an extension of the special authority and continuity which the Dieci di Balia had in war-time to a period of peace.[5] The Otto, indeed, had responsibility for all military affairs as well as foreign policy but could always refer particularly controversial issues to a full debate in the Council of Seventy. The impact of the setting up of the new committee on ambassadorial reporting was immediate. The ambassadors clearly felt freer to report confidential matters direct to the Otto and this accounts in part for the more intermittent

---

[1] For discussion of the conduct of Florentine foreign policy and the role of ambassadors, see E. Santini, *Firenze e i suoi oratori nel Quattrocento* (Florence, 1922) and G. Pampaloni, 'Gli organi della Repubblica fiorentina per le relazioni coll'estero', *Rivista di studi politici internazionali*, xx (1953).

[2] Rubinstein, 'Lorenzo de' Medici' above, p. 129.

[3] N. Rubinstein, *The Government of Florence under the Medici, 1434 to 1494* (Oxford, 1966), pp. 199–201.

[4] ASF, Signoria, Legazioni e commissarie, 21, 7–8ᵛ (to Antonio Ridolfi and Piero Nasi, 2 May 1480), and ASF, Otto di Pratica, Legazioni e commissarie, 1, 7 (to Luigi Guicciardini, 2 May 1480).

[5] *Memorie e ricordi di Ser Giusto di Giovanni Giusti d'Anghiari*, in Biblioteca Nazionale di Firenze, ii. ii. 127, 135ᵛ: 'Quelli trenta della Balia di Firenze elessono otto cittadini di Firenze che havessino la cura del governo loro per di fuori della terra che si può dire sieno in luogo de' Dieci di Balia' (19 Apr. 1480).

quality of the letters of some of the senior ambassadors to Lorenzo in this period.[1] Lorenzo was not a member of the first two groups of the Otto di Pratica, and although he continued to be consulted on all major issues and he clearly had access to the official ambassadorial reports, one gets the impression of him dropping a little into the background in this key area of Florentine policy-making. Undoubtedly there were many occasions within the following two years when there were fierce debates over foreign policy and military affairs; Lorenzo frequently found himself defending a minority position, both inside the Otto and outside, against hardliners who disliked the way in which Florence was seeming to be manipulated and exploited by its allies.

These insights into Lorenzo's role in foreign policy-making within Florence in these years obviously have some bearing on one's view of his influence in Italy as a whole. Foreign observers, in this period, frequently remarked that Lorenzo's reputation and authority within Florence depended to a large extent on his links with other Italian and foreign powers, and that without these his position in the city would be considerably weakened. But it is equally true that the reputation and influence of Lorenzo outside Florence depended on the extent to which he was seen by the powers to have control of the Republic's foreign policy. However, the influence of Lorenzo in the wider 'concert' of Italy was also dependent on the economic and military strengths of Florence itself. But militarily it was clearly the weakest of the five major powers and its growing reluctance actually to contribute money to the leagues in which it was involved tended to nullify its economic strength. The lack of regard for Florentine opinions and interests which was clearly apparent in the intrigues and negotiations of this period tended to negate the value of Lorenzo himself as a sort of arbiter in Italian politics, although this was a role for which both Milan and Naples occasionally cast him.

The fusion of diplomatic and military affairs in peace-time and the need for small long-serving committees that could discuss such

---

[1] The impact of the change in foreign policy direction is most apparent in the letters of Pierfilippo Pandolfini in May 1480 (ASF, Signoria, Otto, Dieci; legazioni e commissarie, missive e responsive, 10, 196–224). When Antonio da Montecatini approached Lorenzo to seek his help in persuading both the Florentine *signoria* and, more importantly, King Ferrante that Ercole d'Este's *condotta* should be agreed before the League was redrafted, Lorenzo referred him to the Otto di Pratica which had been specifically set up 'per fare le cose loro più segrete'. He refused to write direct to Naples because this would 'rompere lo ordine di questo governo apena cominciado' (ASMo, Carteggio degli ambascratori, Firenze 2, 24 May 1480).

matters in confidence and with the benefit of continuity of experience was summed up in the establishment of the Otto di Pratica in Florence. Exactly the same process was taking place in Venice with the gradual involvement of the Council of Ten in such matters. Here the development was more gradual and informal, but it was in 1480 that the Council first began to get involved in secret diplomacy while at the same time it was extending its authority over many aspects of military organization.[1] Foreign policy, diplomacy, and war, were thus playing their parts in that crucial consolidation of power which was so much a feature of the Italian political scene in the later fifteenth century.

[1] Zaccaria Barbaro, sent to Rome at the end of May 1480, was the first Venetian ambassador to write extensively to the Consiglio de' Dieci (ASV, Dieci, misti, 20, 4ᵛ–5f.). For an extended discussion of the growth of the power of the Dieci in military affairs, see J. R. Hale and M. E. Mallett, *Venice: the Military Organisation of a Renaissance State, 1400–1617* (Cambridge, 1984). Other recent discussions of the role of the Dieci are G. Cozzi, 'Authority and the Law in Renaissance Venice', *Renaissance Venice*, pp. 303–8; M. Knapton, 'Il Consiglio dei Dieci nel governo della Terraferma: un' ipotesi interpretativa per il secondo '400', *Atti del convegno 'Venezia e la Terraferma attraverso le relazioni dei rettori'* (Milan, 1981).

THE CONSCIENCE OF THE PRINCE

CONSCIENCE cropped up in so many forms in the literature and records of Western Europe in the fifteenth century
that few people, one might suppose, can have been left without
some awareness of its significance and force. Theologians discussed the ways in which men experience it and the nature of
the obligation it imposes upon them. The burden of conscience,
a man's responsibility for action in accordance with moral
judgements formulated by reason, is mandatory on the individual and must be obeyed. But it is not infallible, conscience
can err, and most of those who wrote on the subject in the lull
before the Lutheran storm stressed the importance of avoiding
error. So there grew up a whole body of case law, records of the
opinions given by bishops or preachers, and encyclopedic
collections of useful examples, the *Summae de casibus conscientiae*,
through which the teaching of theologians was mediated down
to the broadest pastoral level for the benefit of those who consulted their confessors.[1] Laymen too referred to conscience,

Note: I have used the following abbreviations:

Cart. Sf. = Carteggio Sforzesco, Archivio di Stato, Milan;

L. Miss. = Registri Lettere Missive, ibid.;

ASL = Archivio storico Lombardo;

DBI = Dizionario biografico degli Italiani;

Inv. e Reg. iii = Inventari e Regesti del R. Archivio di Stato di Milano,
vol. iii, a cura di N. Ferorelli (Milan, 1920);

Marcora, *MSDM* = C. Marcora, articles on the Archbishops of Milan in
Memorie storiche della diocesi di Milano;

RIS, NS = Muratori, Rerum Italicarum Scriptores, nuova serie.

[1] M. G. Baylor, *Action and Person: Conscience in late Scholasticism and the
Young Luther* (Brill, 1977) (I am grateful to Professor Henry Chadwick for
a reference to this book); R. Creytens, 'Les cas de conscience soumis à St.
Antonin', *Archivum fratrum Praedicatorum*, xxviii (1958), pp. 149–220; M.
Sevesi, 'I "Sermones" ed i "casus conscientiae" del B. Michele Carcano',
Studi francescani, xxviii (1931), pp. 331–2. For the *Summae*, T. N. Tentler,
'The Summa for Confessors . . .', in *The Pursuit of Holiness in late Medieval
and Renaissance Religion*, ed. C. Trinkaus and H. A. Oberman (Brill, 1974),
pp. 103–26.

sought guidance on it, attributed their actions to it, and it is probably from these documents, emanating from every literate level of society and infinitely dispersed, that the response of laymen to the obligation of conscience could best be assessed. From Isabella the Catholic Queen of Castile, whose confessor kept a 'book of the discharges of the conscience of the Queen our Lady', now lost, to the shopkeepers who set out to build the new Jerusalem in Florence under the inspiration of Savonarola, there are probably countless references that show some concern for the obligation of conscience.[1]

The conscientious prince had to take account of his actions in a dual capacity: in his private life, like any other man, and in the field of government where his decisions could affect the lives of all his subjects. There were plenty of academics—humanists and lawyers—eager to bombard the princes of Italy in the fifteenth century with instruction on how they ought to do their jobs. They wrote for the most part in very conventional terms, and were not inclined to question the advantage of a good conscience. Martino Garati, for example, who held a Chair of Civil Law in the University of Pavia in the 1430s, wrote in his treatise *De Principibus*: 'The Prince ought chiefly to seek two things, namely a good conscience and a good reputation in the eyes of men of the world.' And elsewhere, drawing on the earlier commentators: 'The Prince can pass judgement according to his true and just conscience. Let the Prince beware, however, lest his conscience be ill informed.'[2]

This formal attachment to what ought to be done was not universal. 'You can't govern states with paternosters' expressed the traditional pragmatic wisdom of Florentine statesmen, attributed quite appropriately even if incorrectly to the most successful of them all, Cosimo de' Medici the elder. And we have recently been reminded that Cosimo's contemporary, Leonardo Bruni, put the same sentiment into the mouths of those who spoke for Florence in the 1270s: 'aliter enim coelum, aliter terra regitur.'[3] When Francesco Guicciardini, three generations

---

[1] Amalia Prieto Cantero, *Casa y descargos de los reyes católicos* (Valladolid, 1969), pp. 9–11, 466–7 (Dr. Roger Highfield has kindly discussed this with me). Domenico Cecchi, *Riforma sancta et pretiosa*, reprinted in U. Mazzone, '*El buon governo*' (Florence, 1978), 181–206, *passim* (I mention these purely by way of example).

[2] G. Rondinini Soldi, *Il Tractatus de Principibus di Martino Garati da Lodi* (Milan/Varese, 1969), pp. 98 (q. 39), 148 (q. 262).

[3] *RIS*, ns, vol. xix, 3, p. 62. I owe the reference to Professor J. H. Whitfield (in 'The Machiavellian Moment', *European Studies Review*, viii (1978), p. 367).

younger than Cosimo and Bruni, set down in the private pages of his *Ricordi* the realistic experience of the 'new' school of Florentine historico-political writers of the early Cinquecento, that 'one cannot keep control of states by acting according to conscience', he was surely saying much the same thing, and none of them was far removed from Machiavelli's concise defence of the double standard of judgement: 'accusandolo il fatto, lo effetto lo scusi.'[1] The rulers of Italy in the Renaissance were certainly not noted in their behaviour for the tenderness of their response, either as private or as public persons, to the admonitions of virtue that were addressed to them, but they seem to have been less ready than the Florentine writers to associate themselves openly with the recognition of political realities. It hardly needs to be said today that the institutions of the Church embraced them from childhood, and that they continued in regular observance of its outward forms. So the seed was there, sown perhaps in the dry ground of routine habit, but there was always the chance that, watered by adversity or personal loss, it might germinate and grow.

Some twenty years ago Dr Marcora of the *Biblioteca Ambrosiana* referred to *un fattore coscienza*, an element of spirituality that he claimed to have discerned in the conduct of Ludovico Sforza, seventh Duke of Milan, in the last years of the fifteenth century. The proposition, as he recognized, was likely to be received with some scepticism, and the evidence he mentioned—that Ludovico applied to the Pope for dispensation from the Lenten fast, and that he had a *correttore* of his conscience in the person of the Prior of the Dominican convent of Santa Maria delle Grazie in Milan (to whom I shall return)—does not in fact tell us very much about the nature and depth of Ludovico's spiritual commitment. The subject was not particularly close to Dr Marcora's theme, and he did not pursue it further.[2] As it happens, however, the records of Ludovico's government do go some way to illuminate the workings of his conscience, both in his relations with the Church and in his attitude to some of the problems that the habits of society in the Renaissance forced on the attention of a ruler. They cannot of course tell us anything

---

[1] *Ricordi*, ed. R. Spongano (Florence, 1951), p. 159, quoted by M. Phillips, *Francesco Guicciardini: the Historian's Craft* (Manchester, 1977), p. 74 n. 30. Machiavelli, *Discorsi*, bk. I c. 9.

[2] Marcora, *MSDM*, v (1958), p. 341. My debt to Dr Marcora's articles will be evident. I should like to add my thanks to him for courteously responding to an enquiry.

with any certainty about the conscience of any other prince. But the territory is so very faintly charted, as far as I know, that it seems worth while to examine a case history for which a rather unusual body of evidence happens to have survived.

The dynasty that ruled Lombardy in the fifteenth century was fairly consistent in its devotional attitudes. Filippo Maria Visconti, third Duke of Milan, that strange, tormented, and superstitious man, was very punctilious in prayer. His conscience clearly troubled him in 1446, a year before he died, for he posed to a committee of rather distinguished theologians the question whether there was any way in which a ruler who had oppressed his subjects with taxes, beyond the possibility of making restitution, could hope to save his soul. He received a long, careful, and not entirely discouraging response, replete with references to 'li doctori de ragione et sacra scriptura', but the doubt remained to disturb the conscience of those who governed the Duchy for Charles V a century later.[1] Filippo's only fully acknowledged child, Bianca Maria Visconti, was a woman of firm character and devout nature, 'religiosissima et sanctissima' as the Canon Regular Matteo Bossi wrote after an audience with her, and she brought up her children in the same spirit.[2] Some of it too seems to have rubbed off on to her husband Francesco Sforza, who by 1450 had brought under his own control the ten cities of Filippo's dominion and assumed the title Duke of Milan. Francesco, in the course of his earlier career as a *condottiere* had had too much political experience of Popes to treat them with great reverence, but he was careful to seek their approval where appropriate for 'the greater quiet of his conscience' and even, in one matter, 'although we are advised that we could do it without burdening our conscience'.[3]

Ludovico Sforza was probably the most able and certainly the most intelligent of the sons of Francesco and Bianca. Fate appeared to have condemned him to the common lot of younger sons, with no great place clearly reserved for him in either State or Church. But he seems to have believed with a rooted conviction in his own capacity and destiny for the rule of men. By

---

[1] P. C. Decembrio, *Vita Philippi Mariae*, c. lxv, *RIS*, NS, vol. xx, 1, pp. 363–78. E. Verga, 'Un caso di coscienza di Filippo Maria Visconti', *ASL*, xlv (1918), pp. 427–87. For Charles V's Governors, Caracciolo and Del Vasto, see F. Chabod, *Lo Stato e la vita religiosa a Milano nell'epoca di Carlo V* (Turin, 1971), pp. 172 and n. 3, 173.

[2] Marcora, *MSDM*, i (1954), p. 238.

[3] C. Canetta, 'Spigolature d'Archivio', *ASL*, viii (1881), pp. 632–3, 631.

1480, at the age of 28, he had grasped the rule of the dominion by a series of well-taken chances, as Governor and Lieutenant for his ineffectual and sickly young nephew Giangaleazzo. When Giangaleazzo died in 1494, Ludovico brushed aside the claims of his infant son and took the office and title of Duke for himself.

There was a strong element of temperamental insecurity in Ludovico's character that enhanced his need to look to the Church for assurance. There is no doubt that this need conformed to the education planned for him by his mother, and his attachment to the Church was certainly not weakened by his marriage at the beginning of 1491 to a young girl of 15, Beatrice daughter of Ercole d'Este Duke of Ferrara. An observer described Beatrice as 'pretty, dark, a designer of new dresses, given to dancing and amusements day and night', but she was lively and full of character, certainly no nonentity.[1] Her father presided over the most devout court of Italy, and she brought something of its spirit with her. Ludovico and Beatrice accorded special patronage to the new church of the Observant order of the Dominicans in Milan, Santa Maria delle Grazie.

Ludovico had a much-loved illegitimate daughter named Bianca; Beatrice, only four or five years older, also became very fond of the child. Bianca was about sixteen when she married the man who was probably Ludovico's closest friend, Galeazzo di San Severino, the winner of tournaments and pattern of courtly grace. Five months after the wedding Bianca died, quite suddenly, on 22 November 1496. Six weeks later, a more intolerable loss, Beatrice too was dead. Pregnant with her third child, she was taken ill during an evening's dancing and died, in the night of 2–3 January 1497, in giving premature birth to a stillborn son. She was 21 years old. She lies still in effigy by the side of her unfaithful and adoring husband on the great marble tomb, originally in the apse of the church of Santa Maria delle Grazie where she was buried, but now in the left transept of the church of the Certosa of Pavia.[2]

Ludovico, twenty-four years her senior, mourned her with a sincerity it has never been possible to doubt. There are many signs of his grief, but the most consistent information comes from the reports received by the Venetian government and duly

[1] G. Lopez, *Feste di Nozze per Ludovico il Moro* (Milan, 1976), p. 64. J. Cartwright, *Beatrice d'Este Duchess of Milan* (London, 1899), is still useful.

[2] Usually attributed to Cristoforo Solari, but see F. Filippini, 'La tomba di Lodovico il Moro e Beatrice d'Este', *ASL*, NS ii (1937), pp. 198–201.

recorded by the indefatigable Marino Sanuto in his inexhaustible diary. After reporting Ludovico's initial despair, Sanuto noted in April 1497 that the Duke had become very devout after his wife's death, that he observed the fasts and lived chaste *come si divulgava* (and was it divulged without the authority of the Duke?). 'The court is no longer what it was, and at present he seems to show much fear before God.' In August Sanuto noted that the Duke went twice a day without fail to pray by the tomb of Beatrice. In May 1498 Ludovico still set aside each Tuesday as a day wholly dedicated to God, and spent much of it in Santa Maria delle Grazie.[1]

On the day Beatrice died Ludovico ordered the payment of votive offerings she had promised to the Virgin Mary for her safe confinement. A courier rode to Varese with 25 ducats for the famous shrine of Santa Maria del Monte. The church of Santa Maria di Loreto in the March of Ancona received 100 ducats.[2] It was a natural impulse to honour his wife's vows in spite of the tragic non-fulfilment of the hopes that had accompanied them. So, too, filial piety required that a son should fulfil the testamentary dispositions made by his mother for the salvation of her soul. Six months after Beatrice died Ludovico signed with his own hand an order for payment of 2,285 lire 10 soldi to the Abbot of the Cistercian house of Chiaravalle outside Milan. 'They are part of a sum of 11,000 lire for which we are debtor to the Monastery by reason of the will of the late illustrious Duchess our mother, which it is our intention to put into effect.'[3] But in this case Bianca Maria Visconti had already been dead for twenty-eight years, and Ludovico had been effective ruler of the Duchy for sixteen of them. The delay is in some measure explicable. But then, what had belatedly stirred Ludovico's conscience to his duty at this particular moment?

References to the Duke's conscience had in fact begun to appear, in letters issuing from the chancellery, in April 1497. And already before that, in March, there is a change of emphasis in the measures that were being taken to set up a Monte di Pietà in Milan. The campaign to endow these non-profit-

[1] M. Sanuto, *Diarii*, vol. i (Venice, 1879), pp. 457, 575, 746, 960. Other references on pp. 460, 463, 480, 491, 512, 630, 812.

[2] L. Miss. 204, f. 193t, 3 Jan. 1497, to the Archpriest of S. Maria del Monte. A. Luzio and R. Renier, 'Delle relazioni di Isabella d'Este Gonzaga con Ludovico e Beatrice Sforza', *ASL*, xvii (1890), p. 648 n. 1.

[3] L. Miss. 206 *bis*, f. 174t, 7 July 1497, to *Deputatis rei pecuniarie*. Repayment of his mother's and brothers' debts was confirmed in the will of 3 Dec. 1498: C. Cantù, 'Il Convento e la Chiesa delle Grazie', *ASL*, vi (1879), p. 236.

making loan banks, or pawnbroking offices, in the cities and towns of Italy, spearheaded by the mendicant orders, had been in progress for over thirty years. Some cities of the Sforza dominion—Parma, Piacenza, and Pavia where Ludovico had given full support to the efforts of the radical Franciscan preacher Bernardino da Feltre in 1493—had already set them up, while there was still certainly nothing more than a kind of embryonic pre-Monte supposed to have been opened in Milan in 1483. The endowment of a full Monte apparently met objections, perhaps from vested interests. But a group of Milanese citizens threw themselves into the cause, and eventually were able to get the Duke's consent at the beginning of July 1496 to certain specific requests that they put to him. This enabled them to start detailed planning; statutes were drafted, and accepted by the Duke in August.[1]

The terms in which Ludovico expressed his approval at this stage suggest nothing much more than polite acquiescence. Nine months later, after the death of Beatrice, he had transformed himself into the leading champion of the Monte. He allocated the offerings of himself and his court on the first Sunday after Easter 1497 for the endowment of the Monte, and made elaborate arrangements to ensure a generous response. Shortly afterwards, in an ordinance laying down procedures for getting the Monte under way, he was arrogating to himself virtually the whole credit for the enterprise. 'We have thought how much benefit and honour would accrue to our city, if a Monte di Pietà were set up in it. . . . And so for the implementation of this idea of ours (*questo nostro pensamento*) we have put great diligence and study to give beginning and form to the said Monte. And even as the work stemmed from us (*l'opera procedeva da noi*) . . . .'[2] Was it in the eyes of God or of men that

[1] P. Compostella, *Il Monte di Pietà di Milano*, vol. i (Milan, 1966), pp. 37–80, and 159–170 docs. 1–2 (in which, unlike Dr Compostella, I cannot see evidence of Ludovico's special interest). I have not seen F. Calvi, *Vicende del Monte di Pietà di Milano* (Milan, 1871), which refers to the 1483 foundation without identifying the evidence. For general accounts of the Monti, P. Holzapfel, *Die Anfänge der Montes Pietatis 1462–1515*, Veröffentlichungen aus dem Kirchenhistorischen Seminar München, Nr. 11, (Munich, 1903); V. Meneghin, *Bernardino da Feltre e i Monti di Pietà* (Vicenza, 1974); A. Milano, see below, p. 168 n. 1.

[2] Compostella, op. cit., pp. 171–7 doc. 3 (undated). See also pp. 181–3 doc. 5, decree published 17 June (the original is in L. Miss. 206 *bis*, ff. 139–42). For the offerings, Compostella, pp. 80–1, and add L. Miss. 206 *bis*, f. 24 (21 Mar. 1497, to Hieronimo Vincemala), f. 24&t (23 Mar., to Gianfrancesco Vicomercato).

Ludovico was seeking to attach to himself the credit that seems rightly to have been due to the Milanese citizens who had sponsored and worked for the establishment of a Monte?

The manner in which the Duke proceeded during this time to direct his conscience towards two issues closely linked to the foundation of the Monte may suggest the answer. The campaign for Monti di Pietà was fought to relieve the poorer part of the population from the need to have recourse to money-lenders at high rates of interest. Of money-lenders there were two kinds, the Christian and the Jewish. Christian usurers, some of whom lent money on a very large scale, broke the law of their Church, exposed themselves to the consequences of sin, and were liable ultimately to feel the need to make atonement in the hope of saving their souls. They also incurred criminal liability, to the financial profit of the Duke. A very prominent Milanese financier, Gasparino da Casate, who had begun to have mis-givings about his occupation as early as 1477, made provision on his death-bed (1491), 'desiring burial as a good and faithful Christian', for all his profits from usury to be restored. The Archbishop of Milan himself declared that Gasparino had ensured the salvation of his soul by the provision he had made for restoring his ill-gotten gains, and absolved his heirs from all claims for restitution. The government then got to work. The Deputies for Criminal Affairs assessed the usurious profit to be restored at the enormous sum of over 50,000 ducats. The government in accordance with normal practice made a com-position with the heirs for what it was thought they could pay, and agreed to settle for 20,000 ducats. By 1495 the rights of the borrowers seem to have yielded to the advantage of the Duke, who was still pursuing the heirs for 3,000 ducats. Then, four months after Beatrice's death, Ludovico Sforza showed mis-givings about his personal part in these transactions. He set out the details of the arrangement with the heirs in a long letter to the Finance Board, signed *manu propria*—evidence that the Duke was personally dealing with the matter and had read the letter. 'However,' he went on, 'it is not our intention by reason of this to add burden to our own conscience, nor to exonerate or discharge the conscience of the heirs.' The phrases recur later in the letter: 'wishing to discharge our conscience', 'exonerating our own conscience and adding the burden to the conscience of the heirs'. The point, as I understand it, is that if the heirs were morally bound in conscience to repay 50,000 ducats and the Duke had agreed to compound for 20,000, there might still be a moral responsibility for the remaining 30,000 ducats and in that case the Duke wanted to make it clear that it must rest on the conscience of the heirs and not on his own.[1]

This concern to define and limit obligations that might rest on his conscience as a result of the exercise of public authority was underlined three weeks later when Ludovico declared his position *vis-à-vis* the second category of usurers. The Sforza had accepted the presence of small Jewish communities within their dominions, sanctioned their money-lending activities, and given them the full protection of the law against the hostility of their Christian neighbours. The Duke took his profit, for the Jews paid an annual subsidy in return for the concessions granted to them.[2] Each year 'the principals of the banks of the Hebrews' were summoned to 'fare la congregatione loro' at a determined place, where they were told the sum the Duke needed and were required to make the *estimo*, the assessment, that is to allocate the total sum between themselves. Thus in 1480 the 'congregation' was summoned to meet in Piacenza on 5 February. In July the subsidy had not yet been paid in full.[3] And the Jews remained vulnerable. At the end of October, when the dilapidated state of the Ducal revenues had become a political issue, 'all the Jews of the dominion' are said to have been seized on charges of sacrilege, and were only released in December after agreeing to pay a composition of 32,000 lire, presumably on top of the subsidy already paid for the year.[4]

---

[1] Ibid., ff. 68–9t, 2 May 1497, to *Deputatis rei pecuniarie*: 'Nec tamen per questo era la intentione nostra de aggrauare la propria conscientia né exonerare né discaricare la conscientia de predicti heredi che non fossino tenuti alla restitutione de le usure extorte, nec similiter tollere jus tertii.' For the history of the case, G. Barbieri, *Economia e politica nel Ducato di Milano* (Milan, 1938), pp. 122–3; A. Noto, *Gli amici dei poveri di Milano*, 2nd ed. (Milan, 1966), pp. 191–2; L. Miss. 185, ff. 19t–20, 8 November 1491, to *Deputatis super rebus criminalibus;* L. Miss. 184A, 3 June 1491, 21 June 1491.

[2] C. Canetta, 'Spigolature', *ASL*, viii (1881), pp. 632–5. For some indications of the position of the Jews under the Sforza, E. Motta, 'Ebrei in Como ed in altre città del ducato milanese', *Periodico della Società Storica Comense*, v (1885), pp. 9–44; C. Invernizzi, 'Gli Ebrei a Pavia', *Bollettino della Società Pavese di Storia Patria*, v (1905), pp. 191–219; L. Fumi, 'L'Inquisizione Romana e lo Stato di Milano', *ASL*, xxxvii, 1 (1910), pp. 296–313.

[3] L. Miss. 146, ff. 117t–18, 27 Jan. 1480, to all Referendaries; L. Miss. 150, f. 117&t, 26 June 1480, to the Captain of Melegnano (where the 'thesorero de la universitate de li Ebrei' resided); ibid., f. 197t, to the Podestà of Piacenza: 'certe subventioni li hano a fare di proximo'.

[4] *Cronica gestorum in partibus Lombardie*, *RIS*, NS, vol. xxii, 3, pp. 81, 91 (6,000 ducats, but I have preferred the sum stated in a ducal letter of

In the long run, however, the Jews had most to fear from the popular hostility fanned by the violently anti-semitic tone of the immensely effective preacher Bernardino da Feltre and his Franciscan followers, for whom the expulsion of the Jews was a logical consequence of the foundation of Monti di Pietà. Ludovico Sforza seems to have had misgivings from quite an early stage of his rule about the activities of the Jews. There is no doubt that he ordered the expulsion of the Jews from his dominion at some time, probably in 1491 and certainly by 1492. No copy of any edict of expulsion seems to have survived, the immediate cause is totally obscure, and the expulsion was certainly not enforced with absolute rigour, for the finances available to the Monti were probably quite inadequate to take over the functions fulfilled by the Jews.[1] The correspondence about Jews in the government records is much thinner for the 1490s than it had been in the early 1480s, but Ludovico himself made no mention of the expulsion when he turned his attention in May 1497 to those activities of the Jews that lay on his own conscience. A letter addressed to the Exchequer and signed *manu propria* declared that 'our intention is to satisfy and restore everything that has come unduly into our hands'. The money for the annual subsidy paid by the Jews to the Duke could only have been acquired by usury, since they had no other resources—an apparent acknowledgement that all other economic options were closed to them. So the subsidy, paid with the fruits of usury, carried the taint, and when it came into Christian hands the sin of usury with it. 'We have been advised that we cannot keep this money with good conscience.' So 4,000 ducats a year were to be dispensed in alms, until the whole amount of the subsidy received in the years of Ludovico's rule had been paid out. The accounts had been checked, and the total amount to be dispensed added up to 75,587 ducats 40

4 Dec. to the Camera, summarized by C. Cantù in Archivio di Stato di Milano, Registri Ducali 213, p. 43).

[1] 'Essendo per noi ad honore del Salvatore nostro Jesu Cristo cazati li Judei dal Dominio nostro': Ludovico's 'political testament' (*c.*1498), G. Molini, *Documenti di storia italiana*, vol. i (Florence, 1836), p. 327. A quarter of the 'giudei espulsi dal ducato di Milano' had settled in Crema, according to a sermon of Bernardino da Feltre, July 1492: V. Meneghin, *Bernardino da Feltre*, pp. 450–1. In 1491 the community of Alessandria petitioned that a Jew should not have to leave the city: G. Barbieri, *Economia e politica*, p. 127 n. 2. For the limited resources of the Monti in general, A. Milano, 'Considerazioni sulla lotta dei Monti di Pietà contro il prestito ebraico', in *Scritti in memoria di Sally Mayer* (Jerusalem, 1956), pp. 199–223.

soldi. At the rate of 4,000 ducats a year this would take 19 years. Thereafter the payments were to continue until the illicit gains of his father and brother from the same source—amounting to 42,272 ducats—had also been cancelled out. The Pope was consulted, and in September 1497 gave licence thus to commute to works of piety 'agreed between you and your confessor' the restitution due to unknown persons. The arrangement was confirmed by the terms of Ludovico's will drawn up at the end of 1498. Though the souls of his father and brother must wait, wherever they might be, he accepted his responsibility for them in the long run, once he had cleared his own account.[1]

The Duke's conscience had begun to grapple with the sins of the Quattrocento even before he took these steps to escape from the stigma attached to usury. He wrote on 12 April 1497 to Galeazzo Visconti, privy councillor and commissioner-general of men-at-arms, evidently a sort of marshal of the household, 'We have decided not to omit any provision needed to ensure that the sin of sodomy shall not be committed in our household.' The records of lawcourts and denunciations of preachers have suggested a wide diffusion of this practice in the cities of Italy in the fifteenth century, speculatively linked to the relatively late age of marriage enforced on men by the inflationary rise in the rate of dowries.[2] However that may be, it was again the preachers of the mendicant orders who led the attack on it in the 1490s, associating it with the programme of Savonarola and his followers in Florence, leading the Council of Ten to start an inquiry into it in Venice.[3] In Milan a proclamation of 1476 had recalled that the penalty was death by fire, though this was certainly not always imposed.[4] But Ludovico Sforza's

[1] 'Et perché secundo la plena Intelligentia che habiamo hauuto, li prefati ebrei non haueuano altre Facultate saluo quelle che erano extorte et acquisite per usura, et ex consequenti tutti li loro beni erano obligati ad restitutione, ne è stato consiliato che li prefati dinari non possiamo con bona conscientia retenere.' L. Miss. 206 bis, ff. 98t–9, 22 May 1497, to Magistris intratarum ordinariarum. C. Cantù, 'Il Convento . . .', ASL, vi (1879), pp. 232–3 n. 6 (the papal brief), 236 (the will).

[2] D. Herlihy, 'Vieillir à Florence au Quattrocento', Annales, xxiv (1969), pp. 1348–9; R. C. Trexler, 'Ritual in Florence', in The pursuit of holiness, ed. Trinkaus and Oberman, pp. 234–8, 240–2, 255 (and cf. Bouwsma's comment, pp. 270–1).

[3] M. Sanuto, Diarii, vol. i, p. 61 (and p. 704, Marco Corner 'confinato a morir per sodomito', Aug. 1497). For Florence, U. Mazzone, 'El buon governo', pp. 97–111, 194–7; Trexler (see previous note), p. 255.

[4] C. Morbio, Codice Visconteo-Sforzesco (Milan, 1846), p. 483 doc. 290 (7 May 1476). For some cases in the late 1470s, Acta in Consilio Secreto

concern in April 1497 was not with the enforcement of the criminal law or of the penalties laid down in it. Galeazzo Visconti was given authority to expel from the household anyone who committed the offence, 'be he among the first that we have, showing no regard for any one, whoever he may be', and commanded to take all possible steps to ensure that the guilty did not go undetected. It is the last sentence of the letter that reveals the Duke's purpose with unequivocal clarity. 'We give you this task upon the charge of your conscience; excusing ourselves for our part before our Lord God, who has to punish you if this our will be not enforced.'[1] Thus the Prince could sign away the burden of responsibility for sin from his own person to his officer, and leave the Lord God in no doubt what He was to do about it. The sins committed in Ludovico's household troubled him for the potential consequences to himself, not to the offenders.

Ludovico Sforza remained in Milan through the summer of 1497, renouncing the usual summer round of the Duke's country residences for his vigils by the tomb of Beatrice. 'The unburdening of our conscience', the promotion of religious living, 'the advantage of places dedicated to divine worship' figure without any exceptional prominence in the records. But Ludovico now began to frame a series of measures designed to resolve all the major issues in which the authority and interests of the Duke in the rule of his dominion could come into conflict with the rights or claims of the Church.

The Dukes of Milan had always kept practical control of appointments to benefices within their dominion very firmly in their own hands. Their subjects were strictly forbidden to enter into direct communication with the Curia in Rome, and though the rule might occasionally be waived by ducal licence it was otherwise strictly enforced.[2] Throughout the years of Ludovico Sforza's rule a special secretary for ecclesiastical affairs, a minor humanist of some repute in his day called Jacopo Antiquario, dealt with all the paperwork, kept the records, prepared lists of candidates when benefices fell vacant, forwarded the Duke's

---

Mediolani, ed. A. F. Natale (Milan, 1963–9), vol. i, p. 51; vol. iii, pp. 62, 229, 254.

[1] 'Ve dasemo questa cura sopra el carico de la conscientia vostra, excusandosi noi presso nostro Signore dio el quale habia ad punire voi, quando non sia exeguita questa nostra voluntà.' L. Miss. 206 *bis*, ff. 43t–4.

[2] L. Prosdocimi, *Il diritto ecclesiastico dello Stato di Milano* (Milan, 1941), pp. 51–77. Marcora, *MSDM*, ii (1955), pp. 255–9; iii (1956), pp. 307–8.

nominations to Rome, and conducted correspondence with the Curia. He kept a 'book of promises of benefices', for a system of expectatives had grown up, used sparingly at first but rather lavishly by Ludovico Sforza. Ludovico himself was aware that all was not well, for he issued a decree in 1484 and again in 1490, revoking all letters expectative past and future because of the disputes and damage they caused, but the interests vested in the system seem to have proved too strong for it to be implemented effectively.[1]

Three administrative instructions issued in the summer of 1497 aimed at infusing a new spirit and a new order into the exercise of ecclesiastical patronage. The first, addressed to Antiquario and signed *manu propria*, was primarily a declaration of intent to give priority henceforth to the best-qualified candidate: 'so to proceed that the consent we give in the nomination of persons should not have to put us in the wrong with God': *dare graveza con Dio*, a clear reflection of the *carico di coscienza*. This commendable sentiment was hardly compatible with a system of expectatives. Two months later expectatives were abolished by letters patent, backed by letters missive signed *manu propria* to Antiquario and, for good measure, to the chancellor who worked under him. It was to be Antiquario's duty to ensure that expectatives were never again to be mentioned or, if mentioned, put into effect, 'even if we ourselves give you the order for them'. 'Know that this is our will'—the ultimate sanction of the absolute prince, to prevail in this case even against his own countermanding order, for the 'absolute' prince depended on his civil servants to protect him from his inability always to say no to the clamour of powerful subjects demanding favours for themselves and their clientage. Two weeks later, two members of the Privy Council, both trained lawyers and one of them a Bishop, were appointed as 'persons by whom controversies over benefices may be heard'. Antiquario, who was not a lawyer, was to consult them when such problems arose, rather than wrestle with them himself.[2] In fact the only

[1] Prosdocimi, pp. 66–7. *DBI*, vol. iii (Rome, 1961), pp. 470–2 for Antiquario, with very little on his secretarial functions, which can be reconstructed in detail from the records. For the *Liber promissionum beneficiorum*, a note to Bartolomeo Calco, Cart. Sf. 1085, 11 Jan. 1481; Count Giovanni Borromeo to Niccolò Negri, Cart. Sf. 1120, 20 Feb. 1495 ('Libro del Rdo. D. Jacopo Antiquario').

[2] Prosdocimi, p. 68 and n. 66, from the batch of decrees issued on 23 Dec. 1497 (Inv. e Reg. iii, p. 143 no. 13). The original instructions are in L. Miss. 206 *bis*, f. 106 (26 May, to Antiquario), ff. 204–5 (23 July, to Antiquario and

person I know to have had his tenure of a benefice subjected to investigation by this little committee—to his own intense distress and indignation—was poor Antiquario himself.[1]

Meanwhile Ludovico, continuing, as he put it, 'the examination of our affairs, so as not in any way to leave a burden on our soul nor a risk to our conscience', turned his attention to the whittling away of the proprietorial rights of churches 'when they have to do with those more powerful than themselves', whether as tenants or landlords. The extent to which the territorial endowments of the churches of Lombardy were being expropriated by their tenants in the fifteenth century seems to have been exaggerated, but the problem evidently was a substantial one.[2] Ludovico's concern predictably extended only to the 'displeasure and penalty' he himself might incur if this befell in his own dealings, and he proposed to put himself out of risk by a counter-exchange of lands between himself and the churches which held from him or of which he was a tenant. Negotiations were being conducted in Rome during July 1497 by Matteo dell'Olmo, titular Bishop of Laodicea and suffragan to the Archbishop of Milan, but the outcome is unknown to me.[3]

Of all the issues involving the 'freedom of the Church' (that phrase of sinister import to secular powers), what most directly affronted the Curia was probably the legislation, going back at least as far as 1382 and re-enacted in a decree of 1480, that forbade the Duke's subjects to seek favours or resort to the jurisdiction of courts outside the dominion. It is a measure of the seriousness of Ludovico Sforza's concern to rid his conscience of all the burdens that the tasks of government laid upon it that he was prepared to renounce so firmly established a bulwark for the Duke's sovereignty in his own dominion. Late in 1497 he instructed the Privy Council to consider what could be done,

to his chancellor Paolo Biglia), f. 274&t (5 Aug. to Cristoforo Latuada, Bishop of Glandèves, and Gian Andrea Cagnola, and to Antiquario).

[1] Antiquario to the Duke, Cart. Sf. 1139, 16 June 1498.
[2] C. M. Cipolla, 'Une crise ignorée', *Annales*, ii (1947), pp. 317–27. G. Chittolini, 'Un problema aperto', *Rivista storica italiana*, lxxxv (1973), pp. 353–93.
[3] 'Continuando lo examino de le cose nostre, per non laxarne in veruno modo graueza al anima né periculo de conscientia . . .': draft of letter to 'Mro. Mattheo de Ulmo de Como', Cart. Sf. 1137, 10 July 1497; L. Miss. 206 *bis*, f. 194t, instruction to Gualtero Bascapè and Giuliano Guascono, 19 July. For dell'Olmo, F. Ughelli, *Italia Sacra*, 2nd ed., vol. iv (Venice, 1719), pp. 272–3; Marcora, *MSDM*, iv (1957), p. 329, v (1958), pp. 382, 393.

'saving the freedom of the Church and the conscience of the Prince', to protect the Duke's subjects from the demands of foreign courts—largely a euphemism for protecting the Duke from the inclination of his subjects to apply to the Curia behind his back. The Council, in view of the spiritual penalties that could be invoked against the decree of 1480, recommended its unconditional revocation, to be followed by a supplication to the Pope for assurances, backed by an indult for which a precedent had been found, that he would refer ecclesiastical cases to suitable judges within the dominion.[1] An edict dated 28 January 1498 accordingly annulled all decrees against the freedom of the Church, and especially those prohibiting resort to Rome in lawsuits and for benefices, 'for we know not only that this could not be enforced without damage to the freedom of the Church but that it could not be allowed by us to be observed without grave offence.' The new decree, published on 8 February, was issued so as 'not to leave burden on his Lordship's conscience nor on those of his subjects'.[2] It has been supposed that this step was the price for the political support of Alexander VI, and Ludovico wrote to Rome that he had taken this action as a 'catholic and religious prince', to demonstrate his devotion to the Pope, but also 'so that we may remove all scruple from our conscience, and can live in security and tranquillity'.[3] It was the danger to himself, should he offend God's Church, that seems overwhelmingly to have predominated in his mind throughout this time.

There is little evidence to indicate whether these measures made any appreciable difference to the practice of the Duke's government in its relations with the Church, but perhaps the

[1] '. . . de aliquo temperamento per ipsos omnes Senatores cogitari debere, quo, salua libertate Ecclesiastica et Principis conscientia, subditi non trahantur extra Dominium suum ad agendas lites . . .': Cart. Sf. 1138, 4 Dec. 1497 ('Consultatio Senatus de non trahendis subditis extra dominium ad litigandum'). This mentions decrees of 1382 (Inv. e Reg. iii, p. 4 no. 60, mistakenly dated 1392?), and 1480 (ibid., p. 125 no. 46).

[2] Prosdocimi, op. cit., pp. 68–9. The decree (Inv. e Reg. iii, p. 144 no. 14) published by M. Formentini, *Il Ducato di Milano* (Milan, 1877), pp. 212–13 doc. 42, and (from a copy in the Ambrosiana) by Marcora, *MSDM*, v (1958), pp. 459–61 doc. 1. There is a copy dated 6 Feb. in Cart. Sf. 1139.

[3] Letters to the Pope and to Stefano Taverna (*residente* at Rome), 1 Feb. 1498: Marcora, *MSDM*, v, pp. 340–2. Unfortunately there is a lost Register, in the series for Milan–Como–Novara–Lodi, between L. Miss. 206 *bis*, which ends (in its present state) on 10 Oct. 1497, and 207 which opens on 7 June 1498. But I suspect the demands of conscience were largely satisfied by the end of 1497.

treatment of jurisdiction in cases of incest may have been symptomatic. Incest was a sin, it was also a crime punishable by death under Roman law, but local statutory law often gave no guidance on it. So the judges in the secular courts before which cases came tended to consult the Duke about the penalty to be imposed. Thus the Captain of Justice in Milan wrote to the Duke in 1480 about Cristoforo Brambilla, 'a man of rustic nature, a farmworker of primitive mentality', whose wife had left him seven years before and who had been found guilty in the Captain's court of incest with his daughter: 'a case which rarely befalls'.[1] I am not sure that the offence was so rare, at least in the more remote parts of the dominion, nor that it was restricted to men 'of rustic nature and primitive mentality'. The Counts Antonio and Annibale da Balbiano, writing to the Duke about a case that had arisen in their large franchise centred on Chiavenna and extending northwards as far as the Swiss border, warned him that undue leniency would make it difficult to enforce the law in future, and encourage crimes of this kind 'of which in these parts there is no lack'. Their Podestà had passed sentence in a case of confessed incest between a man of the leading family of the little town of Piuro near the border, and his sister who was *non sana de mente*. It is an interesting case, complicated by the aggressive intervention of the Swiss relatives of the man's mother from across the border, and one might suspect that the Duke was not entirely unhappy to accept the existence of powerful franchise-holders on whom the immediate brunt of exercising jurisdiction in these mountainous regions could fall. It shows the readiness of secular courts to take cognizance of cases of incest up to the end of 1497, for there was no suggestion that the judgement of the Podestà was *ultra vires*.[2] A year later, when a case of incest came before the secular court at Domodossola, the government would have none of it. 'The punishment of incest does not attach to your office but to the Bishop and those to whom he delegates it. So you should leave this case to them, and not put your sickle in another man's harvest.'[3] It seems that care was being shown,

---

[1] 'Vir rusticane nature et agricola rudis ingenii': Cart. Sf. 1084, 26 Feb. 1480. Another case in *Acta in Consilio Secreto*, vol. iii, pp. 120–1.

[2] Cart. Sf. 1157, 30 Oct. and 10 Nov. 1497 (the latter addressed to Bartolomeo Calco).

[3] 'Merauegliamo multo de la domanda ce farete: però che el punire li Incesti non specta al officio vostro ma al vescovo et quelli che ne hano carico da sua Signoria, et però uoi doueti lassare questa cura a loro et non

since the repeal of the edict of 1480, to respect the rights of ecclesiastical jurisdiction which formed a part of the freedom of the Church.

Ludovico Sforza, like his predecessors, had always professed to rule 'as a catholic Prince'. Conscience was no newcomer to the language of government in Lombardy, and references to it can be found in the years of Ludovico's rule before 1497, though they seem limited in number and scope. They might reflect no more than the personal style and language of the chancellor who drafted the letters. Three instances within a year, referring not to the Duke's conscience but to that of the recipients of the letters, were all drafted by the same chancellor, Giulio Cattaneo, and he was the kind of man who approved of sermons by radical preachers attacking the vices of the court of Rome.[1] On the other hand, a proposal made in 1484 regarding the use to which a tax on vacant benefices might be put for the benefit of the empty Treasury was referred to the suffragan Bishop of Milan, to say whether it could be done 'without burden of conscience'. He answered, firmly, no, at least not without papal dispensation.[2] Ludovico himself wrote in 1489 of his determination, 'for the discharge of our conscience', to put an end to one of the endless disputes between powerful men and families over land that called for the Duke's personal attention. Fra Giovanni Pagano, a Dominican of the Observance known 'for the purity of his conscience', had already been called on to report what 'in right and conscience' the Duke should do in the dispute, which had been in progress for at least 11 years and blood had flowed, but the involvement of the Prince's conscience probably derived from the fact that one of the parties was a churchman.[3]

mettere la falce in alienam messem.' L. Miss. 207, f. 204, 6 Nov. 1498, to *Vicario Commissarii Domiossule.*

[1] L. Miss. 146, f. 236 (to the Podestà of Milan); 150, f. 238&t (to the Podestà of Novara); 152, ff. 199t–200 (to Giovanni Maria Visconti), 24 March and 27 August 1480, 17 February 1481. P. Ghinzoni, 'Un podromo della Riforma in Milano, 1492', *ASL*, xiii (1886), p. 76. Cattaneo was not in the Privy Council office (C. Santoro, *Uffici del Dominio Sforzesco* (Milan, 1948), p. 33), but in the main chancellery.

[2] Cart. Sf. 1089, 9 Dec. 1484, one of two letters of that date from the *Prefecti rei pecuniarie* to Ludovico Sforza: 'Senza altro carico de coscientia'.

[3] 'Per discarico de la conscientia nostra, et adciò che la controversia quale vertise tra lo Rdo. Vescovo de Piasenza et li Arcelli habia fine': Cart. Sf. 1092 ,30 Apr. 1490, Ludovico to B. Calco. '. . . referatis quid in causa cuius

Between 1492 and 1496 a recurrent problem which had
caused trouble in the 1470s reappeared in the records. The
enforcement on the clergy of the *gabella del sale*, the compulsory
purchase of a fixed quantity of salt at a price decreed by the
government which had the monopoly, and of other excise
duties, was 'contrary to the freedom of the Church' and brought
automatic deprivation of spiritual services on all those involved
in it. So each year, at the beginning of Lent, the tiresome
business began of obtaining a Papal brief of absolution, to
release them from 'the worry over the unburdening of conscience'. In 1495 a suggestion was made that the Pope should
empower the Archbishop of Milan to grant absolution, 'should
your Lordship wish to confess and be absolved so that he can
receive the sacrament, and all the rest of your servants as well'
(the Papal brief had to arrive in time for Easter), but this
proposal was apparently not accepted.[1] It may be that by
1495 Ludovico's conscience, burdened by the awareness that
the recent disinheritance of his young great-nephew had no
moral justification, was becoming increasingly sensitive. There
is a suggestive emphasis in a note that Jacopo Antiquario
attached to a letter he had drafted and sent open to the Duke
for him to see before it was dispatched. The note gives no
inkling what the letter was about, but 'it seems to me',
Antiquario wrote, 'of its kind, conformable to the effect desired
and to the discharge of your Highness's conscience, for the
safeguarding of which we must always be on the alert'. And
he added, with what sounds like a bland understanding of the

fit mentio de Jure et conscientia fieri opporteat': L. Miss. 173, f. 123, 19 Feb.
1489, to 'fratri Johanni Pagnano Ord. Sti. Dominici Obseruantie' (who was
also to be involved in the case of the heirs of Gasparino da Casate). For 'la
sincerità de la cosientia sua', an undated note in Cart. Sf. 1094 to Alberto
(Ferruffino, the financial secretary?).

[1] L. Prosdocimi, *Diritto ecclesiastico*, pp. 122–4 (with references to the 1470s).
'Circa el principio de questa quadragesima, como è consueto, fo scripto alli
Ambassatori de Roma, che operasseno apresso el pontifice fosse dispensato,
che per quelli di questo stato fosse reuscito opera contra libertatem eccle-
siasticam, hauesseno absolutione da li soi confessori': B. Calco to Ludovico
Sforza, 27 Mar. 1492, in Cart. Sf. 1086, folder for Mar. 1482 (there is an
undated draft in Cart. Sf. 1094). '. . . quanto he necessario obtenere de
presente dal pontefice volendo la S. v. confessarse et essere absoluto per
poterse bene comunicare, e noi altri serutori tuti': Cart. Sf. 1120, 27 Mar.
1495, Antonio Landriani (Treasurer General) to the Duke; 24 Mar., the
same; 17 Apr., Ludovico to B. Calco. Cart. Sf. 1134, 30 and 31 Mar. 1496,
Deputati rei pecuniarie to the Duke, and the Duke to B. Calco. There was more
trouble over this in 1510 and 1514: Marcora, *MSDM*, v (1958), pp. 406–11.

Duke's requirements, that by using the procedure he proposed, 'there will be less burden to fear before God, and very certain escape from the blame of men'.[1] By 1495, at least, Ludovico's conscience was already sensitive to particular cases, but it was only during the year after Beatrice's death that general issues confronting his conscience in the context of his responsibilities as a ruler received a concentrated attention to which I think it would be difficult to find a parallel.

Naturally the Duke did not have to discover unaided what measures conscience required of him, though presumably the initiative came from Ludovico himself. He took counsel as a matter of course, and we have seen instances of it, on what in conscience he should do. It is possible to identify with some confidence three men who were close to the spiritual impulses of Ludovico Sforza and who had some influence on the steps he took for the unburdening of his conscience in 1497.

The Duke's confessor of course had a special responsibility in this sphere. Ludovico's confessor in the 1490s was a Tuscan from Montepulciano, an Augustinian Canon Regular called Bernardino d'Ilcino, for whom Ludovico secured preferment to the little see of Bobbio. Ludovico asked him in 1495 to report 'what we can do, with a safe conscience, about the boy that our cousin madonna Beatrice wants to have in her household, and added that 'we place ourselves entirely upon your conscience'.[2] But it seems that the Bishop did not always wait to be asked. A petition came in to the government in April 1497 from an unpaid creditor of the Podestà of Bobbio, who was a protégé of the Bishop. So the letter of complaint was passed on to the Bishop, 'and since you are wont to pass people on to us at times, when you think that in conscience we should make some provision, it has seemed appropriate to pass this one on to you; and when you have studied his petition, you are to report to us

---

[1] 'La quale ad me pare, che in suo genere sia congrua per lo effecto predicto: et per lo discarico de la conscientia de la celsitudine v., ad quam conseruandam est semper aduertendum; che saltem andando la cosa per la via ordinaria, et cum auctorità de lo judice ecclesiastico, se ne pò timere manco graueza apresso Dio, et certissimo effugio del biasmo humano.' Cart. Sf. 1120, 19 Mar. 1495. Ibid., 13 Apr. 1495, Giovanni Molo, secretary for criminal justice, replied to an enquiry from the Duke 'se ho casa alcuna per l'officio mio de recordare de conscientia'.

[2] '... quello che per noi se possi fare salua conscientia nel facto de quello puto ... In questo noi repossaremo in tutto sopra la conscientia vostra': L. Miss. 199, f. 126t, 6 Apr. 1495, to *D. Bernardino Episcopo Bobiensi*. F. Ughelli, *Italia Sacra*, ed. cit., vol. iv, p. 947 for d'Ilcino.

on your conscience what provision you think we should make upon it'.[1] It seems an unlikely point in time for Ludovico to be making sport over a matter of conscience, but one can hardly escape the conclusion that he sometimes found his confessor tiresomely officious in the fulfilment of his duties.

Perhaps this accounts for the appearance of a partner for him, under the terms of Ludovico's will at the end of 1498, in the task allotted to him by the Pope a year earlier of distributing the profits of usury in pious works.[2] The partner was in fact the man to whom Ludovico seems to have transferred some at least of the care of his conscience, Vincenzo Bandelli of Castelnuovo Scrivia, Prior of Santa Maria delle Grazie from 1495 to 1500. Bandelli, butt of one of Vasari's lively and unreliable stories and uncle of Matteo Bandello the writer of *novelle*, was a powerful figure in teaching and government among the Dominicans of the Observance in Italy. He had ample opportunity to bring his influence to bear on the Duke, for Ludovico seems to have welcomed his company and is said to have dined with him twice a week in the course of his visits to the tomb of Beatrice.[3] Ludovico certainly referred cases to him as a moral arbiter at this time. In one case Bandelli gave his opinion on what would win praise 'before God and among men'. In another, he reported, with a secular jurist, what the Duke should do 'in right and conscience'.[4]

A Papal brief of 9 March 1497 instructed fra Domenico Ponzone of the Observant order of St. Francis to go to Milan, at the urgent request of the Duke in view of his high regard for the friar's moral qualities, and to stay there for as long as the Duke wished.[5] Ponzone, who had an academic training, was in very great demand throughout northern Italy, like his fellow

[1] 'Et perché voi sete solito alle volte redriciarne qualchuno, parendoui che per conscientia gli habiamo prouedere, così a noi è parso redriciarui dicto abetore (?), perché examinato la petitione sua, in conscientia ce habiate referire quale prouisione ve pare che lì habiamo fare.' L. Miss. 206 *bis*, f. 54t, 20 Apr. 1497.

[2] See above, p. 169 and n. 1.

[3] D. Pino, *Storia genuina del Cenacolo* (Milan, 1796), pp. 72–3. For Bandelli, *DBI*, vol v (Rome, 1963), pp. 666–7.

[4] 'Ne avrà lode appresso Dio et appresso li homini': C. Santoro, 'Un registro di doti sforzeschi', *ASL*, 8th series, iv (1953), p. 156, doc. 24, 19 Apr. 1497 (but I doubt whether Bandelli was a Councillor). 'An secundum conscientiam vostra Excellentia me habia poduto dare tal licentia': Cart. Sf. 1140, 25 Oct. 1498, Johannes Antonius ex Marchionibus Incise et Rochete to the Duke.

[5] P. Compostella, *Monte di Pietà*, vol. i, p. 21 n. 30.

minorite Bernardino da Feltre, as a radical hell-fire preacher and as a committed champion of Monti di Pietà. He is supposed to have played a large part in the foundation of the embryonic Monte at Milan in 1483 and of the Monte itself in 1496.[1] He was well known in Florence, where his battle against Savonarola from the pulpit of Santa Croce in the overheated politico-religious atmosphere of 1495 led to the allegation, for which no impartial evidence exists, that he was an agent of Ludovico Sforza. In Venice, from the pulpit of San Polo, he led the denunciation of sodomy that moved the Council of Ten in 1496 to initiate a thorough inquiry, as Sanuto recorded, into 'a vice that was very prevalent in this city'.[2] So his affiliation with some aspects of the programme for the unburdening of Ludovico's conscience in 1497 is especially clear. A reference to his intercession with the Duke on behalf of a disloyal subject suggests that he did in fact go to Milan, but we do not know how long he stayed there.[3]

These pointers, however incomplete they may be, do at least give us some idea of the kind of spiritual environment in which Ludovico Sforza chose to immerse himself after his wife's death. There may have been others of their kind near him, like the friar Bernardino Caimi.[4] The Sforza had shown special favour to the Observant orders, which attracted most of what talent and fervour were to be found in the Church in Lombardy in the second half of the fifteenth century. Attempts to purge and reform lax communities, regularly supported by the dynasty, seem to have reached a climax in the 1490s, with the active encouragement of Ludovico Sforza whose intervention might be said to have attained almost caesaro-papal proportions by 1498. Matteo Bandello asserts in one of his *novelle* that Ludovico had formed the intention, in these last years of his rule, 'to reform all the clergy, and every other kind of religious

[1] Ibid., pp. 18–22. Ed. V. Meneghin. *Documenti vari intorno al B. Bernardino Tomitano da Feltre* (Rome, 1966), ad indicem.

[2] M. Sanuto, *Diarii*, vol. i, p. 61. For Ponzone's feud with Savonarola, C. Cannarozzi, 'Il pensiero di fra Mariano da Firenze', *Studi Francescani*, xxvi (1929), pp. 125–32 (not referred to by Ridolfi or Weinstein who accept Parenti's pro-Savonarolan version).

[3] L. Miss. 206 *bis*, ff. 143t–4, 17 June 1497, to *Magistris intratarum extraordinariarum*. Ponzone died in Rome in 1499.

[4] For whom see *DBI*, vol. xvi (Rome, 1973), pp. 347–9. His undated letter of condolence to Ludovico Sforza on the death of Beatrice, written in Venice on his return from the eastern Mediterranean, claims a certain closeness with both of them: Cart. Sf. 1137, folder for Jan. 1497.

persons' in the dominion, and that only his overthrow by the French in 1499 halted the plan. The measures sanctioned by the Duke in many religious houses go some way to justify the claim, at least as a general aspiration if not as a precisely articulated programme.[1] Ludovico Sforza had always taken a passionate interest in sermons and theological debate, and seems to have given an equally warm welcome to every style of preacher.[2] But again it was the Observants who were most favoured, both at court and when the Duke intervened in the selection of preachers for the churches of the dominion. The appointment of preachers was a sensitive area, partly because it afforded cover for the infighting of local parties. But it also gave the Duke an opportunity to express his sense of responsibility for the spiritual as well as the physical well-being of his subjects. At the beginning of 1499, when the local authorities protested that the monopoly granted for many years past to the Franciscan Observants in the pulpit of the Greater Church at Caravaggio infringed 'the liberty of their Church', the government replied that the Duke had acted simply 'to make better provision for the safety of your souls', and not because he wished to interfere with the freedom of the Church.[3] It was not always easy to see where duty ended and encroachment began.

It seems, then, that the death of Beatrice intensified an innate susceptibility in Ludovico Sforza to the teachings of the Church, and an already well-developed inclination to support the work of those elements in the Church that were most actively and directly striving to contribute to the improvement of the

[1] Marcora, *MSDM*, v (1958), pp. 351–62. E. Cattaneo in *Storia di Milano*, vol. ix (Milan, 1961), pp. 574–692, *passim*. Matteo Bandello, *Novelle*, lib. iii. no. 19, ed. Brognoligo, vol. iv (Bari, 1911), p. 247, quoted by Cattaneo, p. 585 n. 6.

[2] e.g. P. Ghinzoni, 'Podromo della Riforma', *ASL*, xiii (1886), p. 87; Marcora, *MSDM*, v (1958), pp. 356–7, 358–9; ed. V. Meneghin, *Documenti vari*, (Rome, 1966), p. 180 doc, 118. For the traditional story of his reception of Bernardino da Feltre, L. Wadding, *Annales Minorum*, vol. xv (Rome, 1736), p. 5.

[3] L. Miss. 207, ff. 235 (25 Nov. 1498, to the *Commissario*), 313t–14 (16 Jan. 1499, to the communtiy): 'non è facta per alterare la libertate sua . . . Nostra intentione non è impedire la libertà de dicta vostra ciesia.' Conflicts over allocation of the pulpit went back well before 1483: 'Per obviare ad omne altercatione potesse nascere tra li homini de quella nostra terra per casone de predicatori gli habiano ad predicare come per altri tempi è nasciuta . . .': L. Miss. 157, f. 113&t, to *Commissario* and Podestà, 13 Feb. 1483, and ff. 121t, 126, 130&t.

spiritual and material condition of the people.[1] Certain reservations have to be made. 'The safety of our state' always came first in the priorities of a prince. There were the inevitable practical dilemmas of power. The threat of arbitrary treatment could often be the quickest way of bringing recalcitrant ecclesiastics to heel. Even among the Observants, some of the leading figures found themselves banned at one time or another from the dominions of the Sforza: the Franciscan Michele Carcano in the 1470s, the Dominican Angelo da Chivasso for a brief time in 1481.[2] It seemed uncertain in 1491 whether Bernardino da Feltre would be allowed to come and preach in Milan, and when he did arrive at the end of the year he was accused of upsetting the people, but Ludovico after hearing him preach for two hours declared himself well satisfied.[3] Even in March 1498 the Vicar General of the Franciscan Observants, Gerolamo Tornielli, was forbidden to set foot in the dominion, for no reason given other than 'because we will not tolerate him', but this may have been no more than a customary way of bringing pressure to bear for the quick settlement of a minor difference, for the Chapter of the Order duly met in Milan a few months later, to the Duke's great satisfaction.[4] In an atmosphere that encouraged authoritarian attitudes, the Duke expected due obedience in return for his support and favour.

When the Archbishop of Milan lay dying at the beginning of October 1497, Ludovico set out to secure the succession to the Metropolitan see for Cardinal Ippolito d'Este, Beatrice's brother, a young man not quite 18 years old. The appointment had unfortunate consequences for the spiritual well-being of the diocese. It is difficult at first sight to understand how it can have seemed compatible with the impulse towards reform of the

[1] See above, p. 180 n. 1. For the spiritual and social climate of the time, G. Barbieri, *Bernardino da Feltre nella storia sociale del Rinascimento* (Milan, 1962), and A. Noto, *Origine del Luogo Pio della Carità* (Milan, 1962). For a less favourable view of Bernardino da Feltre, Matteo Bandello, *Novelle*, lib. iii no. 10 (ed. Brognoligo, vol. iv, pp. 183–9); and no. 14, pp. 205–9, for another Dominican comment on the style of the Franciscans.

[2] *DBI*, vol. xix (Rome, 1976), pp. 742–4 for Carcano. M. Sevesi, 'Beato Michele Carcano: documenti inediti', *Archivum Franciscanum Historicum*, xxxiii (1940), pp. 405–8, docs. 16–21, for Angelo da Chivasso.

[3] L. Wadding, *Annales Minorum*, vol. xiv (Rome, 1735), pp. 516–17; ed. V. Meneghin, *Documenti vari*, pp. 163 doc. 107, 164 n. 2, 178–88 docs. 117–24.

[4] Marcora, *MSDM*, v (1958), p. 358 and n. 46. Tornielli too was a champion of the Monti: P. Compostella, *Il Monte di Pietà*, vol. i (Milan, 1966), pp. 23–4; V. Meneghin, *Bernardino da Feltre* (Vicenza, 1974), ad indicem.

clergy, and one wonders what Ludovico's spiritual advisers can have thought or said about it. A Canon Regular at Verona, outside the dominion, horrified at so blatantly unsuitable an appointment, wrote in protest to the Duke. Ludovico, aware perhaps that some valid grounds for criticism existed, authorized a reply, seeking to explain and justify his action, in measured and reasoned and quite unauthoritarian terms. The arguments seem superficial today, and begged large questions at the time. Even if, as the letter suggests, Ippolito d'Este already displayed those natural qualities that were to earn him the praise of the literary men of the time, of Ariosto and Castiglione and Luigi da Porto, he seems to have given little real ground for supposing that they were likely to be effectively deployed 'for the fulfilment of divine worship'. Nor did the fact that he was a Cardinal give any very certain guarantee of the due performance of his diocesan duties.[1] Had this appointment been promised to Beatrice, and was this another offering to her memory? If it really left no burden on Ludovico's conscience, it was probably because he accepted a limited concept of the functions and responsibilities of an Archbishop that was certainly widely held in the fifteenth century though it was far from universal. The duties of spiritual leader and governor could be delegated to suitable subordinates, leaving the Cardinal Archbishop free to play the part of an ecclesiastical politician and statesman. But in this case one can perhaps see too a confirmation of Ludovico's wish to assume a larger directing part for himself, in the confidence that he himself could direct the Church in his own dominions to its best advantage through a complaisant Archbishop and his subordinates.[2]

One cannot expect that men and women will always act in a consistent way. Cecilia Ady, in her elegant and learned lecture on the morals and manners of the Quattrocento, delivered to this Academy 37 years ago, quoted Castiglione's maxim that 'devotion to God is the duty of all and especially of princes', and added the rider that 'the first duty of the man of the Renaissance was to himself'.[3] She knew Ludovico Sforza well, and saw him

[1] P. Ghinzoni, 'Altre notizie su don Celso Maffei da Verona', *ASL*, x (1883), pp. 86–7. Marcora, *MSDM*, iv (1957), pp. 369–70.

[2] Marcora, *MSDM*, v (1958), especially pp. 342–4. E. Cattaneo in *Storia di Milano*, vol. ix (Milan, 1961), pp. 527–31.

[3] *Ante*, vol. xxviii (1942), p. 188, and (for Ludovico Sforza) p. 189. And in general, for Ludovico and Beatrice, C. M. Ady, *History of Milan under the Sforza* (London, 1907).

as a pattern of the Renaissance prince. The measures for the exculpation of the Duke's conscience that we have examined were certainly consistent in purpose, and their message was unmistakably that his first duty was to himself. The ruler's responsibility before God for the well-being of his subjects was a commonplace in the language of the Duke's chancellery, and there is no reason to doubt Ludovico's good intentions in the field of government. But the unedifying aspects of the morals and manners of the Quattrocento that passed under his review in 1497 alarmed him, so far as our evidence takes us, only out of fear that he might be held to account for the sins of others. His wife's death clearly made a powerful impact on a nature already quite sensitively attuned to the demands of conscience, but the area of government in which the demand was met was so carefully limited as to raise serious doubts about a spiritual change of heart at any but a rather superficial level. Given the constraints of the political environment, it would perhaps be unreasonable to expect more. With all his enthusiasm for radical preachers and all his anxiety over the burdens on his conscience, Ludovico Sforza had neither the courage nor the originality to escape from the cocoon of custom that drained so much of the content out of the religious life of the fifteenth century.

We have gone a long way round and arrived at a rather negative conclusion. But travelling hopefully in the wake of Ludovico's conscience, observing the fears and aspirations that marked its progress and the compromises that attended its discharge, we may perhaps have seen a little more of the pattern of habits and ways of thought which helped to shape the character of the rule of princes in Italy during the Renaissance.

THE VATICAN STANZE: FUNCTIONS
AND DECORATION

I THINK I should begin by defining the scope of this lecture. We shall be looking most closely at the three Vatican Stanze painted by Raphael, and considering the relationship between the design and subject-matter of their decoration on the one hand and their functions on the other.[1] But I should maintain that they cannot be understood in isolation, but they must be read in the context of the whole papal apartment of which they form a minor part; and so we shall begin with a necessarily abbreviated survey of the whole apartment, from which I hope to demonstrate, in two simpler cases, the proposition that a recovery of the functions of these rooms can indeed yield a direct explanation of their decoration.[2] For the title I chose the less elegant plural—Functions—because I wanted to draw attention to one complication among so many which I must pass by, which is that the purposes of the separate parts of the papal apartment are subject to confusing but not casual change, and that these changes must be brought into exact chronological correlation with the decoration if the result is to make any sense. Historians never fail to over-simplify, and I do not expect to be an exception; but one of their worst habits, which in this case we *must* avoid, is the neglect of the intrinsic dynamics of historical problems, by which I mean the assumption that the purposes of enterprises remain the same from start to finish, and that it is only exterior factors, like time, personalities, and politics, that change. What we shall see is that in some papal rooms intentions survived changes of both patron and responsible artist; but in each of the Stanze the decorative enterprise was radically changed, and the function was changed in two of them.

This is a lecture about a problem and not about heroes, so I want to introduce the heroes at this point. I shall be talking about the contributions of only two popes, who were in their profoundly different ways remarkable men. The first was

John Shearman

Giuliano della Rovere, nephew of Sixtus IV, who became Pope Julius II late in 1503; he died in February 1513 and was succeeded in March by Giovanni de' Medici, son of Lorenzo *il magnifico*, who reigned as Leo X until 1521. The elements of continuity and change in the ecclesiological and political ambitions of these two popes are matched by continuity and change in the total programme of reconstructing the papal apartment begun by the first and virtually completed by the second. In somewhat the same way Bramante, who was the chosen director and architect of the Julian programme, and who died in 1514, was succeeded by Raphael, who died in 1520. Raphael had, of course, been active in the programme as a partly independent agent with special responsibilities since the second half of 1508. For the purposes of this lecture I feel that I do not need to distinguish between Raphael and his workshop. I do not know a certain portrait of my fifth hero, the papal Master of Ceremonies Paris de Grassis (Crassus to his enemies), who was, from his appointment by Julius in 1504 to his retirement after the death of Leo, a diligent and, one suspects, reluctant witness of all novelties which might change the proper order of things.[3] He belonged to that blessed and maligned breed of men we call pedants, and he was obsessed by the necessity of being understood; without the manuscripts of his diary and the precision of his notes I should have fewer dates and identifications to give you, and the ice would be too thin even to skate round the edges of this problem.

Julius took up residence in the Vatican with one rare memory: he had been papal legate at Avignon, and thus he had known a papal residence not only considerably larger than the Vatican in 1503, but also one more completely and impressively equipped for ceremonial.[4] I think this memory was crucial when he drew up a programme for modernizing and amplifying the Vatican Palace. It was to include, for example, an enormous and never-realized Hall for Conclaves, a feature at Avignon;[5] and I suspect that his recollection of the grand staircase there prompted his major structural alteration in the Vatican. At all events it was with the staircases of the Vatican that he began. In May 1506, a month or so after laying the foundation-stone of New Saint Peter's, he demolished the old ceremonial staircase (No. 1 on the plan, fig. 1) that led from the portico of the basilica to the Hall of the Royal Consistories, the Sala Regia (No. 2).[6] This was, in fact, the first stage of a total reconstruction of the pontifical route from the private suite to public ceremonies in Consis-

Fig. 1. Plan of the Vatican Palace, *c.* 1506–20, on second and third levels.
Key: (1) Via Iulia nova (staircase from Saint Peter's); (2) Sala Regia (Aula
prima, Royal Consistory); (3) Sistine Chapel (Capella palatina); (4) Sala
Ducale (Aula secunda); (5) Sala Ducale (Aula tertia, Public Consistory);
(6) Cordonata; (7) Sala vecchia degli Svizzeri (Camera de' Paramenti);
(8) Sala de' Palafrenieri (Camera del Papagallo, Secret Consistory); (9)
Camera del Papa (bedroom); (10) Chapel of Nicolas V (Capella secreta);
(11) Anticamera secreta; (12) Sala di Costantino (Aula pontificum superior);
(13) Stanza d'Eliodoro (Audientia?); (14) Stanza della Segnatura (Bibliotheca
Iulia, Studio?); (15) Stanza dell'Incendio (Signatura, Triclinium penitius);
(16) Torre Borgia (Guardaroba); (17) Loggia.

tory (5 or 2), the Sistine Chapel (3), or Saint Peter's; and it
followed from his decision taken some time before November
1505, to remove his living quarters from the Borgia Apartments
on the second level of the palace, back to the third level where
they had certainly been, but perhaps as summer quarters only,
in the time of Nicolas V, fifty years earlier.[7] This decision led to
a staircase of such amplitude that it was possible to ascend on
horseback from Saint Peter's to the top level of the palace; but
it was a decision with several other results, which we can best
approach by starting from the other end, that is the private
papal chambers themselves.

The essential nucleus of a papal private apartment in this period is a bedroom, an *anticamera*, and a *capella quotidiana* where the pope may daily perform the Mass.[8] On the third level these were accommodated at the East side of the central court-yard, known now as the Cortile del Papagallo. His bedroom (No. 9) led on one side directly into the chapel, which is the one decorated for Nicolas V by Fra Angelico (No. 10), and on the other into the *anticamera* (No. 11).[9] The sequence of events, so far as I can reconstruct it, is as follows: after his return from Bologna, on 28 March 1507, Julius did not immediately go back to the upper suite which he had occupied in 1505 and 1506, but he lived in the Borgia Apartments; he abandoned the latter, definitively, in November 1507 when he settled in the *mansiones superiores*.[10] The delay is likely to have been caused by the very finality of that decision, entailing reconstruction and redecoration of the upper suite at this date. In December 1507 the chapel was in use and described as *nuper restaurata*,[11] which I hope means no more than the rebuilding of the entrance doors, particularly the very splendidly framed one from the hall outside which used to have a pair of intarsia leaves with Julius's emblems.[12] (Each arrow on the plan represents a Julian door-frame, and the direction of entrance it implies.) The reconstruc-tion of the bedroom, so far as Julius was concerned, was mainly a matter of woodwork—one half of a ceiling carved with his arms survives,[13] and we learn that it was also lined with wood panelling from a diplomat's description of a comic scene in December 1512 when Julius became so deep in discussion with the Venetian ambassador that neither noticed that the fire had so far escaped the fireplace as to reach the ceiling.[14] Leo X added a majolica tiled floor and a new fireplace.[15]

The *anticamera* (No. 11) has been totally gutted, and its fire-place has been removed;[16] all that remains of the original decoration is a Julian door of white grey-veined marble which leads, by one step up, into the bedroom, another which leads by a passage to the Stanze, and fine stone window-seats like those of the Stanze. Its vault was decorated with 'bellissime pitture'—but perhaps for Leo rather than Julius—and its walls were hung with tapestries which were unequivocally Julian, and so impressive that they came to Michiel's mind as a term of comparison when Raphael's Leonine tapestries were first hung in the Sistine Chapel.[17] Here the pope, seated on his *Sede camerale*, would receive visitors;[18] and it seems to me very probable that it was particularly in this position that Raphael represented him in the portrait in the National Gallery, seated on a *sede camerale* in the corner of a room hung with richly woven green tapestry. The *anticamera* may be the *camera del broccato* for which Leo provided a new floor in 1518, and which I cannot locate elsewhere.[19] By an odd accident a copy of Raphael's portrait now hangs in the *anticamera*.

This private suite must communicate directly, for ceremonial and liturgical reasons, with two semi-public halls which I can best introduce by describing the sequence of events before a Mass or Public Consistory. These two halls are robing-rooms, and in the outer one, the *Camera de' Paramenti* (7), the cardinals receive their robes; they then pass into the inner one, called (as I shall explain later) the *Camera del Papagallo* (8), where they await the pope's appearance.[20] He is provided not only with a throne but also with a ceremonial bed for robing,[21] and when that operation is at length complete[22] the pope and cardinals pass through the *Camera de' Paramenti* to Public Consistory, or through the Consistory Halls (5 and 2) to Mass in the Sistine Chapel (3) or Saint Peter's. It is at this point that we can return to the ceremonial staircase; for the rooms I have described so far were to be, in Julius's new scheme, on the level above the Consistory Halls, and the existing communication between the two was very cramped.[23] Julius required—as Leo, on the whole, did not—to be transported through this long sequence not, indeed, on horseback but on the *sede gestatoria*, which posed some of the same problems. The necessarily moderate slope entailed length, and a staircase of the requisite length could not be accommodated within the existing building. It was provided in a new wing to the South (6), which is buttressed by a new Eastern façade, the second and third levels of which are the celebrated Logge (17). The part of this loggia-façade which masks the main block of the palace in fact replaces a medieval three-tier loggia which, like the loggia of Pius II's palace at Pienza, overlooked the *giardino segreto* and the best view, in this case of Rome.[24] But the new and extended loggia-façade seems to have been intended from the start to mark out the flank of an enormous rectangular courtyard, not unlike the present Cortile di San Damaso but in fact completely enclosed.[25] The staircase (6) which leads down from the third to the second level, and thus via the Consistory Halls (5 and 2) and another new flight (1) to Saint Peter's, also continues directly down to a *portone* in the centre of the loggia-façade, which should be the new principal entrance.[26] The ceremonial staircase, the so-called *cordonata* of Bramante, did in its original form allow ascent to the papal apartment on horseback, as its name implies and as diplomatic correspondence testifies.[27] It was probably begun when the new loggia-façade was begun, also to Bramante's design, and that was some time before the end of 1509.[28] The third flight was under construction in August 1513, that is some six months after Julius's death; the logge themselves had probably been brought to this level before his death.[29]

Now let us return to the two robing-rooms (7 and 8), but noticing first that they and the intimate papal chambers repeat in function and relationship a set of rooms below. There too the first of the big rooms was the *Camera de' Paramenti*, the second the *Camera del Papagallo*, distinguished only by the adjective 'lower'. The name *Camera del Papagallo* refers to one of its trivial but presumably most striking functions, which was—and had been since the medieval period—to house a caged parrot.[30] These two robing-rooms, however, serve other more serious purposes when the pope is not on his way to public ceremonies. The inner room, in spite of the parrot, was the proper location of the Secret (that is to say, normal) Consistory;[31] the outer room at this date housed the guard of door-keepers, *ostiarii*, and here an ambassador would wait before admission to the Consistory.[32]

In April 1506, apparently for the first time, Julius held the Secret Consistory 'in aula Papagalli superiori',[33] and in November 1507—that is to say when he moved into the new private suite—he began to use the two upper halls for robing before Mass.[34] Julius in fact died not in his bedroom (9) but in the upper hall immediately outside it (8).[35] The decoration of these two halls had been begun before his death. The outer one, now known as the Sala vecchia degli Svizzeri, has three Julian doors[36] and a massive stone fireplace which is probably a late work of Bramante's and Julian too. The inner hall, later called the Sala de' Palafrenieri, has three Julian doors, to the chapel, the bedroom and the *anticamera*, and it had a fireplace on the North wall which has disappeared.[37] The outer hall was also given a superb gilt, compartmented, wooden ceiling, which is really one of the most important examples of a type particularly characteristic of Roman Cinquecento architecture (Pl. 21). The arms and emblems, including *bronconi* interwoven along the frames, are those of Leo X, and I see no reason to question Vasari's general attribution of all the gilt wooden ceilings in this part of the palace to Raphael.[38] The rectangular panels of grotesque-relief which include the Medici Yoke are consistent

PLATE 21

a. Raphael and Giovanni Barile, ceiling of the Sala vecchia degli Svizzeri, Vatican Palace (detail); wood, gilt, and painted.

b. Raphael and Giovanni Barile, ceiling of the Sala vecchia degli Svizzeri, Vatican Palace (detail); wood, gilt, and painted.

PLATE 22

Workshop of Raphael, fictive intarsia basamento, Stanza della Segnatura; fresco (*photo*: Archivio fotografico, Gallerie e Musei Vaticani).

PLATE 23

Fra Giovanni da Verona, lining of door of Stanza della Segnatura; intarsia
(*photo*: Archivio fotografico, Gallerie e Musei Vaticani).

PLATE 24

Exterior door to Stanza dell'Incendio, Vatican Palace.

in style with the decoration of the window-embrasures of the Stanza d'Eliodoro, to be dated 1514–15. The ceiling incorporates end-panels the full width of the room, each bearing an inscription. The text over the entrance to the Consistory, from Proverbs 8, was no doubt addressed, in the first place, to the visitor to that assembly: 'Blessed is the man that heareth me, watching daily at my gates, waiting at the posts of my doors' (many an ambassador must have thought that only too pertinent); and the text the other end, which I take to be addressed more especially to those *ostiarii* whom Paris de Grassis describes mounting guard in the *Camera de' Paramenti*, is from Psalm 134: 'Praise ye the name of the Lord, praise him O ye servants of the Lord; Ye that stand in the house of the Lord, and the entrances of the house of our God'.[39] The walls were decorated by Giovanni da Udine, who painted a frieze of lions, *putti*, papal arms, and grotesques, above fictive marble panelling in imitation of wall-surfaces like those of the Pantheon (the absence of any figurative subjects is striking, but appropriate to the transitory ceremonial functions of the room);[40] this decoration probably disappeared about 1558,[41] and the present frescoes were painted for Gregory XIII in 1582.[42]

The Sala de' Palafrenieri, the new Consistory Hall itself, was completed by 2 February 1517, when Paris de Grassis notes that Leo, on his way to and from Mass, passed through the 'nova Aula facta in Aula Concistoriali';[43] its function, therefore, had not changed; on 10 January a notary drew up a document for Raphael in the same room, clearly because that was where he was at work.[44] In this case too, Leo—and, one supposes, Raphael—gave the room a magnificent gilt ceiling, in a superficially less attractive but in fact more advanced style, with much deeper coffering;[45] it bears a good selection of the Leonine emblems, but its meaning is restricted to them. In this room the principal decoration was a frescoed sequence of grisaille figures in pilastered tabernacles—the Apostles and one or two other saints.[46] This decoration was very largely destroyed by Paul IV in 1558, reconstructed for Pius IV by Taddeo and Federico Zuccaro in 1560,[47] and modified once more in 1582 under Gregory XIII, who gave the room the title *Aula Sanctorum Apostolorum*.[48] It is a miracle that anything of the original decoration survives, as in fact it does; this seems to me visually obvious in the case of the *Saint John the Evangelist*, which is almost entirely original, and can be demonstrated conclusively in this case and in that of the *Saint Lawrence* by the technique of graffito-dating (each of them bears inscriptions dated long before Paul IV's destructive intervention).[49]

The subject-matter of this decoration is very directly related to the hall's function as Consistory, for the constitutional role of the College of Cardinals in Consistory with the pope is derived from that of the Apostles in their office of assistance first to Christ, then to Peter.[50] That is a late thirteenth-century formulation, revived in the fifteenth century and established in the two sources that matter most in this context, the *Summa* of Torquemada and the *De Concilio* of Domenico Jacobazzi, whom Leo indeed made a cardinal in 1517.[51] But there was another feature of the room's decoration of which no trace survives: a frieze painted with various animals, but principally parrots, by Raphael's colleague Giovanni da Udine.[52] It is interesting on two counts: first because it must surely have been inspired by the room's popular name, the *Camera del Papagallo*, and second because the sumptuous wooden ceiling of Raphael's was in fact dropped nearly two metres below the full height of the thirteenth-century room in such a way that superimposed thirteenth- and fifteenth-century friezes have been preserved above it; and each of these friezes includes among its decorative motifs a large number of birds.[53]

I have spent a little time on these two big rooms because they show in the clearest and simplest way the specific relationship between the purpose and decoration of rooms in this papal apartment. But I think it is valuable to notice as well how a pre-existing decoration may be recalled in a new one, if only to remind ourselves how much more we might understand about the Stanze if we had a better idea of the earlier decorations there.[54]

When we turn to consider the sequence of rooms which we call the Stanze we move from the thirteenth-century part of the palace to the relatively new North wing, erected about 1450 by Nicolas V; this too was built on three levels, in the lowest of which Sixtus IV had put the papal library while Alexander VI had put his private suite, the Borgia Apartments, in the second.[55] Those apartments continue into the tower in the North-West corner, the Torre Borgia, which was the most recent addition to the fabric. When we examine the Stanze on the top level (13, 14, 15) we have to start by unravelling a confusion that arose by pure accident. Vasari was the first and only sixteenth-century writer (except for his followers such as Borghini) to call the middle room (14) by the name we now use, the *Camera della*

Segnatura;[56] and this was due to the coincidence that during the 1540s, when Vasari first became familiar with the Vatican, the tribunal of the *Signatura gratiae* was for a brief moment established in this room by Paul III. Vasari's name for the room was accurate for the years in which he knew it, but it is worse than misleading when it is applied anachronistically, as it is so often, to the pontificates of Julius and Leo. And while talking of confusions perhaps I should mention that a document that turns up in the literature now and then, purporting to be a credit-note to Raphael, dated 3 January 1516, for painting the *Cubicula signature*, is a Roman forgery of about 1860.[57]

Providentially we can establish from multiple references in Paris de Grassis's diary exactly where the *Signatura* of Julius II was situated, and that was in the third of these Stanze, the one now called the Stanza dell'Incendio (15). The evidence, which comes from the diarist's accounts of four occasions upon which Leo X used this room for the consecration of bishops, is perfectly precise and admits of no wriggling. On the first of these occasions, 12 December 1513, the consecration took place 'in the last of the new upper rooms, that is the one that is painted: the *Signatura* of Julius'.[58] This document has been known for almost a century but it has been misinterpreted with astonishing persistence;[59] the 'last room' is the last topographically, and in Paris de Grassis's terminology it cannot be any other than the Stanza dell'Incendio;[60] and he says that the room *was* Julius's *Signatura*, not that Julius had once thought of putting it there.[61] I think the implication of the retrospective definition, the *Signatura* of Julius, should be that it was not, in 1513, the *Signatura* of Leo. That is quite certainly the case in the last of three other diary references (which I think are not generally known),[62] the one dated 2 July 1519, in which it is called 'cammera in qua *solebat* esse Signatura P.P. Julij': it used to be. . . . So, let us consider the fact that Julius used this end room for his *Signatura*, and return later to the function and decoration of the room under Leo.

The *Signatura* is the supreme tribunal of the Curia;[63] its business had grown during the fifteenth century to the extent that Alexander VI subdivided the pleas between a *Signatura iustitiae*, presided over by a cardinal, and a *Signatura gratiae* of which the president was the pope.[64] It is the latter, then, with which we are concerned, and its composition requires a papal throne and table on a daïs, in front of it a longer table with benches for cardinals, and provision for the accredited prelates and notaries.[65] Since the tribunal must function through the winter it requires a fireplace;[66] and since some of those attending would in fact be external to the papal household it requires access not only directly from the papal chambers and the Consistory, through which the cardinals could pass, but also independently and directly from the public end of the palace. These necessities seem to have conditioned Julius's choice. In his pontificate there would have been uninterrupted passage from the *anticamera* and the robing rooms through the other Stanze; and an exterior route leads along a balcony on the West exterior façade of the palace to a door—not, as is usually said, a window —which is clearly the principal entrance for visitors to the *Signatura* (Pl. 24).[67]

The only part of this room's decoration which survives from the Julian period is the ceiling, which was painted by Perugino, probably in the second half of 1508.[68] The subjects of the four *tondi*, in so far as they can be interpreted, seem perfectly responsive to the room's use. The *tondo* over the West wall illustrates the text of John 20, in which Christ says to His disciples: 'Receive ye the Holy Ghost: Whose soever sins ye remit, they are remitted unto them; and whose soever sins ye retain, they are retained';[69] in a pontifical context this can mean only one thing: the transmission of the authority to loose and to bind, through Peter and the Apostles, to the Church.[70] It seems to me probable from the design of this fresco, and from analogous situations in which the papal throne was placed opposite the fireplace, that the daïs was on this side.[71] The *tondo* over the North or window-wall represents Christ, against a circular gold disc, as *Sol iustitiae*, the fulfilment of an Old Testament prophecy;[72] on his left is His tempter, the devil, and on His right an Apostle, perhaps Saint Matthew who describes the Temptation.[73] To the East is represented the *Pantocrator*, probably opposite the papal throne; and, to the South, Christ is shown in an attitude of mercy between two personifications, one obviously *Iustitia*. A point to notice is that *Iustitia* holds her sword point down, as she does not, for example, on Raphael's ceiling in the next room; Justice with the scales and the sword pointing downwards was the emblem of the *Signatura iustitiae* engraved in later centuries on the calendar of the tribunal.[74] For the other personification the late nineteenth-century interpretation as *Gratia* seems to me marginally preferable on its own merits to the alternative *Misericordia*,[75] and it is also marginally more appropriate to the *Signatura* of Julius. Thus the ceiling as a whole may be taken to illustrate the integrity, plenitude and spiritual grace of divine justice, and its transmission to the institution of the Church through its head.

When Francesco Albertini wrote his *Opusculum de mirabilibus Romae* in 1509 he spoke of the decoration of these rooms by several artists *concertante*, which was more than a pretty metaphor, since he used the same word to describe the relationship of the team of artists employed by Sixtus IV in the Sistine Chapel.[76] It seems that Julius did in fact recall his uncle's technique of patronage, and that he assembled a team of collaborators to conduct a rapid campaign on the ceilings of these rooms; the date of this decision would appear to be about the spring of 1508.[77] As in the Sistine Chapel, so here: Perugino was the only artist to be given a clear field. In the middle room the story was much more complicated. The Sienese painter Sodoma undertook, at some date before October 1508, to paint a relatively small portion of one of these rooms, and certainly less than the whole of this ceiling upon which he began, in the centre;[78] but if it was planned from the start that he should have a collaborator, the plan was changed while he was still at work, for whereas he first painted the *putti* in the centre in a *circular* frame,[79] he also painted the small scenes on the diagonal axes of the definitive design, and his too is the invention—but perhaps not the execution—of the grotesques of the frames.[80] The change of plan is most likely to be connected with the late appointment, towards the end of 1508, of Raphael as his collaborator;[81] and for reasons too complicated to explain here the definitive design of the vault—not the first one—must be connected with a decision to paint the walls.[82] One of the reasons for that decision was the destruction by Julius of whatever had been the decoration of the North and South walls. To the North this happened when he had the segmentally headed window of Nicolas V's room reduced in height and given a more classical, rectangular frame; and to the South it happened when he introduced an entirely new window of the same kind which looks onto the Cortile del Papagallo and bears on that side his name.[83] The new South window could not be centred on this wall because in the thickness of the latter, to the right, was the flue of the fireplace in the room below.

The function of this middle room cannot be established with the same certainty as that of the end room. If you will forgive me the omission of a long and tedious argument I should like simply to say that the documents show very nearly conclusively

that this room was intended to be the *Bibliotheca Iulia*, that is
a new library reserved for the pope's private use;[84] in fact the
documents leave the only alternative site for this library in the
Torre Borgia.[85] So in this case, where the external evidence
is not wholly conclusive, we must reverse the process we have
followed so far, and seek, in the room itself, confirmation or
refutation of the possibility offered by the documents. I should
add that no other possibility arises from the external evidence.

The hypothesis that the room was designed to be a library
was evolved by Grimm, Springer, Wickhoff, and Schlosser, but
most effectively by Wickhoff, late in the nineteenth century;[86]
briefly, what they demonstrated was in part the documentary
argument—but they did not use one crucial document[87]—and
in part the compatibility of the iconography of the decoration
with library conventions. To be still more brutally brief, the
second part of their argument is reducible to two essential
points: that the decoration includes the representation of an
altogether exceptional number of books, and that the division
of the subject-matter, which begins on the ceiling, conforms to
the existing system of organizing libraries, *in facultatibus*;[88] the
Faculties in this case are Theology, *Poesia*, Philosophy, and
Jurisprudence (not Justice). Beneath each Faculty, on the
walls, is a large fresco in which that Faculty is seen to be exercised; so, for example, the *Disputa* is an ideal elucidation of one
of the Mysteries of the Sacrament by the practice of Theology,
which is the titular Faculty on the vault above.

The requirement of an hypothesis is not that it should
resemble a fact, but that it should be consistent with all the
contingent facts; and when it is as old as this one, it should be
consistent with all those many discoveries and observations
which have been made since. This hypothesis has had an odd
history; it has been greeted enthusiastically by some specialists in
library-history,[89] but with hostility by others and by many art-
historians;[90] many objections have been raised but not a single
one survives scrutiny.[91] Rather than rehearsing and refuting
these old arguments I should prefer to check the hypothesis
against some neglected facts. Let us start with practical matters,
and first of all with the books.

By good fortune there exists a list of Julius's books, in which
there were 220;[92] so it was not a great library, but a respectable
one and a good working tool.[93] At Julius's death it was split up,
and the greater part absorbed into the main Vatican library;
thus it follows *ex hypothesi* that if the middle room had been the

library, then it should have lost its original function and furnishings on the accession of Leo. And that did happen in this room.
Any interpretation must take account of one odd circumstance:
that whereas the room appears to have been finished in the
autumn of 1511,[94] it was Leo X who provided, immediately
after his election, the intarsia *basamento*.[95] This celebrated work,
by Fra Giovanni da Verona, was replaced by the present
frescoed one in the 1540s;[96] but because it had been completed
on the North wall by an imitation—also Leonine—in fresco
(PL. 22), we can visualize rather accurately its design;[97] and
because Fra Giovanni also made the intarsia linings of the doors,
which survive, we can assess its beautiful quality (Pl. 23). Now
if, as I believe, it is scarcely credible that the room was left
without a *basamento* for eighteen months after the main frescoes
were completed, it follows that the Leonine intarsie replaced
something Julian; and book-shelves of about the right length
for Julius's collection—either closed *armarii* like those of the
Vatican library or open shelves like those of the Varano library
at Camerino—would fill these spaces.[98]

   Two other points about the room are worth noting. The first
is that this is the only room in the sequence of eight that did
not have a fireplace. Fireplaces have always been unpopular
with librarians, not only because they brought the obvious risk
of fire but also because they were thought to encourage bugs.
The Vatican libraries have never had fireplaces. The second
point arises from a consideration of the *opus sectile* floor, which
can best be studied from a beautiful drawing by John Talman
(Pl. 25).[99] Part of this floor—certainly the whole strip between
the doors—was added by Leo X. But the principal pattern,
the large carpet-like square, bears Julius's name, and the asym-
metrical position of this carpet makes no sense until one notices
that it is exactly centred on the axis of the North window, from
which Julius could see the Villa Belvedere that he loved so much.
A pattern of that kind, like the very similar one in the chancel of
the Sistine Chapel, has a definite significance: it delimits an
open space, an area of free circulation, and it is inconceivable
that a papal throne was placed here, as some would wish,[100] or
for that matter in any other part of the room. A floor of this kind
was placed in the Vatican Library by Sixtus IV.[101] Whatever
function is proposed for the room it must take account of two
facts that eliminate almost every possibility that comes to mind:
the absence of a fireplace and the design of the floor. Both of
these are accounted for by the library-hypothesis.

During Julius's long career as cardinal he had lived in two Roman palaces, at SS. Apostoli and at San Pietro in Vincoli; in each of these he made a library.[102] And for almost as long, from 1476 to 1503, he had been Cardinal-legate of Avignon and had lived in the papal palace there from time to time and particularly in the 1490s. At Avignon he would have seen that the private papal chamber, which was on the third level, was directly connected with the papal library.[103] No doubt the *Bibliotheca Iulia* in the Vatican was intended to be a permanent accession to the papal apartment and, as Bembo said, 'much more convenient for the pope's personal use' than the public library below; and the implication of Bembo's words, that this library was intended by its founder to be an institution (like the tribunal of the *Signatura*), is the necessary condition without which this room's expensive and protracted decoration makes no sense.

Finally I should like to examine more closely the *Parnassus* fresco, because this is the one that has always given the most trouble—understandably—to those who have sought some function for the room in papal ceremonial;[104] indeed it is absurd in that context. The site for this fresco was chosen, I believe, because it frames the view, through the North window, of the Belvedere on the summit of the Mons Vaticanus, and the Mons Vaticanus, as was perfectly well known at the time, had been sacred to Apollo.[105] Yet the prominence of Apollo is only equalled in the room by that of Christ, and it may even seem greater if the viewer's orientation, implied by the floor-design, is taken into account; it demands an explanation which seems to be best supplied by the tradition of dedicating libraries to Apollo and of decorating them with images of Apollo and the Muses. This tradition was exemplified in recent times by a project for the Medici library in the Badia at Fiesole and above all in the Vatican Library founded by Julius's uncle;[106] and it seems very probable that in the case of the latter, the *Bibliotheca palatina*, the inspiration was derived from the greatest in antique Rome, the Palatine Library of Augustus, which was also known as the Library of Apollo.[107] I am not suggesting that Julius's was in any sense a reconstruction of Augustus's library, but rather that the latter, by far the best recorded of ancient libraries, especially by Suetonius, Horace, and Pliny, was a model for the visualization of ancient libraries in general.[108] Julius, by the way, had the texts of Suetonius and Pliny among his manuscripts. And it seems to me important that Bembo's well-known description of the *Bibliotheca Iulia*, which so far as it goes is consistent with this middle room's decoration, is immediately preceded by a passage in which he asserts that in this foundation Julius was emulating the great libraries of antiquity;[109] he mentions, in fact, Alexandria and Pergamum, but of those no visually suggestive descriptions survived.

It will be obvious to you that I am persuaded by the library-hypothesis. It seems to me that there *is* sufficient internal evidence to resolve that choice for its location which is determined by the documents, between this room and the Torre Borgia; it would be astonishing if the latter had been more appropriately decorated, and in fact there is no reason to suppose that it was decorated at all under Julius. But what I want to suggest in particular is that any more elaborate analysis of the so-called Stanza della Segnatura should start from the proposition that Raphael interpreted his task as the animation and orchestration of those conventionally emblematic, serried portraits of the literary heroes and their gods to be found in library decoration in antiquity and in the fifteenth century.

Raphael began work in the remaining room in this suite, the first in ceremonial sequence and the one we call the Stanza d'Eliodoro, in the autumn of 1511.[110] The vault had already been painted in the initial campaign of 1508–9 by Peruzzi, Ripanda and other artists whom I cannot identify;[111] and at least two of the walls had been painted at that time by Signorelli and Bramantino.[112] I shall say very little about this room, not because I think it less interesting than the Stanza della Segnatura, but because within the terms of this lecture there is much less to be said; in other words the function of this room is not moderately but in the highest degree hypothetical. The first positive designation that I can find is on a conclave-plan of 1565, where it is the *Sala dell'Audienza*;[113] there is a series of references, beginning in 1517, to a *Camera de l'Audientia*, which I cannot locate elsewhere,[114] and the anonymous author of a *Memoriale* of 1544 describes a 'belisima udienza, dipinta di mano di Rafaello da Urbino', which is also hard to locate elsewhere unless this was a loose description of the Consistory.[115] So, the only suggestion I can make is that this was the papal audience-chamber; and while on the one hand the evidence is unsatisfactory, on the other hand it is not, so far as it goes, in conflict with the Julian decoration, political and even propagandist in its meaning.

That the subjects of the four main frescoes on the walls of the room were all chosen during the pontificate of Julius II is beyond doubt, and the consistency of the four preliminary projects suggests to me that they were all selected at the beginning of the work, that is to say in 1511.[116] To define the political intent of this programme requires intuition (that is to say, guesswork) and a more careful survey of the political imagery of that precise moment than has yet been made, but a politically allegorical programme it must be, as Vasari saw already,[117] for there is no other conceivable link between the four Julian subjects: one from the Old Testament, the *Expulsion of Heliodorus*, one from the Acts of the Apostles, the *Release of Saint Peter*, one from the early Christian Church, the *Repulse of Attila*, and one from the Middle Ages, the *Miracle of the Mass at Bolsena*. My guess in the case of the *Expulsion of Heliodorus* is that this represents, allegorically, the divine sanction for the Church's right to temporal possessions, since it was upon the presumption of the contrary that Heliodorus attempted to remove the treasure from the Temple. This guess is controlled by the emblematic *Moses* on the keystone above, for Julius was compared with Moses as the leader who made a 'just war' for his people;[118] the apology for the 'just war' was a posture of the Julian panegyrists, for whom one of the appropriate causes was the defence of Church property.[119] More obviously the *Repulse of Attila* refers to the divine sanction for the defence of the States of the Church, and particularly Rome, against the barbarian invasion. The keystone in this case, a young man holding a sphere, is perhaps an emblem of *Imperium*; the barbarians threatening the papal *Imperium* in 1511 were, of course, the French.

Raphael had reached what should have been the definitive design of this fresco, the last of the four, when Julius died in February 1513; and then by a happy but quite characteristic coincidence Leo X stepped into the role of Leo I. This event led to a revision of the design by which the new pope became prominent in the foreground. The revision is accomplished a little awkwardly, but it is once again a political statement; the pacific gesture of Leo is, it seems to me, a record for posterity of his appearance as the man of peace in his triumphal Lateran procession of 11 April, the feast of San Leo, which is recorded for us in a little-known woodcut of the same year (Fig. 2).[120] So in the final fresco, as in historical reality, the political aspiration remains the same but the means of its attainment are different.

Fig. 2. The Lateran Procession of Leo X, 11 April 1513; woodcut, Roman, 1513 (*photo*: Biblioteca Apostolica Vaticana).

And immediately afterwards the whole programme of the room was given a subtly different meaning by the repainting of the ceiling.[121] Of the original ceiling there now remains only the peripheral framing, the central wreath and four of the initially eight ribs. In the four new quadrants are represented symbolic episodes from Genesis and Exodus which function as retroactive titles for the wall-frescoes, to which their relation is that of typological precedents.[122] Thus the Leonine modification of the programme shifts the emphasis away from the contingencies of those political obsessions identified with the personality of Julius towards a more universal and, as it were, neutral theme; for it was only at this stage that the wall-frescoes—in combination with the new ceiling—became most naturally interpreted as illustrations of the intervention of Divine Providence in the affairs of God's people. In the lower sections of the vault Raphael added, at the same time, Medicean *imprese*, emblems, and hieroglyphs which seem to be best interpreted as attributes of the reign of Leo X; Hercules, for example, is probably chosen as the Tuscan hero who first bore the *signum leonis*, and as *exemplum virtutis*.[123] And Raphael finally added the painted *basamento*, where the caryatids stand as allegories of the benefits of good papal government—a New Style of Government, one might say—benefits such as Peace, Commerce, and Law.[124] The final Leonine programme is as appropriate to an audience-chamber as the first one, but for audiences with a very different pope.

Retracing our steps we come back to the Stanza della Segnatura, which was certainly not Leo's library. In order to understand what it might have been in his pontificate we should notice at this point two general changes that Leo brought to the Stanze. Under Julius these three rooms—audience-chamber (13), papal library (14) and *Signatura* (15), if our hypotheses are correct—were semi-public and institutional, and there was passage-like, uninterrupted communication down the enfilade of open doorways from the Sala di Costantino (12).[125] It was Leo who gave to each of these rooms an enclosed, discrete character,[126] for his are the marble door-frames and all the superb wooden doors, carved in high relief by one of the finest craftsmen of the period, Gian Barile.[127] These doors and their frames were designed with a clear implication of the direction of entrance (with the papal arms on the 'outer' side), and when seen together in a plan of the Stanze in their Leonine state (Fig. 3) these directions make a coherent pattern; from that pattern we can deduce that in the hierarchy of privacy the most secret were the middle room and the Torre Borgia (16). Secondly, you will notice that when Leo enclosed the Stanze he provided simultaneously a by-pass, as it were, which is the balcony erected in 1513 to lead from the remaining medieval tower at the North end of the Loggia to a new door cut in the exterior wall of the end room, the Stanza dell'Incendio.[128] This by-pass, for the

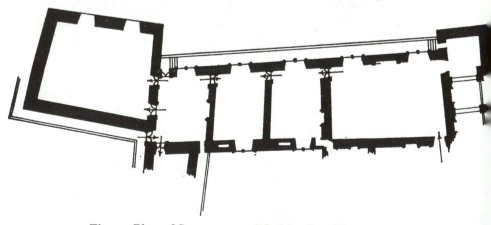

Fig. 3. Plan of Stanze as modified by Leo X, 1513–21.

better protection of privacy, is so designed that the level descends by steps, and no one using it could either see into the Stanze or be seen from them. While we are considering this plan let us notice another new Leonine balcony, on the western interior face of the Cortile del Papagallo, which leads from the *cucina secreta* through a newly cut door into the Stanza dell' Incendio.[129]

When Leo made the Stanze into self-contained rooms he not unnaturally completed, in the case of the middle room, the *opus sectile* floor of Julius which had been no more than a kind of carpet laid over a part of it (Pl. 25); and he provided, as we have seen, a stunning intarsia *basamento* which, by the way, included benches, or the illusion of benches.[130] To what purpose did Leo put this now completely private room? Paolo Giovio simply called it 'the pope's inner chamber'.[131] My suggestion is derived from those intarsie, which must have given the room the character of a *studio*. It is important to remember that Leo's greatest love was not for the visual arts, nor even for letters, but for music;[132] he was patron and composer, performer and listener, and moreover he was a collector of musical instruments. Somewhere, I feel, we have to find a place for his clavichord,[133] his Neapolitan alabaster organ,[134] and the gold and silver instruments imported from Nürnberg.[135] The suggestion that this room became Leo's music-room is based partly upon this necessity, and partly upon two texts. Leo, a compulsively generous man, gave Paris de Grassis a Christmas present in 1518: 'a most beautiful clavichord which [the pope] had kept for his own delight *in sua camera*';[136] and in 1520 a legal document was drawn up in a room described as 'the room towards the Belvedere where His Holiness, during the Summer, relaxes' (it will be remembered that the room still had no fireplace, so that its enjoyment would be limited in winter).[137] But the suggestion may also be supported by an analogy with the practice of other music-lovers, such as Ferdinand of Naples who kept his instruments in his private *studio* in the Castello Nuovo.[138] And perhaps we may take a hint from the doors of this room, all four leaves of which were decorated, on the inside, by Fra Giovanni da Verona with intarsie of musical instruments (Pl. 23).[139]

Passing on through the Leonine suite we cross the Stanza dell' Incendio to the other most private section, the Torre Borgia; and it was indeed so private that it was called the *Sancta Sanctorum* where, in theory, only the pope could enter. For this was the secret treasury, the *Guardaroba*—so described from 1517 until

1541—where Leo kept in chests and cupboards of cypress-wood his tiaras, mitres, and jewelled rings, together with certain documents and an organ (not the Neapolitan one).[140] I find this adaptation of the Torre Borgia interesting because once again it seems to reflect the experience of the palace at Avignon, where there stands, next to the papal chamber, a *turris guardarobae*; and Leo X, like his predecessor, had known the Avignon palace and became much concerned with its conservation.[141]

Now, briefly, back to the end room, the Stanza dell'Incendio, the function of which I think you will have guessed from the new exterior passage from the *cucina secreta*; Paolo Giovio, writing in the 1520s, called it the *triclinium penitius* of Leo, that is to say the secret dining-room.[142] In that case it is likely to be identical with the *tinello segreto* (a less pretentious title) that is mentioned in several documents of the period.[143] But if it was secret it was not by the same token informal, and I suspect that it is no accident that the essential furnishings required for a secret dining-room were the same as those for the *Signatura gratiae*: a papal throne with a small table opposite a longer table for the cardinals.[144] It seems to be clearly stated by Paris de Grassis that this room was no longer used for the *Signatura*, as it had been under Julius;[145] and so—unless Julius had already used this as his dining-room, which is quite possible—Leo adapted its furnishings to another ceremonial purpose. In any case he and Raphael, between 1514 and 1517, adapted the existing decoration to this purpose in a remarkably enterprising way.

It is said that Raphael's wall-frescoes in the Stanza dell'Incendio bear no relation to Perugino's ceiling of 1508 or 1509[146] —a remark so unlikely to be true that one instinctively looks again; and by a magical dexterity of mind Raphael did indeed establish both thematic and visual relationships between his four histories and Perugino's four *tondi*. I take two examples arbitrarily out of the four; Leo, in the person of Leo III in the *Coronation of Charlemagne*, receives the gift of apostolic authority together with the blessing of Christ above, which is one reason why Raphael placed the pope to the right of this fresco; in the opposite scene Leo, in the person of Leo IV in the *Defeat of the Saracens at the Battle of Ostia*, is placed conversely to the left, where he looks directly at Perugino's *Pantocrator* for divine aid against the infidel and duly receives the Father's benediction.

The *Fire in the Borgo*, from which the room takes its name, is, like the Expulsion of Heliodorus, a political allegory. The extinction of the fire by Leo IV is not, as is generally said, a reference to the extinction of the Schism by Leo X, because the contemporary metaphor for the Schism was not fire but pestilence.[147] The flames that Leo extinguishes are, as in so many texts of the period, the Flames of War.[148] In these four frescoes generally Leo is presented—I suspect in reaction to the requirements of the Election Capitulations drawn up at his conclave in 1513—as the bringer of Peace, and of Concord between Christian princes, the man of purity and integrity, and the propagator of the Crusade against the Turk.[149] The ambitions and to some extent the achievements, the ideals and to some extent the realities that are represented here do make, in relation to the expectations voiced at Leo's election, pertinent objects for the contemplation of his cardinals. But more than that (and more importantly) they would have appeared at the time to be more than reactions to the contingencies of a brief moment of history, and to represent the temporal charge laid permanently upon the Vicar of Christ. The choice of incidents from the lives of his Carolingian predecessors Leo III and Leo IV may seem to require no elaborate explanation in the case of this pope, who was more obsessed than most with previous bearers of the name with whom, indeed, he was frequently compared by entirely serious contemporaries.[150] But if we remember that this was Leo's *Triclinium* the choice may seem a little odd unless we also remember what every historian knew from the *Liber pontificalis* (the literary source for the narratives), that is the contributions of Leo III and Leo IV to the earliest Vatican Palace: Leo IV's building operations are recalled in the *Fire in the Borgo*, Leo III had erected and decorated its *Triclinium*, and Leo IV, once more, had restored it.[151]

We could certainly continue, applying the same techniques and principles, to study Raphael's later decorations for Leo X in the Loggia and in the Sala di Costantino; but that would take much longer, and although it would amplify our results so far it would add nothing to the main point. In this survey I have already, perhaps, attempted to show you too much, but the cumulative effect was an essential part of my purpose. We have scarcely considered the decorations of these rooms as works of art. But by tracing the relationship between functions and decoration, and between these two factors and the changing requirements of his patrons, I wanted—indirectly—to draw attention to two neglected aspects of Raphael's qualities as, precisely, an artist: his profound sense of purpose and his extraordinary intellectual agility.

NOTES

1. I have left unaltered the text of the lecture from which, necessarily, much detail was omitted, as well as all documentation; the omission is rectified here, so far as possible, in the annotation which, as I realize, becomes disproportionately elaborate. The only alternatives I can see are to rewrite the lecture itself at greater length, or to edit the documentation to a degree which would give this publication the *ex cathedra* character which lectures have by their very nature; and the latter, in my view, is not an acceptable alternative. In working on this problem I have profited greatly from discussions with many friends, and in particular with Howard Burns, David Chambers, Christoph Frommel, Julian Gardner, Michael Hirst, Konrad Oberhuber, Rolf Quednau, and Ruth and Nicolai Rubinstein. I should like to add at this point that I cannot regard this study as complete. In seeking evidence for a problem of art-history in ceremonial, diplomatic, literary, legal, ecclesiological, and other historical sources, one shakes a cornucopia of information as best one can and with, inevitably, incomplete results. I should hope that the cornucopia will be shaken again by others with more specialized experience, and no one will be more astonished than I if the fruits that fall out do not entail revision of my present conclusions.

2. The only relevant survey of the functions of the apartment that I know is by D. Redig de Campos, 'L'appartamento pontificio di Giulio II', *Bollettino della unione storia ed arte*, N.S. ix (1966), p. 29; this note, although very brief and without documentation, is extremely useful, and the only real changes I have to propose are in the function of the Stanza d'Eliodoro and the location of the *anticamera secreta*.

3. A biography of Paris de Grassis is to be found in the introduction to L. Frati, *Le due spedizioni militari di Giulio II* . . . (Bologna, 1886). A portrait to the left of Leo X's in Raphael's *Repulse of Attila* is conventionally identified as that of Paris (most recently in A. Haidacher, *Geschichte der Päpste in Bildern* (Heidelberg, 1965), p. 280), but this head seems too young; Paris was perhaps born *c.* 1450 (Frati, p. v), and certainly not later than 1470 since in his *Diarium*, 1512, he remarks that he has known Rome for forty years. There exists an extraordinary number of MSS. of the *Diarium*, of which I have used, in most cases, the British Museum copy, Add. MSS. 8440–4. There is no complete printed edition, although excerpts, précis and abridged texts have been published quite frequently. Two much abbreviated 'editions' are by J. J. I. Döllinger, in *Beiträge zur politischen, kirchlichen und Cultur-Geschichte*, iii (Vienna, 1882), pp. 363 ff. (Julius II only) and by Mons. P. Delicati and M. Armellini, *Il Diario di Leone X di Paride de Grassi* (Rome, 1884); of these the second is very misleading.

4. L. -H. Labande, *Le Palais des Papes* . . . *d'Avignon* (Marseilles, 1925), ii, pp. 83 ff.; L. Pastor, *The History of the Popes*, ed. F. I. Antrobus (London, 1950), vi, p. 61.

5. For the Avignon Conclave-hall, see Labande, op. cit. in n. 4, i, pp. 120 ff.; the one projected for the Vatican is referred to in the description of the Belvedere by Francesco Albertini, *Opusculum de mirabilibus novae & veteris Vrbis Romae*

(Rome, 1510), fol. Z. iii, v. ('locum pro conclavi designatum a tua Beatitudine
...'). Albertini's text, dedicated to Julius II, was completed by 3 June 1509.
This Conclave-hall is presumably the huge structure shown, leading off to
the East of the Belvedere, on the drawing Uffizi A287 (J. S. Ackerman, *The
Cortile del Belvedere* (Vatican City, 1954), pp. 199 ff. and Fig. 3); this identification seems justifiable because of the perfect solution the structure provides
for the recurrent problems of conclaves: independence, total security, self-
contained service-rooms and chapel (the latter to be erected on the *Torrione*
of Nicolas V). For earlier attributions of UA287 (Bramante, Antonio da
Sangallo the Younger) see Ackerman, loc. cit., who himself proposes the
name of Peruzzi and a date probably before 1527. More recently C. L.
Frommel, 'Antonio da Sangallos Cappella Paolina', *Zeitschrift für Kunstgeschichte*, xxvii (1964), p. 34 n. 6, has returned to the attribution to Antonio
and suggested a date *c.* 1524. I would suggest that it be dated much earlier.
The drawing is unquestionably before 1521 because it shows the door
between the two parts of the Sala Ducale (4 and 5 on my plan, Fig. 1) to
the South of the dividing wall, whereas it had been moved to the centre by
10 April 1521 (Paris de Grassis, *Diarium*, quoted by E. Müntz, *Les Historiens
et les critiques de Raphaël* (Paris, 1883), p. 132). It is with only a little less
certainty before 1513, because it shows the North wing of the palace at
Stanze-level, but without the Leonine balcony and its access-doors (see
p. 20). On the East side it shows a loggia occupying the length of the
one erected by Bramante, discussed below, but with twelve bays instead of
thirteen; and the staircase-solution in the South-East corner is also different
from Bramante's; thus it is unlikely to be later than 1509 (see below, n. 28).
On the other hand the plan of the Belvedere is probably exactly consistent
with Bramante's definitive plans, so that the drawing is unlikely to be earlier
than about 1508. My colleague Howard Burns, independently of these
arguments, has proposed an attribution to Giuliano da Sangallo, which I
find very convincing (compare the very striking plan for the Conclave and
chapel with his plans for the Neapolitan royal palace and Saint Peter's
reproduced by G. Marchini, *Giuliano da Sangallo* (Florence, 1942), Pls. Xa,
XXIIb). Giuliano was called to Rome by Julius in 1508 and left again—not
to return in this pontificate—in spring 1509 (Marchini, p. 110). I suggest
that UA287 is a plan produced by Giuliano in these months in response to
Julius's new requirements, with solutions in some respects different from
those of Bramante, and that as a whole it represents essentially the same Julian
scheme that Albertini was writing about at the same date. The plan shows
the Julian *serliana* of Bramante at the North end of the Sala Regia (inserted
summer 1508) and the Julian South windows of the Stanze (probably also
1508—see p. 13), but neither of these provides a positive *terminus post*
since—like the Belvedere—they may be represented as parts of a scheme not
yet implemented.

6. Johannes Burchard, *Liber notarum*, 21 May 1506: the staircase 'demolive-
rant pro nova facienda, tali scilicet quod eques ire posset ex aula regali usque
ad S. Petrum' (quoted from F. Ehrle, S. J., and E. Stevenson, *Gli affreschi del
Pinturicchio nell'appartamento Borgia del Palazzo Apostolico Vaticano* (Rome 1897),
p. 11); there are two further reports in the *Diarium* of Paris de Grassis on the
Eve and Feast of Ascension 1506 (Add. MS. 8440, fols. 349ᵛ–351ᵛ). The real
significance of this project may be deduced from the fact that when it was

first used, with explicit personal enthusiasm by Julius himself, at Pentecost 1506, it was entitled *via Iulia nova* (Paris de Grassis, MS. cit., fol. 358ʳ; and again at Easter 1507, Add. MS. 8441, fol. 127ᵛ), and a similar title was evidently in use for some time. When Charles V visited the Vatican in 1536, he and Paul III ascended 'per scalas novas Iulii ad Salam Regiam' (*Diarium* of Biagio da Cesena, 5 April, quoted from B. Podestà, 'Carlo V a Roma', *Archivio della R. società romana di storia patria*, i (1878), p. 331). The Sala Regia is basically a late thirteenth-century room, built by Nicolas III (D. Redig de Campos, *I Palazzi Vaticani* (Bologna 1967), pp. 28 ff.); it has a number of alternative titles in documents of the Renaissance period: Sala grande, Sala Magna, Aula regalis, Aula Regum, Aula prima, Aula major, Magnum atrium inter duas capellas, and Aula prima Caesaris (the latter in Bibl. Vat., MS. Vat. Lat. 3535, *Scripturus quae memoratu digna Romae et in Italia ab excessu Adriani. vj. Pont: Max: gesta sunt*, Anon., *c.* 1523, fol. 96ᵛ, where the title Aula Regum is, unusually, given to the second Consistory-hall, 4 on my plan). The functions of the room, as the site of the reception of ambassadors from the Emperor or kings, are described with particular clarity by Paris de Grassis on the occasion of the arrival of an embassy from Maximilian, 13 January 1509 (Add. MS. 8441, fols. 268ʳ–271ʳ), and in the *Liber Caeremoniarum* of Johannes Burchard and Agostino Patrizi, 1488 (MS. Vat. Lat. 4738; in the edition by Cristoforo Marcello, *Rituum ecclesiasticorum* . . . (Venice, 1516), fols. iᵛ, and xlvᵛ).

7. The first signs that Julius was living on the top level come in two reports of the wedding of Laura Orsini, which was performed in the upper *Aula Pontificum*, that is the Sala di Costantino (12 on the plan), on 16 November 1505; one account is in the *Liber notarum* of Burchard ('. . . Sponsalia in superiori aula Pontificum . . . quo facto papa surrexit et intravit ad suas cameras novas ibidem . . .', quoted from Ehrle–Stevenson, op. cit. in n. 6, p. 22); the other is in the *Diarium* of Paris, under the date 9 November ('Papa in aula alia (sc: superiori) Pontificum . . .; mulieres . . . ascenderunt . . . Quo facto Papa recessit ad suam cameram, et omnes mulieres sequutae sunt eum, et factae sunt nuptiae, et coena nuptialis in eamdem cameram, in qua Papa etiam coenavit . . .': Add. MS. 8440, fols. 282ᵛ ff.). It appears from Paris's later reports that Julius continued to reside in the upper suite until his departure for Bologna, 26 August 1506 (see, e.g., *Diarium*, under 12 December 1505, Epiphany 1506, 26 August 1506: Add. MS. 8440, fols. 242ᵛ, 243ᵛ, 294ʳ, and the passage quoted in C. Baronius, *Annales ecclesiastici*, xi (Lucca, 1754), p. 482); and that would appear to be the implication of Burchard's account, 27 April 1506, of the Secret Consistory 'in aula Papagalli superiori', cited below, n. 33. It is worth noting that not only Nicolas V but also Julius's uncle, Sixtus IV, had lived in the bedroom of the upper suite (Ehrle–Stevenson, op. cit., p. 14). The seasonal use of the different levels of the palace is discussed by G. Dehio, 'Die Bauprojecte Nicolaus des Fünften und L. B. Alberti', *Repertorium für Kunstwissenschaft*, iii (1880), p. 246.

8. A nucleus of this kind was provided (1555–8) for Paul IV in the East wing of the Belvedere when the original apartment was in a dangerous state (D. René Ancel, 'Le Vatican sous Paul IV', *Revue bénédictine*, xxv (1908), pp. 50–7).

9. That the *anticamera* was immediately contiguous with the bedroom is clear from a letter of Stazio Gadio, *c.* 20 December 1512, cited below, n. 14; also, an account, 5 July 1519, of ambassadors visiting Leo X (M. Sanuto, *I Diarii*, xxvii (Venice, 1889), col. 453), the description of Marco Dandolo, 1523, cited below, n. 17, and a letter from Francesco Gonzaga, 17 January 1526, describing Isabella d'Este's visit to Clement VII (A. Luzio, 'Isabella d'Este e il sacco di Roma', *Archivio storico lombardo*, xxxv (Ser. 4, x, 1908), p. 366). The earliest reference to this room's use during the pontificate of Julius II seems to be in the *Diarium* of Paris de Grassis, 25 July 1508 when, the pope being absent from Mass, 'ego ordinavi ut Cardinales omnes ad Anticameram Papae in Paramentis venirent, et ibi expectarent . . .' (Add. MS. 8441, fol. 215ᵛ); on 23 August 1511, when Julius was in bed and exceedingly ill he was visited by Francesco Maria della Rovere, who got as far as the 'Anticamera di N. S.' but was not allowed into the bedroom (A. Luzio, 'Isabella d'Este di fronte a Giulio II', *Archivio storico lombardo*, xxxix (Ser. 4, xvii, 1912), p. 329 n. 1); see also below, n. 17.

10. Paris, *Diarium*, 26 November 1507 (Add. MS. 8441, fol. 170ʳ): 'hodie Papa cepit in superioribus mansionibus Palatij habitare . . .'; this well-known passage continues with Julius's insults against Alexander VI (E. Müntz, *Raphaël* (Paris, 1881), p. 317, n. 1, and op. cit. in n. 5, p. 132; although Müntz took, and usually has received, credit for producing this text it had been known long before; there is a précis published by L. G. de Bréquigny in *Notices et extraits des manuscrits de la bibliothèque du roi*, ii (Paris, 1789), p. 562, whence it was introduced to the Raphael literature by J. D. Fiorillo, *Geschichte der Mahlerey*, i (Göttingen, 1798), p. 97). After this date Paris does not directly specify Julius's continued residence upstairs, but implies it several times, as for example on 12 January 1509 when, for the reception of Cardinal Santa Croce, Legate to Germany, in Consistory (i.e. 5 on the plan), 'Papa . . . in sede per scalas delatus est ad Concistorium' (MS. cit., fol. 267ʳ). A letter from Leonardo Grasso in Rome, 15 December 1512 (Sanuto, op. cit. in n. 9, xv, col. 411) makes it clear that Federico Gonzaga was then lodged in the suite on the second level, below Julius's room on the third. It should be noted, however, that at the height of summer Julius lived in the Villa Belvedere (i.e. *Diarium*, 1 August 1511: after an expedition to San Pietro in Vincoli, 'Papa . . . delatus est ad Palatium, et inde ad Belvedere, ubi solet hoc tempore pernoctare': Add. MS. 8442, fol. 123ʳ). Compare a report of the ambassadors of Orvieto, 6 August 1511: 'Mercordì po' vespero fumo ad Belvedere, dove sta quasi continuo Nostro Signore' (L. Fumi, 'Carteggio del comune di Orvieto degli anni 1511 e 1512', *Archivio della R. società romana di storia patria*, xiv (1891), p. 153).

11. Paris, *Diarium*, 26 December 1507 (Add. MS. 8441, fol. 177ʳ): Julius 'fecit cantari Vesperas in sua parva cappella superiori, quae erat antiqua Nicolai Pape V. dicata S. Laurentio, et per Suam Sanctitatem nuper restaurata . . .' Paris generally refers to this as the 'Cappella quotidiana', but at Christmas 1511 invented an apparently new term: 'in sua parva ante Camerali Cappella' (Add. MS. 8442, fols. 156ʳ, 157ʳ), which rather neatly expresses its symmetry with the *Anticamera* proper. I should like to draw attention to a problem arising from a report of a new chapel: Marin Zorzi wrote from Rome, 8 September 1516, that he had spoken with the French

ambassador 'qual era andato a palazzo a certa capella feva il Papa per sua devution' (Sanuto, op. cit. in n. 9, xxii, col. 567). 'Palazzo' in such a context means specifically the Vatican, and the only suggestion I have to offer is that Zorzi was mistaken, and that the chapel in question was the one begun in 1514, partly to Michelangelo's design, in Castel S. Angelo (J. S. Ackerman, *The Architecture of Michelangelo* (London, 1961), ii, pp. 1 ff.).

12. A. Taja, *Descrizione del Palazzo Apostolico Vaticano* (Rome, 1750), p. 117: 'restando la porticella riquadrata di breccia nera, i cui portelli son di finissimi intagli antichi in legno di noce, e con gli specchi, e i fondi lavorati in bella tarsia con l'arme parimente, e col nome dello stesso Giulio II, che fu ne' suoi giorni il primiero ristoratore della seguente cappella . . .'

13. I have never been in this room, and I rely upon: G. Tesorone, *L'antico pavimento delle Logge di Raffaello in Vaticano* (Naples, 1891), pp. 22 ff. ('L'antico soffitto, uno stupendo soffitto di legno a cassettoni, con ornati rossi e di oro, su fondi di azzurro-scuro, e del quale non esiste ora che una sola metà. Vi sono bellissimi fregi a rilievo, sui quali si ripete il ramo di rovere carico di foglie, e nell'arme centrale vi è la nota quercia d'oro a quattro rami e sei radici in campo azzurro fra il triregno e le chiavi: l'arme di Giulio II.'); E. Steinmann, *Die Sixtinische Kapelle*, ii (Munich, 1905), p. 8; Redig de Campos, loc. cit. in n. 2.

14. Letter of Stazio Gadio to Isabella d'Este, c. 20 December 1512, in A. Luzio, 'Federico Gonzaga ostaggio alla corte di Giulio II', *Archivio della R. società romana di storia patria*, ix (1886), p. 546 ('in camera sua qual è tutta fodrata di asse et soffitata si accese il focho nella soffitta et nelle asse dal canto verso il letto . . .').

15. Tesorone, op. cit. in n. 13, p. 23; he describes the Medici emblem of Ring and Feathers with the motto *Semper*, and the Leonine *impresa* of the Yoke with the motto *Suave*, and gives a coloured drawing, Pl. I. 4 (it should be noted that the reconstruction he proposes for the lost Loggia floor is in many details wrong: an accurate drawing, by Francesco la Vega, 1742, is in Bibl. Vat., MS. Vat. Lat. 13751, fol. 58). A new fireplace was placed 'su ala camera del Papa' during the first nine months of Leo's reign (an item on the account of Giuliano Leno, 1 December 1513, published by K. Frey, 'Zur Baugeschichte des St. Peter', *Jahrbuch der königlich preußischen Kunstsammlungen*, xxxi (1910), Beiheft, p. 22).

16. It is shown in an important and little-studied plan in Ferdinando Caroli, *De Vaticano Templo et Palatio*, (c. 1620), MS. Vat. Lat. 10741, fol. 243a.

17. *Relazione* of Marco Dandolo, describing visit to Adrian VI, April 1523: 'sua anticamera, che è un camerino quadro a volta di bellissime pitture; dal quale insino in terra pendevano da ogni banda bellissimi arazzi nuovi, la maggior parte di seta . . . nella faccia da man manca un baldacchino di bellissimo soprariccio d'oro . . . sotto il quale era una bellissima cattedra di veluto cremisino ricamata d'oro e fornita di pomelli d'argento lavorati d'oro colle arme di papa Leone; e intorno intorno molti scabelli da sedere. Presso alla porta della camera di Sua Santità, v'era una tavoletta sopra tre piedi . . . per riporvi il paramento . . .' (E. Albèri, *Le relazioni degli ambasciatori veneti*,

iii (Florence, 1858), p. 101). Michiel remarked that Raphael's tapestries 'furono giudicati la più bella cosa, che sia stata fatta in eo genere a nostri giorni, benchè fussino celebri *li razzi di Papa Giulio de l'anticamera*, li razzi del Marchese di Mantova . . .' etc. (E. A. Cicogna, 'Intorno la vita . . . di Marcantonio Michiel', *Memorie dell'I. R. istituto veneto di scienze, lettere ed arti*, ix (1860), p. 405; the words italicized here are omitted by V. Golzio, *Raffaello nei documenti* . . . (Vatican City, 1936), p. 103). The necessity for the seating described by Dandolo is exemplified by an occasion when Julius summoned the cardinals 'et in Anticamera sua tenuit consistoriolum' (Paris de Grassis, *Diarium*, 27 December 1511, Add. MS. 8442, fol. 157ᵛ).

18. Biagio da Cesena, *Diarium*, 12 April 1520, describing the reception of an embassy of Charles V by Leo X 'in anticamera sua in sede camerali, assistentibus quindecim, vel sexdecim circumstantibus Cardinalibus' (Bibl. Vat., MS. Chig. L. II. 22, fol. 33ʳ; B.M., Add. MS. 8445, fol. 15ʳ).

19. In the first surviving account-book of Serapica (Archivio di Stato, Rome, Camerale I, 1489, fol. 84ʳ), 1 November 1518; 'E più . . . a mf. Philippo Adimari duc. cinquanta doro larghi, per dar a qual fe el pavimento de la camera del broccato'.

20. For these functions, see Francesco Sestini, *Il Maestro di Camera* (ed. Rome, 1653), pp. 47 ff., and the passages from Burchard's *Liber notarum* cited in Ehrle–Stevenson, op. cit. in n. 6, pp. 13–14; the latter may be supplemented from the *Liber Caeremoniarum*, 1488, of Agostino Patrizi and Burchard (ed. cit. in n. 6, fols. lxixᵛ, and cxxxivᵛ); 'S. D. N. Innocentius VIII pont. max. Ad reformationem Cubiculariorum et camerarium papagalli et paramenti palatii apostolici', in Patrizi–Burchard, *Miscellanea*, MS. Vat. Lat. 5633, fol. 89ʳ ff. (an important text which defines degrees of rank admitted to the two rooms, and which was copied c. 1517 by Paris de Grassis into his *Caeremoniarum opusculum*, MS. Vat. Lat. 5634/1, fols. 169ʳ ff.); Paris de Grassis, *Caeremonialium regularum supplementum et additiones* (1515), MS. Vat. Lat. 5634/2, fols. 4ᵛ–9ʳ (in great detail). Although it is normal in this period to refer to these rooms as *Camera de' paramenti* and *Camera del papagallo*, it should be noted that: (i) either can also be termed *Aula*, or *Sala* (e.g., Paris, *Diarium*, 10 August 1513: 'Aula, sive Camera Papagalli inferior'), and (ii) that they can also be designated *prima* and *secunda camera paramenti* (e.g. by Patrizi–Burchard). There are a great many references to these rooms in normal or abnormal use in the *Diarum* of Paris. There were 'sale del paramento e del papagallo' provided in Palazzo San Marco while it served as the papal residence of Paul II (a payment, 23 July 1471, for the decoration of their ceilings is in A. Bertolotti, *Artisti lombardi a Roma* (Milan, 1881), p. 31).

21. The fullest description of the furnishings is given in Paris de Grassis, *Caeremonialium regularum supplementum et additiones*, MS. Vat. Lat. 5634/2, fols. 5ᵛ (instructions to sacristan for preparing papal *paramenta*) and 7ᵛ (instructions to Master of Ceremonies for preparing furnishings: consistorial throne, benches for cardinals, 'Lectum: ubi papa parandus est', and 'sedes papae cameralis maior, aut minor'); in the *Diarium*, 26 May 1504, he describes Julius 'apud lectum paramenti . . . vestitus iturus ad Vesperas . . .' (Add. MS. 8440, fol. 2ʳ).

22. A fully detailed and illustrated manual for this lengthy operation is a beautiful MS. from the Heineman Collection, on loan (1969) to the Pierpont Morgan Library: *Praeparatio ad missam pontificalem;* the frontispiece, which shows Leo X enthroned during the robing ceremony, is dated 1520; an earlier description is in Patrizi-Burchard, *Liber caeremoniarum*, 1488, ed. cit. in n. 6, fol. cxxviii[r].

23. There exists, so far as I know, no direct evidence on the location or scale of the original staircase; that it could be adapted ceremonially is indicated by Paris de Grassis's record of the first time that Julius used the upper rooms for robing, 26 November 1507: 'Hodie Papa incepit facere Cameram Paramenti in superiori aula, ubi etiam est vestitus, cum hactenus sit solitus in inferiori parari, et per scalas in sede fuit delatus ad Cappellam' (Add. MS. 8441, fol. 169[v]). But in the Eastern part of the palace before Julius's rebuilding there was no space for anything but a very cramped staircase; it is probable, I think, that there was one in each of the towers at the North and South ends of the medieval loggia on the East façade (for which see the next note) and that the southern one was used in 1507. A *lumaca* (spiral staircase) on the East side is mentioned by Paris in 1505 (under the date 9 November: Add. MS. 8440, fol. 282[v]).

24. The literary sources on the earlier loggia are printed in F. Ehrle, S.J., and H. Egger, *Der vatikanische Palast in seiner Entwicklung bis zur Mitte des XV. Jahrhunderts* (Vatican City, 1935), pp. 68–9, and Ehrle–Stevenson, op. cit. in n. 6, p. 14; for visual evidence, a tentative reconstruction, and description of surviving fragments incorporated into Bramante's structure, see D. Redig de Campos, 'Bramante e il Palazzo Apostolico Vaticano', *Rendiconti della pontificia accademia romana di archeologia*, xliii (1971), pp. 283 ff. Trees and topiary in the *giardino segreto* are visible in the view of the old palace from the East in Benozzo Gozzoli's fresco in S. Agostino, San Gimignano (reproduced by Ackerman, op. cit. in n. 5, Fig. 42).

25. Such a courtyard is sketched in black chalk on UA287 (1508–9: see above n. 5); it is obvious from the views of the southern end of the Logge, *c.* 1532, by Marten van Heemskerck (e.g. Redig de Campos, op. cit. in n. 6, Fig. 62), that the structure erected by Bramante and Raphael was a fragment of a larger scheme.

26. The several flights of this staircase are best understood from the plans in P. Letarouilly, *Les Bâtiments du Vatican*, ii (ed. London, 1963), Figs. 114, 116, 118.

27. In addition to the texts of Michiel and Albertini quoted by Redig de Campos, op. cit. in n. 6, pp. 100–1 (see also next note), the letter of Mario Equicola to Isabella d'Este, 23 March 1513: 'Fabrica [Leo] una scala per potesse condurre ad cavallo sino al lecto' (A. Luzio, 'Isabella d'Este ne' primordi del papato di Leone X', *Archivio storico lombardo*, xxxiii (1906), p. 457). The slope of the original *cordonata* (ramp) was about 1:3·5; the flights were rebuilt as steps, of awkward rhythm, under Pius VII (1800–23: Redig de Campos, op. cit. in n. 6, p. 101).

28. In MS. Corsini 2135 (receipts of Girolamo Francesco da Siena, *computista* of St. Peter's, 1508–9), fols. 7ʳᵛ, there are payments from 30 November to 3 December 1509 for *pilastri* of the 'opera horti segreti'. G. I. Hoogewerff, 'Documenti . . . che riguardano Raffaello . . .', *Rendiconti della pontificia accademia romana di archeologia*, xxi (1945–6), p. 265, has suggested that these documents refer to the northern end of the Belvedere; A. Bruschi, *Bramante architetto* (Bari, 1969), p. 933 (following Ackerman), relates them not unreasonably to the Logge. However, the total number of *pilastri* then erected was sixteen, which is too many for the Logge (where, in any case, previous foundations were adapted for at least part of the lowest level); sixteen would be exactly right for the East side of the first (southern) court of the Belvedere, and I think it is probable that these documents should be added to the list in Ackerman, op. cit. in n. 5, pp. 152 ff.; there was, of course, a garden on this side of the palace as well. But even if these documents do not apply to the Logge, a project-date (see below, note 91) of 1509 at the latest is implied by the reference to the new staircase in June 1509 in Albertini, op. cit. in n. 5, fol. Yiᵛ: 'Sunt praeterea aulae & Camerae adornatae variis picturis ab excellentiss. [imis] pictoribus concertantibus hoc anno instauratae. Praetereo [sc: sunt hoc anno instaurati?] faciles ascensus ad commoditatem aedium palatinarum cottile opus ex laterculis & lapide Tyburtino: ut ad summitatem usque tecti facile possit equitari'; and I think that Bruschi (op. cit., p. 934) is right in taking the *deambulatorii* mentioned in another passage of Albertini's (quoted below, n. 84) as the Logge themselves. On the other hand Julius, on 12 January 1509, stood 'in logia superiori sua secreta' to watch a procession, so at that date the demolition of the previous loggia had not begun (Paris de Grassis, *Diarium*, Add. MS. 8441, fol. 267ʳ).

29. Paris de Grassis, *Diarium*, 10 August 1513; 'preparari feci aulam, sive Cameram Papagalli inferiorem, ubi Pontifex parandus esset, propter structuras, et ruinas scalarum superiorum . . .' (MS. Vat. Lat. 5636, fol. 51ʳ). A payment of 27 April 1513 'per 2 ferate, messe a lavoro di palazzo sotto la schala di palazzo' almost certainly refers to the same project (Frey, op. cit. in n. 15, p. 20). In his description of the Conclave arrangements of 1513 (*Diarium*, 4 March), Paris refers to a *logia longa*, which has been taken to be the second level of Bramante's; but it is, rather, the portico of the Cortile del Maresciallo. According to Redig de Campos, the existence of a door of Julius II at the end of the passage that leads from the head of the *cordonata* to the Sala vecchia degli Svizzeri (7 on the plan) implies that construction had reached the third level before Julius's death; but I think that this doorway could as well—in fact must—have been accessible from the previous staircase, and that its dating implications are restricted to the Sala. A passage in a letter from Bibbiena to Giulio de' Medici, 2 December 1511, suggests that part of the loggia, probably on the second level, may then have been usable: 'Essendo la S.tà di N. S. hoggi al tardi venuto nella loggia del secondo giardino secreto et conferendo con quella li R.mi Grimano et Cornaro et il secretario veneto . . .' (G. L. Moncallero, *Epistolario di Bernardo Dovizi da Bibbiena*, i (Florence, 1955), p. 380).

30. See the article, both amusing and scholarly in the highest degree, by H. Diener, 'Die "Camera Papagalli" im Palast des Papstes', *Archiv für Kulturgeschichte*, xlix (1967), pp. 43 ff.

31. Patrizi-Burchard, *Liber Caeremoniarum*, 1488 (ed. cit. in n. 6, fol. xlvi^r):
'Secretum consistorium celebratur in aula aliqua palatii Apostolici remotiori:
hodie Cameram Papagalli appellant'; cf. Burchard, *Liber notarum*, 1 December
1505 (quoted from Ehrle–Stevenson, op. cit. in n. 6, p. 16): 'Papa . . . vocavit
. . . de camera Papagalli sive consistorii . . . singulos cardinales'. On conclave-
plans of 1549–50, 1555, and 1565, the lower Camera del Papagallo is marked
as 'Locus Concistorij Secreti', 'Aula Consistorii Secreti', 'Sala del Con-
cistoro secreto' (F. Ehrle, S. J., and H. Egger, *Studi e documenti per la storia del
Palazzo Apostolico Vaticano, V: Die Conclavepläne* (Vatican City, 1933), Nos. I,
III, VII).

32. Paris de Grassis, *Diarium*, 14 October 1504, the reception of the ambassadors of Rhodes, who 'se firmarunt in prima camera Paramenti, idest non
Papagalli, sed in prima ubi Hostiarii faciunt custodiam, et ibi sedentes in
principali banco, quod est apud ignem, expectarunt finem Consistorij, quo
finito, vocavi eosdem qui intrarunt' (i.e. into the Camera del Papagallo:
Add. MS. 8440, fol. 62^r; at this date the lower rooms were in use); compare
the description of the lower room by Ferdinando Caroli, MS. cit. in n. 16
(*c.* 1620), fol. 436^r: 'Salla che sta avanti a quella del Concistori che serve
ordinariamente dove sta la guardia . . .'. The *ostiarii* had ancient rights and
duties in the *Camera paramenti*, described in a document of 1409 quoted by
F. Ehrle, S. J., *De historia palatii Avenionensis* (Rome, 1890), p. 116n. For
ceremonies of the presentation of ambassadors to the Curia see M. de Maulde-
la-Clavière, *La Diplomatie au temps de Machiavel* (Paris, 1892), ii, p. 215. On
the conclave–plan of 1585 (Ehrle-Egger, op. cit. in n. 31, No. IX) the lower
Camera de' Paramenti is designated simply: *Sala delli Oratori*.

33. Burchard, *Liber notarum*, 27 April 1506 (Ehrle–Stevenson, op. cit. in n. 6,
p. 14): 'fuit secretum consistorium in aula Papagalli superiori'. During the
later part of the pontificate of Julius a particular room—presumably this
one—was customarily used for secret consistories, for example the one held
on 8 October 1511 for the approval of the Bull confirming the League
between the Church, Ferdinand of Aragon and Venice against the Bentivoglio of Bologna: 'Acta fuerunt hec Rome in palatio apostolico in sala, in
qua secretum consistorium *consuevit* . . .' (A. Theiner, *Codex diplomaticus
dominii temporalis S. Sedis*, iii (Rome, 1862), p. 524). On the dispatch of the
Legate to Perugia (Antonio del Monte), 8 October 1511, Paris was called
'in cameram Consistorij', and on 26 December 1511 the cardinals were
summoned 'ad Cameram suam Consistorialem' for discussion on the gift of
the Sword (*Diarium*, Add. MS. 8442, fols. 134^v, 156^v). In these cases, too, it
seems safe to assume that it is the present Sala de' Palafrenieri that was meant
since it is of a size to allow the use of the terms *camera* or *aula* alternatively.
Less certain is the identity of the 'Aula Consistorij Secreti' in which the
ambassadors of Parma were received on 27 October 1512 (MS. cit., fol.
249^r); this should most naturally be the same, but a doubt arises from the
record of the reception of the Piacenza embassy, 26 July of the same year,
for which Julius decided 'potius fieret secretum consistorium . . .' (it would
normally have been public). 'Et cum multi [Prelati, etc.] vellent ingredi,
Papa inhibuit propter debilitatem solarij Aulae, quod tremere videbatur,
quinimo feci, quod omnes Prelati, et quicunque aderant, non essent in
medio Aulae stantes, sed in extremitatibus circa parietes adhaerentes . . .'

(MS. cit., fol. 240ᵛ ff.); this account particularly recalls Paris's remark in 1510 that the upper Aula Pontificum (i.e. the Sala di Costantino) had a 'solarium . . . ligneum quasi curvum, et debile . . .', and another in 1513 that it was 'vacillans, & male firma, & in periculo ruinae' (Add. MSS. 8442, fol. 31ᵛ, 8443, fol. 18ʳ); there had been general fear of the collapse of that floor since the notorious occasion in 1500 when a good part of it fell, with the chimney and roof above, very nearly killing Alexander VI enthroned below (some of the accounts are reprinted in Ehrle–Stevenson, op. cit. in n. 6, p. 17). And it should be noted that the Sala di Costantino was undoubtedly used for the reception of the embassy from Reggio, 3 September 1512, 'in Consistorio semipublico . . . in Aula Pontificum *Consistoriali*, et superiori . . .' (Add. MS. 8442, fol. 247ʳ). However, a semi-public Consistory is perhaps sufficiently distinct to make its occurrence in the 'Aula Consistorij Secreti' incorrect; and it is worth noting too that on 27 June 1513 Paris expected the collapse of all the upper *Aulae* (Add. MS. 8443, fol. 52ᵛ), so that the fears expressed by Julius on 26 July 1512 could indeed have been caused by the floor of the Sala de' Palafrenieri. I have not yet found a text to contradict the assumption that after 1506 the Sala de' Palafrenieri was the normal location of the Secret Consistory.

34. See the text of Paris de Grassis quoted in n. 23, above; from this date his references to the two robing-rooms are to be read as applying to the third level unless he specifies otherwise. The sequence of events at Easter, 1508, will illustrate this point, and also the trials of a Master of Ceremonies: *Tenebrae*, Wednesday in Holy Week: 'Papa voluit parari in aula inferiori cum prius à multis mensibus citra in superiori paratus fuerat . . .'; Thursday: 'tandem hora 12 Papa paratus in aula superiori cum in inferiori sacristae omnia praeparaverunt, sed iussi superius paramenta portari et Cardinales ascendere . . .'; Good Friday: 'Papa voluit in inferiori aula paramenta parari . . .'; Saturday: 'Papa . . . venit in aulam inferiorem ubi accepit paramenta . . .'; Sunday: 'Omnes Cardinales et Prelati ac Oratores accesserunt ad superiorem aulam Paramenti ubi Papa vestiri debuit . . .' (Add. MS. 8441, fols. 195ʳ–203ᵛ).

35. Paris de Grassis, *Diarium*, 21 February 1513: 'Tandem circa horam noctis decimam, quae est inter dies 20. et 21. Februarij S. D. N. Julius Papa ij mortuus est . . . in Aula Superiori apud aulam Pontificum, ubi solitus est habitare. . . . Et postquam vestivimus cadaver de toto Pontificaliter iussi illud ad Aulam Paramenti deferri, quae omnibus commodior fuit.' The 'Aula Pontificum' in this account is the present Sala di Costantino, and hence the 'Aula Superior' must be the present Sala de' Palafrenieri (already interpreted so by Steinmann, op. cit. in n. 13, ii, p. 8).

36. The door on the West wall (well illustrated in J. Hess, *Kunstgeschichtliche Studien zu Renaissance und Barock* (Rome, 1967), ii, Pl. 36) leads to the 'stanze de' camerieri di Sua Santità' over the Public Consistory (Vasari, *Vite*, Florence, 1550, p. 875); in a plan of this part of the palace *c.* 1580, attributed to Ottaviano Mascarino (Accademia di San Luca G. 113) the corridor leading off from this door is designated 'Andito per andare a la cucina secreta' and the rooms over the Public Consistory are the apartment of the

Maestro di Camera; the hall itself is given its present name, 'Sala de li Svizzeri'. It may be convenient at this point to outline the history of the nomenclature of this room in the sixteenth century. Under Leo X and Adrian VI it continued to be called the 'aula paramenti' or 'camera paramenti in prima sala superiori' (Paris, *Diarium*, 1 November and 31 December 1517, Add. MS. 8444, fols. 41ᵛ, 54ᵛ, and Biagio da Cesena, *Diarium*, 30 August 1522, Add. MS. 8445, fol. 32ᵛ). It is the 'Sala de' Lanzi', the furnishings of which are recorded in the account-books of Paul III in 1536 and 1538 (L. Dorez, *La Cour du Pape Paul III d'après les registres de la trésorerie secrète* (Paris, 1932), ii, pp. 19, 250; cf. Vasari's description, quoted below, n. 40); and it is called 'stanza . . . dove sta la guardia de svizzeri' in reports of the destruction threatened by Paul IV in 1558 (letter of the Bishop of Anglone, 10 August, quoted by Ancel, op. cit. in n. 8, p. 67, and the *Avviso da Roma*, 13 August, quoted by E. Rossi, 'Roma ignorata', *Roma*, vii (1929), p. 565); the same title is used by Caroli, *c.* 1620 (MS. cit. in n. 16, fols. 243a, 445ᵛ). The only contradiction I know comes in a plan by Pirro Ligorio, 1560–1 (Ackerman, op. cit. in n. 5, Fig. 31), where it is called 'Sala de Palafrenieri'; this plan is, however, inaccurate in almost all respects that matter in our context.

37. This fireplace is shown in the plan by Caroli, *c.* 1620, MS. cit. in n. 16, fol. 243a; it is described by Taja, op. cit. in n. 12, p. 113: 'un focolare di portasanta masiccio alla moda antica'.

38. G. Vasari, *Le Vite . . .*, ed. G. Milanesi (Florence, 1906), iv, pp. 362–3: '. . . oltre che di grottesche e vari pavimenti egli tal palazzo abbellì assai, diede ancora disegno alle scale papali ed alle logge cominciate bene da Bramante . . . E fu cagione la bellezza di questo lavoro, che Raffaello ebbe carico di tutte le cose di pittura ed architettura che si facevano in palazzo . . . Egli fece fare a Gian Barile, in tutte le porte *e palchi* di legname, assai cose d'intaglio lavorate e finite con bella grazia'. It is worth noting that visitors soon after Raphael's death were at least as impressed by the lavishly carved and gilt ceilings as by his paintings; e.g. Francesco Novello, *Vita Leonis X.* (*c.* 1525), Bibl. Vat., MS. Barb. Lat. 2273, fol. 8ᵛ: 'Augustum palatium pontificum in politiorem formam magnificentissime eximia operis elegantia instauravit, ac egregiis picturis superbisque auratis laquearibus splendidissime exornavit: et auxit . . .'; Stephanus Ioanninensis, *In Mediceam Monarchiam pentateuchus* (Ancona, 1524), fol. cxᵛ: 'faustissima illa Vaticani laquearia quae in porticibus illis in excaelsam illam aeminentiam vergentia conspiciuntur: opulentissimo nitore expolivit: quibus videre nihil augustius est' (he makes no mention of paintings); Andrea Fulvio, *Antiquitates urbis* (Rome, 1527), fol. xxvi: 'Leo X insignem porticum triplicem & Zetas [sc: Dietas] & picturam & lacunaria aurea omnia ab eminentissimis artificibus comparata adiunxit'.

39. The texts as carved are, respectively: BEATVS HOMO QVI AVDIT ME E QVI VIGILAT AD FORES MEA / QVOTIDIE ET OBSERVAT AD POSTES HOSTII MEI (Proverbs 8: 34), and LAVDATE NOMEN DOMINI LAVDATE SERVI DOMINVM / QVI STATIS IN DOMO DOMINI IN ATRIIS DOMVS DEI NOSTRI (Psalms 134: 1–2). For texts relating to the *Ostiarii*, see above n. 32.

40. Vasari, *Vite*, ed. cit. in n. 38, vi, p. 554: 'Volendo poi papa Leone far dipignere la sala, dove sta la guardia de' Lanzi . . . Giovanni, oltre alle fregiature, che sono intorno a quella sala, di putti, leoni, armi papali e grottesche, fece per le faccie alcuni spartimenti di pietre mischie finte di varie sorti, e simili all'incrostature antiche che usarono di fare i Romani alle loro terme, tempj ed altri luoghi, come si vede nella Ritonda e nel portico di San Piero.' This room was 'accanto' to the Sala de' Palafrenieri, and there is no doubt of its identity. It is worth noticing that here—as again in the Stanza della Segnatura—Vasari gives the room a title that was out of use in 1568, but conforms to usage in the Vatican under Paul III (1534–49; see above, n. 36), when he had made his closest acquaintance with the palace. The lost frieze may be visualized on the basis of the splendid Leonine frieze in S. Maria in Domnica (the pope's former titular church, the restoration of which he continued until at least 1518); the treatment of the wall-surfaces, as described by Vasari, recalls the real marble panelling of Raphael's Chigi mausoleum. I know of no positive evidence for the date of the Leonine decoration of the Sala degli Svizzeri. In MS. Vat. Lat. 13751, *Disegni della prima e seconda loggia Vaticana*, by Francesco la Vega, 1745, there are, on fols. 25 and 45, very clear records of the lost shutters of this room and of the Sala de' Palafrenieri respectively, all Leonine; the difference in design between them, when related to the changing style of the doors of the Stanze, suggests that those of the Sala degli Svizzeri are earlier, as I should judge its ceiling to be earlier too. This conclusion is consistent with the only document I have found which refers to structural alterations in this room, which is from the first year of Leo's pontificate; in an account submitted by Giuliano Leno, 1 December 1513, is this item: 'Uno finestrone rimurato inella sala prima del papa, lugho palmi 16, alto palmi 30, grosso palmi $3\frac{1}{2}$ (Frey, op. cit. in n. 15, p. 25); in a *Ricordo* of 19 June 1514 (Frey, p. 26) it is specified that the 'sala prima del papa' is beneath the apartment of Cardinal Bibbiena, which was then under construction in the southern half of the Eastern tract of the palace, on the fourth level, and so it is clear that the *sala* in question was the Sala degli Svizzeri.

41. In the campaign of destruction initiated by Paul IV in that year, documented by Ancel, op. cit. in n. 8, pp. 65 ff.; it is to be identified with the 'sala della guardia de Zanti' mentioned, as due for demolition, in Vincenzo Buoncambi's letter of 13 August 1558.

42. J. Hess, 'Gli affreschi nella Sala vecchia degli Svizzeri al Palazzo Vaticano', *L'Illustrazione Vaticana* (1935), pp. 713 ff. (reprinted in op. cit. in n. 36, i, pp. 99 ff.), and M. V. Brugnoli, 'Un palazzo romano del tardo' 500 e l'opera di Giovanni e Cherubino Alberti a Roma', *Bollettino d'Arte*, Ser. 4, xlv (1960), p. 244, n. 21. Hess stated that the room had been the *anticamera* of Julius II, which is not strictly correct (see above, p. 188), and he curiously misread the emblems on the ceiling so as to conclude that it was a contribution of the penultimate Medici pope, Pius IV (1559–65). The evidence of the imprese is confirmed beyond all doubt by a passage in Paolo Giovio's *Vita Leonis* (Florence, 1548), p. 105: 'conclavia quoque per quae aditus est ad intimum cubiculum, laquearibus auratis & iucundissimis signis albario opere depictis in luculentiorem formam redegerat . . .' The term *Conclavia*

(i.e. rooms closed to the public) is also used by Michiel to describe the Sala degli Svizzeri and Sala de' Palafrenieri (27 December 1519: he describes the inner wall of Raphael's Loggia 'contiguo alle camere, et conclavi concistoriali del Papa'—quoted from Golzio, op. cit. in n. 17, p. 104).

43. Add. MS. 8443, fol. 207ᵛ. Under Leo X this room was generally so described (e.g. Paris, *Diarium*, 27 September 1513, 'In aula superiori Consistoriali fecerunt prandium') and this was the 'place of the [private] Consistory' in which John Clerk presented Henry VIII's *Assertio septem sacramentorum* to Leo (letter to Wolsey, 10 October 1521, with description of papal throne, baldacchino, cardinals' 'stolys', in B. M., Cotton MS. Vitellius B. IV, fol. 194ʳ); similarly, under Clement VII, Cardinal Cornaro was 'ordinatus in Presbiterum per Papam in camera Concistoriali, seu alia ante Capellam suam . . .' (Biagio da Cesena, *Diarium*, 1 April 1524, Add. MS. 8445, fol. 56ᵛ); in 1532, however, this room and the Sala degli Svizzeri were together termed 'camerae suae Cubiculariae' (ibid., fol. 232ᵛ), anticipating Vasari's title for the former: 'salotto . . . dove stavano i cubicularii' (*Vite*, ed. cit. in n. 38, vi, p. 555); in the accounts of Paul III, however, it is already, in 1536 and 1538, the 'saletta dove li parafrenieri fanno la guardia in Palazzo' and 'la sala de' . . . parafrenieri' (Dorez, op. cit. in n. 36, ii, pp. 54, 250), and similar titles are commonly used in later Cinquecento sources. For a new use for the room in the 1530's, see below, n. 65. A payment of 1517 often, but wrongly, related to this room's decoration is discussed below, n. 140.

44. The formal acknowledgement of a loan (Golzio, op. cit. in n. 17, p. 52), 'Actum in palacio apostolico in sala ante Cameram pape . . .'. Hess, in *Studien*, cit. in n. 36, i, p. 415, suggested that this *sala* was made for Leo X out of two rooms of the suite of Julius II; this idea does not appear illogical structurally, when the walls on this level are compared with those below (cf. the plan in Letarouilly, op. cit. in n. 26, Fig. 200), where the 'anticamera' or 'Camera Audientiae' was a long narrow room separating the Camera del Papagallo from the Sala de' Pontefici (Ehrle–Stevenson, op. cit. in n. 6, pp. 13–16). But on the upper level, at least under Julius, the Sala de' Palafrenieri was already directly adjacent to the Sala di Costantino (see the report of his death quoted above, n. 35). Hess's suggestion would also appear to be contradicted by the fragments of thirteenth- and fifteenth-century friezes remaining above the ceiling (see below, n. 53). The present division by supporting piers was added by Pius VII in 1816 (Hess, p. 416).

45. On 8 December 1518 Antonio da Sangallo was commissioned to make a ceiling for S. Maria della Quercia in Viterbo 'de quella richezza che è quello de camera de Papa Leone in Palazzo di Papa in Roma, dove se fa concistorio . . .' (C. Pinzi, 'Memorie e documenti inediti sulla Basilica di Santa Maria della Quercia in Viterbo', *Archivio storico dell'Arte*, iii (1890), p. 322); the model was undoubtedly this one (H. van Dam van Isselt, 'I soffitti della Sala del Concistorio e della Sala Regia in Vaticano', *Rendiconti della pontificia accademia romana di archeologia*, xxviii (1955–6), pp. 101 ff., discusses the document and the Viterbo ceiling, without realizing that the prototype still exists). The wording of the Viterbo contract may well imply that Antonio had constructed the ceiling of the Sala de' Palafrenieri (as he made, in 1518–19, the similar ceiling—now destroyed—of the Sala di

Costantino), but it remains probable that, as Vasari seems to say (see above, n. 38), Raphael made the design and Gian Barile the carvings. A payment to Antonio for the ceiling of the Sala di Costantino is dated 14 March 1519 (200 ducats 'per conto del palco della gran sala'); another of 10 September 1518 (300 ducats 'per el Palco') perhaps also applies, as does one to Penni, 25 December 1523 'pro pictura Palci Aule Consistorialis' (Archivio di Stato, Rome, Camerale I, 1490, fol. 9^r, 1489, fol. 67^r; Archivio segreto vaticano, Introitus et exitus 561, fol. 126^r; the Sala di Costantino was used for Public Consistories under Clement VII). I should like to add a brief reference to this important ceiling: 'le imprese del suave nel suffito d'oro tutto' (c. 1585: R. Lanciani, 'Il Codice barberiniano XXX. 89', *Archivio della R. società romana di storia patria*, vi (1883), p. 459).

46. Vasari, *Vite*, ed. cit. in n. 38, p. 555 (continuing the description of the 'Sala, dove sta la guardia de' Lanzi', quoted above, n. 40): 'in un altro salotto accanto a questo, dove stavano i cubicularii, fece Raffaello da Urbino in certi tabernacoli alcuni Apostoli di chiaroscuro, grandi quanto il vivo e bellissimi; e Giovanni sopra le cornici di quell'opera ritrasse di naturale molti pappagalli di diversi colori, i quali allora aveva Sua Santità, e così anco babuini, gattimamoni, zibetti, ed altri bizzari animali . . .' (see also 1550 ed., *Vita di Rafaello*, p. 663).

47. For the destruction see Vasari, loc. cit. in previous note, Ancel, op. cit. in n. 8, and Rossi, op. cit. in n. 36. For the reconstruction under Pius IV see J. Gere, *Taddeo Zuccaro* (London, 1969), p. 91, and in addition a payment in A. Bertolotti, *Artisti urbinati in Roma* (Urbino, 1881), p. 17, dated 3 May 1560.

48. On the painted architrave on the South side is the inscription: AVLA SANCTORVM APOSTOLORVM IN AMPLIOREM HANC FORMAM RESTITVTA AN MDLXXXII; this last phase of the work was done by Giovanni Alberti and Egnazio Danti (Brugnoli, op. cit. in n. 42, p. 230). A further restoration by Maratta for Clement XI is recorded by Taja, op. cit. in n. 12, p. 116.

49. D. Redig de Campos, 'Relazione dei laboratori di restauro', *Rendiconti della pontificia accademia romana di archeologia*, xxvii (1951–4), p. 403, and C. L. Frommel, *Baldassare Peruzzi als Maler und Zeichner* (Vienna–Munich, 1967), p. 88, n. 395. Parts of the original Corinthian fluted pilaster-framing of the niches are now visible once more behind the gridiron of the *Saint Lawrence*. Three drawings for SS. John, Matthew, and Luke (Louvre 28954 and 4261, British Museum 1959–7–11–1) have been published (S. J. Freedberg, *Painting of the High Renaissance in Rome and Florence* (Cambridge, Mass., 1961), ii, Figs. 396, 395; P. Pouncey and J. Gere, *Italian Drawings . . . in the British Museum: Raphael and his Circle* (London, 1962), pp. 52–3), of which the *Saint John* seems to me to be by Raphael himself. An apparently unrecorded study for the *Saint Lawrence* (probably by Penni) is in Vienna (Albertina ScR. 117).

50. H. Jedin, *A History of the Council of Trent* (London, 1957), i, pp. 77 ff., with further bibliography.

51. For Torquemada and earlier sources, see Jedin, loc. cit. in n. 50. Domenico Jacobazzi, *De Concilio* (ed. C. Jacobazzi, Rome, 1538), especially p. 32: '. . . Cardinales loco apostolorum successerunt' (the *De concilio* was begun not later than 1512). This doctrine is recalled in the papal address to newly created cardinals: 'successores Apostolorum circa thronum sedebitis' (Patrizi–Burchard, *Liber Caeremoniarum* (1488, ed. cit. in n. 6), fol. xl^r—see also ii^v).

52. See above, n. 46. According to Taja, op. cit. in n. 12, p. 115, the two parrots over the door to the Sala vecchia degli Svizzeri are fragments of Giovanni's original decoration.

53. D. Redig de Campos, 'Di alcune tracce del Palazzo di Niccolò III nuovamente tornate alla luce', *Rendiconti della pontificia accademia romana di archeologia*, xviii (1941–2), pp. 71 ff., and 'Les constructions d'Innocent III et de Nicolas III sur la colline Vaticane', *Mélanges d'archéologie et d'histoire*, lxxi (1959), pp. 369 ff.

54. Another case may be mentioned here, since we shall not meet it later, the Leonine decoration of the Sala di Costantino, begun by Raphael in, probably, 1519; here again one part of the decoration—the series of portraits of the *sainted* popes—repeats the previous one, which is specified most clearly in Sigismondo de Conti, *Le storie de' suoi tempi* (ed. Rome, 1883), ii, p. 269: 'tectum superioris aulae Pontificum (hoc enim nomen habet a Pontificibus in numerum Sanctorum relatis in eo depictis) . . .'

55. Ehrle–Stevenson, op. cit. in n. 6, pp. 31 ff.; Redig de Campos, op. cit. in n. 6, pp. 46 ff.

56. 'Rafaello . . . cominciò nella camera della segnatura . . .'; 'Fu fatto levare per ordine di Papa Paulo un cammino che era nella camera del fuoco: et metterlo in quello della segniatura: dove erano le spalliere di legno in prospettiva, fatte di mano di fra Giovanni intagliatore per Papa Iulio: et avendo nell'una et nell'altra camera dipinto Raffaelle da Urbino, bisognò rifare tutto il basamento alle storie della camera della segniatura' (*Vite* (1550), pp. 641, 939).

57. I would not mention this document, which has generally lapsed into an appropriate oblivion, if it had not recently been pressed into service again by J. Pope-Hennessy, *Raphael*, London, n.d. (1970?), p. 138. It is written in the form of a *Mandato camerale*, that is a credit-note addressed to Agostino Chigi, informing him on the authority of the treasurer Ferdinando Ponzetti that he should pay Raphael thirty ducats 'pro coloribus et alijs rebus necessarijs in depingendo cubicula signature palatij S.mi dnj nrj . . .', from which Pope-Hennessy would draw the conclusion that 'the term Segnatura is applied to the whole suite of rooms'. If this were indeed the case the term would also have become meaningless; but it is not the case. I have examined this document and I am convinced that it is a forgery. There are a surprising number of these spurious *mandati*, and they are not all by the same hand; this one, however, is identical in all physical respects (including its rather good Ponzetti seal) with another in the same collection dated 1 June 1518 (100

ducats 'pro sua provisione . . . per duos menses . . . in operibus picture palatij . . .') which is much more interesting because its author tried to be more specific; in doing so he made a number of mistakes: (i) Raphael was *not* paid by *provisione* (a technical term); (ii) Ponzetti is described as 'electus melphitanus', inappropriate after 21 December 1517 when he was consecrated; (iii) reference is made to a *cedula* by 'r. d. J. magistri domus Sanctitatis sue', probably meant to be Johannes de Ferraria; he, however, had been replaced late in 1515, and in any case was *Magister sacri palatii*, a very different post; the *Magister domus* throughout Leo's reign was Alessandro Neroni. The *mandato* of 3 January 1516 has a notarial reference to one Nicia; there was no notary of this name active in the period, so far as I can discover, and I suspect that the author was amusing himself (and perhaps discreetly warning Italian collectors) by taking to Rome the best-known of all Renaissance lawyers, the cuckold of Machiavelli's *Mandragola*. I should like to acknowledge that I have discussed these documents with Christoph Frommel, who has worked on others in the group; his negative opinion in this case is cited by H. von Einem, *Das Programm der Stanza della Segnatura im Vatikan* (Opladen, 1971), p. 17 n. 45 (with earlier bibliography). For the probable origin of the group, see D. Farabulini, *Saggio di nuovi studi su Raffaello d'Urbino* (Rome, 1875), p. 334n.

58. 'In festo Sanctae Luciae . . . Papa in camera ultima superiori nova idest in ea quae est picta Signatura S.tae me[moriae] Julij ij. consecravit R.mum D. Laurentium Puccium Cardinalem Sanctorum quatuor Coronatorum' (Add. MS. 8443, fols. 85ᵛ–86ʳ; essentially the same text in MS. Vat. Lat. 5636, fol. 71ʳ).

59. It was published simultaneously by Müntz, op. cit. in n. 5, p. 132 (without comment), and J. Hergenroether, *Leonis X . . . regesta* (Freiburg-im-Breisgau, 1884), p. 361.

60. Paris de Grassis and, so far as I know, all other Masters of Ceremonies, invariably described rooms from the point of view of the visitor to the pope, that is to say in anti-clockwise sequence in the Vatican Palace. Thus, for a parallel to his meaning for the word *ultima* in this text, he calls the Sala Ducale (5 on the plan), the third of the Public Consistory Halls, 'ultima sala' (e.g. 18 August 1504, Add. MS. 8440, fol. 50ᵛ). It would never occur to him to count rooms in chronological order of their decoration, like an historian— or like Vasari, who called the Stanza d'Eliodoro (13) 'la camera seconda, verso la sala grande' (12). Sellaio, writing to Michelangelo, 1 January 1518/ 19, also described the Stanza dell'Incendio as 'l'ultima stanza di palazo' (quoted from Golzio, op. cit. in n. 17, p. 65).

61. Steinmann, op. cit. in n. 13, ii, pp. 99–110, did not mistake the room that Paris meant, but his interpretation was as follows: the Stanza dell'Incendio was initially to house the *Signatura*; Perugino's commission was transferred to Raphael when the *Signatura* was moved from the end room into the middle one; but in 1513 the *Signatura* was still convened in the end room because Raphael's was not finished. There is no evidence for the second step in the argument, and the third seems to do violence to the text. Broadly similar is the derivative argument of von Einem, op. cit. in n. 57, pp. 16 ff.; von

Einem is one of the few recent scholars to have remembered that Steinmann wrote about the Stanze, and so he too realized that Paris was describing the end room; but in following Steinmann's assertion that Julius moved his *Signatura* from there into the middle room he eventually left unexplained the plainly contrary evidence of Paris.

62. They are, in sequence: 17 December 1513: 'quia non videbatur conveniens ut [Papa] illum insigniret minoribus ordinibus in publico, suasimus, quod similiter in secreta Cappella sua paucis presentibus ordinaret, prout fecit, et etiam ibidem, postea legit psalmos cum orationibus paramentorum, et induit calciamenta, et venit ad locum, ubi in die S.tae Luciae consecravit illum, et ibi indutus de toto sicut tunc dixit missam . . .' (Add. MS. 8443, fol. 87ᵛ). 21 December 1517: two cardinals were consecrated 'in Episcopos . . . in camera superiori, in qua olim etiam Cardinalem sanctorum quatuor consecraverat . . .' (Add. MS. 8444, fol. 51ᵛ). 2 July 1519: 'Papa consecraverat cardinalem de Farnesio in Episcopum . . . in cammera in qua solebat esse signatura PP. Julij . . .' (MS. Vat. Lat. 5636, fol. 285ᵛ, poor text in Add. MS. 8444, fol. 163ᵛ). It will be noticed that these uses of the room fall, as they must, outside the period of Raphael's occupation, approximately midsummer 1514 to midsummer 1517.

63. The most helpful source of information on this subject is still G. Moroni, *Dizionario di erudizione storico-ecclesiastica*, xliii (1853), pp. 210 ff. For a more modern (but still incomplete) bibliography: I. Gordon, S. J., 'Normae supremi tribunalis signaturae apostolici', *Periodica de re morali canonica liturgica* (Rome, Pontificia universitas Gregoriana), lix (1970), pp. 75 ff., 112 ff., and also D. S. Chambers, 'The economic predicament of Renaissance Cardinals', *Studies in Medieval and Renaissance History*, iii (1966), pp. 300, 307.

64. B. Katterbach, O. F. M., *Referendarii utriusque signaturae*, Vatican City (1931), p. xiv (who also, p. vii, makes a clear statement of the relation between the *Signatura* and the other curial tribunals); in conformity with this subdivision, Paris de Grassis distinguished between the 'Signatura Cardinalis Alexandrini' and the 'Signatura Papae', or 'Signatura Papalis' (*Diarium*, 17 March and 26 May 1506, Add. MS. 8440, fols. 347ʳ, 356ʳ).

65. Moroni, op. cit. in n. 63, xliii, p. 223; since his sources were inevitably no earlier than the seventeenth century there is an element of hypothesis in the assumption that requirements were essentially the same in the early sixteenth century (most scholars who have worked with materials relating to papal ceremonial would, I think, agree on the probability while acknowledging the possibility of change). I have been unable to discover where the *Signatura gratiae* was convened in the pontificates of Leo, Adrian, and Clement (the *Registri* do not, like Privy Council Registers, specify the location of meetings). In the case of Clement I suspect that it was in the Sala de' Palafrenieri, because his corpse was prepared for lying-in-state—a ritual previously performed in the hall outside the bedroom (cf. n. 35, above)—in his *Signatura* ('Obijt Clemens in camera magna superiori, et in alia camera ubi solet fieri Signatura extractis visceribus fuit lotus, et indutus, ac per scalas secretas, et secretiores portas [i.e. via the *anticamera*, 11], ad cameram

Papagalli inferiorem' (Giovanni Francesco Firmano, *Diarium*, 25 September 1534, Add. MS. 8447, fol. 9ᵛ—this text was known to Steinmann, op. cit. in n. 13, ii, p. 110, but I think he was wrong to associate it with the Stanza dell' Incendio). Early in Paul III's reign the *Signatura* was quite certainly in the Sala de' Palafrenieri (Biagio da Cesena, *Diarium*, 17 February 1538: 'S.D.N. . . . exivit de thalamo suo penetrali (9) in Aulam ubi fit Signatura prope Cappellam suam parvam' (10); Add. MS. 8446, fol. 222ᵛ). This makes sense since the requirements described by Moroni's sources approximate those of a consistory. The following payments, trivial in themselves, are helpful in being consistent with such requirements (and in confirming the common meaning of the word): 23 December 1524, 'per uno Busselo di polvera per mettere al calamaio della signatura . . .' (A.S.R., Camerale I, 1491, fol. 68ʳ); 25 June 1537, 'per uno tavolino . . . per uso della Signatura'; 15 October 1538 'per un tavolino . . . per sua Santità per la Signatura' (Dorez, op. cit. in n. 36, ii, pp. 132, 250).

66. Hence, when Paul III converted the middle room, in 1541, to be the Camera della Segnatura that Vasari knew, he had the fireplace of the Stanza dell'Incendio moved to the other side of the dividing wall so that it fed the same flue: 26 July 1541, 'A. M.ro Francesco Salviati pittore per suo pagamento del Re Pipino che ha depinto nella Camera inanti la Guardarobba di Palazzo dove stava il camino che N.S. se fece levare et metter in la camera della Tarsia, scudi 15' (A. Bertolotti, 'Speserie segrete e pubbliche di Papa Paolo III', *Atti e memorie delle RR. deputazioni di storia patria per le provincie dell' Emilia*, N.S. iii (1878), 1, p. 180); for commentary on the titles given to these rooms, see below, nn. 96, 140. The fireplace was of a height to cause the destruction of the lowest, central part of the *Disputa*, later restored; the fireplace was moved back quite soon, and now nothing survives of Salviati's *Pepin* in the Stanza dell'Incendio but the titular inscription formerly over his head.

67. The exterior frame of the door was clearly erected in two stages, and from the inside it is obvious that the upper extension must have been made before Raphael painted the *Coronation of Charlemagne* (probably early in 1516). I think it is likely that the lower door-frame was Julius's and that the heightening was done, under Leo, in connection with the room's redecoration; but other solutions are possible. The present balcony along the West façade at this level was erected under Clement XI (1700–21), but it must have replaced one existing *c.* 1515 since at its southern end there is a door-frame identical on the exterior to that which leads into the Stanze; this door would have led via a corridor to the Julian door on the West side of the Sala vecchia degli Svizzeri (see above, n. 36); I think it is probable that there was already (as there has been since early in the eighteenth century) a small staircase in the South-West corner of the block which would give direct access from the Sala Ducale (4) but the evidence is not clear, at least to me. An alternative route to the exterior door of the Stanze is by a short balcony that leads from a *ballatoio* around the South and West sides of the Torre Borgia and appears to be original; by this route the Stanze could be reached via the staircase in the Torre Borgia and the Borgia Apartments below.

68. There is still, so far as I know, no direct evidence to date this ceiling. Documents testify to Perugino's presence in Perugia on 27 May 1508 and in

Florence on 18 February 1509, but there is another gap between February and December 1509. F. Canuti, *Il Perugino*, Siena (1931), i, pp. 194 ff., favours the earlier date on the grounds that Perugino is likely to have begun when Sodoma did in the middle room; if a passage in Albertini's *Opusculum*, cit. in n. 5, fol. Yi^v ('Sunt praeterea aulae & Camerae adornatae variis picturis ab excellentissimis pictoribus concertantibus hoc anno instauratae') is taken to embrace Perugino, it may be argued with about equal success that this should mean 1508 (when Sodoma began) or 1509 (hoc anno). The earlier date can be supported by the evidence (discussed by Canuti) that Perugino's work was contemporaneous with Signorelli's; in the case of the latter artist the only possible gap in his documented career appears to be the second half of 1508.

69. John 20: 21–22; this identification also in Canuti, op. cit. in n. 68, p. 196.

70. The sources on this subject are extremely numerous; the commentaries of Gregory and Chrysostom quoted in Thomas Aquinas's *Catena aurea* are characteristic of an exegetical tradition. Perhaps I may refer the reader to J. Shearman, *Raphael's Cartoons* . . . (London, 1972), pp. 68 ff., for a discussion of the text, but for a theologian at Julius's court interpreting it in the sense outlined here, see Giovanni Gozzadini, *De electione romani pontificis*, quoted by H. Jedin, 'Giovanni Gozzadini, ein Konziliarist am Hof Julius II', *Kirche des Glaubens, Kirche der Geschichte* (Freiburg-im-Breisgau, 1966), ii, p. 33.

71. For example, the Sala de' Pontefici, where the 'sedes Papae Consistorialis' was opposite the fireplace (a description in Paris, *Diarium*, Thursday after Easter 1510, Add. MS. 8442, fol. 32^r). On the other hand in the Camera del Papagallo on the second level the papal throne was placed against the wall at right angles to the fireplace (idem, 24 August 1505, Add. MS. 8440, fol. 230^r); with this kind of arrangement the throne of the *Signatura* could have been placed against the South wall (later painted with the *Fire in the Borgo*), but clearly not against the window in the North wall.

72. Isaiah 60: 1–2.

73. Matthew 4: 3–11; Canuti suggests that the saint is the Baptist, which is reasonable textually but not, I think, visually.

74. Moroni, op. cit. in n. 63, xliii, p. 213.

75. *Grazia* was proposed by J. Klaczko, *Rome et la renaissance: Jules II* (Paris, 1898), p. 189; Steinmann, op. cit. in n. 13, p. 99, suggested *Hope*, and Canuti, op. cit. in n. 68, p. 196, *Misericordia*. A few more exotic identifications have been suggested but they are, I believe, best forgotten.

76. See above, n. 28; the passage on the Sistine Chapel (ibid., fol. Xiii^v) reads: 'Capella PP. Syxti. iiij. in palatio apostolico perpulchra in qua sunt picturae novi & veteris testamenti cum pontificibus Sanctis, manu & arte mirabili nobilium pictorum concertantium videlicet. Petri de castro plebis . . .' (etc.).

77. The basis for this date is in part an interpretation of a passage in Raphael's letter to his uncle, 21 April 1508, which I should explain; he writes: 'averia caro sefosse posibile davere una letera direcomandatione al gonfalonero difiorenza [Piero Soderini] dal .S. Prefetto [Francesco Maria della Rovere] . . . me faria grande utilo per linteresse de una certa stanza dalavorare la quale tocha a sua .S. de alocare...', which is, obviously, extremely ambiguous —above all in the identity of 'sua .S.'; it makes no sense to suggest, as does Golzio, op. cit. in n. 17, p. 19, that the *stanza* might be the enormous Sala dei Cinquecento in Palazzo Vecchio in Florence. On the other hand the possibility that Soderini might have acted as agent for Julius arises from the parallel between the latter's patronage in 1508–9 and Sixtus IV's in 1481–2, when the decoration of the Sistine Chapel could not have been achieved without the active co-operation of the Florentine government; and the fact that Raphael's letter was written, probably, only a few months before Perugino, Signorelli, and perhaps also Sodoma actually began work (above, n. 68), makes me think that the task to which Raphael aspired was also the one in the Vatican.

78. 'Die xiii. Octobris 1508 Ma.cus D. Sigismundus Chisius permisit quod magister Io: Ant. de Bazis de Vercellis pictor in urbe pinget in Cameris S.D. papae superioribus tantam operam quae extimabitur fact. per 50 ducatos de carlinis x per ducatum, quos praefatus Io. Ant. confessus fuit recipisse . . . ad bonum computum . . .' (G. Cugnoni, *Agostino Chigi il Magnifico* (Rome, 1878), p. 82; a seriously abridged reading in Golzio, op. cit. in n. 17, p. 21). Fifty ducats is a small amount in relation to other Stanze payments.

79. This important detail is rarely noticed; I am fairly certain that I am not the first to notice it, but I cannot now trace the source to which an acknowledgement is due.

80. A candidate for the execution, on documentary grounds, is Johannes Ruysch (J. Shearman, 'Raphael's Unexecuted Projects for the Stanze', *Walter Friedlaender zum 90. Geburtstag* (Berlin, 1965), p. 160, n. 12).

81. The first known payment is dated 13 January 1509, and is 'ad bonum computum picture camere de medio eiusdem Santitatis testudinate' (an essentially correct transcription of the whole document in Golzio, op. cit. in n. 17, p. 370). I should like to take this opportunity to correct a mistake in the article cit. in n. 80, p. 160, n. 13, which arose from inability to read my own notes and which has so far escaped castigation, except by my students; I argued that Raphael could not have arrived in Rome in the summer of 1508 as, before going to Rome, he did an appreciable amount of work on an altarpiece provided for in a will of 20 July 1508, but in terms that imply no contract at that date. The proper date for the will is 1506.

82. A brief outline of this argument is in J. Shearman, 'Raphael as Architect', *Journal of the Royal Society of Arts*, cxvi (1968), p. 396; but it will be set out in more detail in a book on the Stanza della Segnatura.

83. D. Redig de Campos, *Raffaello nelle Stanze* (Milan, 1965), p. 18; I should like to thank Professor Redig de Campos for kindly giving me access to the

records of the recent campaign of restoration. A problem to notice is that the profiles of the external window-frames on North and South sides are quite different; it seems to me probable that those on the North are earlier, and that they may have been inserted by Alexander VI (without, however, altering the outline of the internal embrasure at that time).

84. The title comes from the first literary reference, in Albertini's *Opusculum* (cit. in n. 5, fol. Zii^r): 'De Bibliotecis novae urbis ... Est praeterea biblioteca nova secreta perpulchra (ut ita dicam) Pensilis Iulia: quam tua beatitudo construxit signisque planetarum & coelorum exornavit, additis aulis & cameris ornatiss[imis] atque de ambulatoriis auro, & picturis ac statuis exornatis non longe a capella syxtea.'

85. A documentary argument is set out in Shearman, op. cit. in n. 80, p. 160, but I would now express it differently. The crucial document remains the record, 9 March 1509, of payment to Lorenzo Lotto 'ad bonum computum laborerii picturarum faciendarum in Cameris superioribus papae prope librariam superiorem' (Golzio, op. cit. in n. 17, pp. 20–21); the same treasurer had noted on 8 October 1508 that Sodoma had received 50 ducats for painting 'in Cameris S.D. papae superioribus', from which it follows that this treasurer understood that Sodoma and Lotto were at work in the same suite of rooms; and further it follows that one of these rooms was next to an upper library. Albertini refers to a new upper library in 1509 (previous note). On 20 January 1513 Bembo described this library in terms so specific, and in such a context, that it is clear that he had seen it complete (see below). In January 1513 only two rooms in the suite could conceivably be so described, the present Stanza della Segnatura or part of the Torre Borgia (an extremely unlikely alternative—see below, n. 140—but logically admissible); the Stanza d'Eliodoro was at that time very obviously incomplete, and the Stanza dell'Incendio, although it might have appeared complete for all we know, was, as we have seen, the *Signatura* of Julius. The passage in Bembo's letter reads as follows: 'Ptolemaeum quidem Philadelphum, Aegypti, atque Attalum Pergami regem laudamus; quod in comparandis ad eas bibliothecas celeberrimas, quas instituerunt, libris omnem operam adhibuerint: ita pulchrum semper maximis, & in summo imperio constitutis hominibus fuit, iuvisse studia litterarum, et ingenijs materiam suppeditavisse optimis se in artibus exercendi. Eam tu curam, & diligentiam eorum aemulatus, ad illam egregiam bibliothecam Vaticanam ab ijs, qui fuerunt ante te Pontificibus maximis comparatam, addis, adiungisque alteram, non illam quidem librorum numero; sed cum eorum, quibus est referta, probitate atque praestantia, tum loci commoditate, amoenitateque propter elegantiam marmorum & picturarum, speculasque bellissimas, quas habet; ad usum Pontificum multo etiam amabiliorem. Huic tu bibliothecae quod ornamentum, quam venustatem, quam etiam auctoritatem addere atque tribuere maiorem possis ...' (*Epistolae familiares* (Venice, 1552), p. 188).

86. In the progressive solidification of this hypothesis the position of the unfortunate Hermann Grimm is remarkable, was unacknowledged by his contemporaries, and has more recently been forgotten. Already in *Das Leben Raphael's* (Berlin, 1872), pp. 206 ff., he made the explicit suggestion that the Stanza della Segnatura was a library, comparing its decoration with

that of other libraries (in most detail, with that of the Escorial), and noting its four-fold subject-division. A. Springer, *Raffael und Michelangelo* (Leipzig, 1878), i, pp. 149, 156, basing himself on the pioneering work of J. D. Passavant (*Rafael von Urbino* . . ., i (Leipzig, 1839), p. 138: 'Zimmer . . . der Facultäten') came near to restating the proposition when he rightly stressed the recognition of the four personifications on the ceiling as Faculties, and compared the subject-matter of the wall-frescoes with the portrait-cycle of the *studio* of Federico da Montefeltro at Urbino (the heroes of his library). A. Schmarsow, *Melozzo da Forlì* (Berlin–Stuttgart, 1886), p. 231, n. 3, quoting the payment to Lotto, 9 March 1509, cited above, n. 85, asked parenthetically after the words 'prope librariam superiorem': 'Wo lag diese?' His question was in effect answered by F. Wickhoff, 'Die Bibliothek Julius II.', *Jahrbuch der k. preußischen Kunstsammlungen*, xiv (1893), pp. 49 ff., who first brought together the documentary evidence and the iconographical indications. In the meantime J. von Schlosser, 'Beiträge zur Kunstgeschichte aus den Schriftquellen des frühen Mittelalters', *Sitzungsberichte der k. Akademie der Wissenschaften: phil.-hist. Classe*, cxxiii (Vienna, 1891), pp. 147 ff., had placed the iconographical proposition in the context of encyclopaedic decorative cycles in medieval libraries; and later, in 'Giusto's Fresken in Padua und die Vorläufer der Stanza della Segnatura', *Jahrbuch der kunsthistorischen Sammlungen des allerhöchsten Kaiserhauses*, xvii (1896), pp. 83 ff., combined this approach with Wickhoff's. Since that date the argument has not been advanced in any important respect, except for one practical suggestion by Georg Leyh (see below, n. 98).

87. A payment of 100 ducats 'Johanni pictori in camera Bibliothece' (A. Zahn, 'Notizie artistiche dall'archivio segreto,' *Archivio storico italiano*, Ser. III, i (1867), p. 181, and Frey, op. cit. in n. 15, p. 15; for an interpretation, Shearman, op. cit. in n. 80, p. 160.).

88. The term is used in the inventory of Cardinal Fieschi, 1524, printed by E. Rodoconachi, *Rome au temps de Jules II et de Léon X* (Paris, 1912), p. 397. Raphael's father, Giovanni Santi, had described the library of Federico da Montefeltro as 'in tucte facultà universale . . . Theologi . . . Philosophi antichi . . . le storie tucte . . . Poeti . . . Legisti . . . Medici . . .' (and Arabic, Greek, Italian divisions: the whole text in Passavant, op. cit. in n. 86, i, p. 460); this description accords reasonably well with subdivisions of the *Index Bibliotecae Ill.mi Ducis Urbini* (MS. Vat. Lat. 3960, fols. 94 ff.): Theology, Philosophy, *Iuriste*, Cosmography, History, miscellaneous, Greek and Hebrew (for another description of the library of Federico, see C. H. Clough, 'The Library of the Dukes of Urbino', *Librarium*, ix (1966), p. 102). For other examples, varying in detail but not in principle: the inventory of Piero di Cosimo de' Medici's books, 1456 (E. Piccolomini, 'Ricerche intorno alle condizioni e alle vicende della libreria medicea privata', *Archivio storico italiano*, Ser. III, xxi (1875), pp. 106 ff.); a reconstruction of the *segnature* of the books of Alfonso I of Naples (T. de Marinis, *La biblioteca napoletana dei Re d'Aragona*, i (Milan, 1947), pp. 176 ff.); the *Canone bibliografico* of Nicolas V, sent to Cosimo de' Medici in 1463 (Piccolomini, p. 111—already adduced in this context by Wickhoff, op. cit. in n. 86, p. 53); the *Index* of Alfonso II of Naples, c. 1515 (De Marinis, op. cit. ii, pp. 193 ff., whose date—before 1458—must be corrected on the basis of the contents); and the inventories of

two ecclesiastical libraries, at the monastery at Bobbio, 1461 (D. M. Robathan, 'Libraries of the Italian Renaissance', in *The Mediaeval Library*, ed. J. W. Thompson (New York, 1957), p. 523); and of the church of the Incoronata at Lodi, 1518 (E. Motta, 'I libri della chiesa dell'Incoronata di Lodi nel 1518', *Il libro e la stampa*, i (1907), pp. 105 ff.). The inventory of the Vatican Library under Leo X, 1518 (MS. Vat. Lat. 3948) provides subject-classifications of this kind which correspond fairly neatly to the actual location of books in the presses.

89. O. Hartwig, in *Zentralblatt für Bibliothekswesen*, x (1893), pp. 140 ff.; G. Laschitzer, ibid. xiii (1896), pp. 272 ff.; and, more recently, G. Leyh 'Die Camera della Segnatura — ein Bibliotheksraum?', *Festschrift für Georg Leidinger* (Munich, 1930), pp. 171 ff. A silent, symbolic testimony to the same approval is the decoration of the vault of the entrance-hall of the Pierpont Morgan Library (painted by H. Siddons Wombray, 1906), a close imitation of that of the Stanza della Segnatura in which the four faculties are *Religio, Philosophia, Ars*, and *Scientia*.

90. The counter-attack from which most others take their inspiration was by J. Klaczko, 'Dans la "Camera della Segnatura"', first published in *Revue des deux mondes*, 15 July 1894, and reprinted in *Rome et la Renaissance: Jules II* (Paris, 1898), pp. 207 ff.; the success of Klaczko's article is a lesson in the advocative efficacy of wit and charm in scholarship, but I think it is seldom read now; it is greatly to his credit that he was, it seems, the first to take the trouble to find out the true meaning of *Signatura*; for his principal arguments, see the next note. His immediate (but less good-tempered) followers were P. Fabre, 'La Vaticane de Sixte IV', *Mélanges de l'École Française*, xv (1895), pp. 476 ff., and L. Dorez, 'La Bibliothèque privée du Pape Jules II', *Revue des bibliothèques*, vi (1896), p. 107. Steinmann, op. cit. in n. 13, ii, pp. 44 ff., 109 ff., was also in opposition, but independently; he thought that he had found another place for the library, on a still higher level where Julius had built a corridor up by the roof with bird-cages and so on for his leisure-hours. This conclusion was based upon two misconceptions, I think: the first that the *Bibliotheca Iulia* was in that sense private, and the second that Albertini's epithet *Pensilis* ought to imply something like a hanging garden; on the contrary—as Bembo makes clear (above, n. 85)—Julius's new library was put where it was for the greater convenience of popes in general (*ad usum Pontificum*), and the limited force of the adjective *Pensilis* may be judged from its use by Andrea Fulvio (*Antiquaria Urbis* (Rome, 1513), fols. 36ʳᵛ): *Pensilibusque viis* for the corridors of the Belvedere, *Pensile . . . iter* for the corridor to Castel Sant'Angelo; Albertini and Fulvio meant to express nothing by the word except their mild surprise at not finding at ground-level something normally to be found there. Steinmann's arguments have been recently restated, but without any useful addition, by von Einem, op. cit. in n. 57, pp. 11 ff. I see no point in assembling a long list of authors who have opposed the library-hypothesis, but it would be misleading to imply that there have not been others to support it, among the more serious of whom have been H. Weizsäcker, 'Literarisches in Raphael's Gedankenwelt', *Jahrbuch der preußischen Kunstsammlungen*, lviii (1937), p. 59; O. Fischel, *Raphael*, London, 1948, pp. 72–3; W. Schöne, *Raphael*, Darmstadt (1958) p. 11; and Redig de Campos

consistently in several publications. One of the least justifiable positions
seems to me the apparently neutral one of Pastor, op. cit. in n. 4, vi, pp. 582
ff., who thought that the room could have served both as a library and as a
Signatura; the furnishings necessary for the two functions would indeed be
hard to combine.

91. Two of Klaczko's are worth dealing with: (i) that the room in question
was already termed *Camera signaturae* by Paris de Grassis in 1513; after Steinmann, in 1905, had shown that this text referred to the Stanza dell'Incendio,
the repetition of this point by later (even present) authors has been inexcusable;
(ii) that the *Bibliotheca Pensilis Iulia* described by Albertini appears, from the
text itself (dated June 1509), to be complete, as is indeed the case; but after
nearly a century historiography has at least advanced by the general
acknowledgement of a rule, that evidence must be weighed by the standards
of the context from which it is taken. To read a little more of Albertini's
Opusculum is to find—to take three fairly adjacent examples—the following:
fol. Xiii^v, in the Sistine Chapel 'superiorem partem testudineam pulcherrimis
picturis & auro *exornavit* [sc: Julius] opus praeclarum Michael. Archangeli
floren.' (completed 1512); fol. Yi^v, in the Vatican Palace 'laquearia pul-
cherrima auro & picturis *exornata* in ipsis aulis' (all these have, or had,
Leonine emblems); and fol. Xii^r, S. Maria in Domnica 'quam nuper
Reverendissimus Ioannes de Medicis Florentinus . . . collapsam in pristinam
formam *restituit*' (restoration in fact continues until at least 1518). Obviously
Albertini anticipates—as authors of other guide-books have done—the completion of enterprises, and to take his book as an accurate *terminus ante* for all
he describes is quite unjustifiable. It is quite clear that he had no idea what
Michelangelo was doing on the Sistine Ceiling—only that he was at work
there—and thus, by analogy, his description of the *Bibliotheca Iulia* is not
only no *terminus ante* but also no obstacle to Wickhoff's thesis on the grounds
that its details do not conform to Raphael's decorations. I think it is better
to read the text (above, n. 84) as a generalized, rhetorical vision of the proper
appearance of libraries based upon humanistic experience, and particularly,
perhaps, that of reading Vitruvius vi. 3 or Plutarch, *Lucullus* xlii, on the
library of Lucullus, whence he might have taken the stress on the contiguity
of logge; and from his own experience of real libraries, like that of the Vatican
itself, he could have been led to expect celestial and terrestrial globes as
furnishings (*signe planetarum & coelorum*: cf. Fabre, op. cit. in n. 90, pp. 21, 26,
and E. Müntz and P. Fabre, *La Bibliothèque du Vatican au XVe siècle* (Paris,
1887), p. 152). At the same time it is as well to be precise about what Albertini
did say; Pope-Hennessy, op. cit. in n. 57, p. 138, uses his account of the
Bibliotheca Iulia as a disqualifying *terminus ante*, but also thinks it means that
it 'had a ceiling with planetary symbols, and frescoed and gilded walls'
(from which the critical reader will, I think, want to draw conclusions
different from Pope-Hennessy's).

92. MS. Vat. Lat. 3966, fols. 111^r ff., *Inventarium librorum a Iannocto Robera ex
custodia rerum secretarum Pape habitorum* (a transcription in Dorez, op. cit. in n. 90,
pp. 109 ff.). The list is divided about two-thirds of the way through, the second
section being headed: *Inventarium librorum Iulii Pape ii R.mo Car.li* [*Luigi*] *de
Aragonia de mandato Collegii consignatorum*, which suggests that the list was

drawn up during the *sede vacante* after Julius's death; and it cannot be complete since it does not include copies of all books dedicated to the pope (a conspicuous absentee is Albertini's *Opusculum*).

93. It seems very limited, for example, when compared with the library of Cardinal Giovanni de' Medici, then reintegrated in Rome, or with that of Cardinal Domenico Grimani (inventory in MS. Vat. Lat. 3960, fols. 1ʳ ff.), but each of those was exceptionally rich.

94. This date, which marks the approximate time when Raphael directed his own energies to the next stanza, must not be taken as too rigid a guillotine upon ancillary decoration of the Stanza della Segnatura; but the *basamento* is not in that category. The date 1511 inscribed over each window does not refer directly to the immediately superimposed frescoes, but rather to the decoration of the room as a whole (the further indication: PONTIFICAT. SVI. VIII, gives the latest possible date of 26 November 1511: Pastor, op. cit. in n. 4, vi, p. 590). On the other hand Grossino writes to Isabella d'Este, 12 July 1511, that Julius 'in palazo fa depenzer due Camere a un Rafaello da Urbino . . .' which, if accurate, should indicate that Julius and Raphael had turned their attention to the Stanza d'Eliodoro by that date (A. Luzio, 'Isabella d'Este di fronte a Giulio II', *Archivio storico lombardo*, xxxix (Ser. 4, xvii), 1912, p. 326 n. 1).

95. Vasari, *Vite* (1550), p. 647: Julius . . . 'per fargli le spalliere di prezzo, come era la pittura, fece venire da Monte Oliveto di Chiusuri . . . Fra Giovanni da Verona . . . il quale vi fece non solo le spalliere, che attorno vi erano, ma ancora usci [doors] bellissimi et sederi lavorati in prospettive' (see also p. 939). Vasari not unnaturally assumed that the *basamento* was part of the Julian scheme, but two payments to 'fratre Iohanne de Verona che lavora di tarsie . . ., che lavora de intaglio' are dated 28 May and 26 June 1513 (A. Mercati, *Le spese private di Leone X nel maggio-agosto 1513* (Vatican City, 1928), pp. 101, 102), and the *usci*, which survive, are Leonine too. These indications are consistent with the break (1512–15) in Fra Giovanni's work in the choir of San Benedetto a Porta Tufi, near Siena (1511–16: P. Lugano, O.S.B., *Fra Giovanni da Verona . . . e i suoi lavori alla Camera della Segnatura* (Rome, 1908), p. 4, who, however, did not question the date implied by Vasari for the *basamento*). The date of the doors is discussed further in n. 127.

96. In the payment to Salviati, 1541 (above, n. 66) the room is called the 'Camera della Tarsia', a title already used in the accounts of Paul III in 1537 (Dorez, op. cit. in n. 36, p. 110); and I think it is probable that a passage in the anonymous *Memoriale* of 1544 (part of a description of this part of the palace) also applies: 'E inn sala, che si dice dj Farnese, e 1.o belisimo quadro [i.e. table], tutto storiato di figure e ucegli e anjmagli. E 1.o belo frego è fatto di legniamj dj piu cholorj e in prospettjva' (C. Frey, *Il Codice Maglia-bechiano* (Berlin, 1892), p. 134). It was suggested by Klaczko, op. cit. in n. 75, p. 218, that the intarsie disappeared in the Sack of Rome, 1527, and this is stated as a fact by Fischel, op. cit. in n. 90, p. 72, but almost certainly they survived until the insertion of the fireplace from the Stanza dell'Incendio, 1541; Perino del Vaga's *basamento* was undoubtedly executed after that, some

time in the early 1540s (B. Davidson, *Mostra di disegni di Perino del Vaga . . .* (Florence, 1966), p. 49). It is probable that Vasari had never seen the intarsie. However the room retained its previous name; there is a document of 31 March 1551, a payment for a 'studio [i.e. desk] di legniame . . . nella tarsia stanza di N. Signore' (Bertolotti, op. cit. in n. 20 , p. 339), and this room is marked as the 'sala della Tarsia' on a conclave-plan of 1565–6 (Ehrle–Egger, op. cit. in n. 31, No. VII).

97. Comparison between this fictive intarsia and the choir-stalls by Fra Giovanni at Monte Oliveto Maggiore, 1503–05 (an excellent reproduction in G. Kauffmann, *Die Kunst des 16. Jahrhunderts* (Berlin, 1970), Fig. 313) confirms strikingly the accuracy of the former as a copy of the Frate's lost work, while at the same time suggesting that he was only at liberty to invent within a fictive architectural framework designed by another artist with a stronger sense of classical style (perhaps Raphael).

98. For the housing of the books in the Vatican Library see Fabre, op. cit. in n. 90, p. 18, and J. W. Clark, 'The Vatican Library of Sixtus IV', *Proceedings of the Cambridge Antiquarian Society* (1898–9), p. 43. Wickhoff, op. cit. in n. 86, p. 56, and more recently Fischel, op. cit. in n. 90, p. 72, visualized the books in the Segnatura in free-standing desks (presses) like those of the Laurenziana; but Leyh, op. cit. in n. 89, p. 176, had already suggested alternatively that they were on shelves against the wall; his reasoning was in part invalid, but I think nevertheless that he was right. It is generally believed that the wall-shelf system begins with the library of the Escorial (J. W. Clark, *The Care of Books* (Cambridge, 1901), p. 266), but to the known partial exceptions to this rule, in the *Bibliotheca secreta* of Sixtus IV and at Urbino, I should like to add one unambiguous example, the library of the Varano (connected by marriage with the Della Rovere) at Camerino, as described in the inventory of 1502: 'una stantia dove stava la libraria suffictata con soe schaffe atorno da ponere libri et cassoni in torno da ponere libri doi fenestre et uscio' (R. Romani, 'Il palazzo dei Varano a Camerino', *Rassegna marchigiana*, vi (1927–8), p. 380). The papal library at Avignon already had shelves for books (documents of 1349 in Ehrle, op. cit. in n. 32, p. 63). A representation of such a system can be found in the anonymous *Portrait of a Librarian* in the private apartments of Palazzo Doria-Pamphilj in Rome (by the same hand, I think, as the *Lutenist* in the Musée Jacquemart-André, probably a Lucchese artist *c.* 1540–50).

99. Ashmolean Museum, Gibbs Volumes, IV, No. 62, 106×76·5 cm.; for the attribution and date (1710–15) see H. M. Colvin, *A Biographical Dictionary of English Architects* (London, 1954), pp. 589–90.

100. Most recently von Einem, op. cit. in n. 57, p. 19, who visualizes Julius enthroned with his back to the South window, which is improbable from several points of view. I have come across no text describing such an arrangement. The functional design of the similar floor in the Sistine Chapel is described by Shearman, op. cit. in n. 70, p. 22.

101. Redig de Campos, op. cit. in n. 6, p. 62.

102. Albertini, op. cit. in n. 5, fol. Zii^r; Steinmann, op. cit. in n. 13, ii, p. 43.

103. The *Camera* and the library at Avignon occupied the third and fourth levels of the Tour du Pape (Tour des Anges): Ehrle, op. cit. in n. 32, pp. 127 ff., and Labande, op. cit. in n. 4, i, pp. 98 ff.

104. At this point, for example, Steinmann's interpretation becomes noticeably impressionistic (op. cit. in n. 13, ii, p. 115), and von Einem's (op. cit. in n. 57, p. 32) decidedly wilful: he finds that *Parnassus* holds its place logically in the now-fashionable Platonic *ascensus* culminating in the *Disputa*, whereas perhaps the one certain thing about the relationship between *Parnassus* and the *Disputa* is that they are on the same level.

105. E.g. Fulvio, op. cit. in n. 90 (1513), fol. 33^v ('Vaticanus apex, phoebo sacratus'); the importance of the view of Bramante's Belvedere-complex from the Stanza della Segnatura has been stressed by Ackerman, op. cit. in n. 5, p. 125; I would simply extend this to the villa of Innocent VIII, to which Julius was devoted. When Bembo (above, n. 85) said that Julius's library had 'speculas bellissimas' he might perhaps have meant windows (as Pliny in his description of the *porticus* of the Laurentinum villa, protected 'specularibus ac multo magis imminentibus tectis'—*Epistulae* ii. 17), and it is possible that stained-glass windows by Guglielmo da Marcillat were already in place (Vasari, *Vite* (1550), p. 676); but I think it is more probable that Bembo was talking of the view—for a contemporary example of this usage, from the same circle, cf. Petrus Valerianus's description, in a letter of 13 November 1512, of the Belvedere 'in speculam cui ab amoenitate pulchrae nomen inditum est' (M. Freher, *Germanicarum rerum scriptores*, ii (Frankfurt, 1602), p. 293).

106. E. H. Gombrich, 'Alberto Avogadro's descriptions of the Badia of Fiesole and of the Villa of Careggi', *Italia medioevale e umanistica*, v (1962), p. 219; Aurelio Brandolini, quoted by Redig de Campos, op. cit. in n. 6, p. 47 ('Nunc Phoebo est, Sixti munere, sacra domus').

107. R. Lanciani, *Ancient Rome in the Light of Recent Discoveries* (London, 1888), p. 112; Clark, op. cit. in n. 98 (1901), pp. 14 ff.

108. Suetonius, *De vita Caesarum*, Augustus xxix; Horace, *Epistolae* I. iii. 16–17; Pliny, *Historia naturalis*, vii. 58 (210), xxxiv. 7 (43).

109. See above, n. 85.

110. See above, n. 94.

111. A summary of the arguments for this dating of the ceiling, and of earlier approaches to the same conclusion, is in Shearman, op. cit. in n. 80, pp. 173–5; the parts attributable to Peruzzi include the corner triangles with grisaille figures against a blue ground; the pseudo-antique 'reliefs' in the broad arches over the North and South walls seem to be rightly attributed to Ripanda, the pairs of *putti* in the same place to one or more artists strongly influenced by Verrocchio.

112. This conclusion arises from collation of two texts from Vasari's *Vite* of Piero della Francesca and Raphael (1550 ed., pp. 361, 641). Vasari also said that there had been one or two frescoes by Piero della Francesca; he was much confused by their dates, which he believed the same as that of Bramantino's (documented by a payment of 4 December 1508: Golzio, op. cit. in n. 17, p. 21). Vasari's reference to Signorelli is confirmed by a statement, which Steinmann interpreted rightly, and which alone suggests the subjects, in Paolo Cortese, *De cardinalatu* (Castro Cortese, 1510), fol. clxxxviii[r]: 'Iulius Secundus Lucae Cortonensi homini in pingendo frugi & naturam verecunde imitanti divorum Imagines pingere in cella Vaticana iubeat'; there is a gap in the documentation of Signorelli in Tuscany in the second half of 1508. Vasari's notice in the *Vita* of Piero indicates that the two frescoes by Piero were on the two window-walls, but one may doubt that he was well informed; it is more natural that the frescoes added in 1508 by Bramantino and Signorelli should have been on the window-walls, since the previous decorations there would have been more or less destroyed by the changes in fenestration carried out under Julius, similar to those in the Stanza della Segnatura.

113. Ehrle–Egger, op. cit. in n. 31, No. VII.

114. Marco Minio, Venetian ambassador in Rome, wrote on 11 March 1517 that he had had an audience with Leo 'in la camera di la audientia, dove erano molti cardinali e altri'; on 19 May 1517 that Cardinals Cornelio and Sauli 'erano in la camera di la audientia' waiting to introduce Cardinal Petrucci (this was the time of the plot against Leo); and on 25 June 1517 that he and the other ambassadors had been 'reduti in la sala di l'audientia per udir lezer il processo contra li cardinali . . . [Leo] vene, e sentato in cao di tavola . . .' (Sanuto, op. cit. in n. 9, xxiv, cols. 102, 288, 419). On 6 March 1525 Isabella d'Este presented herself to Clement VII 'qual era a sedere, in la camera sua grande de la audientia . . .' (Luzio, op. cit. in n. 9 (1908), p. 363). Under Paul III there are payments of 1536 and 1538 for furnishings of the 'Camera della Audienza' (Dorez, op. cit. in n. 36, ii, pp. 19, 189). It should be noted that there exists the hazard of an alternative *udienza*, or *Audientia rotae*, a very large hall in the so-called palace of Innocent VIII behind the Benediction Loggia (H. Egger, 'Das päpstliche Kanzlei-gebäude im 15. Jahrhundert', *Mitteilungen des österreichischen Staatsarchivs* (1951), pp. 487 ff.), but I do not think that that can be meant in any of these cases; more real is the possibility, especially in the case of Isabella's reception, of a loose use of terms by which a room like the Sala de' Palafrenieri might be meant. The earliest reference to (apparently) the Stanza d'Eliodoro is in the text of the formal protest of 28 September 1515, against Francis I's intention to seize Milan, drawn up in 'camera nova versus Belvedere' (C. Guasti, 'I manoscritti Torrigiani', *Archivio storico italiano*, Ser. 3, xxvi (1877), p. 184; see also pp. 186, 364, 403, for other legal documents of 1517 that may indicate a similar use by Leo for this same room); at this date the Stanza dell'Incendio was not usable, and the Stanza della Segnatura seems to have been differently described by the same notary (see below, n. 137).

115. Frey, loc. cit. in n. 96; the description continues: 'e evj 1.0 belisimo quadro d'ebano chomeso chon molte belle parte', which is consistent with the

description of a table in the time of Leo X (previous note); but the ebony table described in 1544 was very probably a replacement, the gift of Bindo Altoviti in 1541 (documents in Bertolotti, op. cit. in n. 66, pp. 180, 185, 187, 190).

116. The arguments for this view, and for others in the following paragraphs, are set out in Shearman, op. cit. in n. 80, pp. 166 ff.

117. In the *Expulsion of Heliodorus* he saw 'papa Giulio che caccia l'avarizia della Chiesa' (*Vite*, ed. cit. in n. 38, iv, p. 345).

118. Aegidius of Viterbo, *Oratio prima synodi Lateranensis*, Rome, 1512.

119. See, for example, Paolo Cortese, *De cardinalatu* (dedicated to Julius) (Castro Cortese, 1510), fol. vi^v; but this is a generous list of legitimate circumstances, notably irrelevant to the author's main theme.

120. The woodcut is the frontispiece to the very rare pamphlet published in Rome by Giovanni Giacomo Penni, 27 July 1513: *Cronicha delle magnifiche & honorate Pompe fatte in Roma per la Creatione & Incoronatione di Papa Leone .X. Pont. Max.* (the text is the familiar one reprinted in F. Cancellieri, *Storia de' solenni possessi . . .*, Rome, 1802).

121. This revision of the conventional chronology was suggested independently (and for different, complementary reasons) by K. Oberhuber, 'Die Fresken der Stanza dell'Incendio im Werk Raffaels', *Jahrbuch der kunsthistorischen Sammlungen in Wien*, lviii (1962), p. 35, and by myself, op. cit. in n. 80, pp. 173 ff.; subsequently there appeared a confirmation of our hypothesis (which was not in all respects new) in a sheet of studies datable to the summer of 1514, in the corner of which is a record of the ceiling of the Stanza d'Eliodoro with eight ribs (K. Oberhuber, 'Eine unbekannte Zeichnung Raffaels in den Uffizien', *Mitteilungen des Kunsthistorischen Institutes in Florenz*, xii (1966), pp. 225 ff., fig. 13).

122. Steinmann, op. cit. in n. 13, ii, p. 124; and in detail by F. Hartt, 'Lignum vitae in medio paradisi: The Stanza d'Eliodoro and the Sistine Ceiling', *Art Bulletin*, xxxii (1950), p. 127. These and other authors, basing their interpretation on a quite different chronology, naturally drew very different conclusions.

123. Hercules is described as the antetype of Leo, in this sense, by Aegidius of Viterbo, *Historia viginti saeculorum* (addressed to Leo, begun 1513), Rome, Biblioteca Angelica, MS. Lat. 351, fols. 6^v, 36^r, 316^r; Hercules as *exemplum virtutis* is familiar in many commentaries, of which the most relevant is the *Herculis vita* of Lilio Gregorio Giraldi, dated in the colophon 'Romae ex Vaticanis Pontificis Max. aedibus, mense Octobri MDXIII' (*Opera omnia*, Basle, 1580, i, p. 545). Other hieroglyphs are clearly identifiable as *Concordia* (or *dextrarum coniunctio*), *Applicatio* (a young man painting), and Chastity or Innocence (a girl with a unicorn); and Moses appears once more with, in Leo's case, however, the likely role of the gentle ruler (cf. Pietro Delphin, *Oratio ad Leonem X. Pont. Max.*, 13 March 1513, Bibl. Laurenziana, MS.

Plut. xlvii.17 (presentation copy), fol. 134^r: 'sicut de Moyse legitur, mitis-simus es super omnes homines qui morantur in terra'). These lower sections of the vault were painted at this point because the structure itself was an addition, arising from the removal of consoles at a higher level, like those that remain in the Stanza dell'Incendio; the structural modification is essentially similar to that which was made earlier in the Stanza della Segnatura (this point is discussed in more detail in Shearman, op. cit. in n. 82, p. 396).

124. For a list of these personifications, which must be approximately correct, see J. D. Passavant, *Raphael d'Urbin* (Paris, 1860), ii, p. 135; I have adapted my interpretation of them from one originally produced by a former student, Kirstine Brander.

125. One does not imagine, of course, that previously there was no enclosure of any kind; I think it is probable that the doorways were hung with 'portiere', of which a number are recorded in the *Inventarium omnium bonorum existentium in foraria S.mi D. Leonis* . . . (1518–21), A.S.R., Camerale I, 1557/1, fol. 15^r ('Portere' of Julius), 50^r ('Antiportae . . . in diversis portis palatij', no pope specified). Since the shutters in the Stanze (and formerly those in the Sala vecchia degli Svizzeri and the Sala de' Palafrenieri) are all Leonine the question naturally arises as to how the windows were screened in the time of Julius. *Impannate* (waxed or oiled cloth or paper on wooden frames) may be taken for granted, but there were probably also woven curtains, like those recorded in the same inventory, fol. 20^r: 'Tappeta sex parva per fenestris.'

126. Neither the extent nor the novelty of the enclosure should be exaggerated. On the one hand the Stanze were already, in Julius's time, known as 'salae . . . suae occultae' (Paris de Grassis, *Diarium*, 28 June 1510, Add. MS. 8442, fol. 47^v), and even in the approach to them there were, in theory, several degrees of hierarchical obstruction to be negotiated. The difference between theory and practice is, of course, considerable, and although it is ceremonial theory that concerns us the contrast of reality must not be overlooked. Thus a passage in Valeriano's *Simia* recalls that 'la turba importuna de' poeti . . . miseramente lo [Leo] affligono in ogni luogo, nei portici [logge], in letto, nelle intime stanze, in Belvedere . . .' (ed. D. Gnoli, in *La Roma di Leon X*, Milan, 1938, p. 133); and the impression gleaned from diplomatic sources is confirmed by an observation by P. Mattheus, *Encomion in Leonem X. Pont. Max.* (Milan, Biblioteca Ambrosiana, MS. H. 35 inf. (4), fols. 78 ff.): 'Pavimenta, aulae, thalami, camerae, pontificie domus omnis tota die Cardinalium Salutationibus patescunt'. On the other hand the informality suggested with irresistible charm by Francesco Vettori in a letter to Machiavelli, 23 November 1513, should be taken with salt since the impression was supposed to be so irresistible that Machiavelli would leave Florence for the papal court: 'La mattina, in questo tempo, mi lievo a 16 ore e, vestito, vo infino a Palazzo; non però ogni mattina, ma delle due o tre una. Quivi, qualche volta, parlo venti parole al Papa, dieci al Cardinale de' Medici, sei al magnifico Iuliano; e, se non posso parlare a lui, parlo a Piero Ardinghelli, poi a qualche imbasciatore che si truova per quelle camere; e intendo qual

cosetta, pure di poco momento. Fatto questo, me ne torno a casa . . .'
(A. Moretti, *Corrispondenza di Niccolò Machiavelli con Francesco Vettori dal 1513
al 1515* (Florence, 1948), pp. 21–2).

127. The primary evidence for this statement is in the passage from Vasari
quoted above, n. 38. The door between the Stanza della Segnatura and the
Stanza d'Eliodoro, at least, is to be dated after 27 September 1514, since it
shows the *Archipoeta* (*Architutto*) Baraballo hoist on Leo's elephant, *Annone*, a
heartless but clearly unforgettable event of that date (Sanuto, op. cit. in n. 9,
xix, col. 74; a solemn description in Pastor, op. cit. in n. 4, viii, pp. 154 ff.,
a much funnier one in Gnoli, op. cit. in n. 126, pp. 108 ff., or M. Winner,
'Raffael malt einen Elefanten', *Mitteilungen des kunsthistorischen Institutes in
Florenz*, xi (1964), pp. 87 ff.). Lugano, op. cit. in n. 95, p. 20, n. 4, refers to
Gian Barile's doors a record of a *provisione*, or salary, to him, to run for seven
years from 1 November 1514 (while arguing that it refers not to the Segnatura
doors, but to the rest); this document seems to me to be wrongly invoked
here; it is more likely that this is the same salary that is provided for in a
motu proprio of 1 December 1514 'Dilecto filio Magistro Johanni Barilla
senensi Modelli fabrice nostre Sancti Petri' (i.e. Raphael's model: A.S.R.,
Camerale I, 859B, fol. 12^r).

128. Claims for payment for the erection of this balcony, or *coridoro picholo*
(which bears Leo's name), and for piercing the door into the Stanza dell'Incendio and another (perhaps into the tower at the North end of the Loggia),
are included in a statement presented by Giuliano Leno, December 1513
(Frey, op. cit. in n. 15, p. 23, and Ackerman, op. cit. in n. 5, pp. 52, 156).
At some point there was also access from this balcony directly into the Torre
Borgia (a doorway is now bricked up), but this was not necessarily the case
originally.

129. This balcony bears Leonine emblems but it is not, so far as I know,
documented; I once suggested that its design might be attributable to Raphael
(op. cit. in n. 82, p. 402), but I now feel that Giuliano de Sangallo is more
likely to be responsible; Giuliano was back in Rome and working for Leo
upon a scheme for remodelling the Torre Borgia in 1513 (Ackerman, op. cit.
in n. 5, p. 52). The location of the kitchen in the South-west corner of this
level of the palace, and at this date, is not, I think, demonstrable; it is assured
about 1580 by the inscription marking the passage leading off in this direction
from the Sala vecchia degli Svizzeri on Mascarino's plan (see above, n.
36): *Andito per andare a la cucina secreta*. In Caroli's plan, *c.* 1620 (above,
n. 16) the room at the end of this passage, occupying the southern half of the
West wing, is shown with what appears to be a very large oven. The door
from this balcony into the Stanza dell'Incendio is now bricked up; the door-
frame in the Stanza (under the left side of the *Fire in the Borgo*) is a late
insertion in imitation of the other Leonine frames and doors in the room
(this is clear both from the technique of the door and frame, and from the
interruption of the original painted *basamento*).

130. Vasari, quoted above, n. 95.

131. He was telling the story of Baraballo and Annone, 'cuius triumphi memoriam lignarii caelatores quum tesselato opere lascivirent, in interioris pontificii cubiculi foribus scitissime inscriptam reliquerunt' (*Vita Leonis* (Florence, 1548), p. 103).

132. A collection of sources on this point in Shearman, op. cit. in n. 70, p. 13.

133. See below, n. 136.

134. H. W. Frey, 'Leo X', in *Die Musik in Geschichte und Gegenwart*, viii (Kassel, 1960), cols. 619 ff.; he dates the acquisition to 1519.

135. Archivio segreto vaticano, Introitus et exitus 557, fol. 157^v, 30 September 1517: 1,000 ducats 'domino Corrado Trompa de Nolirbergo pro uno horologio et certis instrumentis musicis per eum datis S.D.N. et auro, et argento laboratis . . .'.

136. *Diarium*, 26 December 1518: 'Hodie mihi papa pro mantia donavit pulcherimum clavicembalum sive monochordum optimum quod ipsemet in sua camera tenere solatus est valoribus centum ducati hoc autem ideo dixit se libenter servisse quia intellexit me multum in tali sono delectari prout in veritate delector' (MS. Vat. Lat. 5636, fol. 249^r). In many cases 'sua camera' should be understood as a specific term, indicating the papal bedroom; but it is unlikely to be so in this case.

137. 27 June 1520: 'in camera versus Belvedere ubi Sanctissimus D.N., tempore estivo, commoratur' (passes the time, not at work: Guasti, op. cit. in n. 114, p. 369).

138. Raffaello Brandolini, *De musica et poetica opusculum* (dedicated to Leo), Rome, Biblioteca Casanatense, MS. 805, fols. 17^v-18^r.

139. These are the *usci* in Vasari's account, above n. 95; it should be noted, however, that there are also musical instruments on the 'inner' faces of the Leonine doors between the Stanza d'Eliodoro and the Sala di Costantino.

140. On 1 July 1517 Raphael's *garzoni* were given a substantial tip while working in 'la stanza avanti la guardaroba' (A.S.R., Camerale I, 1489, fol. 24^v); this document has been referred to the Sala de' Palafrenieri (e.g. by E. Müntz, *Raphaël* (Paris, 1881), p. 466, n. 1, and by Golzio, op. cit. in n. 17, p. 56), in which case it makes no sense whatever; the identity of the room as the Stanza dell'Incendio will be established in the following documents, but it may be noted that on 16 June 1517 Raphael said he had 'anchor che fare dui dì ne la Camera del Papa', clearly the same (Golzio, p. 54). On 15 May 1518 'Ubaldini d'Antonio Ubaldini, pictor fiorentino' was paid 50 ducats 'per resto di pictura del organo di guardaroba' (an earlier payment for the same work, 8 September 1517, does not specify its location: A.S.R., Camerale I, 1489, fols. 52^r, 28^r); and on 3 July 1518 there is a payment of 88 ducats to 'M.o angelo fa legniame ... per manifactura di dui armarij di cipresso stanno in guardaroba et ... per tante tavole comprate per dicti armarij' (ibid., fol.

57^r). This *guardaroba* may be visualized from a description of the death of Adrian VI (1523); the body was taken to Saint Peter's, 'Et paulo post ut pecuniam, ac caeteras res in Iudicem (sicuti mortuo Pontifice mos est) referrent sancta Sanctorum sunt ingressi, quod erat secretius cubiculum in Turri, cui à conditore Alexandro vj. Borgiae nomen est, in quo Adrianus pecuniam, et quicquid preciosi ad eum deferebatur adservabat, et quasi illuc nemini mortalium (Judeorum more) ingredi liceret nisi Pontifici Maximo, hoc est sibi, sic locum appelabat. . . . Cum igitur Sancta sanctorum patuissent, sperabant homines veluti de Caci speluncha fabulantur Poetae, ingentem gazam, et congestas apparituras rapinas: sed longe aliter evenit. Duas namque Tiaras, nonnullos calices, et vascula quaedam argentea, ne magni quidem pretij inventa sunt. Verum multum librorum impressorum nullius momenti inerant volumina. Praeterea erat eodem in loco scrinium multis forulis distinctum, ex his quae Neapoli advehentur (quae studiola nuncupantur) obsignatum, et cum claves non adferrentur, Camerarius claustra refringi iussit, in quo plurimae diversorum epistolae, nonnullae gemmae, et duodecim anuli, qui Leonis X.mi fuerant . . . et duo aureorum millia reposita fuerant.' (Anon. MS. cit. in n. 6, fols. 86^r ff.) In 1541 the Stanza dell' Incendio was still referred to as 'la Camera inanti la Guardarobba di Palazzo' (see above, n. 66), so that a number of payments for work done in the *guardaroba* under Clement VII and Paul III may be connected with the same; however in 1546 there is a reference to a *guardaroba nova* (Bertolotti, op. cit. in n. 66, p. 190). I think it is likely that two items on Giuliano Leno's account of 1 December 1513, refer to the conversion of this part of the Torre Borgia into the secret treasury: 'Per rovinare e tramezi e le volte degli anditi, che vano a la tore di Borges', and 'Per levare 3. porte in detto luogho di porfido et porle altrove' (Frey, op. cit. in n. 15, p. 23). And if that is so, then when Isabella d'Este was shown, on 26 October 1514, 'el palazzo, et el guardarobba del Papa et li regni et mitre et altre zoglie pontificale' she was presumably taken to the same place (letter from Gabbioneta, in Luzio, op. cit. in n. 27, p. 468). It is not clear how much of the Torre Borgia on this level was taken up by Leo's *Guardaroba*, but it should have been in the Northern part. There was probably always a staircase in the South-West part; in the South-East corner there is a now a chapel, accessible through another Leonine door in the centre of the West wall of the Stanza dell'Incendio (see the plan, p. 20), which is, however, so small that it is unlikely to be the *Guardaroba* converted.

141. Ehrle, op. cit. in n. 32, pp. 48, 111 ff.; Labande, op. cit. in n. 4, i, pp. 98 ff. In this case the *guardaroba* after which the tower was named provided storage for, probably, less precious objects; the secret treasury, more nearly equivalent to Leo's, was immediately above the papal chamber, next to the library, in the Tour du Pape (Tour des Anges). For Leo's interest in the palace at Avignon, see Labande, ii, pp. 81, 85–6.

142. Paolo Giovio, *Raphaelis Urbinatis Vita* (*c.* 1527), reprinted in Golzio, op. cit. in n. 17, p. 192: 'In penitiore quoque Leonis X triclinio Totilae immanitatem, ac incensae urbis casus, atque pericula rapraesentavit . . .' (this is not uncharacteristic of his iconological limitations, but in its context the passage is unambiguous in the sense that matters here).

143. For example (from the *Foraria* inventory of 1518–21, above, n. 125, fol. 20ʳ, an entry from 1518): 'Tapete [sc: pro tabula] unum magnum cum tribus rotis magnis, et alijs parvis in fundo viridi in Tinello secreto'. At Avignon the function of the *parvum tinellum* is perfectly clear from a document: 'in quo pontifex solebat comedere' (Ehrle, op. cit. in n. 32, p. 117). However a *tinellum* is not always (and not even usually) a dining-room; and during the pontificate of Paul III there were *Tinello secreto, tinello maggiore*, and *tinello minore* (Dorez, op. cit. in n. 36, ii, p. 176); he also had a *credenza secreta* (ibid., pp. 281, 300), and Leo had had one too (*Foraria* inventory, fols. 20ʳ, 50ʳ). A *credenza*, properly a serving-table, can by extension be the title of a serving-room and in rare cases of a dining-room. Clearly these problems are hard to resolve: and it is far from certain that the Stanza dell'Incendio is the *tinello secreto* of the documents, and that the room between this and the kitchen is the *credenza secreta*; what is not in doubt is that Leo had a room specifically reserved for dining, and Giovio (writing in this case very soon afterwards) makes it clear that this was the Stanza dell'Incendio.

144. In the room directly beneath the Stanza dell'Incendio, that is the Sala delle Arti Liberali in the Borgia Apartments, Julius had lunch after consecrating Burchard as bishop, 9 April 1504: 'Papa fecit prandium in camera *consueta* ante turrim in mensa quadra solus et post eum in mensa longa decem cardinales . . .' (*Liber notarum*, quoted from Ehrle–Stevenson, op. cit. in n. 6, p. 21).

145. See above, n. 62, the reports of consecrations of bishops by Leo; it may be observed (if not explained) that while Julius had used the room below for his dining-room (see previous note), Pius III also used it for the consecration of a bishop (1 October 1503: Ehrle–Stevenson, op. cit. in n. 6, p. 21).

146. Pastor, op. cit. in n. 4, viii, p. 285, and recently von Einem, op. cit. in n. 57, p. 9.

147. So, for example, in Julius II's Bull *Salvator Dominus*, 13 April 1512, summoning the Lateran Council; and in Cardinal Antonio del Monte's preface, 1521, to the official *Acta* of the Council (republished in J. Hardouin, *Acta conciliorum* . . ., ix (Paris, 1714), col. 1563).

148. The imagery of Leo's pontificate is very richly documented in contemporary sources, and so this point is capable of lengthy illustration; the following are selected examples: Aldus Manutius, *Supplicatio* to Leo, published as preface to *Platonis omnia opera* (ed. Marco Musurus), Venice, 1513: 'sicut paulo post mortem Patris tui [i.e. Lorenzo il magnifico] tanta incendia belli exorta sunt, sic te illius filio, creato Pontifice Max. brevi, tua opera, tuo unius studio penitus extinguentur'; Leo's own letter to Sigismund King of Poland, 18 March 1513 (P. Bembo, *Epistolae Leonis Decimi* . . ., Lyon, 1538, p. 8); Raffaello Brandolini, *Oratio de laudibus Cosmi Medici* (1515, dedicated to Leo), Bibl. Laur., Plut. xlvi.2, fol. 22ᵛ ('Universa Cristianorum pax, & concordia successit. Imminuta vel extincta potius Italiae totius flamma . . .'); Filippo Donati, dedication to Leo, c. 1515, of Girolamo Donati's *De processione Spiritus Sancti* (MS. Vat. Lat. 4326, fol. 1ᵛ); Cristoforo Marcello, *Oratio ad Leonem X*, MS. Vat. Lat. 3646, fol. 5ᵛ.

149. For the Election Capitulations (*Capitula publica*), see Sanuto, op. cit. in n. 9, xvi, cols. 101 ff. Leo's preoccupation with the Crusade has now been thoroughly documented by K. M. Setton, 'Pope Leo X and the Turkish Peril', *Proceedings of the American Philosophical Society*, cxiii (1969), pp. 367 ff. Of the four achievements or ambitions mentioned in the text above, the one that may not be self-evident is *Concordia* in the *Coronation of Charlemagne*. The 'key' to the interpretation of this fresco is given by the group of musicians in the choir-gallery, one of whom carries a text, now fragmentary, which may be reconstructed as the familiar epigram *Harmonia est discordiae concors*. It was seriously believed (and stated in public) that Leo's training in musical discipline gave him a special aptitude for the attainment of *concordia* (for example by Marcello, MS. cit. in n. 148, fol. 16ᵛ); the word crops up repeatedly in panegyrics and prayers of the period (with good reason) and the final agreement between the Pope and Francis I (adumbrated so clearly in the fresco) was generally known as the *Concordia*-Bull (e.g. Sanuto, xxiii, col. 394). This is not the place for an elaborate analysis of the iconography of the room; I should only like to indicate briefly the secondary meaning of the *Fire in the Borgo*. The 'key' in this case is the 'Aeneas-Anchises' group, a clear metaphor of *Pietas*, which was believed to be an attribute of Leo X, Leo IV (the 'hero' of the fresco) and of the lion itself ('tanta est pietas leonis'). This *pietas* is shown principally to suffering humanity, but also to the basilica of Saint Peter; it was in fact required, in the Election Capitulations of 1513, that the new pope should continue the rebuilding of the church (symbol of the Church), and although under Leo there may have been less vigour than under Julius, there was notably more *pietas* towards the ancient monument and its relics. The façade of Saint Peter's that is shown in the fresco did already carry a rather surprising Medicean donation, marked by coats of arms: a set of windows built by Michelozzo for Cosimo (Vasari, *Vite*, ed. cit. in n. 38, ii, p. 443); and it is Cosimo's profile—as Johannes Wilde was the first to recognize—that Raphael gave to 'Anchises'; familial *pietas*, also a genuine emotion of Leo's, may thus close the circle of meaning.

150. Shearman, op. cit. in n. 70, pp. 18 ff.

151. In the *Fire in the Borgo* the tower, in which Leo IV appears, bears his name not only to identify him but also to recall that he in fact built it; for this is the base of the campanile erected in 863 (*Liber pontificalis*, ed. L. Duchesne (Paris, 1955), ii, p. 119), the position of which is correct and was already known to Flavio Biondo (Ehrle–Egger, op. cit. in n. 24, p. 92). For the *triclinium* of Leo III, see *Liber pontificalis*, ed. cit., ii, pp. 8, 109 (restoration of Leo IV); this text is recalled and discussed at length in Michelangelo Lualdi's *Memorie istoriche, e curiose del Tempio, e Palazzo Vaticano*, Bibl. Corsiniana, MS. 275, fols. 26ᵛ ff., which is perhaps the earliest attempt at a comprehensive history of the palace (*c.* 1640).

THE DECORATION OF THE SISTINE CHAPEL

THE curious visitor to the Vatican who penetrates to the Sistine Chapel, and is able to raise his eyes above the turmoil of pious and worldly pilgrims and shut his ears to the babel of their authorized guides, finds himself surrounded by three outstanding works of church decoration (Pl. 26). To his right and left the walls, up to the highest cornice, are covered with fresco-cycles ordered by the founder of the chapel, Sixtus IV, and executed by Florentine and Umbrian artists; above him is Julius II's and Michelangelo's ceiling; and in front of him the giant fresco of the Last Judgement, commissioned by two popes, Clement VII and Paul III, and also painted by Michelangelo. Of course, whatever position on the floor the visitor occupies, the range of his vision will be more limited than that of the camera which, from a scaffolding just inside the entrance and some 20 feet high, took this picture. But the overwhelming presence of the works will soon confirm the view with which, thanks to the advance art history has made in our century, he is likely to have been long familiar. It then depends on his personal taste and interest where his attention will settle first; but if he is influenced by his reading he will, in all probability, contemplate the three works one by one, separately. For very good reasons. Their styles are distinctly different, no less so than the moral, religious, or philosophical messages which they convey, and the fact that, in addition to their inherent qualities, they are monuments of three definite periods in the progress of Renaissance art offers opportunities for aesthetic and historical considerations of all sorts.

There is, however, one aspect which my imaginary visitor might miss because he would have found little encouragement for it in his reading, and that is to look at these three works in their relation to each other as parts of the overall decoration of the same interior. As such they were certainly intended by those who ordered them. It may seem strange to refer to Michelangelo's 'Last Judgement' as a piece of decoration; yet Paul III, who was responsible for its execution, spoke of his predecessor's commission as given 'decori et ornamento . . . capelle . . . Sixtine intendens',[1] and Julius II in the last of his edicts defined his and his uncle's common aim not only in erecting, but also in embellishing, churches as that of fostering piety through works of art.[2] So, a continuity of purpose prevailed in the attitudes of the four Renaissance popes to whose ambition the present complex whole is due. This is the more important since the two later components were not additions to something incomplete: the ceiling *replaced* the corresponding part of the original scheme, and the altar fresco replaced parts of both—they did so, as we have heard, with the aim of making the whole interior more ornate. In other words, when Michelangelo executed his paintings on the vault, as well as when he planned his 'Last Judgement', the original, Sistine, decoration of all four walls up to the level of the highest cornice still existed unaltered and could not be ignored: the new works had to fit not only the building but also the rest of its decoration. This positive relation of works to a comprehensive whole of which they are parts was a general postulate in Renaissance art. I believe that, in spite of their rightly emphasized 'otherness', it is not entirely absent from Michelangelo's works in the chapel.

My talk will approach the problem from this angle. It can offer no new source material, only a few observations which may help to explain the nature of this extraordinary juxtaposition. I am encouraged by the thought that they concern a monument which was dear to the remarkable woman who founded these lectures.

The palace chapel erected by Sixtus IV in the residence of the popes was unique among the major creations of Quattrocento art in the completeness and accuracy of its planning. This was doubtless partly due to the fervour of the patron, who resolved to make the new chapel the most splendid monument of his reign, surpassing everything popes had done so far for *Roma Restaurata*. Our earliest source on his undertaking, a poem of 1477, calls Sixtus the 'author' of both the building, then in progress, and the plans for its decoration.[3]

[1] *Motuproprio* of 17 November 1536, published by H. Pogatscher in E. Steinmann, *Die Sixtinische Kapelle*, ii, Munich, 1905, pp. 748 ff.

[2] See L. von Pastor, *Geschichte der Päpste*, iii[5-7], Freiburg, 1924, p. 930; Steinmann, op. cit., ii, p. 48.

[3] See Pastor, op. cit., ii[8-9], pp. 457 n. 1, 689 n. 2, and for the more recent literature, the article quoted below in note 3 on p. 244.

There is no reason to doubt this statement. Although the pope must have been assisted throughout the work by a master-mind, who was able to give shape to his ideas and to survey and control their execution, the fact remains that it was thanks to the patron's determined planning that his artist-deputy carried the complex whole to termination in the surprisingly short period of six or seven years.

But this careful planning was necessitated by the double purpose which the structure was to serve (Pl. 27c). For, apart from replacing the thirteenth-century *cappella maior* of pope and cardinals, it was to be a powerful defensive bastion, projecting

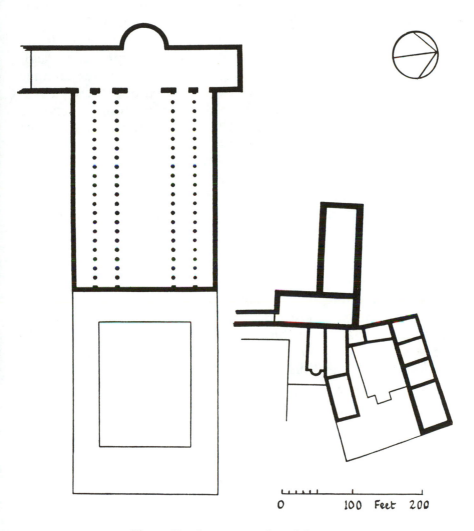

Fig. 1. Sketch reconstruction of the site.

from the south-west corner of the palace quadrangle and commanding its approaches from two directions: the north and the
west, where the terrain is closed by the Vatican hills (Fig. 1).[1]
In fact, when it was erected it was by far the tallest building of
the whole fabric and was only rivalled by the old basilica on the
western skyline of the Borgo: a sober, rectangular mass, with a
high sloping base, narrow windows high up, and projecting
battlements. But for this row of windows the exterior does not
differ from that of the fortress designed a little later by Giuliano
da Sangallo for the papal port of Ostia.[2]

The prism-like shape of the block and the straight course of
its extremely massive walls prescribed a plan for the interior
not to be found elsewhere in church architecture (Pl. 27a, b).
The chapel was to be on the first floor, on the same level as the
palace's state-rooms through which it could be entered. Though
wider and longer than any of these, it is in plan yet another
aula; but, in contrast to them, it was vaulted and there can be
no doubt that its imposing proportions were chosen to express
its different purpose. The length of this interior is twice its
height and three times its width, which is 44 feet.—It has
recently been pointed out by an Italian scholar[3] that the proportions of the chapel's groundplan are the same as those of
Solomon's temple as described in the First Book of Kings. He
could have added that the same is true as regards the height
(though the temple was, of course, not vaulted). One should not
try to deduce too much from this fact. The commemorative
inscription on Perugino's fresco in the chapel[4] refers to Solomon's
building (and this tends to prove that that identity of proportions was not fortuitous), but also states that Sixtus erected
his sanctuary *opibus dispar* (although *religione prior*). There was
to be no emulation in this case, whereas Julius II, in his bull
already mentioned,[5] deliberately compared his New St. Peter's
to the temple of the king.

[1] Figure 1 is a sketch reconstruction of the site drawn by Mr. Kerry
Downes. On the defensive purpose of the new structure cf. Steinmann, op.
cit., i, 1901, pp. 146 ff., and P. Tomei, *L'architettura a Roma nel Quattrocento*,
Rome, 1942, p. 141. Plate 27c is a reconstruction of the original state of the
exterior drawn by the architect G. B. Giovenale for Steinmann's work (pl. ii).

[2] G. Marchini (*Giuliano da Sangallo*, Florence, 1942, pp. 83 f., pl. xiia)
dates the design of this fortress in 1483.

[3] E. Battisti, 'Il significato simbolico della Cappella Sistina', *Commentari*,
viii (1957), pp. 96 ff.

[4] See Steinmann, i, p. 333.

[5] See above note 2 on p. 242.

Nevertheless, it is clear that all the surfaces which Solomon had covered with cedar and gold were, in the chapel of Sixtus, meant from the beginning to be covered with paintings, every square inch of them (Pl. 28a). For below the level of the clerestory and ceiling the architecture provided no articulation, and these large surfaces of plain wall would have been dead without decoration. Apart from this, paintings were necessary to express the sacred purpose of the hall. Its liturgical division into presbytery and space for the laity was structurally expressed by means which, in their lack of emphasis, may be called symbolic. First, the presbytery was slightly longer than the other half of the room (69 feet as to 64). This reconstruction of the interior in Steinmann's standard work on the chapel shows the dividing screen, the *cancellata*, in its right place;[1] it was moved much nearer to the entrance in the second half of the sixteenth century, obscuring some significant features of the intended arrangement. Originally the *cancellata* was linked with the *cantoria*, which was entirely within the eastern half of the room, while allowing it to belong to, and be a bridge between, the two sections. (The reconstruction is incorrect in some other particulars, but it is an excellent help in illustrating the system as a whole.) Secondly, the floor of the presbytery was raised by one step, and another step marked the area of the altar and the papal throne. I should also like to mention a small but characteristic detail: the marble seats which ran along the walls had in the presbytery, in distinction from those outside it, a step for the feet, that is to say, the cardinals and prelates were seated two steps higher than the laymen. Finally, the presbytery was lighter, being illuminated by two additional windows, those in the altar-wall.[2] There were no windows in the entrance wall.

Another structural division, more marked than this, is the halving of the height of the hall by the entablature: the distance from the floor to the latter's cornice is equal to the distance from the level of this cornice to the apex of the vault. The upper half of the hall is flooded with light. Here the walls are set back by a few inches so as to allow for the projection of pilaster-strips, which are flush with the walls below the entablature and which

[1] Steinmann, pl. vii, and vol. i, pp. 160 f.

[2] Although no archaeological evidence for it is at present available, the former existence of these windows can, on other considerations, be regarded as certain. They are also indicated in a plan of the Vatican attributed by J. S. Ackerman (*The Cortile del Belvedere*, City of Vatican, 1954, pp. 199 f., fig. 3) to Baldassarre Peruzzi.

carry the vault, a low-pitched barrel coved at the ends, with lunettes cutting into it. A narrow cornice marks the bottom of the lunettes and the springing of the pendentives. So walls and vault interpenetrate, while keeping to a simple ratio: the height of the window openings is equal to the actual height of the vault (that is to say, to the distance from the level of the upper-most cornice to the apex of the vault).—There is another cornice below the entablature, halving the distance between the heads of the people seated on the benches and the architrave. A painted frieze and architrave were added to this lower cornice. While the exterior is unfaced brick, with the few architectural members of travertine, inside the latter are of marble and all the rest is covered with paintings.

Now I come to the main question: how to organize the decoration which had to transform this well-proportioned but bare interior into one both ornate and expressive of its function. There is no time to discuss the models to which the pope turned, the monumental church interiors of the late-thirteenth century in Rome and Assisi; they were in any case basically transformed to meet the requirements of the papal sanctuary. As we have seen, owing to the placing of the windows and the correspond-ing system of vaulting the chapel walls were, in their uppermost register, divided into equal bays, six on each of the long sides, two on each of the smaller sides. These bays were extended right down to the benches by centring pilasters with capitals and bases in the lower registers, in the lowest register also with plinths, on the pilaster-strips of the clerestory. By these means the walls were transformed into a sequence of identical bays of classical articulation and proportions (Pl. 28b).[1]

The decoration of the sixteen bays was organized horizontally (Pl. 29a, b). The spaces in the lowest register were filled with hangings of gold or silver brocade, the two kinds not alternating but following a symmetrical scheme round both axes; I shall return to it later. Though the hangings have folds to show their weight, the brocade pattern ignores the folds; and there are broad, dark-green borders, the top ones forming curves which harmonize with the pilaster capitals, while the side-borders link up with the pilasters themselves. On these the relief ornament appears against a dark ground which hardly allows cast shadows to be noticed. And so in this register everything

---

[1] This diagram, and others which follow, illustrate points which cannot be shown in photographs. They are the work of my colleague Dr. John Shearman.

PLATE 25

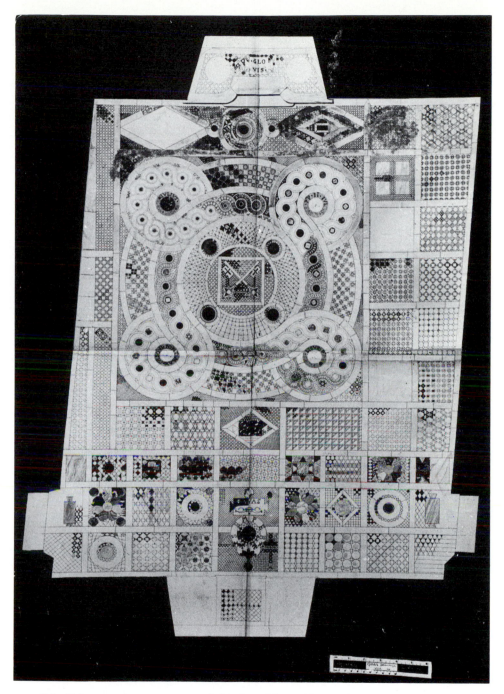

John Talman, *c.* 1710–15, measured drawing of floor of Stanza della Segnatura; Oxford, Ashmolean Museum (*photo*: Courtauld Institute).

PLATE 26

The Sistine Chapel

PLATE 27

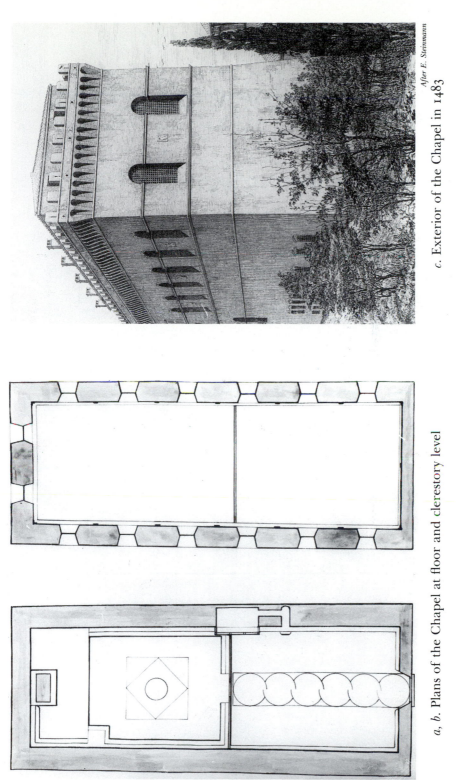

After E. Steinmann

c. Exterior of the Chapel in 1483

a, b. Plans of the Chapel at floor and clerestory level

PLATE 28

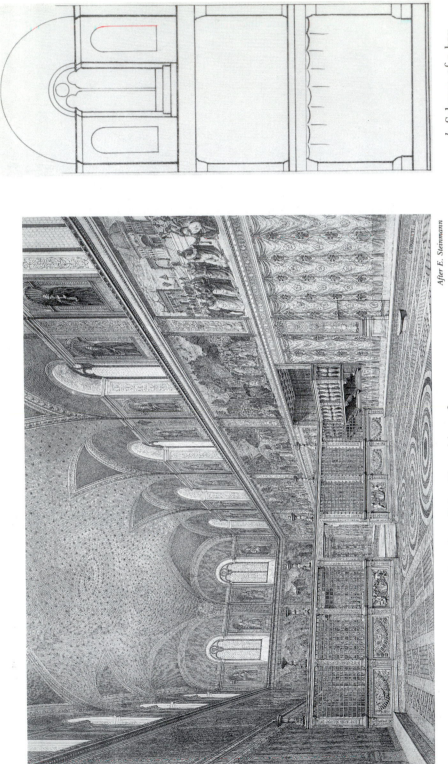

b. Scheme of a bay

After E. Steinmann

a. Interior of the Chapel in 1483

PLATE 29

After E. Steinmann

b. Upper half of a bay

After E. Steinmann

a. Lower half of a bay

PLATE 30

a. Scheme of an 'interior façade'

b. Botticelli, 'The Temptation of Christ'

PLATE 31

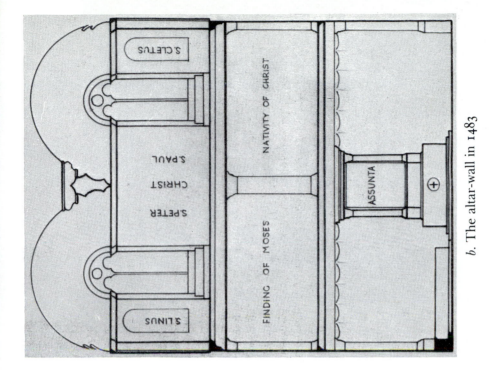

b. The altar-wall in 1483

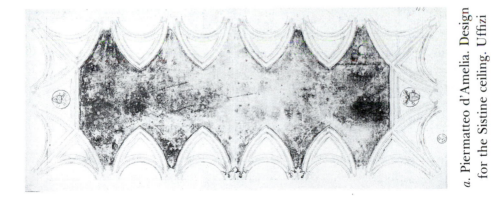

a. Piermatteo d'Amelia. Design
for the Sistine ceiling. Uffizi

PLATE 32

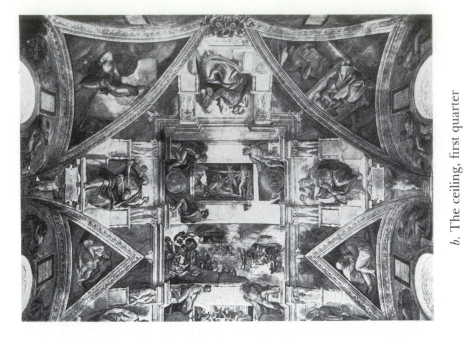

b. The ceiling, first quarter

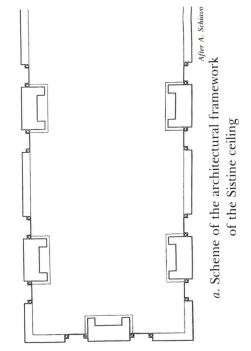

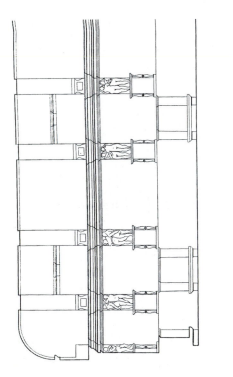

After A. Schiavo

a. Scheme of the architectural framework
of the Sistine ceiling

PLATE 33

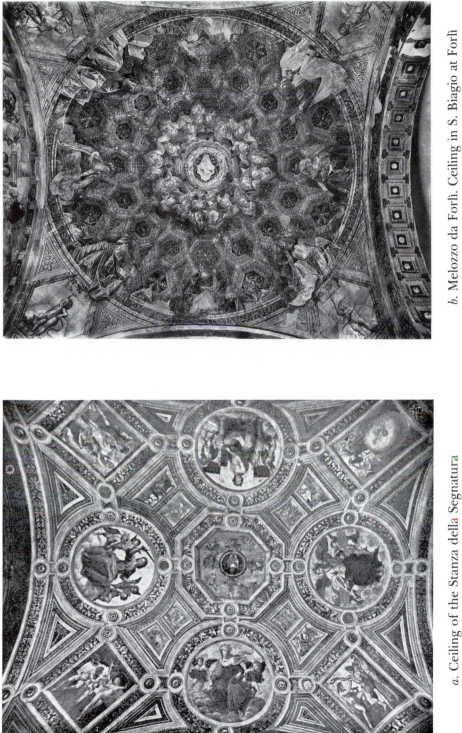

b. Melozzo da Forlì. Ceiling in S. Biagio at Forlì

a. Ceiling of the Stanza della Segnatura

PLATE 34

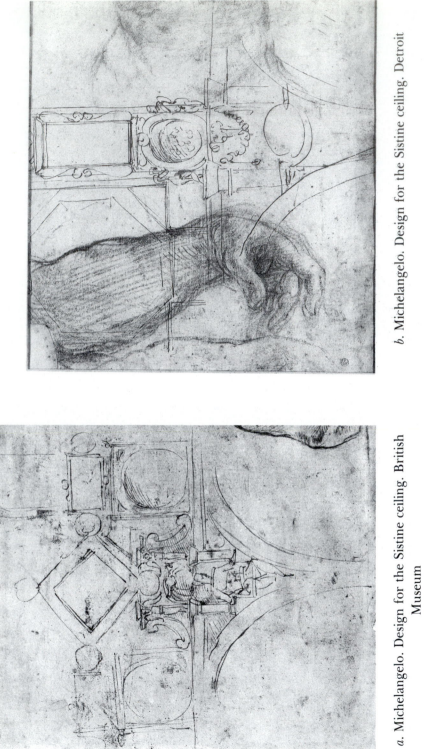

b. Michelangelo. Design for the Sistine ceiling. Detroit

a. Michelangelo. Design for the Sistine ceiling. British Museum

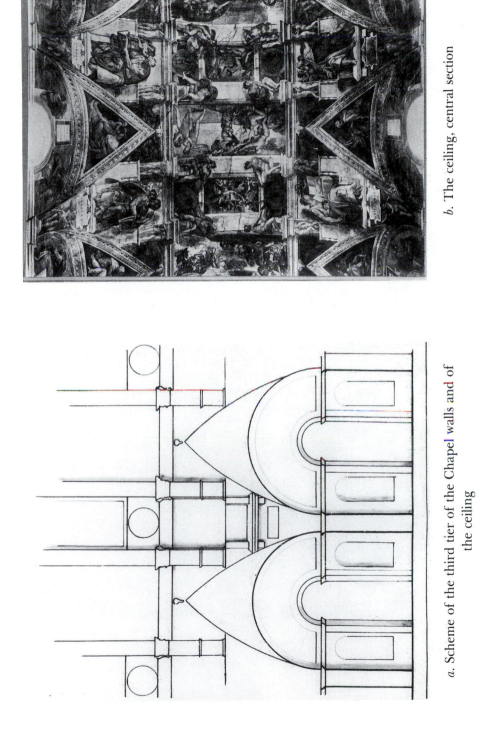

PLATE 35

b. The ceiling, central section

a. Scheme of the third tier of the Chapel walls and of the ceiling

PLATE 36

The Erythraean Sibyl. (See also Pl. 70).

PLATE 37

View of the second half of the ceiling

PLATE 38

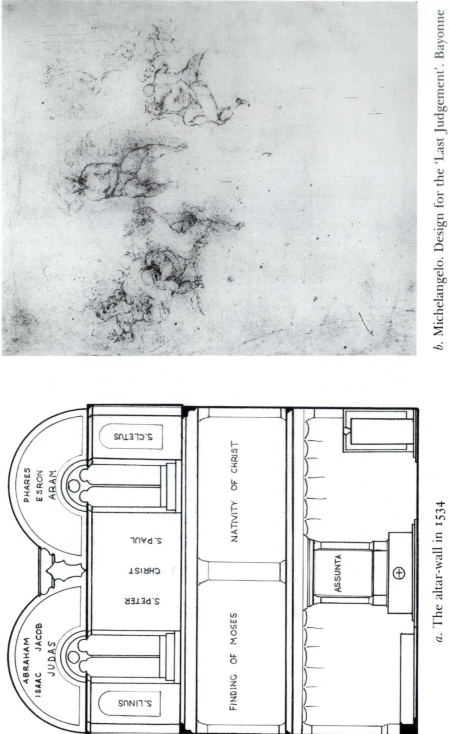

b. Michelangelo. Design for the 'Last Judgement'. Bayonne

a. The altar-wall in 1534

PLATE 39

Michelangelo. Design for the 'Last Judgement'. Casa Buonarroti

PLATE 40

The 'Last Judgement'

appears to have been done to preserve the flat reality of the wall.

The oblongs between cornice and entablature contained the main part of the decoration: two concordant cycles of histories, each beginning above the altar and ending above the entrance. They were called by a contemporary 'pictura qua omnia veteris novique Testamenti mysteria representantur',[1] and Ludwig Pastor has shown how they were selected to show the threefold authority of the primate: as a priest, as a teacher, and as a ruler.[2] It is worth noticing that, contrary to tradition, the New Testament scenes occupy the Epistle side: facing south, this side is much better lit, and it is the one opposite the pope *in cathedra*. As to the form, the picture planes seem to have been slightly stepped back, for the histories are surrounded by a plain frame which disappears from sight at the bottom. In effect, on the three other sides this dark frame fulfils the same function of connecting rather than detaching, like the borders of the hangings below. This and the compositional schemes adopted for the individual paintings, usually with large picture-parallel groups placed right in the foregrounds, go far towards restoring the flatness of the surface.

In the third register, above the real entablature, the wall is treated as a relief (Pl. 29*b*). Here the window openings with their splayed sides and arches take up a third of the total width of each bay. They are accompanied by round-headed niches, and the rest of the wall is faced with richly carved slabs and panels. And here, framing the bays, are the projecting pilaster-strips, with an additional cornice running above them. One can say that, as the wall rises, its real and suggested plasticity increases.—The niches contain images of pre-Constantine popes; they are larger than the figures in the histories. We possess no evidence about the original decoration of the lunettes. It may also have consisted of sculptured panels; but it is possible that it also included medallions with half-length figures. If the latter was the case, the figures may have been those of Prophets and Sibyls.

The description would be quite inadequate without including some of the principles of the visual order on which the system is based. First, it should be noted that each section of a bay, as

---

[1] Sigismondo de' Conti, *Le storie de' suoi tempi*, Rome, 1883, i, p. 205, quoted by Steinmann, i, p. 136 n. 1. About the author see ibid., pp. 594 f., and Pastor, ii, p. 665, iii, pp. 901 f.

[2] Pastor, ii, pp. 706 ff.

well as each individual form within it, has its own viewpoint. In all the histories the perspective point lies on the centre line, and in most of them rather more than half-way up. No account is taken of the spectator's position. The comparatively low point from which the scalloped shell of the niche is viewed appears to be a means used to make it recognizable as such. The figure is not foreshortened.

This, then, is a principle of objectivity and clarity by which each section tells with equal weight. The disjointed effect of its strict application is counterbalanced by two others. One is that of unified lighting. The light falls throughout the chapel as if its source lay in the two windows of the altar-wall (the windows which no longer exist). On the two long walls all the plastic forms, representational as well as ornamental, cast shadows in the same direction. This helps the eye to link them one with another and to disregard the divisions. It is also a means of increasing the harmony between building and decoration.[1]

Another device which works in the same direction is the formation of larger units by subtle compositional means. On closer examination the sequence of uniform bays breaks up into groups of two or three—into units which may best be called *interior façades*. So, clearly conforming to the liturgical division of the room, each of the long walls consists of two such groups (Pl. 30*a*).[2] What makes them appear distinct in this sense is the symmetrical arrangement round a central axis followed in the two lower registers. The central hanging has a pale-gold ground and a white pattern; in those to right and left the ground is a dark, warm gold and the pattern a deep red. Above, the composition in the middle depends on an emphatic central feature (the façade of the temple) which is the peak of a pyramid of figures (Pl. 30*b*), while each of those to right and left shows two groups in balanced symmetry. In addition, in the central fresco the cool colour harmony of the silver brocade below it is, as far as possible, taken up and expanded. There can hardly be any doubt that all this is intentional, for the scheme is repeated, with only slight variations, four times on the long walls.

[1] The device was not new, see the Arena Chapel at Padua. About its use by Giotto in S. Croce cf. John White, *The Birth and Rebirth of Pictorial Space*, London, 1957, p. 72. Another famous instance was the decoration of the Brancacci Chapel.

[2] The diagram represents the right-hand wall of the presbytery. The histories are (from left to right): Perugino and Pinturicchio, 'The Baptism of Christ'—Botticelli, 'The Temptation of Christ and the Cleansing of the Leper' (Pl. 30*b*)—Ghirlandaio, 'The Vocation of Peter and Andrew'.

Moreover, the central pieces of the 'façades' were given to the two best artists at Sixtus IV's disposal: three to Botticelli, one to Perugino, who also painted the frescoes on the altar-wall. Finally, these four pieces are distinguished iconographically. Perugino's 'Traditio clavium' contains the commemorative inscription already mentioned, and its counterpart across the chapel, Botticelli's 'Punishment of Korah' (Pl. 29*b*), contains the only explanatory inscription of the cycle, a sentence on the divine calling of the priest from the Epistle to the Hebrews.[1] The two central pieces in the presbytery contain references to the pope's activity: the temple-front in the 'Temptation of Christ' is that of the Ospedale di S. Spirito just built,[2] and the well in the 'Daughters of Jethro' recalls, as it has been convincingly suggested, the bringing back of the *Aqua Virgo* to the Romans.[3] Here a canopy of trees takes the place of the central architectural feature.

The most important 'interior façade' was that of the two-bays-wide altar-wall, which was later sacrificed to the 'Last Judgement'. Its reconstruction is a key to apprehending the whole system (Pl. 31*b*). The centre of the lowest register, between two silver hangings, was occupied by the mensa and the altar-piece, the latter painted on the wall[4] but framed, as can be gathered from a casual remark in a contemporary diary, by columns or pilasters.[5] The composition of the altar-piece—the chapel was dedicated to the Assunta—is known from a precise copy.[6] Not so the frescoes of the Finding of Moses and the Nativity of Christ, which began the cycles of histories above

---

[1] NEMO SIBI ASSVMM|AT HONOREM NISI VOCATVS A DEO | TANQVAM ARON (Hebrews 5. 4).

[2] See Tomei, op. cit., fig. 93.

[3] Pastor, ii, p. 703, with reference to an article by Hilgers.

[4] Vasari, ed. 1550, p. 548; ed. 1568 (Milanesi), iii, p. 579.

[5] Describing in his diary the *matutina*, with the traditional donation of sword and biretta, which was celebrated in the chapel on Christmas Eve in 1504, the Master of Ceremonies, Paris de Grassis, writes: 'Ipsum ensem . . . portavit acolitus et reposuit in altari in cornu epistolae erectum cum cuspide sursum, habente in summo biretum, et adherebat columnae quadraturae altaris extra picturas' (quoted from Codex Vaticanus 5635 by Steinmann, i, p. 567 n. 2; ibid., on p. 182, an obviously mistaken interpretation of the last phrase). The type of altar-frame which this text suggests was fairly common in the late Quattrocento; compare, for instance, the original framework of an altar-piece now in the City Art Museum at Saint Louis, U.S., painted by Piero di Cosimo soon after he had finished work in the Sistine Chapel.

[6] Albertina, iii. 41 (Sc. R. 100). Identified by F. Wickhoff, *Zeitschr. f. bild. Kunst*, xix (1884), p. 56. Steinmann, i, fig. 119.

the altar.[1] And even less is known about the decoration of the third tier, that of the early popes. But, I think, the deviation from the architectural system of the vault which is to be found on this wall enables us to form a reasonable hypothesis and piece together a mental picture of this section. In the centre the pendentive does not reach down to the cornice: it is met about 7 feet higher by a console formed of acanthus leaves.[2] This could only have one purpose: to eliminate the corresponding pilaster-strip and to obtain in this way a flat surface on which to paint, between the windows. This observation can be complemented by another. The gallery of popes which proceeds crosswise on the long walls begins with the images of Clement I and Anacletus respectively. Now, according to the *Vitae Pontificum* compiled for Sixtus IV by the humanist Platina, these two popes were preceded by two disciples of St. Peter, Linus and Cletus.[3] They were doubtless given niches similar to the others in the two corners of the altar-wall. This leaves a group of three to be represented in the central space: Our Lord, who had to be in the centre, with the Princeps Apostolorum on His right and, I think the conclusion is inevitable, with the Apostolus Segregatus on His left. Although St. Paul never was the head of Christ's Church, he was one of its founders and his representation in this context was natural.[4] So the group placed above the altar was a second focus of this 'façade'. What kind of setting it may have had must remain a matter of mere speculation.

And finally, the other part of the original decoration which was entirely destroyed: the ceiling. For this, by good fortune, we possess a well-authenticated source in the form of a preparatory design (Pl. 31a).[5] The artist was Piermatteo d'Amelia, a former

[1] Vasari, loc. cit.

[2] Cf. J. Wilde, 'Der ursprüngliche Plan Michelangelos zum Jüngsten Gericht', *Die graphischen Künste*, N.S., i (1936), pp. 7 ff. Similar consoles occur in the Belvedere built by Innocent VIII in the 1480's (in the room which is now Stanza i of the Galleria dei Busti).

[3] *Platynae Hystoria de Vitis Pontificum*, chaps. iii and iv.

[4] Platina's first chapter is on Christ, the second on St. Peter, but the latter contains a paragraph which in the Italian version is inscribed 'S. Paolo Apostolo, chi fosse, e suoi fatti', and which concludes with this sentence: 'Quelli che questa Chiesa ne stabilirono, Pietro e Paolo senz' alcun dubbio furono.'

[5] Uffizi, 711; 39 by 17 cm. (Pl. 31a shows two-thirds of the sheet.) First identified by C. von Fabriczy, and published by Steinmann, i, fig. 92. See also U. Gnoli, 'Piermatteo da Amelia', *Bolletino d'Arte*, 2nd ser., iii (1924), pp. 391 ff., and C. de Tolnay, *The Sistine Ceiling*, Princeton, 1945, pp. 13, 123, 166, fig. 253.

garzone of Fra Filippo, who later specialized in this branch of painting. His drawing was done to scale with the greatest precision (1 inch in the drawing is equal to 10 feet). A rectangle in black chalk marks the outer limits of the vault proper; to this is added, in a strongly foreshortened projection, the area of the lunettes, in order to show how the pendentives and the vaulted triangles, which connect the lunettes with the vault, end. The vault is painted ultramarine and is sprinkled with yellow dots. A most remarkable feature is the series of large acanthus leaves which mask the springings of the pendentives, thus detaching the ceiling from the walls.[1] The same was done at the two ends by large, plastic coats-of-arms of the pope. (In this respect d'Amelia's design was not carried out.) The starry sky was an old device of ecclesiastical art. Pius II, who used it in his church at Pienza, described it in these words: 'fornices'—that is, the sections of the cross-vault—'in quis stellae affixae aureae et color impressus aereus veram coeli faciem emulabantur'.[2] But in this case the symbol is so explicit that it almost became the thing itself. There were no divisions in this vast expanse of calm blue, no ribs cut through it, and even the dichotomy was absent. The heavenly tent, as though descending upon the walls, gave its protection equally to the presbytery and to the people outside it.

There may have been a number of reasons for Julius II's decision to have this ceiling replaced less than a quarter of a century after its unveiling. One certainly was the pope's determination to keep Michelangelo in his service, and occupied, while the project of a papal mausoleum was shelved. It is a new situation in which the artist's personality could become all-important. The patron chooses the task, but then the initiative passes to the artist and, once in his hands, the task itself could be changed beyond recognition.

Another reason probably lay in the increase in the practice of decorating ceilings with painting which marked the decades following the completion of the Sistine Chapel in Rome. The ornate new ceilings, many of them in the Vatican, may have made d'Amelia's plain firmament look mean. The pope's programme was self-explanatory: to continue the monumental cycles of the chapel by adding to them, in a third series, the

---

[1] They first appear, on a modest scale, in Mantegna's Camera degli Sposi at Mantua, and became a fashion in Rome after the completion of the Sistine Chapel.

[2] *Pii Secundi Pontificis Max. Commentarii*, book ix.

images of the twelve apostles painted on the twelve pendentives, and filling the rest of the vault with ornamented compartments.[1] There were two ways of doing this. One was advocated by Bramante who, in painting, was a follower of Melozzo da Forlì. 'The figures are high up and [must be shown] foreshortened', he said.[2] The last work of Melozzo, formerly in S. Biagio at Forlì (Pl. 33*b*),[3] illustrates what he meant. The figures do strike the eye—perhaps too much. There is always something theatrical in the relation between representation and spectator established by the *di sotto in su*. It is opposed to the principles on which the Sistine decoration was based, and it fatally clashed with Michelangelo's ideals as a sculptor.

The other method, almost universally followed in Rome, was different. It consisted in making the figures parts of a general design which treated the vault as if it were a flat surface. Its finest example is the ceiling in the Stanza della Segnatura (Pl. 33*a*), begun by an unknown artist probably at the very moment when Michelangelo was planning his. Here the figures occupy rectangular or circular spaces, each having its own viewpoint. There is an octagonal opening in the centre—it was called *sfondato* by the theorists—in which *putti* appear holding up the papal emblem against the sky; they are shown abruptly foreshortened. All the compartments are held together by a richly ornamented frame which is continuous, and the spaces between them are filled with emblems or minute compositions.

There are two drawings by Michelangelo which prove that he honestly tried to comply with the terms of his commission and adapt this accepted system to the conditions prevailing in the chapel (Pl. 34*a*, *b*).[4] Common to both is the intention to link the niches in which the apostles are seated on to the decoration of the central area which, in one case, consists of diamonds connected by smaller compartments, in the other, of large octagonal *sfondati* and again smaller spaces forming transverse belts. The niches are round-headed like those in the third tier of the chapel. Adjoining niches are linked together by a length of cornice at a tangent to the vaulted triangles above the lunettes.

[1] See G. Milanesi, *Le lettere di Michelangelo*, Florence, 1875, p. 427.

[2] See the letter of Pietro Roselli to Michelangelo, of 10 May 1506, published by H. Pogatscher in Steinmann, ii, p. 695.

[3] Painted in 1493–4, cf. C. Gnudi–L. Becherucci, *Mostra di Melozzo*, Forlì, 1938, p. 12, pls. 104–8. Destroyed in the Second World War.

[4] Cf. C. de Tolnay, op. cit., pp. 14 f.; J. Wilde, *Italian Drawings in the British Museum: Michelangelo and his Studio*, London, 1953, pp. 17 ff.

The axes of the bays and pilasters are respected, but otherwise the references to the decoration of the chapel are slight. Although both designs look convincing on paper, it is not easy to visualize either of them carried out on the prescribed scale. First of all, it is difficult to imagine how those dominating lozenges, or octagons, could be filled: they are much too large to be treated as ornamented panels and their shapes are not very suitable to figure compositions.

Michelangelo, we know from his own admission, felt that the problem could not be satisfactorily solved in this way,[1] and he tried his own method. The desire for a more significant and a more comprehensive programme may well have been a much stronger factor in this change than his dissatisfaction; but of this he does not speak, and I cannot even touch upon this immense theme today. 'His own method' in our context means only certain aspects of his final design. Studying this design it should be remembered that the central problem of the period in Michelangelo's career to which it belongs was a new relation between figures and architecture. His activity was concentrated on large-scale projects in which assemblies of statues and reliefs were to be placed in architectural frameworks designed by him for the purpose. One can clearly see from his own statements how much these works meant to him, and one can understand why a commission of a different character was transformed into one of this particular kind.

The Sistine ceiling has been called Michelangelo's substitute for the project of a papal mausoleum abandoned at the patron's whim.[2] Doubtless to some extent this is true. Plate 32a is an architect's design demonstrating in plan and elevation what the framework of the ceiling would be like if it were carried out as architecture.[3] The experiment is legitimate, for the artist clearly conceived this framework as a kind of attic storey added to the chapel walls. This attic consists of very plastic walls erected on a podium which has no mouldings. Pier-like projections, with balustered plinths and sculptured shafts, divide the walls into alternating wider and narrower sections. Seats are inserted in the narrower sections. The elaborate cornice breaks forward above the piers, but the latter are continued across the low barrel

[1] See the letter quoted in note 1 on p. 252, and W. Maurenbrecher, *Die Aufzeichnungen des Michelangelo im Britischen Museum*, Leipzig, 1938, p. 69.

[2] Cf. C. Justi, *Michelangelo: Beiträge zur Erklärung der Werke und des Menschen*, 2nd ed., Berlin, 1922, pp. 15 ff.

[3] A. Schiavo, *Michelangelo architetto*, Rome, 1949, fig. 83.

vault in plain marble ribs against the sky. For in Michelangelo's final design the chapel again became hypaethral. This is clearly shown at the two ends of the ceiling, where the narrow strips between the shorter courses of the cornice and the ribs next to them are painted pale blue (Pls. 32*b*, 37). Although we see only sections of it, Michelangelo's open sky is infinite, as was the *vera coeli facies* it replaced. It is peopled not with golden stars but with a great artist's visions of biblical mythology. Figures are placed in front of the attic, which appears to have been made thus plastic in order to provide appropriate places for them. They are seated or standing on the benches, and are also seated on cubes which, centred on the piers, surmount the cornice. Figures and architecture appear to speak the same language.

It is not surprising to find that this system corresponds much more closely with the original decoration than the schemes embodied in Michelangelo's earlier designs. Of course, owing to the interpenetration of clerestory and vault, there was no question of directly continuing the third tier of the chapel walls. On the contrary, Michelangelo used his predecessor's method to secure a separate existence for his ceiling. As the large acanthus leaves did before, standing *putti* with inscribed tablets above them mask the nearly vertical springs of the pendentives. This actually severs the vault from the walls and makes it appear floating above the chapel space.[1] But, unlike his predecessor, Michelangelo included in his system the vaulted triangles, by giving them broad marble frames to match their surroundings, and he used them, as well as the lunettes, which he also redecorated, as a transition to the increased scale and plasticity of his principal figures.

The correspondence consists, first of all, in continuing certain divisions of the third tier on the curved surface of the vault, divisions which become arresting by the exigencies of lighting. If one wants to see the portraits of the popes, one has to take up a position *between* two windows. Then two niches with a plastic pilaster between them will form a natural unit, separated from the next of its kind by a framed window opening. The units are about a third wider than the sections between them. The diagram Plate 35*a* shows how the acceptance of these divisions resulted in the rhythm of Michelangelo's system (Pl. 35*b*)—the rhythm praised by Condivi as a means of avoiding the monotony

---

[1] Cf. C. de Tolnay, op. cit., pp. 16 f.

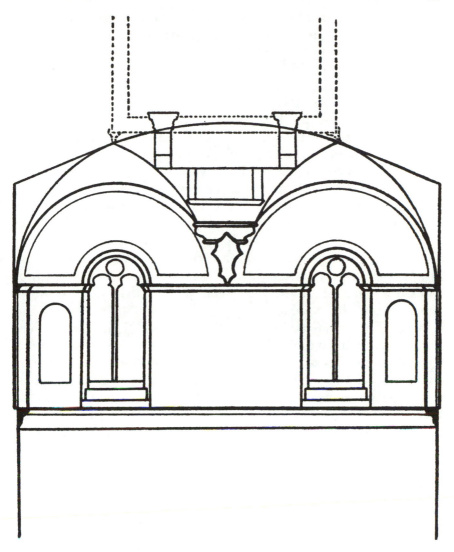

Fig. 2. Position of the painted cornice.

resulting from repetition.[1] Appropriately, the centres of greatest plasticity in the attic are above the plastic units of the third tier, while the large rectangles of the ceiling open above the voids of the windows.

Another dominant feature of the new ceiling is the cornice of its attic (Pl. 37). Most of the other architectural members depend on this one. It runs mathematically straight—no small

---

[1] 'E questo ha fatto per fuggir la sacieta che nasce dalla similitudine': Condivi, ed. Frey, p. 98.

achievement, considering that it had to be painted piecemeal, and that the building is full of irregularities: the interior is 36 inches wider at the entrance than on the altar side; not all the bays are of equal width; the vaulted triangles are not of the same height; and so on. Now, the long courses of the cornice were determined by taking up the centres of the two windows once in the altar-wall (Fig. 2). This can only be indicated in drawing; but it can be *seen* at the two ends of the ceiling where the short courses of the cornice are similarly orientated on the first and last windows of the long walls.

A more important point of agreement between the two systems is their adoption of the same visual order. As on the walls, each section and each frame on the ceiling has its own viewpoint. Outside the histories linear perspective was used only for one purpose: to mark the narrower sections of the attic as forming, together with the piers at their flanks, distinct units: the thrones of the Seers (Pl. 36). Vertically, these units extend from the slabs on which the figures' feet rest to the cornice. The *ignudi* are outside the scope of their perspective, and in order to avoid a break at this point, the upper, inner edges of the cubes on which they are seated—which one would expect to be receding—are masked, in all twenty cases. The vanishing point lies on the vertical axis about one-third of the way up, at the level of the seat. This is the ideal viewpoint for the figures and, thanks to the ingenious choice of the place they occupy on the vault, the spectator actually does see them from this very viewpoint. The figures are large, from 9 to $11\frac{1}{2}$ feet high, and one needs to look at them from the maximum distance. Taking one's position by the opposite wall, one views them at nearly right angles—that is to say, one is looking at them under the same conditions as if they were painted on a vertical surface with the vanishing point at eye-level (Fig. 3). This device partly accounts also for the fact that the eye has little difficulty in accepting Michelangelo's attic as a continuation upwards of the chapel walls.

Horizontally, in consequence of the multiple viewpoint, the attic is cut up into independent sections. To secure continuity in this direction Michelangelo applied the means used with the same object in the Quattrocento decoration: unified lighting. This meant, for him too, the acceptance of the two windows in the altar-wall as the sources of light: all the plastic forms of the long sides of his attic, and all the figures placed in front of them, cast shadows in the same direction, from left to right on

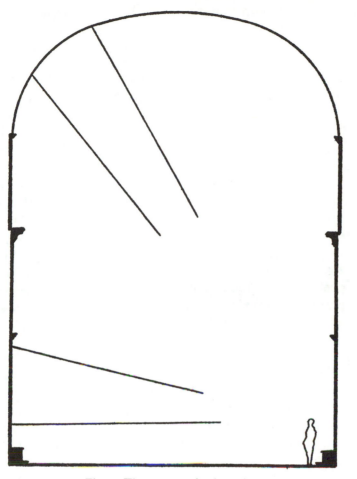

Fig. 3. The spectator's viewpoint.

the north side, from right to left on the south side (Pl. 37). This
consistency of lighting not only helps the eye in moving from one
section to the next within the system; it is, at the same time, the
most effective factor in harmonizing the two systems. But since
the two windows have gone it is easy to overlook both the effect
and its reasons.

This view of the second half of the ceiling[1] illustrates one
more important point: the relation of the ceiling frescoes to the
liturgical division of the chapel. A clear reference to this division
was contained for the theologically minded in the iconography:
all the scenes in which Almighty God appears are above the

[1] It is from C. de Tolnay's book (see note 5 on p. 250) and is the only
one which shows this section from the spectator's viewpoint. The book also
contains a similar view of the whole ceiling (figs. 2 and 3).

original area of the presbytery, while the scenes depicting human misery were above the part left to the people.[1] But it also appears that Michelangelo found a way of indicating the prominence of the chancel by compositional means. It is known that he began work on the entrance side, and that three years later the then completed part was unveiled. This part ends, I believe, at the line which marks the top edge of the 'Creation of Adam' (Pl. 35*b*). There are stylistic changes in it which indicate that he worked in transverse belts; but the system of horizontals and verticals, of forms exactly at right angles to each other, was strictly observed throughout. In contrast to this, the section carried out *after* the partial unveiling (Pl. 37) appears to have been conceived, in its whole length and width, as a unit and to have been done all in one piece.[2] One factor in this unity seems to me to be relevant in our context. There are fewer but much larger figures in the central area, and all of them are in movement, the force of which increases from picture to picture. The direction of the movement alternates in right and left turns as it is carried by the diagonals or, in the large spaces, double diagonals of the figures. The result is a gigantic compositional zigzag for the eye: it connects all four frescoes and it ends, almost like a stroke of lightning, in the contorted figure of Jonah.[3] As Jonah is a symbol of the Resurrection, he was given the place above the image of Christ, the focus in the upper region of the Sistine altar-wall. And his figure is lit, through the narrow opening at the end of the vault, by the light which God divided from the darkness on the first day.

From an aesthetic point of view Clement VII's plan to have the Last Judgement painted on the Sistine altar-wall may be truly called barbarous, for it meant, in any case, the destruction of quite essential parts of the chapel's decoration. It dated from the troubled time following the Sack of Rome and its immediate

[1] Cf. Steinmann, ii, p. 220.

[2] There is no room here to discuss the highly important question of the phases of the work. The line of demarcation between the two main sections suggested above is confirmed by Condivi's statement (ed. Frey, pp. 112 f.) that in the part painted after the unveiling of 1511 Michelangelo did not use gold. Considerations regarding the scaffolding as well as stylistic evidence suggest that the lunettes and vaulted triangles are not later than the central parts of the ceiling corresponding to them. As for the assumption that the whole of the later section was conceived as a unit, I should like to refer to the testimony of Michelangelo's small sketchbook now in the Ashmolean (K. T. Parker, *Catalogue of the Collection of Drawings*, ii, Oxford, 1956, nos. 299–306).

[3] Cf. the article quoted in note 2 on p. 250.

political effects. We are told by a well-informed source of a vow made by the pope to commemorate his own deliverance from the Sack by erecting a group of the Deadly Sins overthrown by angels, composed of gigantic bronze figures, on the tower of the Castel Sant'Angelo.[1] It may well be that this vow in fact resulted in the work which associated the name of the second Medici pope with the chapel in the Vatican. But he must also have felt that, at least in his choice of subject, he was the exponent of a mood more or less general in Italy.

I have got to be very brief. The earliest mention of Clement's plan speaks of a picture to be painted *above* the altar,[2] and Michelangelo's first designs seem to have conformed to this. According to this sketch (Pl. 38*b*)[3] the celestial group was apparently intended to fill the space between the centres, or the outer frames, of the two filled-up windows, the figure of Christ thus taking exactly the place of its Quattrocento predecessor (Pl. 38*a*). The groups of the Elect and Damned would probably have formed columns reaching down to the first cornice, and the whole, a framed square *sopra l'altare* filled with a symmetrical and essentially static composition. The format of the second drawing (Pl. 39),[4] a complete composition study, is a rectangle of the proportions 3 to 4. In this case there is no doubt about how to project it on to the altar-wall. The fresco would have extended from the third cornice to the mensa and again from one outer window frame to the other, that is to say, ending on the right short of the door to the sacristy built by Innocent VIII. The altar-piece, framed by narrow mouldings, is preserved: a small rectangle within the large, of the same proportions; notice how ingeniously the mighty S-curve of the groups has been drawn round it. The top of the altar-piece is used as a platform for an angel fighting the Evil One. But this would not have made the contrast between the subjects of the two compositions, the Glory of the Virgin and the Final Judgement, less abrupt or less disturbing. And both this design and the previous one involved a serious technical difficulty. The altar-wall was not even, its clerestory was stepped back by 5 inches. How to redress this, and what to do with the remaining parts of the wall, the lunettes and the broad strips on the right and the left?

[1] Vasari (Milanesi), vi, p. 153.

[2] See Pastor, iv–2, 1923, p. 567 n. 2.

[3] Musée Bonnat, Bayonne, 1217; B. Berenson, *Drawings of Florentine Painters*, amplified edition, Chicago, 1938, no. 1395B.

[4] Casa Buonarroti, 65; Berenson, no. 1413. For the following remarks cf. the article quoted in note 2 on p. 250.

Evidently, the idea of a separate picture above the altar could not be satisfactorily realized.

In Michelangelo's final design (Pl. 40) the original conception of the palace chapel as a vast rectangular *aula* surrounded by interior façades has been carried to its logical conclusion. One single pictorial composition, *la facciata del Giudizio* as Vasari called it,[1] has replaced the whole of the altar-wall. All that remained of this wall is a dado behind, and to the right and left of, the mensa, and this was to be covered by a decorative tapestry.[2] The painting is not an illusionist extension of the chapel room. It opens up the view of a second reality independent of ours, of a world governed by its own rules. No perspective was used for organizing this view: the scale of the figures increases upwards from tier to tier, and the viewpoint shifts from group to group both horizontally and vertically. It is a façade entirely composed of plastic figures, with that crushing weight of the upper half which is known to us from Michelangelo's previous façade projects, that for the Julius Monument of 1516, and that for S. Lorenzo of 1517.[3]

However, in working out his composition the artist found ways of taking into account the suppressed articulation of the altar-wall and of bringing his fresco into some kind of visual harmony with the chapel room (Pl. 26). The scenes on earth and in hell reach the level of the first cornice. The division between the two higher registers exactly corresponds to the level of the entablature. In the lunettes the *Antenati* have been replaced by groups which link up with the compositions painted on the spherical triangles at the end of the vault: the Cross and the Column of the Passion form parallels to Haman's cross and the pole of the Brazen Serpent, both of which are symbols of the Redemption. And finally, for the two arched windows one similar opening in the centre, on the same level, is substituted. It is the golden-yellow mandorla of light behind the group which replaced the former centres of the altar-wall: Christ and His Mother. This window-like mandorla is a focusing break in the

---

[1] Vasari, ed. 1550, p. 939; ed. 1568 (Milanesi), v, p. 623.

[2] See Vasari, loc. cit., and the documents published by H. Pogatscher in Steinmann, ii, p. 770. The cartoon for the tapestry, which was commissioned by Paul III, 'col consenso di Michelagnolo', from Perino del Vaga in 1542, was discovered by H. Voss (*Die Malerei der Spätrenaissance in Rom und Florenz*, Berlin 1920, ii, p. 74) in the Palazzo Spada. It seems to suggest that already at that time a second door to Innocent VIII's sacristy was planned. This door (on the Gospel side) was built under Clement XI.

[3] Cf. J. Wilde, *Michelangelo's 'Victory'*, Oxford, 1954, pp. 5 ff.

deep blue of the fresco ground and is, by virtue of its position, the centre of the entire tripartite decoration as we possess it.

Subtle adjustments, like those we have observed in Michelangelo's ceiling—no mere technicalities. They are welcome to the eye, even if it is not conscious of them, because they are factors in the visual order which creates harmony between the parts and the whole and helps us to read the message the works were intended to convey. This is the double significance of the visual order. It explains why the finding of the appropriate order was of real concern to the artist. It should, I think, justify our earnest attention.

MICHELANGELO'S PROPHETS AND SIBYLS

THE official *Life of Michelangelo*, written with the artist's approval by his pupil Ascanio Condivi, includes a short and simple statement on Michelangelo's religious readings: 'With deep study and attention, he read the Holy Scriptures, both the Old and the New Testaments, as well as those who have expounded them, such as the writings of Savonarola, for whom he always had a great affection, keeping always in mind the memory of his living voice.'[1]

Charles Holroyd, who was the first to translate Condivi's *Life* into English, supplied this passage with a cautious commentary, warning against the opinion that Michelangelo's general views of the Church were formed—or transformed—by Savonarola: 'No doubt, like all the other citizens, the master listened to the voice of the preacher, but we have no evidence that he was particularly influenced by his teaching, though many of his biographers would have us believe that Savonarola made him Protestant, Lutheran, or what not, according to the sect of the biographer. Michael Angelo loved the sermons of the eloquent Frate as works of art; no doubt, if the prophets of the Sistine could speak, they would preach with the voice of Savonarola.'[2]

Whether anyone in Florence could have listened to the fulminations of Savonarola as works of art is doubtful. His style was abrupt, and his delivery so direct that it offended the poetic sensibilities of Politian, who preferred the mellifluous, well-balanced sermons of Savonarola's enemy, Fra Mariano da Genazzano.[3] But the last sentence in Holroyd's comment is true in a more literal sense than he may have intended: Michelangelo's characterization of the prophets in the Sistine Chapel rests on a theological doctrine of prophecy that can be learned, in

---

[1] Tr. Charles Holroyd, here quoted from the second edition (1911) of Holroyd's *Michael Angelo Buonarroti*, p. 74, § lxv.

[2] Ibid., p. 90.

[3] Politianus, *Epistolae* IV. vi (*Opera* i, 1519, fol. 36ʳ); *Miscellanea*, Praefatio (ibid., fols. 125ᵛ f.).

a most handy form, from one of the popular tracts of Savonarola, his *Dialogo della verità profetica*.[1]

That this text appears not to have been seriously considered by any of the numerous commentators on Michelangelo's Prophets is easy enough to understand. The paintings of the Sistine Ceiling were begun in 1508, ten years after Savonarola's death, and their style is informed with a Roman grandiloquence for which he would have had little use. Indeed, a glance at the simple woodcut that illustrates the tract (Pl. 41) would be sufficient to dispel any thoughts of the Sistine Ceiling.

Savonarola is seen seated under a large tree on the outskirts of Florence, conversing with a group of seven strangers dressed in exotic costume, while the dove of the Holy Ghost floats uneasily above him. The text begins with a lyrical invocation of nature, clearly borrowed from the scene in the *Phaedrus* in which Socrates chooses a grassy slope near a fresh spring, under a lofty spreading plane-tree, as the most auspicious place for discussing divine Beauty. 'Here is the place', writes Savonarola, 'that invites us to sit down near that spring in the fresh grass and under this plane-tree rich with foliage: so that we may converse more quietly and with more pleasure (*con maggiore iocundita*) on divine illuminations.'

In the ensuing dialogue the seven strangers, examined firmly by the Friar, behave very much like pupils of Socrates, surprised by the simplicity of the examiner's questions: ' "I ask you, what is the colour of the lily?"—"It is white."—"Would you think that you could be mistaken in this?"—"No."—"Why not?"—"Because I see it."—"In that case you know for certain that the lily is white?"—"Yes, certainly."—"If all the people of our city were to affirm with one voice that the lily is not white, whom would you rather trust: all the people or your own eyes?"—"Certainly my own eyes."—"But if the sages with many reasons and proofs were to tell you that the lily is black, would you believe them?"—"Not in truth." '

Under the pressure of Savonarola's interrogation, the strangers gradually reveal their identity: they are the Seven Gifts of the Holy Spirit, disguised for Savonarola's benefit as picturesque orientals and bearing mysterious Hebrew names—Uria, Eliphaz, Rechima, Iechima, Thoralmed, Abbacuc, Saphtham—that form the acrostic VERITAS. They discuss with Savonarola his prophetic calling, and after feigning (semi-

---

[1] Hain, *Repertorium bibliographicum*, no. 14341, originally in Latin (nos. 14339 f.), *De veritate prophetica dialogus*.

Socratic in their turn) to disbelieve the rumour of his divine inspiration, proceed to supply him with splendid credentials attesting the supernatural source of his visions.

Savonarola must have written this little fantasy with the Florentine Platonists in mind. The literary form, the idyllic location, the charade performed by oriental mystagogues, reveal an unexpected taste for the arcane vagaries that flourished in Ficino's Villa di Careggi. While it is known that Savonarola made a strong impression on some members of that circle, in particular on the two Benivienis and on Pico della Mirandola, the fanciful nature of this pamphlet makes one wonder whether there was not also some influence in the reverse direction,[1] although Savonarola never favoured the secretive Pythagorean manner. In his hands the cryptic pomp of the pagan mystics dissolves into popular imagery, Zoroaster and Hermes Trismegistus giving way to the magi of the miracle plays. The scene in the woodcut seems far removed from awesome rites or secret societies: it merely suggests that an argument on a difficult subject can be enhanced by a pleasant setting.

It would be agreeable to think that it was in this handy form of a vernacular tract, rather than in the recondite jargon of the higher learning, that Michelangelo first encountered the doctrine of prophetic powers, which the Roman theologians later taught him to expand. The Seven Gifts cited by Savonarola—Wisdom and Understanding, Deliberation and Might, Science and Compassion, and Fear of the Lord—are the canonical gifts of the Holy Spirit listed in a famous prophecy of Isaiah (xi. 1–3):

And there shall come forth a rod out of the stem of Jesse and a branch shall grow out of his roots: And the spirit of the Lord shall rest upon him, the spirit of wisdom (*sapientia*) and understanding (*intellectus*), the spirit of deliberation (*consilium*) and might (*fortitudo*), the spirit of science (*scientia*) and compassion (*pietas*), and he shall be filled with the spirit of the fear of the Lord (*timor Domini*).[2]

---

[1] Petrus Crinitus, *De honesta disciplina* III. ii (ed. C. Angeleri, 1955, pp. 104 f.), describes a debate he had witnessed between Savonarola and Pico della Mirandola in the library of San Marco in Florence, where a small academy used to assemble ('in Marciana academia apud Hieronymum Savonarolam'). At the start of the discussion Savonarola objected to the pride caused by too much emulation of pagan philosophers, but when Pico opposed him by reciting the mystical insights of the pagans, Savonarola replied by embracing Pico and praising his speech. However idealizing in retrospect, Crinitus's account was published in 1508, that is, within living memory of Savonarola and Pico.

[2] The text given here follows that of the Vulgate. In the King James version the gift of *pietas* is not mentioned, so that the canonical seven gifts

In the Sistine Ceiling the Prophets alternate with Sibyls, but although it was customary to group them in pairs, in this instance their numbers do not match: seven prophets are set against five sibyls. In the lunettes below the Prophets and Sibyls Michelangelo painted the Genealogy of Christ according to Matthew, that is, precisely the Tree of Jesse on which, as Isaiah said in the passage quoted, the gifts of the Holy Spirit are supposed to rest. Leaving the sibyls aside for the moment, it can be shown that the seven prophets, beginning at the entrance and ending at the altar, express the Biblical 'gifts of the spirit' in the same order as they appear in Isaiah: *sapientia—intellectus—consilium—fortitudo—scientia—pietas—timor Domini*. A lesser artist might have despaired of visualizing such a set of abstractions. How was he to distinguish, for example, between the spirits of Understanding (*intellectus*), Science (*scientia*) and Wisdom (*sapientia*)? To represent them disguised as mysterious orientals or, according to medieval custom, by a group of white doves perched on a tree,[1] was a delightful way of dodging the problem which only a bolder imagination would attack: could human features, expressions, and gestures be used to characterize the seven gifts of the Spirit as specific moods of prophetic seizure?

In the beginning with Zechariah, who represents *sapientia* (Pls. 42, 43), it is important to suspend judgement on his spiritual temperament until the character is seen as part of the series. Taken by itself, the profile of an elderly sage, reading attentively in his papers while two companionable spirits stand musingly behind him, may or may not be an illustration of Wisdom; but the doubt will diminish, or perhaps even vanish, on seeing how *intellectus*, which follows after *sapientia*, appears in the determined physiognomy of Joel (Pl. 44). With his clean-shaven face and high Ciceronian forehead, framed by flamboyantly receding hair, he embodies the type of a humanist critic, judiciously examining his text with a touch of the vanity and self-esteem that often adhere to the character of an 'intellectual'.[2] The cool

---

appear as six. On the history of this version, see A. Gardeil, 'Dons du Saint-Esprit', *Dictionnaire de théologie catholique* iv, cols. 1728–81. St. Ambrose's listing of the seven gifts (*De spiritu sancto* i, xvi. 159; *Patr. lat.* xvi, col. 740) corresponds closely to that of Jerome: *spiritus sapientiae et intellectus, spiritus consilii atque virtutis, spiritus cognitionis atque pietatis, spiritus timoris Dei*. See also his *Expositio in Psalmum cxviii*, 38 (*Patr. lat.* xv, col. 1265).

[1] Arthur Watson, *The Early Iconography of the Tree of Jesse* (1934), p. 168, with illustrations (cf. p. 280, n. 1, below).

[2] Michelangelo had ample opportunity for observing the type, not only in the average run of contentious humanists, but in an outstanding intellectual

eyes and tight lips, the shapely nose dominated by a frowning brow, suggest force of understanding, mental acumen. To illustrate his state of mind, the pair of spirits behind him enact a little pantomime of intellectual demonstration (Pl. 45): the one putto lectures to the other with a superior air, his authority visibly buttressed by a large volume under his arm.

After *sapientia* and *intellectus*, the mood of deliberation prescribed by *consilium* appears in the attitude of Isaiah (Pl. 46). Reluctantly turning from his half-closed book, the prophet listens to the call of the spirit with an expression of mingled doubt and concern. He hesitates to follow, deliberates, 'takes counsel'. Although appointed to be a 'crier in the wilderness', Isaiah remains a reflective prophet (xl. 6): 'A voice said, Cry! And I said, What shall I cry?' (*Vox dicentis: Clama! Et dixi: Quid clamabo?*). The tension within the prophetic seizure, between an active call and a retarding thought, defines the inspired state of suspense which belongs to the gift of Counsel.

Ezekiel, who follows, is impulsive Might (Pl. 47). The force and rage, concentrated in the bull-like neck, are threateningly expressed by the gesture of the hand, the lips being pressed together in a state of prophetic fury (Pl. 48). Of the two spirits, one has lodged himself impishly behind the prophet's neck, driving him forward (Pl. 49), while the other, more benign and idealistic looking, guides him upward (Pl. 47). Ezekiel's name is translated 'God gives strength'. In a famous passage he refers to 'the form of a man's hand' (*similitudo manus hominis*) as a threatening apparition (x. 8, resumed x. 21), and St. Gregory quotes the image (*Moralia* VII, xxviii) as meaning an active force under divine guidance. *Quid per manus nisi operationes?* As Durandus succinctly put it: 'the hand signifies the deed.'[1]

Science (*scientia*) is represented by Daniel (Pl. 50), zealously engaged in transcribing a text: 'I, Daniel, understood by books' (ix. 2). He appears here as the skilled interpreter, explaining the difficult word in the large volume by transferring it to a little book. 'I have heard of thee', Belshazzar said to Daniel, 'that thou canst make interpretations of obscure meanings and untie

whom he disliked: the sharp-witted Bramante. As shown on two medals, his features resemble those of Joel (see Hill, *A Corpus of Italian Medals*, 1930, nos. 657 f.). Even more pertinent are the classical busts of Cicero (Capitoline Museum, Rome, no. 75; Vatican, no. 698; also Apsley House, London).

[1] 'Manus enim opus significat' (*Rationale divinorum officiorum*, IV. xvii. 2). In Pagnini's *Isagoge ad mysticos sacrae scripturae sensus* (1536) the chapter *Quid manus mystice significet* (x. xliv) begins with St. Gregory's explanation (*Moralia* VII. xxviii) of the image in Ezekiel x. 8: *similitudo manus hominis*.

knots' (*audivi de te quod possis obscura interpretari et ligata dissolvere,*
v. 16). In writing his commentary Daniel is assisted by a spirit
who illustrates the weight of learning by supporting the large
heavy volume, but there is another spirit lurking behind the
prophet's shoulder, a ghost-like figure covered by a cloak,
suggestive of the visionary dreams that were vouchsafed to
Daniel as part of his science. As St. Augustine explained,
Daniel was distinguished among the prophets by the fact that
he combined imaginative vision and probing intelligence:

> . . . and a greater prophet is he that interprets what another has seen,
> than he that has merely seen it. . . . Hence Joseph, who understood what
> was meant by the seven ears of corn and the seven cows, was a greater
> prophet than Pharaoh who had seen them in a dream . . . for in the one
> was only the image of the things, in the other the interpretation of the
> image . . . but the greatest is the prophet that excels in both, so that he
> will both see in his spirit the similitudes of things, and understand them
> by the vivacity of his mind: thus Daniel's excellence was tested and
> proved, because he both told the king the dream he had seen, and
> revealed to him what it signified.[1]

The pair of *Ignudi* who are set above Daniel[2] seem to cele-
brate his scholarly victories with fierce joy and wild jubilation
(Pl. 51), particularly eloquent as they sit on the top of Caryatids
that perform a drastic scene of castigation (Pl. 52), a *drôlerie*
depicted with the grim felicity that distinguishes Michelangelo's
sense of humour.[3] Since it was customary for Renaissance
commentators to refer to their textual emendations as *castigationes* (witness Ermolao Barbaro's *Castigationes Plinianae* or Pierio
Valeriano's *Castigationes Virgilianae*), it is not impossible that an
allusion was intended to the discipline of textual criticism in
which Daniel is engaged as an assiduous scholiast. In the Vulgate Daniel says in praise of the Lord that he gives 'science to
those that understand discipline': *et [dat] scientiam intelligentibus
disciplinam* (ii. 21).

A marginal gloss on Daniel's zeal for scientific clarification is
supplied by the pair of figures that appear below him in the
lunettes (Pl. 71). Although the emaciated scribe and the
spinning woman belong to a separate cycle—a moral account of

---

[1] Augustine, *De Genesi ad litteram* xii. ix (*Patr. lat.* xxxiv, col. 461).

[2] The significance of the youths sitting on the cornice is a nice theological
problem that we shall try to solve below. In art-historical literature their
designation as *ignudi* ('nudes') derives from Condivi (*certi ignudi*) and from
Vasari (*belli ignudi*).

[3] Cf. Daniel vii. 11: 'I beheld even till the beast was slain' (*et vidi quoniam
interfecta esset bestia*).

the Genealogy of Christ, in which Virtues and Vices oppose each other until Christ is born in the human soul[1]—the particular Vice or Virtue under each Prophet or Sibyl is like a homely echo of the prophetic mood. In the case of Daniel the connexion is sufficiently simple not to require any long explanation (by moralizing the names in Matthew i) of why the man writes and the woman spins. Suffice it to say that he is an ascetic judge plagued (like Daniel) with an itch to clarify his thoughts with the help of a pen,[2] while the woman (again like Daniel explicating a text) draws out the spun yarn neatly on a skein-winder. That Michelangelo's contemporaries recognized in these accompanying figures a running commentary on the Prophets and Sibyls is shown by a series of engravings, by Giorgio Ghisi, in which each Prophet and Sibyl is attended by the two adjacent figures from the Genealogy (Pls. 58, 79).

Jeremiah (Pl. 54), the author of the Lamentations, is the prophet of compassionate sorrow (*pietas*): 'For who shall have pity upon thee, O Jerusalem, or who shall bemoan thee?' (xv. 5). Withdrawn into the gloom of his meditation, he has let his

---

[1] On the custom of translating and allegorizing the Hebrew names in Biblical genealogies and itineraries, cf. Pagnini, *Isagoge*, p. 9, with reference to Augustine, *De doctrina Christiana* II. xvi: 'nomina Hebraea non est disputandum habere non parvam vim atque adiutorium ad solvenda aenigmata scripturarum.' It was with the intention of assisting the allegorical interpretation of the Bible that Pagnini compiled, on the model of Jerome's *Liber interpretationis Hebraicorum nominum* (for which see *Onomastica sacra*, ed. Paul de Lagarde, 1870, pp. 1–159), a new and philologically more ambitious *Liber interpretationum Hebraicorum Graecorumque nominum quae arcanis sacrisque in literis inveniuntur* (attached to Pagnini's translation of the Bible, 1528, fols. n ii–x vi); cf. Wind, 'Sante Pagnini and Michelangelo', *Gazette des beaux-arts* xxvi (1944, Focillon Memorial Volume), particularly pp. 218–32: 'The Genealogy of Christ in Renaissance Theology'. To satirize the cult of mystical etymologies, Ben Jonson made a female impostor feign the obsession: 'If you but name a word touching the Hebrew,/she falls into her fit and will discourse/so learnedly of genealogies/as you would run mad, too, to hear her, sir' (*The Alchemist* II. i). As late as 1704 there appeared in Naples a most ponderous specimen of that extravagant literature by a Spanish Franciscan, Isidorus a S. Michaele, entitled *De temporali, humana, et mystica D.N. Jesu Christi generatione observatio genealogica, panegyrica, mystica, dogmatica et moralis super primum caput S. Matthaei* (copy in the Bibliothèque Nationale, D. 3156); reviewed in *Acta eruditorum* (1711), Supplementum iv, pp. 342–6, with some astonishment at the survival of this *ingeniosa pietas*—which 'non ignoramus . . . compluribus Ecclesiae Patribus arrisisse'.

[2] His name, Josaphat, was translated *ipse judicans*, for which the moralization is: *librum scribat ipse qui iudicat* (Job xxxi. 35; cf. St. Gregory, *Moralia* XXII. xix; also Pagnini, *Isagoge* IX. xxxv).

aged head sink down on his hand, in the traditional posture of melancholy: 'I am the man that hath seen affliction by the rod of his wrath. He hath led me, and brought me into darkness, but not into light' (*me minavit, et adduxit in tenebras, et non in lucem*, Lamentations iii, 1 f.). Placed next to the picture of the *Fiat Lux*, in which God divides Light from Darkness (Pl. 80), Jeremiah sits on the side of Darkness. Below him are two figures from the Genealogy who are doomed by the obscurity that has invaded their minds (Pl. 59): a superstitious carpenter who looks like a wrathful gnome, cursing the image of his own face that is carved on his stick,[1] and a man lost in a stupor of forgetfulness.[2] They seem to illustrate the prophet's words: *in tenebris collocavit me quasi mortuos sempiternos* (Lamentations iii. 6).[3] In a chapter on *Abdita Dei* and mystical silence, Francesco Giorgio reflected on the oppressive load that the Lord has put 'on the shoulders of those to whom he has confided his secrets', and he referred as an example to the solitary Jeremiah who had written in the Lamentations (iii. 28): *sedebit solitarius et tacebit* ('he sitteth alone and keepeth silence').[4] Of the two spirits attending Jeremiah, the more remote looks cold and impenetrable like a Fate, while the one closer to the prophet expresses the profoundest pity (Pl. 54). 'And this is the condemnation, that light is come into the world, and men loved darkness rather than light' (John iii. 19). Between the *Ignudi* above the prophet (Pls. 56, 57) the same kind of disparity prevails as between the two spirits behind him: one of them is bent under a heavy burden, the other looks impenetrable and impassive, his expression arrested in a fixed

[1] The name is Boas, but except for the name the figure has nothing in common with the wealthy and generous Boas in the Book of Ruth. 'Boas' was translated *in quo est robur*, and taken to mean 'he in whom there is wood'. For the superstitious carpenter see Wisdom of Solomon xiii. 11–19; Isaiah xliv. 13–18.

[2] Named Aminadab (= *populus meus*), he appears next to a youthful woman, with a veil on her lap, who combs her hair: 'Can a maid forget her ornaments, or a bride her attire? Yet my people (*populus meus*) have forgotten me days without number' (Jeremiah ii. 32). In the Vulgate the bride's 'attire' is specified in this passage as a shawl (*fascia pectoralis*).

[3] That Jeremiah reflects with gloom on the Day of Judgement, prophetically foreshadowed in the first Day of Creation when God divides Light from Darkness (Augustine, *De Genesi ad litteram*, *Patr. lat.* xxxiv, cols. 228–30), is further suggested by the fiery chariot of Elijah in the medallion above Jeremiah: 'Behold I will send you Elijah the prophet before the coming of the great and dreadful day of the Lord' (Malachi iv. 5).

[4] *Harmonia mundi totius* (1525) III. viii. 20, fols. 134ᵛ ff.: 'De pausa, quiete, et silentio.'

gaze like a mask: the face of one who fathoms the abyss (Pl. 55).

The series ends with the prophet Jonah (Pl. 60), exemplifying Fear of the Lord (*timor Domini*): 'I am an Hebrew; and I fear the Lord, the God of Heaven, which hath made the sea and the dry land' (i. 9). Indeed, no prophet was more fully possessed of that fear than the obstinate fugitive and mutineer, who first fled from the presence of the Lord unto the sea, then cried to the Lord out of the belly of the great fish, and finally put the fear of the Lord into Nineveh, so forcefully that the city repented: 'Yet forty days, and Nineveh shall be overthrown', etc. (iii. 4 ff.). Christ himself, to rebuke the scribes and pharisees who had asked him to produce a sign, gave them 'the sign of the prophet Jonah' by which he foretold the Day of Judgement (Matthew xii. 38–41): 'The men of Nineveh shall rise in judgement with this generation, and shall condemn it: because they repented at the preaching of Jonah; and, behold, a greater than Jonah is here.' The passage would suffice to explain why Michelangelo, some twenty years after he had finished the Sistine Ceiling, painted the Day of Judgement directly below the figure of Jonah, thus bringing the spectator face to face with the terrible event which the prophet of the Fear of the Lord foreshadows.

Attended by the whale from whose belly he was resurrected after three days and three nights (Pl. 60), and by the gourd which came up in a night and perished in a night, Jonah is seen in the dialectical moment (related in the Book of Jonah with laconic astuteness) of arguing with God about Justice and Grace, demanding the destruction of the wicked, while he himself becomes through his conduct an object-lesson of divine mercy. If he seems the most turbulent of the seven prophets—unbalanced in the strict sense of the word—it is because he speaks to God directly and thus experiences the terrible disproportion between the divine will and its human vehicle. His absurd attempts to flee from the Lord, defended by truthful but surly remarks on the unsatisfactory state of his employment, are a convincing demonstration that the character best suited to know and preach the fear of the Lord is the most impertinent of all his prophets. Michelangelo did not shrink from this astounding piece of religious logic: he painted Jonah's disequilibrium, his titanic form thrown back by the overwhelming impact of the divine command, which he obeys with reluctance and in fear. While the hands make the gesture of the dialectical reckoner

(Pl. 60), the face is transfigured by an amazed awareness of the incalculable nature of the final judgement, an entranced admission of *timor Dei* (Pl. 61), dramatically reflected in the emotion of awe that animates the attending spirits.

No doubt, the iconographic plan provided that Jonah, the last and most agitated of the prophets, should lead back to Zechariah, the most self-contained (Pls. 42, 43): 'The fear of the Lord is the beginning of wisdom' (Proverbs ix. 10). St. Ambrose quoted that proverb in his classical demonstration that all the other gifts of the spirit originate in the fear of the Lord, that they rise from it as a column rises from its pedestal, and that, again like a column, they transfigure the support on which they rest: the Fear of the Lord, he said, is 'informed by Wisdom, instructed by Intellect, guided by Counsel, made firm by Might, governed by Cognition, enhanced by Pity. Take these away from the fear of the Lord, and it is an unreasonable and incipient fear'.[1] In summarizing these reflections St. Augustine found that in 'these seven operations' the divine forces act from above and below: 'Descending to us, the Holy Spirit begins from Wisdom and moves toward Fear. We however, in ascending, begin with Fear and are perfected in Wisdom.'[2]

In the Sistine Chapel the ascending order would be the sequence that conforms with the liturgical orientation: in facing the altar one sees Jonah, but it is only on turning round to leave the Chapel that one becomes aware of Zechariah throning peacefully above the principal door: after the upheaval of worship the end is quietude. Moreover, along the middle of the vault the stories from Genesis, and in the lunettes the names from the Genealogy of Christ, progress again from the altar toward the entrance, coming toward the spectator while he faces the altar; and the same orientation governs also the Quattrocento frescoes below: the parallel lives of Moses and Christ, and the apostolic succession of the Popes. A purely linear reading, however, whether in one direction or the other, will not do justice to Michelangelo's plan. In contrast to the narrative procession of the large frescoes below, arranged along the walls

---

[1] Ambrose, *Expositio in Psalmum cxviii*, 38 (*Patr. lat.* xv, col. 1265).

[2] Augustine, *Sermones* (*Patr. lat.* xxxviii, cols. 1161 ff.). Durandus (*Rationale divinorum officiorum* II. i. 52) reads the 'gifts' only in ascending order, *a timore incipiens* and ending with *sapientia*. See also Pagnini, *Isagoge* VI. xiv (pp. 320 f.: *Quid gradus mystice significent*): 'Propheta ergo, quia de coelestibus ad ima loquebatur, coepit magis a sapientia et descendit ad timorem. Sed nos qui a terrenis ad coelestia tendimus, eosdem gradus ascendendo enumeremus, ut a timore ad sapientiam pervenire valeamus.'

like a series of monumental tapestries, Michelangelo's ceiling is composed contrapuntally, and this involves all the actors in dynamic cross-correspondences. Just as Jonah's turbulence calls for its complement in the quietude of Zechariah, who is the prophet furthest removed from him, so each of the other prophets finds his spiritual partner not so much in his immediate neighbour on the canonical list as in the figure that answers him by providing a symmetrical counterforce. Given the length of the chapel (cf. Pl. 88), the eye may stall at conceiving of Zechariah and Jonah as a pair, but once this feat of the imagination is achieved, it ought not to be too difficult to recognize that Isaiah, as the hesitant prophet, is counterbalanced by Daniel, the zealous one, and that the sanguine acumen of Joel contrasts with the apathy of Jeremiah. Despite the vast stretch separating these figures, the weight of Ezekiel's fury binds them together: the extremes are centred in his strength.

However, the tensions and correspondences that connect the prophets are less obvious, and perhaps less important, than those introduced by the presence of the Sibyls. What is their part in the prophetic plan? What kind of 'spirits' do they represent, and how do they enter into converse with the seven gifts assigned to the prophets?

While the prophets were appointed to preach to the Jews, the Sibyls prophesied to the Gentiles. Together, they foreshadow the division of the Church into *Ecclesia Iudaeorum* and *Ecclesia Gentilium*, a distinction suggested by Christ himself when he instructed the disciples, before his death, to teach the new gospel only to the Jews, but urged them later, after his resurrection, to spread the good tidings to all the nations. The contradiction between these two commands (Matthew x. 5 f. as against Mark xvi. 15) is resolved by the mystery of the 'supplantation': as heirs. According to the promise the Gentiles displaced the Chosen People, to whom the Word was originally given. In the liturgy of the Sistine Chapel, this particular point of doctrine was of central importance: for, as Durandus explained in the *Rationale divinorum officiorum*, it is peculiar to the mass celebrated by the Roman pontiff that the Apostolic Creed is recited in two stages: first, before the Pope's salutation of peace, by the subdeacons alone who, as Durandus says, represent the Church of the Jews (*Iudaeorum ecclesia*), and afterwards by the choir, which represents the Church of the Nations (*ecclesia Gentium*).[1]

[1] Durandus, *Rationale divinorum officiorum* IV. xxv. 4: 'Et idcirco, Romano pontifice solemniter celebrante symbolum fidei, non cantores in choro sed

The geographical names assigned to the Sibyls reveal the range of their mission to the nations: Greece is represented by the Delphic Sibyl, Ionia and Asia by the Erythraean and Persian Sibyls, Africa by the Egyptian or Libyan Sibyl, and Rome—in the centre—by the sibyl from Cumae, who had instructed Aeneas about the golden bough and was later to force the Sibylline Books on Tarquin. Although all their Christian prophecies were apocryphal,[1] the fact that these uncouth and often garbled texts had been preserved by the efforts of Lactantius and Augustine[2] was sufficient to secure for them a religious

subdiaconi ad altare decantant, et generaliter ipsi ad universa respondent, usque dum ipse pontifex dicit: *Pax Domini sit semper vobiscum*: quoniam usque post Christi resurrectionem sola Iudaeorum Ecclesia, quae per subdiaconum, qui sursum ad altare consistit, designatur, corde credidit ad iustitiam et ore confessa est ad salutem [cf. Romans x. 10]: sed ex tunc cantores in choro respondent, et universa decantant, quia post resurrectionem Ecclesia Gentium, quam cantores, qui deorsum in choro subsistunt, designant, fidem Christi recipit et laudum praeconia personuit Salvatori.'

In another chapter, describing the entry of the procession (IV. vi. 17: *De accessu sacerdotis ac pontificis ad altare*), Durandus refers to a group of seven subdeacons: they represent the prophets who foretold the incarnation through the 'septiform gift of the Holy Spirit'. Throughout the ritual the subdeacon enacts, as it were, the Epistle side, that is, *figuram legis et prophetiae* (IV. xv), hence called in England 'the epistoler' (*OED*, 1440).

On the history of Durandus and his *Rationale*, written about 1286 and printed in 43 editions before 1500, with 13 further editions in the sixteenth century, see J. Sauer, *Symbolik des Kirchengebäudes* (1902), pp. 28–37.

[1] On the origin and growth of these Hellenistic fabrications, conflated (presumably by a Byzantine compiler) into an epic aggregate of fifteen books, of which twelve survive today comprising more than four thousand hexameters (the first eight books having been published in 1545, the last four in 1828), see the classic edition of C. Alexandre, *Oracula Sibyllina* (1841–56), with a deceptively elegant Latin translation and invaluable commentaries and bibliography. A fair sample, translated into English, was included by Montague R. James in *The Apocryphal New Testament* (1924), pp. 521 ff. For the impressive number of fifteenth-century manuscripts see the list in J. Geffcken, *Die Oracula Sibyllina* (1902).

[2] Lactantius, *Divinae institutiones* I. vi, an account of the ten Sibyls listed by Varro (in the lost *Antiquitates rerum divinarum*), with Christian passages from Sibylline prophecies dispersed throughout the book (e.g. IV. vi, xv–xviii; VII. xvi–xxiv, etc.); Augustine, *Civitas Dei* XVIII. xxiii, a discussion of a Christian acrostic ascribed to the Erythraean Sibyl (of which the Greek text is given in Eusebius, *Constantini oratio ad sanctorum coetum* viii), followed by a list of Sibylline prophecies from Lactantius. Isidore of Seville's chapter on the Sibyls (*Etymologiae* VIII. viii) derives, like most of the later statements, from Lactantius and Augustine. For a Renaissance view, see Ficino, *De christiana religione* xxiv f., 'Autoritas Sibyllarum', 'Testimonia Sibyllarum de Christo' (*Opera*, 1561, pp. 28 ff.). An illustrated block book of *Oracula Sibyllina*,

authority close to that of sacred script. Few humanists thought
of questioning their authenticity,[1] while many were engaged in

preserved in a unique copy at St. Gallen (eds. P. Heitz and W. L. Schreiber,
1903, with an important essay on Sibylline iconography), is typical of the
sets of Sibylline quotations that were circulated in the fifteenth and sixteenth
centuries, before the first comprehensive edition of Books i–viii was published
in 1545 (see preceding note). Émile Mâle, with an excusable preference for
'nos Sibylles françaises' (*L'art religieux de la fin du moyen âge en France*, 1925, pp.
256 ff.), dismisses the block book as of uncertain date (p. 267, note 2) and
possibly later than 1480, but in fact it is inscribed by a monk of St. Gallen who
is known to have been dead by 1477 (Heitz and Schreiber, op. cit., pp. 18 f.;
also Schreiber, *Basels Bedeutung für die Geschichte der Blockbücher*, 1909, p. 45).
There is thus no certainty that this branch of the tradition is of French
origin, as Mâle surmised. As for Italian engravings of the Sibyls, A. M. Hind
has shown (*Early Italian Engraving*, i, 1938, pp. 155 ff.) that the 'Baccio
Baldini' series antedates by about ten years the publication of Filippo
Barbieri's illustrated tract *Duodecim Sibyllarum vaticinia* (1481), whose historical influence, although very great (cf. Alexandre, op. cit. iii, pp. 301 ff.;
Heitz and Schreiber, op. cit., pp. 7 ff.), was not quite so decisive as Mâle
believed (op. cit., pp. 258–64). The increase from ten Sibyls to twelve, for
example, was not an innovation by Barbieri but had appeared, some fifty
years earlier, in a Roman cycle of frescoes commissioned by Cardinal Giordano Orsini, since destroyed, but mentioned by Poggio and fully described
in three fifteenth-century manuscripts (cf. Lothar Freund, *Studien zur Bildge-
schichte der Sibyllen in der neueren Kunst*, 1936, pp. 22 ff.). Perhaps the oddest
consequence of Mâle's belief in Barbieri as a fountain-head is his attempt to
explain the presence of Jonah in the Sistine Ceiling by a printer's error in
Barbieri's book, where a picture of Jonah and the whale appears by mistake
over a text concerning Gideon's fleece: 'Jonas s'est donc introduit, à la faveur
d'une faute d'impression, dans la compagnie des Sibylles. Michel-Ange, qui
n'a pas regardé de très près le livre de Filippo Barbieri, a aperçu une gravure
représentant Jonas et la baleine, cela lui a suffi' (p. 264; also p. 260, note 1).
Nevertheless, Mâle's chapter on Sibylline iconography remains fundamental
to any study of the subject—its chief rivals being Mâle's own dissertation
Quomodo Sibyllas recentiores artifices repraesentaverint (1899), and two considerably
older but very substantial studies: Ferdinand Piper, *Mythologie und Symbolik
der christlichen Kunst*, i. i (1847), § 43: 'Von den Sibyllen', pp. 472–507 and
X. Barbier de Montault, 'Iconographie des Sibylles', *Revue de l'art chrétien* xiii
(1869), 244–57, 321–56, 465–507, 578–82; xiv (1870), pp. 290–317; 326–
41, 385–406.

[1] A notable case is L. G. Gyraldus, *De poetarum historia*, Dialogus ii (*Opera*
ii, 1696, col. 112). In the midst of an arduous struggle with Sibylline traditions, Gyraldus reveals that he and his interlocutor, Piso, despair of dis-
entangling the literary history of the Sibyls: '"So much for the Cumaean
Sibyl".—"And enough", said Piso, "for I begin to see what you mean: that
Virgil spread confusion about the Sibyls."—"Not only Virgil, Piso," said I,
"but all the other writers as well: for it is evident that they all produced
concoctions and failed to report with candour" (*omnes enim miscuisse, nec
sincere narrasse videmus*).' This judgement is the more remarkable as Gyraldus
was sufficiently touched by the poetic aura of the Sibyls to attempt a Latin

lending a touch of Virgilian grace to those unwieldy lumps of oracular verbiage,[1] excusable enough in untutored visionaries who were presumably 'speaking with tongues', as did the Gentiles in Acts x. 45 f.[2] The frequency with which some coarse bit of Sibylline fustian appears transfigured in Renaissance books and paintings shows that the Sibyls, particularly among men of elegant erudition, satisfied a profound and genuinely humanist craving: they bore testimony against the prejudice that Christian prophecy had been withheld from the pagans.

That these mantic women had preached the divine word without preparation by Mosaic disciplines seemed only to increase their prophetic stature. As the quality of Mercy is superior to Justice, and Grace stands higher than the Law, so the Sibyls—as prophetesses to the heathen—seemed more miraculous than the Hebrew prophets. A painting by Mantegna that shows a Sibyl conversing with a Prophet leaves no doubt as to which is the superior spirit (Pl. 62). While the Prophet holds the sacred script, the Sibyl explains it to him with persuasive clairvoyance, *numine afflata*, touching the crucial passage like a divine enchantress, while he listens with awe to her inspired utterances.[3]

translation of the Erythraean acrostic (op. cit., col. 108) and to climb into the cave of the Cumaean Sibyl, at that time a more hazardous undertaking than it is today: 'ad quae visenda subterranea crypta ego ipse cum studiosis plerisque comitibus aliquando non sine horrore descendi' (col. 112). On the grotto in question, see below, p. 299, n. 2. An elegiac allusion to it in Sannazaro, *Ad ruinas Cumarum, urbis vetustissimae* (*Elegiae* II. ix. 9 f.).

[1] Politian, *Nutricia* 218–25, gives a catalogue of Sibyls (derived from Pausanias x. xii), cleverly versified as a mnemonic aid. In Sannazaro's *De partu Virginis*, the traditional image of the Annunciation, in which the Virgin is found reading as the Angel approaches, is enriched by a significant detail: the Virgin reads the prophecies of the Sibyls (i. 93). Of peculiar interest is a miscellaneous volume of classical texts published by Aldus in 1495: it begins with Theocritus's *Idylls* and ends with Hesiod's *Works and Days*. In the middle of it, following on *Aurea carmina Pythagorae* and *Phocylidae poema admonitorium*, one can read *Carmina Sibyllae Erythraeae de Christo Iesu domino nostro*, that is, the Greek acrostic of the Erythraean Sibyl, taken from Eusebius.

[2] 'On the Gentiles also was poured the gift of the Holy Ghost. For they heard them speak with tongues, and magnify God'.

[3] The diadem she wears is a Sibylline attribute derived from Eusebius' description of the Erythraean Sibyl (*Constantini oratio ad sanctorum coetum* viii); see also the diadem of the Cumaean Sibyl in Castagno's fresco in Sant' Apollonia, Florence. The old title of Mantegna's painting, *Sibyl and Prophet*, is certainly preferable to the more recent suggestion that the scene represents the Cumaean Sibyl instructing Tarquin. Neither the man's physiognomy nor his costume suggests a Roman. Besides, the Sibyl taught nothing to Tarquin

Even in the spectacular setting of Titian's *Gloria* (Pl. 63), designed for Charles V as a celestial vision of the triumphant Church, a mysterious Sibyl, known as Noah's daughter-in-law,[1] appears near the centre in the part of a jubilant prophetess, directing Noah toward the Holy Trinity above the clouds, with a protective gesture as if she were interceding for him. Yet Noah was an inspired prophet in his own right: with fore-knowledge of the Passion, he had produced a model of divine salvation in his construction of the Ark,—its wood signifying the wood of the Cross while the Ark itself was a figure of the Church floating securely on the waters of tribulation.[2] In a Florentine engraving of the fifteenth century he appears with the inscription *Noe profeta*, pointing to a small model of the Ark which he holds as his prophetic emblem (Pl. 65*a*). It is in the same role that he is seen in Titian's painting, raising the emblem of the Ark ecstatically toward heaven: and yet he seems to need the Sibyl's assistance. Her superiority over the prophet is here as marked as it was in Mantegna's painting.[3]

—except to buy three books for the exorbitant price that he had refused to pay for nine.

[1] Cf. Gyraldus, *Opera*, ii, col. 106. For the full text see *Oracula Sibyllina* iii, 822 ff. (ed. Alexandre, i, pp. 162 f.). A handy summary was accessible in the *Scholia Platonica* (ed. G. C. Greene, 1938, pp. 79 f., on *Phaedrus* 244B); the same also in Photius, *Amphilochia* 60 (cf. Alexandre, op. cit. iii, p. 427).

[2] Augustine, *Civitas Dei* xv. xxvi f.; Hugh of St. Victor, *De arca Noë morali* i. viii; cf. Wind, 'The Ark of Noah: a Study in the Symbolism of Michelangelo', *Measure* i (1950), pp. 411–21.

[3] As Noah is supported by the Sibyl, so Moses on his left is assisted by John the Evangelist in holding up the inspired Word (Genesis i. 1 = John i. 1). The devout youth next to the Sibyl is perhaps meant to represent her spouse, Noah's youngest son Japheth, from whom descended the race of the Gentiles. These appear as worshippers on the upper right, among them Charles V and his family, and a more humble group that includes Titian. In the foreground, David, covered by a shroud of royal ermine, plays the psalter. While Titian called this picture simply *The Trinity* (cf. Crowe and Cavalcaselle, *Titian*, ii, 1881, p. 231), Charles V referred to it as *The Last Judgement* (ibid., p. 236)— 'teste David cum Sibylla'. The presence of the Virgin and John the Baptist as intercessors (on the upper left) would seem to confirm that interpretation, even though the scene is confined to the blessed who enjoy the beatific vision. In the Kingdom of Heaven, according to Romans xiv. 17, the souls are moved by three divine forces that emanate from the Trinity: *iustitia et pax et gaudium in spiritu sancto* (cf. Pagnini, *Isagoge*, p. 252). These phases of ecstasy seem illustrated in the three central characters of the painting: Moses holding the tables of the Law (*iustitia*), Noah raising up the Ark, with the dove and the branch of olive (*pax*), and the Sibyl filled with jubilation (*gaudium in spiritu sancto*). Since all three proclaim by their hymnic gestures the *Gloria Deo in*

Michelangelo, too, paid homage to this Sibyl. In the picture of *Noah's Sacrifice,* which appears in the Sistine Ceiling next to the figure of the Erythraean Sibyl, the 'eight souls' that 'were saved by water' (1 Peter iii. 20)—Noah and his wife, and his three sons and their wives—are assembled around the altar (Pl. 64). While the sons and two of the daughters-in-law are busy with the paraphernalia of the sacrifice (carrying wood, fanning the fire, and preparing the victims), the third daughter-in-law stands on Noah's right side behind the altar where she officiates like a priestess: she solemnly places a burning faggot on the altar, while shielding her face with an ominous oracular gesture (derived from classical representations of the Death of Meleager in which Althea thus lights the enchanted faggot that causes the death of her son[1]). Noah, attended by his wife who listens intently, enacts the part of *Noe profeta.* His gesture of promise, pointing to heaven, unites with the compassionate and mournful, almost protesting gesture of the Sibyl.[2]

With a fine sense for the future union between the Church of the Gentiles and that of the Jews, this particularly clairvoyant Sibyl had married into an Old Testament family before the Flood. As she explains in her prophecy, she had come from Babylon, although 'the mortals in Hellas will call me by another city, saying that I am from Erythrae'. The world, she says, 'was flooded with water, and only one man remained pious, who drove over the waters in a house of cut wood with the beasts and fowls so that the world would be filled again: of him am I a

excelsis, the traditional title *La Gloria* is not mistaken, although deficient in theological detail. Vasari notes that, 'secondo che gli fu comandato da Cesare', Titian represented the emperor in his shroud: this defines the scene as a funerary pageant, comparable to a Requiem.

[1] Michelangelo almost certainly saw this figure on a Roman sarcophagus formerly in the Palazzo della Valle in Rome, now in the Villa Albani. For a sixteenth-century drawing of it see Codex Coburgensis as reproduced in C. Robert, *Die antiken Sarkophag-Reliefs* (1904), no. 278; cf. E. H. Gombrich, 'A Classical Quotation in Michelangelo's "Sacrifice of Noah"', *Journal of the Warburg Institute,* i (1937), p. 69.

[2] Among the animals that have issued from the Ark, a lowing ox and a braying ass (interpreted as emblems of Jew and Gentile by St. Gregory, *Moralia* VII. iv) stand out as prophetic images, as in Job vi. 5 and Isaiah i. 3. According to St. Gregory, whose argument was adopted by Pagnini, *Isagoge* IV. iii. 218, the braying of the ass and the lowing of the ox express the longing for the incarnation and the eucharist 'by which Jews and Gentiles are equally nourished'. On ox and ass as Jew and Gentile, see also Egidio da Viterbo, *Historia viginti saeculorum,* cod. Angel. 502, fol. 32ʳ: 'Hebraeos bovi, gentes asello comparant.'

PLATE 41

Frontispiece to Savonarola's *Dialogue on Prophetic Truth, c.* 1496

PLATE 42

The Prophet Zechariah. Sistine Ceiling

PLATE 43

Head of Zechariah. Detail of Pl. 42

PLATE 44

Head of Joel. Detail of Pl. 45

PLATE 45

The Prophet Joel. Sistine Ceiling

PLATE 46

The Prophet Isaiah. Sistine Ceiling

PLATE 47

The Prophet Ezekiel. Sistine Ceiling

PLATE 48

Head of Ezekiel. Detail of Pl. 47

PLATE 49

Spirit driving Ezekiel. Detail of Pl. 47

PLATE 50

The Prophet Daniel. Sistine Ceiling

PLATE 51

Ignudo above Daniel. Sistine Ceiling

PLATE 52

Caryatids next to Daniel. Detail of Pl. 50

PLATE 53

Head of *Ignudo*. Detail of Pl. 51

PLATE 54

The Prophet Jeremiah. Sistine Ceiling

PLATE 55

Head of *Ignudo* above Jeremiah. Detail of Pl. 56

PLATE 56

Ignudo above Jeremiah. Sistine Ceiling

PLATE 57

Ignudo above Jeremiah. Sistine Ceiling

PLATE 58

Engraving by Giorgio Ghisi, after the Sistine Ceiling

PLATE 59

Jeremiah, with adjacent figures from the Genealogy of Christ. Sistine Ceiling

PLATE 60

The Prophet Jonah. Sistine Ceiling

PLATE 61

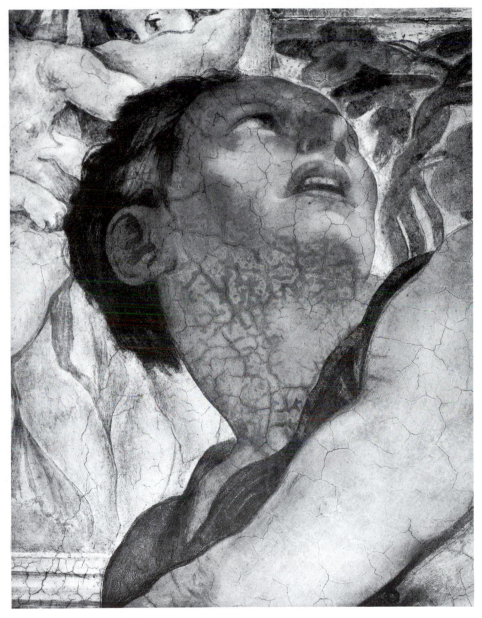

Head of Jonah. Detail of Pl. 60

PLATE 62

Mantegna: Sibyl and Prophet.
(Cincinnati Art Museum)

PLATE 63

Titian: La Gloria.
(Prado, Madrid)

PLATE 64

Michelangelo: Noah's Sacrifice. Sistine Ceiling

PLATE 65

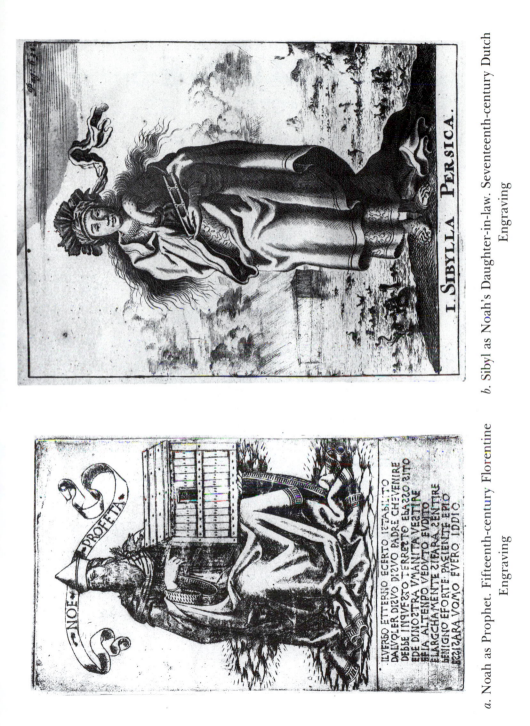

a. Noah as Prophet. Fifteenth-century Florentine
Engraving

b. Sibyl as Noah's Daughter-in-law. Seventeenth-century Dutch
Engraving

PLATE 66

'Sybilla': Title-page of Savonarola's *Sermons on the Ark of Noah*, 1536

PLATE 67

The Delphic Sibyl. Sistine Ceiling

PLATE 68

Head of the Delphic Sibyl. Detail of Pl. 67

PLATE 69

Putti next to the Delphic Sibyl. Detail of Pl. 67

PLATE 70

The Erythraean Sibyl. Sistine Ceiling. (See also Pl. 36).

PLATE 71

The Prophet Daniel, with adjacent figures from the Genealogy of Christ.
Sistine Ceiling

PLATE 72

The Cumaean Sibyl, with adjacent figures from the Genealogy of Christ.
Sistine Ceiling

PLATE 73

The Cumaean Sibyl. Sistine Ceiling

PLATE 74

Creation of Eve. Sistine Ceiling

PLATE 75

The Fall of Man. Sistine Ceiling

PLATE 76

The Persian Sibyl. Sistine Ceiling

PLATE 77

Ignudo above the Persian Sibyl. Sistine Ceiling

PLATE 78

The Persian Sibyl, with adjacent figures from the Genealogy of Christ.
Sistine Ceiling

PLATE 79

Engraving by Giorgio Ghisi, after the Sistine Ceiling

PLATE 80

Division of Light from Darkness. Sistine Ceiling

PLATE 81

The Libyan Sibyl. Detail of Pl. 83

PLATE 82

Head of the Libyan Sibyl. Detail of Pl. 83

PLATE 83

The Libyan Sibyl. Sistine Ceiling

PLATE 84

Caryatids next to the Libyan Sibyl. Detail of Pl. 83

PLATE 85

Putti next to the Libyan Sibyl. Detail of Pl. 83

PLATE 86

a. Bernardo Rossellino: Detail from the Tomb of Leonardo Bruni.
(Santa Croce, Florence)

b. Michelangelo: Detail (enlarged) from a Sketch for the Sistine Ceiling.
(British Museum, London)

PLATE 87

a. Ignudi, above Isaiah. Sistine Ceiling

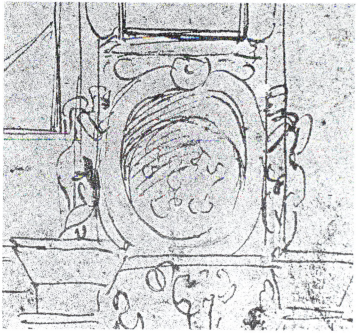

b. Michelangelo: Detail (enlarged) from a Sketch for the Sistine Ceiling.
(Institute of Arts, Detroit)

PLATE 88

Schema of the Sistine Ceiling. After an engraving by Domenico Cunego

daughter-in-law'.[1] How closely the Biblical account of the Flood became associated with this apocryphal legend may be seen from the fact that a Venetian printer, in publishing Savonarola's sermons on the Ark of Noah in the sixteenth century, decorated the title-page with an image of Noah's daughter-in-law, inscribed *Sybilla* (Pl. 66), her figure framed by a quotation from John (xv. 5) printed in Greek, Latin, and Hebrew, which says that without her spiritual gift the books that surround her would be useless.[2]

Fortunately, the Bible could be said to have lent some support to these poetic divagations in praise of sibylline intruders. A few verses after his prophecy on the Tree of Jesse and the Gifts of the Spirit, Isaiah had returned to the same theme, repeating the prophecy in a form that included the Gentiles (xi. 10):

And in that day there shall be a root of Jesse, which shall stand for an ensign of the people; to it shall the Gentiles seek: and his rest shall be glorious.

St. Paul, as apostle to the Gentiles, quoted this passage from Isaiah as part of his evidence when he wrote to the Romans (xv. 12), while in the epistle to the Galatians he traced the promise to the heathen as far back as Abraham:

And the scripture, foreseeing that God would justify the heathen through faith, preached before the gospel unto Abraham, saying, In thee shall all nations be blessed (*benedicentur in te omnes gentes*). . . . That the blessing of Abraham might come on the Gentiles through Jesus Christ. . . . Now to Abraham and his seed were the promises made. . . . And if ye be Christ's, then are ye Abraham's seed, and heirs according to the promise [iii. 8–29].

If thus by the strength of faith alone the Gentiles could become 'descendants of Abraham', with whose name the Genealogy of

---

[1] The quotation in Gyraldus (cf. above, p. 277, n. 1) is important because it shows that the passage was known before the full text appeared in print. For the latter see *Oracula Sibyllina* iii. 808–26 (ed. Alexandre, i, pp. 160 ff.); also J. A. Fabricius, *Codex pseudepigraphus Veteris Testamenti*, i (1722), pp. 278 ff.; F. Blass, 'Die Sibyllinischen Orakel' in E. Kautzsch, *Die Apokryphen und Pseudoepigraphen des Alten Testaments*, ii (1900), pp. 200 ff.; R. H. Charles, *The Apocrypha and Pseudoepigrapha of the Old Testament*, ii (1913), pp. 392 f. In a Dutch *Spiegel der Sibyllen* by J[ohannes] A[itzma] (Amsterdam, 1685), Noah's daughter-in-law, by now known as the Persian Sibyl, is pictured against the background of the biblical Deluge, with Noah's Ark impressively afloat (Pl. 65b). On Noah's connexion with the Sibylline tradition, see also E. Sackur, *Sibyllinische Texte und Forschungen* (1898).

[2] Published in Venice, 1536, by Pietro de' Nicolini da Sabio; cf. Piero Ginori Conti, *Bibliografia delle opere del Savonarola*, i (1939), p. 109, no. 9.

Christ begins in Matthew i, then 'the spirit of the Lord', described by Isaiah as resting upon the Tree of Jesse (xi. 2), may fill the Sibyls with 'spiritual gifts' as it did the Prophets, and both will belong to the 'Genealogy of Christ'.[1]

A list of 'spiritual gifts', specially designed for Gentiles, was drawn up by St. Paul in 1 Corinthians xiv. 26. They are five in number, and sound so abstract that, like the seven gifts in Isaiah, they might seem at first like unpaintable subjects. St. Paul calls them Psalm, Doctrine, Tongue, Revelation, and Interpretation. In his commentary on the Epistles of Paul,[2] Thomas Aquinas explained the nature of these five gifts, whose part in the prophetic dispensation he defined in the *Summa theologica* as follows: 'It belongs to the perfection in the operation of the Holy Spirit that it not only fills the mind with prophetic light, and the imagination with fantastic visions, as was the case in the Old Testament, but also outwardly informs the tongue how to produce a variety of signs through speech: All of which is done in the New Testament according to 1 Corinthians xiv: Each of you has a psalm, has a doctrine, has a tongue', etc.[3]

Since the account given by Aquinas of these new gifts of the spirit is a tough theological demonstration, one must be grateful to Erasmus (who happened to be in Rome as Cardinal Riario's guest when Michelangelo began painting the Sistine Ceiling[4]) that he paraphrased the doctrine with such elegance and lucidity that the five gifts are easy to distinguish. '*Psalmus*', he says, is 'a mystic song in praise of God' (*canticum mysticum quo lubet canere*

---

[1] For rare instances of a Sibyl or a pair of Sibyls associated with a Tree of Jesse in medieval representations, see Watson, op. cit., pp. 169 f.; Heitz and Schreiber, op. cit., p. 14. It should be noted, however, that the corresponding Prophets (Watson, op. cit., pp. 54 ff.) attend the Tree of Jesse not as representatives of the 'Gifts of the Spirit', from which they differ in number as well as in character, but simply as prophets of the incarnation, of which the Tree of Jesse is a figure. It would seem to follow that the occasional Sibyl owes her presence near a Tree of Jesse likewise to a prophecy of the incarnation rather than to any particular 'spiritual gift'. Seven doves remain the current symbol for the 'gifts of the Spirit', visibly separated from Prophets or Sibyls even when they appear on the same page (ibid., pl. xv: Lambeth MS. 3, fol. 198ʳ). Nevertheless, the Renaissance fusion of 'spiritual gifts' with representative prophets or sibyls was prepared by their medieval juxtaposition as separate images.

[2] *Super epistolas S. Pauli lectura* v. 867 (ed. P. P. Cai, i, 1953, p. 400).

[3] *Summa theologica* ii, ii, q. 176, art. 2.

[4] Erasmus stayed in Rome in 1509. In a letter addressed to Riario in 1515 he recalled his sojourn there with more affection than one would expect from him (*Epistolae*, ed. Allen, no. 333).

deum). *Doctrina* he defines as moral instruction, or indoctrination, which relates to the good conduct of life (*ad instituendam vitam*, or *ad bonos mores pertinet*). *Lingua* is of course 'the gift of tongues', which calls for *Interpretatio* (exposition) to make the strange voices intelligible. *Revelatio*, finally, is the exegetic power to 'detect concealed and remote meanings in sacred script' (*eruere abstrusa reconditaque in sacris literis*) or, as Erasmus put it with deliberately occult intonation, to 'open up an arcanum by the gift of apocalypse' (*aperire arcanum per apocalypsis donum*).[1]

Two of these gifts, that of 'mystic song' (*psalmus*) and the 'gift of tongues' (*lingua*) stand out as extremes of prophetic exaltation against the more reflective moods of the other three (*interpretatio, doctrina, revelatio*). The sequence embodied in Michelangelo's Sibyls, if read from the entrance towards the altar, begins with *lingua* and ends with *psalmus*, while the three temperate phases are placed between.

It is fairly obvious from 1 Corinthians xiv that St. Paul was driven to distinguish between these five gifts because of the excessive use that had been made of the 'gift of tongues'. Although an important part of prophecy, and sanctioned as such by Christ himself (Mark xvi. 17), St. Paul wrote that it was of no use in the Church unless it was followed by interpretation: for 'if I know not the meaning of the voice, I shall be unto him that speaketh a barbarian, and he that speaketh shall be a barbarian unto me. . . . Wherefore let him that speaketh in an unknown tongue pray that he may interpret' (ibid. 11–13). Erasmus made much of St. Paul's passing remark that he himself spoke with tongues 'more than ye all', but that in the Church he would

---

[1] Erasmus, *Paraphrasis in omneis epistolas apostolicas* (1539), xiv, pp. 276 f., also p. 272; derived from Thomas Aquinas, *Super epistolas S. Pauli*, loc. cit., where these gifts are explained in the same way; e.g. *Psalmus* = 'canticum ad laudandum nomen Dei'; *Doctrina* = 'praedicatio ad instructionem morum', etc. Although it did not occur to Aquinas to associate the gifts to the Gentiles with Sibylline inspiration, it should be noted that he included the Sibyls with Balaam among the indigenous *prophetae daemonum* who were chosen by God to speak not *ex daemonum revelatione* but *ex inspiratione divina* (*Summa theologica* II. ii, q. 172, art. 6; cf. also II. ii, q. 2, art. 7). The parallel with Balaam makes it clear that he treated the Sibylline evidence as marginal, true enough to be respected ('Sibyllae multa vera praedixerunt de Christo') but not so fascinating as it proved to the Renaissance, when the naming of Balaam together with the Sibyls could not but enhance his reputation. In the spirited procession of Titian's woodcut, *The Triumph of the Cross*, a figure inscribed 'Balaam propheta' brings up the rear of a battalion of Sibyls waving flags. In the vanguard Noah and Moses raise the Ark and the tables of the Law like trophies (compare Pl. 63).

rather speak five words with his understanding than ten thousand of the unintelligible kind (18 f.). In Erasmus's paraphrase this short passage was expanded as follows: 'for in the Church and in the concourse of saints I would rather speak very few words in such a way that, by understanding my own language, I would achieve that it was understood also by others, than pronounce ten thousand words in such a manner that none of the others could understand them, and perhaps not even myself (*ac fortasse ne ipse quidem*)'.[1] The last phrase, which is not in St. Paul, adopts the Platonic view that, in the state of prophetic seizure, the person who suffers these fits is demented and does not himself know what they mean.[2] Erasmus was doubtless aware that his reading of St. Paul in this Platonic sense had the support of Augustine and Thomas Aquinas. In the 'gift of tongues', they say, the prophetic attack gets caught in the imagination so forcefully that it cannot rise to the mind. The uttering of unintelligible words results from hallucinatory states of vision in which the inspired person sees 'images' and 'similitudes' with too much vivacity to be able to grasp their meaning.[3]

The eyes and mouth of the Delphic Sibyl appear to be moved by a violent inspiration which struggles in vain to become articulate (Pls. 67, 68). The tongue is seen pressing against the teeth, and the phrases that escape from the half-open lips are presumably as unintelligible as the visionary figments at which the eyes are staring. No doubt the face was modelled on Virgil's verses (*Aeneid* vi. 46 ff., 79 f.) describing the derangement suffered by the Sibyl as the god takes possession of her frame (*fatigat os rabidum, fera corda domans, fingitque premendo*):[4] but

[1] Erasmus, op. cit., p. 274.

[2] *Timaeus* 71D–72B; see also below, p. 290, n. 4.

[3] Augustine, *De Genesi ad litteram* XII. viii (*Patr. lat.* xxxiv, cols. 460 f.), credits St. Paul with a distinction between *spiritualis visio* and *mens*, the former being confined to 'significationes velut imagines rerum ac similitudines'. He infers that in a figurative sense St. Paul's term *lingua* refers to any subrational projection of signs: 'translato verbo *linguam* appellavit quamlibet signorum prolationem priusquam intelligantur'. See also Thomas Aquinas, *Summa theologica* II. ii, q. 176 (*De gratia linguarum*), art. 2: 'Augustinus, *xii super Genesim ad litteram* (cap. viii), comparat donum linguarum visioni imaginariae.'

[4] Matteo Palmieri (*Città di vita* i. 20 ff.) tried to translate Virgil's description of the raging Sibyl (*pectus anhelum . . . adflata est numine*) into *terza rima*: 'ma di furor piena incensa ed anhela . . .', 'ne viso el suo terror ne pecto cela . . .', 'comincio cosi grande ombra si svela'. In this visionary theological epic, ambitiously modelled on the *Divine Comedy*, the parts of Virgil and Beatrice are fused in the divinely inspired Sibyl—a pagan guide even to the beatific vision.

equally relevant is a more figurative passage that alludes, through a magnificent metaphor, to the disappointments caused by the Sibyl's madness (iii. 443 ff.): Winds blow through the desolate cave of the Sibyl, catch the loose leaves inscribed with her words and put them into a state of disorder which the distracted prophetess does not amend—whence men go away disillusioned and resentful: *inconsulti abeunt sedemque odere Sibyllae* (452).

The two spirits attending the Delphic Sibyl illustrate that fatuous state of expectation that is aroused by incommunicable words (Pl. 69). One putto is engrossed in reading a text while the other waits to hear it, suggesting by his stolid expression that he has been waiting a long time. Indeed, the word will not be delivered until Intellect supervenes, as it does—on the opposite side—in the two putti attending Joel (Pl. 45). The clarity and sharpness of Joel's reason offset the raving of the Sibyl, so that the signs of things that were formed in the spirit 'would beam with intelligence in the mind': *ut et signa rerum formarentur in spiritu, et eorum refulgeret intellectus in mente.*[1]

Yet Joel's intellectual penetration remains a private exercise of the understanding. *Interpretatio*, as practised by the Erythraean Sibyl (Pl. 70), is enlightenment addressed to the assembled Church: she speaks (to use Erasmus's words) *in ecclesia coetuque sanctorum.*[2] Her formal posture in pointing to the text, which is displayed wide open on a lectern that has been ceremoniously covered with linen, suggests the performance of a communal duty; she provides demonstrable authoritative evidence, and thus serves the purpose of illumination, engagingly illustrated by the attending putto who is preoccupied with lighting a lamp: his companion rubs his eyes.

The question whether so rational a process as Interpretation deserves to be called a 'prophetic gift' was raised by Thomas Aquinas in the *Summa theologica*, and answered in the affirmative with considerable vigour. The words addressed by Belshazzar to Daniel seemed to him a conclusive proof: 'I have heard of thee that the spirit of the gods is in thee. . . . And I have heard of thee that thou canst make interpretation of obscure meanings and untie knots' (*audivi de te quod possis obscura interpretari et ligata dissolvere*, v. 16). Aquinas inferred from this text that *interpretatio*

[1] Augustine, *De Genesi ad litteram* XII. ix (*Patr. lat.* xxxiv, col. 461).
[2] Erasmus, *Paraphrasis*, p. 274. Cf. Thomas Aquinas, *Summa theologica*, loc. cit., where *interpretatio* is defined as 'utilior ad aedificationem Ecclesiae: ad quam qui loquitur linguis nihil prodest, nisi expositio subsequatur'.

sermonum involves the *donum prophetiae*: 'inasmuch as the mind requires illumination to understand and expound whatever is obscure in speech, whether because of the difficulty of the things signified, or because the words themselves are unfamiliar, or because of the strange use of imagery'.[1]

The reference to Daniel in this context is of importance to the Sistine Ceiling, since it was Daniel who represented Interpretation among the Prophets (Pl. 71): the very word *Scientia*, which designated his 'spiritual gift', recurs in the Vulgate as a synonym for *Interpretatio* among the 'five gifts' listed by St. Paul (I Corinthians xiv. 6). Thus Daniel and the Erythraean Sibyl, placed diagonally across from each other (see Pl. 88), are meant to be seen as equivalent forces: if the zeal of Daniel counteracts the suspense of Isaiah, Isaiah's hesitation is equally opposed by the positivism of the Erythraean Sibyl whose assertive gesture appears directly opposite to him.

After the frenzied prophecy of the Delphic Sibyl and the Erythraean's enlightening interpretation, *Doctrina* appears in the Cumaean Sibyl as a solid and homely kind of foresight, concerned with nurture and tutelage *ad instituendam vitam* (Pl. 73). Like a primeval nurse or *alma mater*, this muscular woman of gigantic age is distinguished from all the other Sibyls by being visibly endowed with breasts, an attribute that belongs to her as prophetess of the 'celestial milk' (*lac de coelo missum*) which is the future food of salvation.[2] What Michelet said mistakenly of the Delphic Sibyl (at which he cannot have looked very closely) applies almost literally to the Cumaean: 'gonflée de ses pleines mamelles.'[3] Having nursed the Romans with the Sibylline Books, from which they drew advice in critical hours, she looks, with an expression of maternal care, at a weighty sample of codified doctrine. The children watch her benevolently,

---

[1] *Summa theologica*, loc. cit.

[2] The 'Cimmerian' Sibyl, to whom this prophecy was ascribed by Barbieri and others (Mâle, pp. 259, 269 f.), was commonly identified, or 'confused', with the Cumaean, as Gyraldus explained (*Opera* ii, col. 109). See also Alexandre, op. cit. iii, pp. 49–61, Excursus I, vii: 'De Sibylla Cumana seu Cimmeria, . . . sive quorumdam Itala'. Even Virgil's line in the Fourth Eclogue: *iam nova progenies coelo demittitur alto*, although introduced in the original by *ultima Cumaei venit iam carminis aetas*, was ascribed alternatively to the Cimmerian and the Cumaean Sibyl (Mâle, pp. 256, 259). Both were of course known as 'Italic' (see Lactantius I. vi, after Varro). Because of her prophecy about the milk, the Cimmerian Sibyl often carries a nipple (Mâle, loc. cit.).

[3] *Histoire de France* vii: 'La Renaissance' (1855), pp. 315 f., an ebullient description of the Delphic Sibyl, *vierge et féconde, débordant de l'Esprit*.

and with a leisurely touch of condescension; one of them carries a second volume, presumably from the Sibyl's library. She is the weightiest prophetess of the five, and placed in the centre of the series, opposite to the mighty and firm Ezekiel, whose active energy she offsets by a display of monumental quietude.

For a confirmation of her role as prophetic 'nurse' or 'mother', it should be observed that in the lunettes below the Cumaean Sibyl the scenes allegorizing the Genealogy of Christ provide the only instance, in the whole cycle, of two contiguous groups of a nursing mother: they supply a marginal gloss on the Sibyl's character (Pl. 72). Furthermore, in the cycle from Genesis the scene adjacent to the Cumaean Sibyl represents the Creation of Eve, the first mother (Pl. 74). Foreshadowing the Birth of the Church (the second Eve), who was to issue from the side of Christ (the second Adam), the picture occupies the centre of the Ceiling for prophetic reasons that are clearly indicated by the dead tree against which the sleeping Adam leans.[1] The sacraments that were born from the side of the dead Christ for the remission of sin are the 'milk sent from heaven' that the benevolent nurse administers in her 'doctrine':[2] she prophesies

[1] As in Donne's verses on 'Christ's cross and Adam's tree' (*Hymn to God my God, in my sickness*, 21–25), Michelangelo's image of Paradise as a desolate landscape was meant to foreshadow Golgotha. On the sacramental meaning of Adam's sleep, and of the opening in his side, see Augustine, *De Genesi contra Manichaeos* II. xxiv (*Patr. lat.* xxxiv, col. 215 f.), 'Adam Christus, Eva Ecclesia': '. . . soporatus est dormitione passionis, ut ei conjux Ecclesia formaretur . . . de latere eius . . . .'; also Dante, *Paradiso* xvii. 37 ff. For illustrations cf. A. de Laborde, *La Bible Moralisée illustrée* i (1911), pl. 6; v (1927), p. 158; Henrik Cornell, *Biblia pauperum* (1925), pl. 39, with corresponding scene of the Passion and explanatory text: 'Adam dormiens Christum significat, de cuius latere fluxit sanguis et aqua in signum illius ut intelligamus omnia sacramenta de latere Christi effluxisse.' The prophet Ezekiel, seated across from the Cumaean Sibyl on the other side of the Creation of Eve, supports the sacramental interpretation of that scene: 'Et tu dormiens super latus tuum sinistrum . . . assumes iniquitatem eorum' (iv. 4 ff.). See also Ezekiel xvii. 24, on the dry tree as an emblem of redemption, contrasted with the green tree as an emblem of sin: 'I the Lord . . . have dried up the green tree, and have made the dry tree to flourish.' In the background of Michelangelo's painting of the Fall of Man, the dry tree reappears as a meek rod offsetting the rich foliage of the Tree of Knowledge (Pl. 75). For a comprehensive bibliography on the dry and the green tree in Paradise see G. B. Ladner, 'Vegetation Symbolism and the Concept of Renaissance', in *Essays in Honor of Erwin Panofsky* (1961), pp. 302–22, particularly notes 26, 32, 36, 39, 41, 43.

[2] On the relation between 'celestial milk' and 'sacramental wounds', commonly symbolized by Mary pointing to her breast while Christ points to the wound in his side, see Ernaldus, *Liber de laudibus Mariae* (*Patr. lat.* clxxxix,

of the Motherhood of the Church—the most staid and least mantic of subjects, which Michelangelo managed to endow with a monstrous sort of solidity.

The Persian Sibyl (Pl. 76), who exhibits the gift of *Revelatio*, is an old prophetess like the Cumaean, but slender and spinsterly, slightly hunch-backed like a gentle witch, her face foreshortened in a lost profile and covered by a shadow. Straining her short-sighted eyes, she divines some 'concealed and remote meaning' that is 'adumbrated' in her book. The revelatory guess-work, in which she excels, does not prosper in the clear light afforded by her Erythraean sister, with whom she is connected by antithetical symmetry. Mysteries belong to the hour of dusk and disclose their presence only to those who retain a sense of the indefinable: *vaticinari videtur sub nubilo*, 'she appears to prophesy under a cloud'.[1] Her attendants act like somnambulists, and the ancestral figures in the lunettes below her seem lost in sleep and dream (pl. 78). The Caryatids, too, with veils on their heads, are in the mood of sleep-walkers, but above them one of the *Ignudi* (Pl. 77), seized with a cryptic madness, rages in the posture of a classical figure that Michelangelo had seen on a Bacchic relief.[2] The reason is not far to seek. In the Renaissance the supreme model of a veiled theological style, shunning the cold use of positive definitions, was admired in the works of Dionysius the Areopagite, translated and interpreted by Marsilio Ficino who, seizing on the name Dionysius, had characterized the author as a Bacchic spirit: 'Inebriate with this Dionysiac wine our Dionysius expresses his exaltation. He pours forth enigmas, he sings in dithyrambs. . . . To penetrate the profundity of his meaning, . . . to imitate his quasi-Orphic manner of speech . . . , we too require

col. 1726), illustrated in *Speculum humanae salvationis*, eds. J. Lutz and P. Perdrizet (1907), pl. 78. In a predella by Francia (Pinacoteca, Bologna, inv. 570) a figure of St. Augustine, placed between the bleeding Crucifix and the Virgin nursing the Child, points to these contrasting images, while the two scrolls above his hands read: HIC AB UBERE LACTOR—HIC A VULNERE PASCOR. On a third scroll the dilemma of the saint, caught between joy and agony, is resolved into prayer: 'POSITUS IN MEDIO, QUO ME VERTAR NESCIO. DICAM ERGO: JESU MARIA MISERERE.'

[1] Heitz and Schreiber, op. cit., s.v. 'Sibilla persica'; also Mâle, op. cit., pp. 267 f.

[2] Vatican, Galleria delle statue (W. Amelung, *Die Sculpturen des Vaticanischen Museums* II. iii, 1908, pp. 440 ff., no. 261*a*, pl. 52); cf. A. Hekler, 'Michelangelo und die Antike', *Wiener Jahrbuch für Kunstgeschichte* vii (1930), p. 213, fig. iii. 2*b*; A. von Salis, *Antike und Renaissance* (1947), pp. 182 f., 265, with further references and illustrations.

the divine fury.'[1] The excited youth above the Persian Sibyl exhibits the prescriptive Dionysian rage that issues in dithyrambic declamation. Pictured in the act of 'pouring forth enigmas' (a very different matter from 'speaking with tongues'), he is counterbalanced not so much by his dazed companion as by the violently jubilant spirit (above Daniel) diagonally across from him (Pl. 51, see also Pl. 88), these two being related to each other as metaphorical darkness is to logical clarity. Prophesying *sub nubilo*, the Persian Sibyl dimly weaves the kind of knot which Daniel is so skilled to untie. Yet Daniel's scientific explanation is not what the Sibyl seeks. Her aim is to reach the 'cloud of unknowing' by the methods of 'negative theology'—to which the Erythraean Sibyl opposes the 'positive theology' of her authorized book. Yet the belief that 'God resides in darkness' could invoke biblical authority in its turn: *Et posuit tenebras latibulum suum* (Psalms xvii. 12).[2]

In the Libyan Sibyl, prophecy transcends the cloud of adumbration and reaches the state of pure ecstasy—the 'mystic canticle' or 'psalm' (Pl. 83). She was famed as conveyor of a joyous message: *Ecce veniet dies et illuminabit condensa tenebrarum* ('Behold there will come the day and illuminate the density of darkness'),[3] and she is placed next to the *Fiat Lux*, on the side to which God, as divides Light from Darkness, pushes the light (Pl. 80), while the side of darkness is given to Jeremiah. Rising from her seat with downcast eyes, like one who has been struck by a blinding light, and feeling her way with her toes, again like one blinded, but moving with the ease of a dancer, she closes her book and turns away from it.[4] Divine love is above understanding: *amor est supra intellectum*.[5] That she shuts her eyes

[1] Ficino, *Opera*, p. 1013 (preface to Dionysius Areopagita, *De mystica theologia*).

[2] Pico della Mirandola, *De ente et uno* v (*Opera*, 1557, p. 248).

[3] Heitz and Schreiber, op. cit., s.v. 'Sibilla Libica'; also Mâle, op. cit., pp. 258 (Barbieri), 268.

[4] As Vasari explained, the Libyan Sibyl is about to rise from her seat while shutting the book: 'in un medesimo tempo mostra volere alzarsi e serrare il libro' (ed. Milanesi, vii, 1881, p. 184). The common belief that she takes the book down, expressed most forcefully by Taine—'emportant l'énorme livre qu'elle a saisi' (*Voyage en Italie*, 1866, p. 284)—is certainly mistaken: the left hand (Pl. 81) holds the pages, not the cover, which remains resting on its stand (cf. C. de Tolnay, *The Sistine Ceiling*, 1945, p. 158).

[5] Pico della Mirandola, *Conclusiones . . . in doctrinam Platonis*, no. 6 (*Opera*, p. 96); also *De ente et uno* v (ibid., p. 248): 'for we have not reached God so long as we understand and comprehend what we say of God.' Although Ficino was less radical than Pico in his pursuit of a *docta ignorantia* (cf. Wind,

(Pl. 82) is proof of her mystical exaltation: 'for to close the eyes in initiation', Hermias wrote in his commentary on the *Phaedrus*, 'is no longer to receive by sense those divine mysteries, but with the pure soul itself'; and Proclus in the *Platonic Theology* described the supreme mystic surrender as 'giving ourselves up to the divine light, and closing the eyes of the soul, after this manner to become established in the unknown and occult unity of being'.¹ If in her blind ecstasy the Sibyl seems curiously light-footed, stepping with an eerie grace, it is because of a prophetic verse (taken from Habakkuk iii. 19) by which Thomas Aquinas, in his commentary of 1 Corinthians xiv. 26, illustrated the gift of *psalmus*:

> Et ponet pedes meos quasi cervorum;
> et super excelsa mea deducet me
> victor in psalmis canentem.

'And he will set my feet like the feet of hinds, and lead me away captive upon my high places singing psalms.'² In Jerome's gloss on that passage (quoted in full in Pagnini's *Isagoge*, with references to Psalms xvii. 34: *qui perfecit pedes meos tanquam cervorum, et super excelsa ponet me*, and xxviii. 9: *vox Domini perficientis cervos*), the prophetic ecstasy that walks *super excelsa* is infused with the joyful tidings of the new faith: 'And he will set my feet among his other hinds, and lead me to celestial places so that I may sing the glory of the Lord among the angels, and announce peace on earth to men of good will.'³

The two forms of madness distinguished by Plato, the one below reason, the other above it, appear in the Delphic and Libyan Sibyl as mantic obsession and mystic release, 'demonic' as against 'angelic' ecstasy.⁴ Related to each other like the

---

Pagan Mysteries in the Renaissance, 1958, pp. 65 ff.), he endorsed the doctrine in his commentaries on Plotinus and on Dionysius the Areopagite (e.g. *Opera*, pp. 1066, 1793) as well as in his excerpts from Proclus (ibid., pp. 1911 f.); cf. also his commentary on Plato's *Parmenides* (e.g. *Opera*, pp. 1017 f.).

¹ Hermias, *In Platonis Phaedrum* 250B (ed. P. Couvreur, p. 178); Proclus, *In theologiam Platonis* I. xxv (ed. A. Portus, p. 61). For further sources, see Wind, op. cit., pp. 57 ff.

² *Super epistolas S. Pauli* loc. cit. 'exponit Abac. iii. 19: *super excelsa mea deducet me*,' etc.

³ Jerome, *Commentaria in Abacuc* II. iii (*Patr. lat.* xxv, col. 1336); Pagnini, *Isagoge* I. xxxiii (p. 89). The words from Psalms are here given as in Jerome and Pagnini, numbered according to the Vulgate. In the King James version, where the corresponding verses are Psalms xviii. 33 and xxix. 9, the meaning is not the same.

⁴ It is significant that the Libyan Sibyl has removed her gown, which is seen hanging from her seat (Pl. 83). The act of putting on, or throwing

opposite extremes of the same passion, the anxiety in the wide-open eyes of the Delphic Sibyl (Pl. 68) is answered by the weirdly quiet joy with which the Libyan Sibyl closes her eyes (Pl. 82). These 'deranged' states of mind are pagan forms of prophetic excess unknown to the Hebrews: none of their prophets, not even the unbalanced Jonah, surrenders his reasoning powers to that extent. Nevertheless, Jeremiah seems to draw his compassionate silence from the same depths that blind the Libyan Sibyl with joy. In the presence of the ultimate arcanum, both word and vision are transcended. As Pythagorean Platonists and Dionysian mystics taught, the only proper way of meeting the ineffable is by silence and by closing the eyes.[1]

In reflecting on the theology of the Sistine Ceiling, it is important to avoid the misapprehension that, on reaching the mystical Sibyl and the silent Prophet, Michelangelo must have felt that the rest no longer counted. Radical Platonists would indeed have taken that view, which Giordano Bruno was to express with characteristic candour: 'wherefore the most

off, a garment or material vesture (χιτών) is a Neoplatonic image for the soul's descent into matter or ascent from it (cf. E. R. Dodds's commentary on Proclus, *The Elements of Theology*, 1964, pp. 307 f., referring to proposition no. 209). If the Libyca appears 'divested' as compared with the other Sibyls, it is because of her departure *super excelsa*. Among the attending spirits the leader has rolled up the scroll, as if there was no more reading to be done, and admonishes the other putto, who wears a cloak (Pl. 85), to throw it off like the Sibyl. The cloaked putto should be compared with the chief figure attending the Persian Sibyl (Pl. 76): as Ghisi's engraving shows very clearly (Pl. 79), this figure also clutches a cloak, a significant attribute for a spirit attached to a 'veiled' form of initiation, to be abandoned in the final, 'disrobing' ecstasy. The Libyan Sibyl's act of 'transcendence' is illustrated also by the Caryatids engaged in a complicated mock-battle (Pl. 84): one of them forces the other, by kicking his thigh from below, to turn around, while the victim raises his arm to his eyes as if to shield them against the light—a remarkable parody of the Platonic ἐπιστροφή. Justi, *Michelangelo* (1900), p. 177 ('Die Grisaillen der Kinderpaare') described the action correctly: 'Dann versuchen sie es gar sich im Kreise zu bewegen, was anfangs zwar bei dem engen Raum entsetzliche Schwierigkeiten und Verrenkungen kostet (Libyca).'

[1] Ficino, *In Dionysium Areopagitam* (*Opera*, pp. 1018 f.): 'Quomodo Deus apparet in silentio, et post transitum summitatum, et in caligine'; also Pico, *De ente et uno* v (*Opera*, p. 250): 'Tibi silentium laus'; Celio Calcagnini, 'Descriptio silentii', *Opera aliquot* (1544), p. 494: 'in silentio summum bonum'; Francesco Giorgio, loc. cit.: 'arcana et abdita Dei quae (teste Paulo) non licet homini loqui'; Egidio da Viterbo, *Historia viginti saeculorum*, Cod. Angel. 502, fol. 256ʳ (*arcanum, silentium*), also fol. 291ʳ on Pythagorean silence; cf. Iamblichus, *De vita pythagorica* xxxii, 226 f. On 'closing the eyes in initiation', see the sources quoted above, p. 288, n. 1.

profound and divine theologians say that God is better honoured and loved by silence than by words, and better seen by closing the eyes to images than by opening them: and therefore the negative theology of Pythagoras and Dionysius is so celebrated and placed above the demonstrable theology of Aristotle and the Scholastics.'[1] In the Sistine Ceiling 'positive' and 'negative' theology are held in balance: the Erythraean Sibyl is as important as the Persian; nor do Joel and Ezekiel yield to Jeremiah. Without the open eyes of the Delphic Sibyl, the closed eyes of the Libyan would lose part of their meaning, and both these Sibyls would appear uprooted without the central weight of the Cumaean.

A word may be added here about the distinction between male and female prophets. To conceive of the Gentile prophecy as essentially feminine accorded with mantic practice among the pagans. Tiresias and other augurs notwithstanding, the unenviable power to commune with the gods was preferably assigned among the ancient Greeks to women,[2] either simple women susceptible to trance, like the Pythian priestess who uttered oracles that had to be interpreted by men, or women of a perspicacity that was more than masculine, like Socrates's friend Diotima.[3] While Plato said in the *Timaeus* that the gods prefer weak vessels for their infusions,[4] he referred in the

[1] *Eroici furori* ii. iv.

[2] Pausanias's account of ancient diviners (x. xii) is typical in that it places the women ahead of the men: γυναῖκες καὶ ἄνδρες (x. xii. 11). In fact, the whole chapter is devoted to prophetic women while the male prophets are listed summarily in one sentence near the end. See also A. Bouché-Leclercq, *Histoire de la divination dans l'antiquité* ii (1880), pp. 134 ff., with special reference to the Sibyls.

[3] As if to certify her mantic powers, Plato made her a native of Mantineia (*Symposium* 201D). Socrates revered her as 'the Mantineian stranger', ἡ Μαντινικὴ ξένη (211D).

[4] 71D–72B: 'For the authors of our being . . . placed in the liver the seat of divination. And herein is a proof that God has given the art of divination to the foolishness of man (ἀφροσύνη ἀνθρωπίνη). No man, when in his wits, attains mantic truth and inspiration; but when he receives the inspired word, either his intelligence is enthralled in sleep, or he is demented by some distemper or possession. And he who would understand . . . the apparitions . . . must first recover his wits. But while he continues demented, he cannot judge of the visions. . . . And for this reason it is customary to appoint interpreters. . . . Some persons call them diviners; but they are quite unaware that they are only expositors of dark sayings and visions, and are not to be called diviners at all, but only expounders of divinations (προφῆται μαντευομένων).' To judge by the derogatory tone of these remarks, they were probably directed primarily against popular prophets who made business by peddling

Phaedrus with some respect to 'the Sibyl' (Σίβυλλα) as an inspired woman.[1] In Rome the care and consultation of the treasured Sibylline Books was entrusted first to two, later to ten, and ultimately to fifteen men (*quindecimviri sacris faciundis*), whose combined male efforts were directed toward understanding a feminine oracle. Even St. Paul, although he wrote peremptorily to the Corinthians, on finding that there was too much 'speaking with tongues': 'Let your women keep silence in the churches: for it is not permitted unto them to speak' (1 Corinthians xiv. 34), acknowledged in the Epistle to the Galatians that the distinction between Jew and Greek corresponded to that between male and female which, like the division between free and slave, was to vanish in the apostolic church: 'There is neither Jew nor Greek, there is neither bond nor free, there is neither male nor female, for ye are all one in Christ Jesus' (iii. 28).

oracular books (cf. *Republic* 364B–E). Nevertheless, Plato's distinction between two levels of prophecy applies also to the practice at Delphi, where the prophetess, exposed to the fumes that rise from the tripod, produces dark sayings that the priests interpret and edit. Plato's argument was followed closely by Augustine in his distinction of the same two levels in Biblical prophecy (see above, p. 282), St. Paul having likewise insisted (1 Corinthians xiv) that 'speaking with tongues' must be followed by 'interpretation'. In fact, the Greek word for 'expounder', the easily mistranslated προφήτης, is in St. Paul the same as in Plato, as Erasmus noticed in a gloss that he added to his translation of 1 Corinthians xiv. 1: 'Hoc loco Paulus *prophetiam* vocat non praedictionem futurorum, sed interpretationem divinae scripturae. Quemadmodum et Plato discernit vates a prophetis. Vates arrepti numine, nec ipsi quid loquantur intelligunt, ea prudentes interpretantur caeteris.' Near the end of the *Praise of Folly* Erasmus describes the 'maggoty and crack-brained' state of frenzy at some length, admitting that 'persons thus affected shall have . . . mantic ecstasies of foretelling things to come, shall in a rapture talk languages they never before learned, and seem in all things actuated by something divine and extraordinary.' In the conclusion he makes much of the grammatical fact that Folly (*moria*) is a woman.

[1] 244B. For Neoplatonic commentaries see Hermias, *In Platonis Phaedrum* (ed. Couvreur), p. 94; Proclus, *In Timaeum* iv. 288E; v. 325E, 326C (cf. Alexandre, op. cit. iii, pp. 15, 116); *Scholia Platonica* as quoted above, p. 277, n. 1; also Photius, *Amphilochia* 60. Perhaps these Neoplatonic and Byzantine texts should be added to the quotations from Varro in Lactantius to account for the marked interest in the Sibylline revival among the Italian followers of Gemistus Pletho: cf. the cycle of the Sibyls in the Tempio Malatestiano in Rimini. As stated in Platina's Life of Paul II (*Opera*, 1511, fol. x 1ᵛ), Sigismondo Malatesta entertained relations with the academy of Pomponius Laetus, which was equally renowned for its study of Varro (edited by Laetus) and for its part in the Platonic revival: see Platina's panegyric on Bessarion, with its reference to Pletho as *doctissimum et secundum a Platone* (*Opera*, fol. F 5ᵛ; also fol. x 2ʳ on the Roman Academy's Platonism).

In surveying the Sistine cycle as a whole, it may be noted that along the left wall (which is, ritually speaking, the inferior side) the dominant places are held by prophets: Joel's intellect, Ezekiel's might, and Jeremiah's pity mark the beginning, middle, and end of that sequence while the two sibylline gifts of 'interpretation' and 'revelation' support the prophetic trio as secondary voices. Further weight is given to the Hebrew prophecy by the addition of a separate Prophet at each end of the chapel, raising the Old Testament gifts of the spirit numerically above those of the New. Nevertheless, along the right wall, which is ritually superior to the left, the Sibyls play the dominant parts: the beginning, middle, and end of that section are marked by the Delphic, Cumaean, and Libyan gifts, whereas Isaiah's 'counsel' and Daniel's 'science' seem to support them by holding the intermediate seats. Within a system of compelling symmetries, these inequalities and dominations correspond to the irregular concord between the two churches, which rests on the law of 'supplantation': the greater visible strength belongs to the Prophets because they represent the Chosen People to whom the Word was originally given; but the Sibyls, who enter dispersedly and in lesser force, are the true heirs according to the promise. As was explained above on the evidence of Durandus, the division and concord between the two churches was ritually enacted in the Sistine Chapel by a peculiar way of reciting the Apostolic Creed: first as a solo-chant confined to a group of subdeacons who signify the beginnings of the Church among the Jews, then by the choir representing the Church of the Nations.

In view of the ritual prominence given in the Sistine Chapel to the recitation of the Apostolic Creed, it is not surprising to learn that the first and comparatively simple programme for the Ceiling, which Michelangelo persuaded the Pope to abandon, provided for a series of the Twelve Apostles in the places now occupied by the Prophets and Sibyls.[1] In such a series it would be the custom to associate each Apostle with one of the twelve articles of the Creed—the one which he was believed to have spontaneously uttered when the Holy Spirit descended at Pentecost.[2] The schema of this older programme also underlies

[1] *Lettere di Michelangelo Buonarroti*, ed. G. Milanesi (1875), p. 426, no. 383. Written sixteen years after the event and under the threat of a lawsuit by the heirs of Julius II, the letter must be read with some caution, but there is no reason to doubt Michelangelo's statement that there was a change of programme and that the original version provided for a representation of the Twelve Apostles.

[2] On this legend and the customary distribution of the twelve Articles

the new. In the texts of Michelangelo's Prophets and Sibyls prophetic words corresponding to the twelve articles of the Creed can be found without difficulty, and even in the right order: the third article, for example, on the Virgin Birth, would correspond to a famous prophecy of Isaiah (vii. 14), who is the third prophet in the series; or the seventh article, on the Last Judgement, would fall very properly to Jonah. Daniel, who descended into the lion's den and was resurrected, holds the fifth place: and it is the fifth article that says *Descendit ad inferos* and *resurrexit*. With the resumption of the word *Credo* in the eighth article, the final section of the Creed would start with the Delphic Sibyl (*credo in spiritum sanctum*), continue with the Erythraean, who represents the *sancta ecclesia communioque sanctorum* (cf. above, p. 283), and end with the promise of *vita aeterna* (Libyan Sibyl). Being endowed with the gifts of the Holy Spirit, the Prophets and Sibyls would thus foreshadow the pentecostal inspiration of the Apostles.[1]

From an iconographic point of view, the spelling out of the series in that form would neither increase nor diminish the visual eloquence of the figures and might for that reason be dismissed as artistically irrelevant, even though the association of the twelve Articles of the Creed with Prophets and Sibyls was not uncommon in Michelangelo's time.[2] Perhaps the right method is to recognize the twelve Articles for what they are in this context: theological rubrics, comparable to the tablets that carry the names of the Prophets and Sibyls, and of the same use as titles on poems: without being themselves part of the poetry, they set the poetic reading on the right course. In that sense the very first words of the Apostolic Creed: 'I believe in God the Father Almighty, creator of heaven and earth' (*credo in Deum Patrem omnipotentem, creatorem coeli et terrae*),[3] not only direct the mind to the cycle of the Creation represented along the middle of the vault, but also invite the imagination to expect that,

among the twelve Apostles, see Durandus, *Rationale divinorum officiorum* IV. xxv. 7; cf. J. Sauer, *Symbolik des Kirchengebäudes* (1902), pp. 67, 298, with further literature; Mâle, op. cit., pp. 246–53.

[1] Durandus, op. cit. IV. xiv. 9, gives an interesting, if strained, example of how the Seven Gifts of the Holy Spirit, by being associated with the seven salutations of mass, might be seen to imply the corresponding articles of the Creed.

[2] For a parallel instance see Benoît Montenat, *Traité de la conformité, concorde et consonance des prophètes et sibylles aux douze articles de la foi*, dated 1505 (MS. français 949, Bibliothèque Nationale).

[3] For the wording, cf. Durandus, op. cit. IV. xxv. 7: 'De symbolo.'

following the sequence of the Creed, the Creation will fore-shadow the Redemption.

To reinforce that expectation is precisely the *raison d'être* of Michelangelo's Prophets and Sibyls: they prophesy, inspired by the Holy Ghost, and the theme of their prophecy is the inter-connexion between the Creation of the World and the Genealogy of Christ. Occupying a zone between these two cycles, they bear witness to 'a certain analogy between the economy of the incar-nation and the first setting in motion of the world' (*ut incar-nationis oeconomiam quandam proportionem cum prima mundi molitione habuisse credamus*).[1] Although the argument implies that the whole Sistine Ceiling was designed as a vast prophetic pro-gramme, the system rests on a relatively simple theological thought. According to a doctrine of concordance that goes back to the early Fathers, the beginnings of the Old and New Testa-ments—the first Book of Moses and the first chapter of Matthew —were prophetically connected by the word *generation*: what Moses had called 'the generation of Heaven and Earth' re-appeared in Matthew as 'the generation of Jesus Christ': 'whence it was provided (as Peter Damian put it) that both should inscribe their books with the same heading, saying *Book of Generation*.'[2] While St. Paul's and Isaiah's 'gifts of the spirit' continue to rest on the genealogical Tree of Jesse, the enlarged concept of 'generation' links them to the first Acts of Creation represented above.

In the Sistine Ceiling the connexion between Acts of Creation and Gifts of the Spirit is made visible by the *Ignudi*. Hovering above the Prophets and Sibyls, in whose moods they seem to share, they form a living frame for the primeval images in which God is seen setting the world in motion. What kind of theological creatures are these *Ignudi*? The question may sound a little odd since no one seems to have wondered seriously to what part of the theological world they belong. They have been accepted as figments of Michelangelo's imagination, invented freely to enrich the design and to enliven the spectacle by a dis-play of beautiful youths in athletic postures. For want of a better name it has become customary to call them *Genii*, *Athletes* or *Slaves*. An otherwise sensible and learned critic has even dis-

---

[1] Hieronymus de Guevara, *Commentaria in Matthaeum* (1640), p. 19. See also Bernardino de Busti,*Mariale* (1496), II. iii, 1: 'pars prima . . . quae dicitur creatonis.'

2 *Sermo de Sancto Matthaeo (Patr. lat. cxliv, col. 778).*

tinguished in their attitudes different aspects of labour:[1] do they not attach festoons of oak leaves to the cornice, burdening themselves also with heavy medallions which they hold with bands?

It is one of the idiosyncrasies of Michelangelo's art that, except for a very early example in which he was commissioned to supply a companion-piece to a given sculpture,[2] he avoided representing angels as winged. (Like Hogarth, he seems to have recoiled from the idea of disfiguring a human body with the appurtenances of a fowl.) Not only are the angels of the Last Judgement and in the Cappella Paolina wingless, but even in so early a work as the *Madonna della scala* the angels are playing on the celestial staircase without benefit of wings.[3] In the Sistine Ceiling itself, the halo of attendants surrounding God as he creates sun and moon, moves over the face of the waters, or infuses life into the body of Adam, consists of a group of wingless children; and because of this well-known peculiarity of Michelangelo's it has been suspected that the little spirits behind the Prophets and Sibyls might qualify as angels.[4] Strangely enough, this theory has not been extended to the *Ignudi*,[5] although in this instance two preparatory sketches by Michelangelo's own hand give conclusive evidence of his intention.

[1] Justi, op. cit., pp. 172–6: 'Die Sklaven.' Tolnay's bold attempt to invest them with the functions of the *anima razionale* (op. cit., pp. 63 ff., 159 ff.) rests on a misreading of Pico, *Commento* I, ii (ed. Garin, p. 463), where the *anima razionale* is placed below, not above, the *natura intellettuale*. The confusion is increased by quoting Pomponazzi among the Neoplatonists (pp. 48, 159).

[2] The second Angel for the Arca di San Domenico in Bologna.

[3] While the number of steps on the heavenly ladder is no less than thirty in Johannes Climacus's *Scala Paradisi* (cf. M. Vloberg, *La Vierge, notre médiatrice*, 1938, pp. 189–96: 'La Vierge à l'échelle'), they are reduced in Michelangelo's staircase to five—the same as in Domenico Benivieni, *Scala della vita spirituale sopra il nome di Maria* (1495), where this number is associated with the letters in the name MARIA. The author of this devotional tract is mentioned in Pico della Mirandola's dedication of *De ente et uno* to Politian as *utrique nostrum pro sua et doctrina et integritate carissimus*. Since Condivi says that at this period Politian spurred the young Michelangelo by 'always explaining things to him and giving him subjects' (ed. cit., p. 12), it is probable that Politian's friend Domenico Benivieni did likewise.

[4] C. Heath Wilson, *Michelangelo Buonarroti* (1876), pp. 143, 145; Mâle, op. cit., p. 264, note 3; also Barbier de Montault, op. cit. xiii, p. 336.

[5] J. A. Symonds (*Renaissance in Italy, The Fine Arts*, 1877, ch. viii) seized on an appropriate simile for the *Ignudi* in Psalms civ. 4, but denied a few years later (*Life of Michelangelo Buonarroti* i, 1893, pp. 245 f.) that they signified anything of the kind. The first statement is nevertheless worth quoting: '"He maketh his angels spirits, and his ministers a flame of fire": this verse rises to our lips when we seek to describe the genii that crowd the cornice of the Sistine Chapel'.

Apparently he did not hesitate, in his short-hand notations, to designate angels by roughly sketched wings, which he then omitted in the execution. The first design for the Sistine Ceiling, in which the roles of Caryatids and *Ignudi* were not yet distinguished, shows the medallions flanked by a pair of terminal figures which are characterized as angels by wings (Pl. 86*b*). In a later sketch the flanking figures are no longer herms, but their vestigial wings still define them as angels (Pl. 87*b*). The configuration resembles a heraldic type of Renaissance design in which a pair of winged figures hold a medallion that they decorate with a festoon (Pl. 86*a*). This is exactly the function of the *Ignudi* (the oak leaves and acorns being the Rovere symbol), and it is not difficult to recognize in some of them a development of the traditional formula for emblem-bearers (Pl. 87*a*). As for the scenes in the medallions, they represent the Ten Commandments, exemplified in part by Maccabean Histories and related in all cases to the adjacent prophecies.[1] These sacred Tables of the Law, here cast in bronze, would traditionally have to be held by angels.[2]

On the role that angels were thought to play in the formation of prophetic thoughts Savonarola made a significant remark in answering some of his detractors who had accused him of arrogance and blasphemy because he had suggested in a sermon that he had been mysteriously transported to Paradise, where all the enchanting amenities of the place were shown to him: 'Had they listened attentively, they would have understood that I did not mean to say that my mortal body had been in Paradise, but only that I had seen it in a mental vision. Assuredly, in Paradise there would be neither trees nor waters, nor stairs, nor doors, nor chairs; therefore, but for their ill-will, these men might have easily understood that all these things were formed in my mind by angelic intervention.'[3] He consistently maintained that his visions were formed 'by God through the ministrations of angels' (*a Deo per ministeria angelorum formari*): 'for since the angels are intermediate between God and men, prophetic illuminations coming from God himself are subserved by angelic

---

[1] Wind, 'Maccabean Histories in the Sistine Ceiling', in *Italian Renaissance Studies*, ed. E. F. Jacob (1960), pp. 312–27.

[2] The biblical prototype is Exodus xxv. 16–21.

[3] P. Villari, *Life and Times of Girolamo Savonarola*, tr. L. Villari (1897), pp. 320 f. The full text of the sermon—according to R. Ridolfi 'perhaps more than the full text' (cf. Ginori Conti, op. cit., p. 57)—was inserted at the end of Savonarola's *Compendium revelationum* (1495).

spirits who not only inform and arouse the imagination internally towards various apparitions but also address the prophets from within (*sed etiam intrinsecus prophetas alloquuntur*).'[1]

It was generally agreed that during a prophetic seizure the agitation of angels could make itself felt on several different levels.[2] Clearly, the *Ignudi* are spirits superior to the little imps behind the Prophets and Sibyls and to the Caryatids that decorate their seats. Perhaps it is not too fanciful to suppose that Michelangelo intended them for Seraphs, as distinguished from Cherubs and Thrones.

That angels feel sorrow, anger, pity, and joy (Pls. 53, 55, 87*a*) is in keeping with theological tradition; and in states of ecstasy they even rage. As St. Ambrose explained in *De Spiritu Sancto*, the gifts of the Spirit, as they descend into men, become channelled to suit earthly limitations, but in the hierarchy of the angelic spirits the Holy Ghost overflows like an abundant river that soars over the embankments:

But that Sacred Spirit proceeding from the fountain of life, from

---

[1] *Compendium revelationum.* In conformity with Thomas Aquinas (*Summa theologica* II. ii. 171–6) Savonarola distinguished between three kinds of prophecy: (1) by direct infusion into the intellect, as when God poured wisdom into Solomon; (2) by the intervention of angels, who fill the imagination with holy figments; (3) by portents visible to the outward eye. His own prophetic calling was of the second kind. He did not presume that God would speak to him intellectually, nor did he base his predictions on comets, floods, or monstrous births (let alone on astrology, which he despised). He relied on his inward visions. In Leone Ebreo's *Dialoghi d'amore* the philosopher is asked whether any prophet ever attained an intellectual vision of God; to which he answers: 'None, except Moses, who was the first of the prophets, because all the others received their vision through an angel, and their imagination shared with their intellect' (tr. F. Friedeberg-Seeley and J. H. Barnes, 1937, pp. 325 f.). Despite the biblical evidence for this view (Numbers xii. 6–8; Deuteronomy xxxiv. 10) Dionysius the Areopagite denied, as Augustine had done before him (*De Trinitate* II. xvi f.; III. xi; *Patr. lat.* xlii, cols. 862 f., 881 ff.), that even Moses could have seen God without the intervention of spirits: 'Now, if anyone should say that God had shown himself without intermediary to certain holy men, let him know beyond doubt, from the most Holy Scriptures, that no man has ever seen, nor shall see, the hidden Being of God; but God has shown himself, according to revelations which are fitting for God, to his faithful servants in holy visions adapted to the nature of the seer' (*De coelesti hierarchia* IV. iii; *Patr. graec.* iii. col. 179).

[2] Dionysius the Areopagite explained in *De coelesti hierarchia* XI. ii (*Patr. graec.* iii, col. 285) that to ignore distinctions of insight and energy between holy Powers 'would bring confusion into the clear and harmonious order of the angels'. What Savonarola calls 'angelic intervention' is characterized by the presence of dream-like shapes or riddled fancies, and these admit of different degrees of lucidity.

which we are satiated after a short draught, is seen to flow more redun-
dantly in the celestial Thrones, Dominions, Powers, Angels and Arch-
angels as a stream filled with the seven spiritual virtues. For if an
overflowing river rises above its banks, how much more will that Spirit
which rises above all creatures, in leaving the lower stretches of our
minds flooded behind, elate the celestial nature of those angels with an
effusive wealth of sanctification.[1]

Even Jerome, who disliked the verbosity of Ambrose, grew
ecstatic in writing a philological gloss on the word *effusio*: 'That
word "effusion", which in Hebrew is called ESPHOCH and which
all translate in the same way, denotes the plenitude of that
donation which descends not only on a few Prophets (as was
once the case in the Old Testament), but on all believers in the
name of the Saviour as gifts of the Holy Spirit—not only here and
there, but on all flesh. For there is no longer any distinction
between Jew and Greek, bond and free, male and female: for we
are all one in Christ.'[2]

There can be no doubt that the Roman theologians who
planned the programme of the Sistine Ceiling for Michelangelo
conceived the cycle as a hymn to the spirit that confers divine
gifts by effusion. To establish the historical identity of Michelangelo's mentor is too complex a task to be attempted here.
Circumstantial evidence points to the religious circle of Sant'
Agostino in Rome, which in the early sixteenth century was also
the centre of the Roman Academy.[3] Julius II's cousin, Raffaele
Riario, who had arranged for Michelangelo's first visit to Rome
in 1496, was cardinal-protector of the Augustinian order; and
at the time when the Sistine Ceiling was painted, their prior-
general was the neo-classical orator Egidio da Viterbo, Julius
II's chosen preacher, a philological explorer of Hebrew and
Platonic arcana and a Latin lyricist of considerable polish.

[1] Ambrose, *De spiritu sancto*, i. xvi. 158 (*Patr. lat.* xvi, col. 740).

[2] Jerome, *Commentaria in Joelem* ii. 28 ff. (*Patr. lat.* xxv, col. 978).

[3] See Jacopo Sadoleto, *Epistolae* v. xviii, a nostalgic letter to Angelo
Coloccio on the Roman Academy they had known before the Sack of Rome;
Egidio da Viterbo, *Historia viginti saeculorum*, MS. Angel. 502, fols. 197 f., on
the poetic ritual of the *Coryciana*, enacted by the Roman Academy in the
church of S. Agostino. In the late seventeenth century, well after the dis-
solution of the academy described by Sadoleto, the academic associations of
S. Agostino were renewed by members of the former circle of Christina of
Sweden: the famous *Accademia degli Arcadi* (with its enchanting garden on the
Gianicolo, the Bosco Parrasio) still holds regular meetings in the Biblioteca
Angelica at S. Agostino, the former (now secularized) Augustinian Library,
which possesses the bulk of the manuscripts left by Egidio da Viterbo.

Sadoleto referred to him in 1512 as *clarissimum huius seculi tamquam obscurascentis lumen*.[1] The pursuit of a bold and erudite, poetically elegant theology, which drew from some of the Greek and Latin Fathers the authority to revive apocryphal traditions, spread from these adventurous academicians far beyond Rome.[2]

[1] Letter to Bembo (*Epistolae* XVII. xx; *Opera* ii, 1738, pp. 165 f.). Even as early as 1505, Sadoleto had written about Egidio as 'de homine sanctissimo longeque aetatis nostrae doctissimo' (MS. Angel, 1001, fol. 31; cf. G. Signorelli, *Il cardinale Egidio da Viterbo*, 1929, p. 209, note 43). It has not escaped either contemporary or later critics (see F. X. Martin, *The Problem of Giles of Viterbo, a Historiographical Survey*, 1960, pp. 35 ff., 42) that this eminently civilized and eloquent mystic, of whom Giovio spread the malicious gossip that he inhaled wet straw in order to acquire a saintly pallor (*Elogia virorum literis illustrium*, 1577, p. 103), was the general of the Augustinian Order in 1511—the year in which Luther, staying in Rome at the Augustinian monastery next to S. Maria del Popolo, formed his unflattering opinions of the Roman clergy. Some reflections in Erasmus's *Ciceronianus*, on a Roman sermon delivered before the Pope in a portentous classical diction, may also have been inspired by Egidio: cf. the genial pastiche of an Egidian sermon in Pontano's *Aegidius*, prefaced by Petrus Summontius, who addresses Egidio *Christiane mi Cicero* (Pontanus, *Opera* ii, 1519, p. 154). Sannazaro added his praise in *Elegiae* I. ix. 79 f.: 'Quid loquar, ut sacros Mariani exhauriat amnes / Aegidius, verum dum canit ore deum?' Surprising is the impatience of Gregorovius, who admired Egidio's candour and energy as an ecclesiastical statesman but, glancing at a manuscript of the *Historia viginti saeculorum*, found its erudition monstrous and 'not worth printing' (*Geschichte der Stadt Rom im Mittelalter* XIV, 1872, i. 6; iv. 2; vi. 4).

[2] As Sannazaro said (cf. G. Signorelli, op. cit., p. 107; J. A. Vulpius, *Vita Sannazarii*, in *Sannazarii Opera*, ed. J. Broukhus, 1728, p. 514), the thought of composing a neo-pagan epic on the Incarnation (*De partu Virginis*, written in Naples) had come to his mind on hearing Egidio da Viterbo quote a verse from Virgil in a sermon. Egidio himself, on a visit to Cumae, descended frequently (*saepissime*) into what he believed to be the cave of the Sibyl. In a weird letter dated 'from Lake Avernus' he described the grotto as decorated with shells and mosaics and pervaded by a stifling air that he found conducive to spells of fainting and of hallucination: 'visi nescio quod et plus sapere et vaticinari' (Cod. Angel. 1001, fols. 25 f.; cf. E. Martène and U. Durand, *Veterum scriptorum et monumentorum collectio* iii, 1724, col. 1252; also Signorelli, op. cit., p. 130, note 23). The cave in question was probably on the site, near Lake Avernus, that A. Maiuri (*The Phlegraean Fields*, 1937, pp. 136 ff.) calls 'the pseudo-grotto of the Sibyl' because it appears to have been part of a Roman tunnel presumably built by Agrippa. Traces of mosaics in a cavernous chamber below the tunnel (the so-called 'bath of the Sibyl') were still visible in the mid-nineteenth century: see A.-J. du Pays, *Itinéraire descriptif, historique et artistique de l'Italie et de la Sicile* (1855), whose account is quoted in Barbier de Montault, op. cit. xiv, p. 387. According to Maiuri (op. cit., p. 139), a more direct access to that deep part of the cave has been blocked up by a modern wall. It is curious to reflect that while the Renaissance assumed that the deepest and darkest place in the grotto must have been the dreaded

Their theological *Summa* emerged from Lyons in Sante Pagnini's *Isagoge ad mysticos sacrae scripturae sensus*, dedicated to Cardinal Jean du Bellay but presumably compiled for the most part in Lucca and of primary importance for the study of Michelangelo because its author, at one time Prior of San Marco in Florence, was a disciple of Savonarola.[1] Like Egidio da Viterbo, Pagnini favoured a use of religious metaphor in which the prophetic learning of the Hebrews was heightened by the felicities of pagan intuition: 'ab ethnicis siquid bene dictum, in nostrum usum esse convertendum.'[2]

adyton where the Sibyl raved, the Nineteenth Century was satisfied that this would have been the right place for a bath.

[1] Wind, 'Sante Pagnini and Michelangelo: a Study of the Succession of Savonarola', op. cit., pp. 211–46.

[2] *Isagoge*, p. 28.

ACKNOWLEDGEMENTS

Albertina, Vienna (Pl. 65*a*), Alinari (Pl. 86*a*), Anderson (Pls. 42–57, 60*f*, 64, 67–70, 73–77, 80–85, 87*a*), Bibliothèque Nationale, Paris (Pls. 58, 79), British Museum, London (Pl. 86*b*), Cincinnati Art Museum (Pl. 62), Detroit Institute of Arts (Pl. 87*b*), Houghton Library, Harvard University (Pls. 41, 66), Prado, Madrid (Pl. 63).

INDEX